AF789470

Empire and the Peasant Proprietor

Empire and the Peasant Proprietor

Inter-Colony Land Reform in the Victorian Era

PREET S. AULAKH, PHD

Professor and Pierre Lassonde Chair in International Business, York University, Canada

OXFORD
UNIVERSITY PRESS

OXFORD
UNIVERSITY PRESS

Great Clarendon Street, Oxford, OX2 6DP,
United Kingdom

Oxford University Press is a department of the University of Oxford.
It furthers the University's objective of excellence in research, scholarship,
and education by publishing worldwide. Oxford is a registered trade mark of
Oxford University Press in the UK and in certain other countries.

© Preet S. Aulakh 2025

The moral rights of the author have been asserted

This is an open access publication, available online and distributed under the
terms of a Creative Commons Attribution-Non Commercial-No Derivatives 4.0
International licence (CC BY-NC-ND 4.0), a copy of which is available at
https://creativecommons.org/licenses/by-nc-nd/4.0/.
Subject to this license, all rights are reserved.

Enquiries concerning reproduction outside the scope of this licence should be sent
to the Rights Department, Oxford University Press, at the address above.

Public sector information reproduced under Open Government Licence v3.0
(https://www.nationalarchives.gov.uk/doc/open-government-licence/)

Published in the United States of America by Oxford University Press
198 Madison Avenue, New York, NY 10016, United States of America.

British Library Cataloguing in Publication Data
Data available

Library of Congress Control Number: 2025938820

ISBN 9780198928263

DOI: 10.1093/9780198928270.001.0001

Printed and bound by
CPI Group (UK) Ltd., Croydon, CR0 4YY

MIX
Paper | Supporting
responsible forestry
FSC® C013604

The manufacturer's authorised representative in the EU for product safety is
Oxford University Press España S.A., Parque Empresarial San Fernando de Henares,
Avenida de Castilla, 2 – 28830 Madrid (www.oup.es/en or product.safety@oup.com).
OUP España S.A. also acts as importer into Spain of products made by the manufacturer.

For Nandi and Arif

Contents

Figures

Tables

Acknowledgements

This book is based on my thesis that was completed at the Osgoode Hall Law School of York University. Pursuing a graduate degree in a new subject area (Law) after being an academic for over two decades in another discipline (Management) created numerous challenges, not least of which was getting a handle on another discipline's conceptual and methodological domains. I wish to thank several people who helped me navigate these challenges. First and foremost, I am grateful to my supervisor, Philip Girard, who provided constant support over the years for my shifting academic goals and the topics for the thesis. I thank him for his time commitment and guidance. As members of my dissertation committee, Jim Phillips and Jennifer Nedelsky provided critical feedback at various stages. I appreciate their time commitment and encouragement during the different stages of the thesis. I appreciate the input from my examining committee members, William Wicken and Shaunnagh Dorsett. Their critical comments and pointed questions were immensely useful as I reworked the thesis into the book.

I wish to thank several people associated with the Osgoode Graduate Program. Sonia Lawrence, as the Graduate Program Director, for admitting me to the programme despite my lack of formal law education, as well as for her help in developing my thesis proposal in the two graduate seminars; Craig Scott and Jennifer Nedelsky for leading the excellent study groups that introduced me to the vast theoretical and colonial literatures; and fellow students in the various courses whose diverse perspectives helped me make sense of the literature.

This work involved extensive archival work at various sites. I thank the staff at the India Office Records of the British Library and National Archives at Kew in London, the Prince Edward Island Archives in Charlottetown, the National Archives of India in Delhi, and the Library of Congress in Washington, DC. I am especially indebted to John Boylan at the PEI Archives, who took immense interest in my work and helped me access the relevant materials during my visit to Charlottetown during the difficult period of Covid lockdowns. Special thanks to Summaiya Zaidi for helping me access some of the archival materials from the National Archives of Pakistan housed in Lahore. Ramanpreet Kaur and Danna Deutsch helped me access and make sense of the various archives, and their assistance is appreciated.

Numerous people provided invaluable guidance in preparing the book. I wish to thank Renisa Mawani and Mitra Sharafi for their encouragement and for pointing me to appropriate presses that would be receptive to my work; I am grateful to

John McLaren, Rusty Bittermann, and Saptarishi Bandopadhyay for reading different versions of the work and providing valuable feedback.

Throughout the project, I received support from numerous friends and colleagues. Constant interest in my progress and encouragement from Yuval Deutsch, Anoop Madhok, Charles McMillan, Ashwin Joshi, Hildy Teegen, Teresa Hubel, Prabhjot Parmar, Aanchal Singh, Sougata Ray, and Ravee Chittoor kept me motivated over the last few years.

Thanks to my mother for her encouragement despite being perplexed by my decision to pursue another degree, Nandi for the numerous discussions that helped shape and sharpen my arguments, and Arif for his appreciation of my lifelong learning goal. I appreciate the interest and support of my extended family. I am grateful to the Oxford University Press team: Brian Stone, as Commissioning Editor, for showing interest in my work and facilitating a timely and helpful review process and Paulina dos Santos Major, as Project Editor, for her guidance that helped me navigate various aspects in bringing the project to fruition. Finally, I want to thank two anonymous readers who reviewed the manuscript for their detailed comments and suggestions. Their encouragement and guidance were invaluable in sharpening my arguments and revising the manuscript to broaden its appeal to readers across disciplines and geographic contexts.

PART I

BRITISH EMPIRE'S LAND QUESTION IN THE NINETEENTH CENTURY

1
Introduction

> It is time to revert to just principles, and to regulate the supposed right of the owner in such a manner as to make it at least consistent with the essential conditions of industry, prudence, and material comfort, in the agricultural population.
>
> —J. S. Mill (1848)[1]

> It is hoped that Her Majesty's Government will not consent to any compulsory interference with the laws and rights of the proprietors ... and any measures for the benefit of the tenantry must result from an amicable arrangement with the proprietors.
>
> —Prince Edward Island Landowners (1859)[2]

If possession of distant lands led to the formation of colonial empires, then the efficacy in governing these lands was critically important for their sustenance. Given the agrarian nature of its numerous colonies, the British Empire instituted elaborate administrative and legal mechanisms to map and categorise boundaries, allocate land, and collect revenues. Defining the rights and obligations was essential for the functioning of this system because clarity in the structure and associated incentive systems in land tenure relationships allowed imperial governments to achieve their economic objectives of improvement and development and political goals of effectively governing and controlling the disparate colonial subjects.

The dominant belief in earlier colonial thinking was that a powerful landowning class was essential for furthering the economic and socio-political objectives of the Empire. Accordingly, tenurial arrangements in its numerous colonies privileged the landowners and prioritised their property rights. In the nineteenth century, several liberal thinkers increasingly asserted 'that large, privileged landlords were

[1] Letter from J. S. Mill to the *Daily News* on August 12, 1848, where he lamented the miseries of the Irish peasants, in John Stuart Mill, 'Landed Tenure in Ireland', in *Newspaper Writings December 1847–July 1873, in Collected Works of John Stuart Mill, Volume XXV*, ed. Ann P. Robson and John B. Robson (Toronto: University of Toronto Press, 1986), 1114–15.

[2] Letter dated May 13, 1859, to the Queen by a group of proprietors in Prince Edward Island regarding land tenure legislation being contemplated in the colony. Reproduced in Despatches from the Governor (No. 1, 13 May 1859) in 'Prince Edward Island' (House of Commons Parliamentary Papers Online, 1864), 1–2.

Empire and the Peasant Proprietor. Preet S. Aulakh, Oxford University Press. © Preet S. Aulakh 2025.
DOI: 10.1093/9780198928270.003.0001

a prop of tyranny and a heavy burden on agricultural productivity'.[3] Attributing much of the agricultural improvement in the colonies to the users (tenants) rather than the owners of land (landlords), they called for land reform that would institutionalise some form of proprietary rights of the peasant cultivators.[4] Landlords and their supporters in the colonies and the metropole invoked the owners' sanctity of rights to property to resist such reform, encapsulated by British Prime Minister Palmerston's declaration in parliament as late as 1865 that *tenant-right is equivalent to landlords' wrong*.[5] How could the seemingly contrary objectives of maintaining landlords' existing rights and granting new rights to the tenants on the same piece of land be reconciled? This was the Empire's land question in the nineteenth century.

During a short period between 1868 and 1875, however, several laws were enacted in three far-flung colonies of the British Empire, which established some form of security of tenure for the actual cultivators of land by either recognising co-proprietorship of tenants and landlords or by transferring proprietorship from landlords to tenants.[6] Despite being characterised as 'socialist', 'mischievous', and 'the most radical attack on the rights of property' by landowners and their supporters, these laws (Punjab Tenancy Act of 1868, Land and Tenant (Ireland) Act of 1870, Prince Edward Island Tenants' Compensation Act of 1872, and Land Purchase Act of 1875) represented a vital triumph for those land reformers who saw peasants' wellbeing as critical to the economic progress of the colonies and the political stability of the Empire.

The land reforms had significant political implications for each colony. In Punjab, the Tenancy Act stalled the post-1857 Mutiny momentum in British India towards restoring the political and economic influence of the landed aristocratic classes. The Irish Land Act responded to a growing political agitation in Ireland that demanded, among other things, a resolution to the centuries-old land question. In Prince Edward Island, the conversion of leasehold to freehold tenures through the compulsory Land Purchase Act of 1875 was a momentous step in satisfying the aspirations of the colony to get rid of the beneficiaries of the eighteenth-century

[3] C. A. Bayly, *The Birth of the Modern World 1780–1914* (Malden, MA: Blackwell Publishing, 2004), 296.

[4] The primary focus of the current study are land tenure relationships where landowners (landlords) differed from the actual users or cultivators of land (tenants). As argued by Andrew Sartori, the liberal impulse in the middle of nineteenth century 'to extend rights of property more broadly throughout society . . . could find more plausible traction . . . [in] those colonies where peasant agriculture still predominated'. Andrew Sartori, *Liberalism in Empire: An Alternative History* (Oakland: University of California Press, 2014), 200.

[5] Lord Palmerston speech during debate on the Irish land question, February 27, 1865. House of Commons Hansard Archives. Italics mine.

[6] Peasant proprietorship is the broad umbrella term used which encompasses both the transfer of ownership to the tenant (full proprietor) and the recognition of shared rights between the landlord and tenant (co-proprietor). As discussed in Chapter 2, co-proprietorship could take various forms, including compensation for improvement and the 3Fs (fixity of tenure, fair rents, freedom of sale).

Figure 1.1 Map of the British Empire (circa 1850)
Library of Congress, Geography and Map Division.
Bartholomew, John, and A. Fullarton & Co. *British Empire throughout the world exhibited in one view.* [S.l., 185] Map. <https://www.loc.gov/item/98687124/>.

land grants and align its land tenure system with that of the Empire's other North American colonies to which it had decided to join in Confederation in 1873.

Empire and the Peasant Proprietor examines this vital disjuncture in the British Empire's governance of land tenure. It probes how proponents of peasant rights overcame long-standing resistance to any encroachment upon landowners' rights to property in these socio-politically diverse[7] and geographically dispersed colonies (see Map of the British Empire circa 1850 in Figure 1.1) and the implications

[7] Punjab being a non-white and non-settler province of British India with class and to some extent religion distinguishing the landlords and tenants; Ireland as a 'not quite-white' (Catherine M. Eagan, '"White," If "Not Quite": Irish Whiteness in the Nineteenth-Century Irish-American Novel', *Eire-Ireland* 36, no. 1 (2001): 66–81) but semi-settler colony which was a part of Great Britain where religion was the central distinction between the two groups; and Prince Edward Island as a white settler colony in British North America with emerging class and religious distinctions that needed to be addressed. Besides these differences, the colonial administrative structures differed across the three, which had implications for the extent of local agency afforded in discussions about land tenure.

of this movement towards peasant proprietorship in the three colonies during the mid-Victorian period on the subsequent trajectory of land tenure reform across the Empire.

Land Reform in England and the Colonies

The nineteenth-century impetus for land reform and peasant proprietorship came from shifting intellectual currents about property rights and political economy (fully explored in Chapter 2), which considered the possibility of shared rights between landlords and peasant cultivators, saw an essential role of the state in reallocating property rights for the public good, and foregrounded the economic and political benefits of broadly held rights by tenants and owner-cultivators of small farms. The underlying rationale was that security of tenure would provide peasants with the necessary incentives to invest both labour and capital in the improvement and development of the land. Supporters of landlord interests countered each of the rationales behind peasant rights on the grounds of landowners' absolute rights to property, the laissez faire principle of non-interference of the state in the relationships between landlords and their tenants, and the superiority of large-scale capitalist farming. Land reform in the colonies was contested around these competing perspectives about property rights and political economy for much of the nineteenth century. Until the 1860s, for the most part, landlords' interests in the colonies remained prioritised over peasant rights because of the support of the landowning class in England, which used its power and influence in the British Parliament to thwart efforts to establish security of tenure for the peasants that were central to the Empire's land question.

Understanding the roots of the English landowners' resistance to land reform in the colonies requires an analysis of the Empire's land question in conjunction with the concurrent nineteenth-century contestations around England's land question.

At the end of the eighteenth century, England had 'an insular consensus' that 'approved the existing agrarian system. Just as large farms cultivated by substantial tenant farmers holding long leases from improving landlords were believed to be the most productive units of cultivation, so large, landed estates held together by primogeniture and entail were supposed essential to the maintenance of a beneficent political order'.[8] The institutional arrangements in England at the time favoured its landowning class: the Corn Laws (that reduced global free trade) protected it from international competition; the inheritance laws of primogeniture and entail reduced free trade in land and ensured that the land ownership

[8] Clive J. Dewey, 'The Rehabilitation of the Peasant Proprietor in Nineteenth-Century Economic Thought', *History of Political Economy* 6, no. 1 (1974): 17.

stayed concentrated;[9] contracts between landlords and tenants governed the land relationships; and restrictions on political participation based on land ownership maintained the political power of the landowning class.[10]

Within the context of 'a growing desire for reform of the whole system of English Law',[11] and inspired by the success of alternative land tenure arrangements from Continental Europe to the Americas, several influential activists, intellectuals, and politicians started questioning the existing practices 'concerning the use, distribution, and ownership of landed property'[12] in the early part of the nineteenth century. Concerns about the concentration of wealth and political power in England's landed aristocratic class were at the heart of the ensuing debates and became known as England's 'land question'.

If the land question in the colonies entailed improving the material conditions of the vast number of peasant cultivators via secure property rights, the land question in England encompassed breaking the hold of the 'aristocracy over the destinies of the country' by dismantling the large landholdings that were the source of its economic and political power.[13] Although the objectives of land reform in the colonies and the metropole were somewhat different (improving the peasants' economic wellbeing versus diminishing the political power and influence of the landed aristocracy), the means through which each could be accomplished converged. Both entailed some form of redistribution or reassignment of property rights, which caused the concerns of English landlords to converge with the landowners in the colonies.

The English landowning class fought vigorous battles with land reformers in the first half of the nineteenth century on multiple fronts. It suffered a major defeat when the parliament repealed the Corn Laws that had protected landowners' economic interests since 1815 by putting quantitative restrictions and duties on corn imported from abroad. Restrictions on cheaper imported corn meant that

[9] 'Entail' in English law, was the practice which removed the power of alienation from the owner of the estate and placed it in trust for the eldest son. 'Primogeniture' was the practice whereby the estate of an intestate (that is, without a will) passed to the eldest son. These practices supported a landed aristocracy because they prevented the disintegration of large estates. In the nineteenth-century England, 'entail and primogeniture ensured that the aristocracy remained landed, just as the great estates remained aristocratic'. A. R. Buck, 'Property, Aristocracy and the Reform of the Land Law in Early Nineteenth Century England', *Journal of Legal History* 16, no. 1 (1995): 69.

[10] For detailed description on English land, see F. M. L. Thompson, *English Landed Society in the Nineteenth Century*, 1st ed. (London and New York: Routledge, 2007); F. M. L. Thompson, 'Changing Perceptions of Land Tenures in Britain, 1750–1914', in *The Political Economy of British Historical Experience, 1688–1914*, ed. Donald Winch and Patrick K. O'Brien (Oxford: Oxford University Press, 2002), 119–38; M. Cragoe and P. Readman, eds., *The Land Question in Britain, 1750–1950* (New York: Palgrave Macmillan, 2010); A. W. B. Simpson, *A History of Land Law* (Oxford: Oxford University Press, 1986).

[11] Simpson, *A History of Land Law*, 273; Sir Llewellyn Woodward, *The Oxford History of England: The Age of Reform 1815–1870* (London: Oxford at the Clarendon Press, 1962).

[12] Matthew Cragoe and Paul Readman, 'Introduction', in *The Land Question in Britain, 1750–1950*, ed. Matthew Cragoe and Paul Readman (Hampshire: Palgrave Macmillan, 2010), 1.

[13] Cragoe and Readman, 4.

English consumers paid a higher price. The Anti-Corn Law League, formed in the 1830s and led by Richard Cobden,[14] saw the landed aristocracy as a 'rapacious set of tyrants who deprived the people of food'[15] and mobilised public and political opinion on the free trade principle to ensure the repeal of the Corn Laws in 1846.[16]

Emboldened by its success in repealing the Corn Laws, Cobden and his supporters set their sights on reducing the power of the landowning class by dismantling the structural factors that formed the basis of its power and influence: primogeniture and entail. Under the 'free trade in land' banner, the movement hoped that dismantling the system would lead to a sub-division of land, which was crucial for economic and social progress. Cobden was influenced by the peasant proprietorship model prevalent in Continental Europe and believed that free trade in land would create similar peasant proprietors in England. According to him, the 'possession of a piece of land has a tendency to create self-respect, prudence, & self-control – & these are the root of all wisdom & virtue'.[17] However, he did not favour forcing subdivision through compulsion and believed that changes in the inheritance laws would naturally lead to free trade in land.[18]

Numerous attempts to abolish entail and primogeniture in the nineteenth century failed.[19] The landowning class resisted structural changes to land ownership by resorting to the findings in the four reports between 1829 and 1833 of the Real Property Commission.[20] The Commission, tasked to look at all aspects of real property, including inheritance, registration, tenures and wills, emphatically conveyed satisfaction with the state of real property law in England:

[14] Richard Cobden (1804–1865) was a British politician and a free trade advocate who led the Anti-Corn Laws league, and subsequently followed up with an agitation for free trade in land. His overall objective was to reduce the influence of the landed aristocracy, and the Cobden Club, founded in his name, continued to promote peasant proprietorship after his death through advocacy and publications. 'Richard Cobden | British Politician & Free Trade Advocate | Britannica', accessed May 30, 2024, <https://www.britannica.com/biography/Richard-Cobden>; Cobden Club (London, England) et al., *Systems of Land Tenure in Various Countries* (London: Macmillan, 1870).

[15] Anthony Howe, 'The "Manchester School" and the Landlords: The Failure of Land Reform in Early Victorian Britain', in *The Land Question in Britain, 1750–1950*, ed. Matthew Cragoe and Paul Readman (Hampshire: Palgrave Macmillan, 2010), 74.

[16] There is some debate amongst historians about the detrimental effects of the repeal on the landowning class. According to Aydelotte, 'the repeal of the Corn Laws is now more generally regarded not as a victory of the "middle classes", whoever they were, but as a skillful and successful holding operation by the old governing class, the landowners . . . By this means the landed classes, without sacrificing and real economic advantage, retained control of political power'. William O. Aydelotte, 'The Country Gentlemen and the Repeal of the Corn Laws', *The English Historical Review* 82, no. 322 (1967): 50.

[17] Cobden's letter to George Combe, February 29, 1848. Cited in Howe, 'The "Manchester School" and the Landlords: The Failure of Land Reform in Early Victorian Britain', 81.

[18] Howe, 'The "Manchester School" and the Landlords: The Failure of Land Reform in Early Victorian Britain'.

[19] Simpson, *A History of Land Law*.

[20] Buck, 'Property, Aristocracy and the Reform of the Land Law in Early Nineteenth Century England'.

> [T]he Law of England except in a few comparatively unimportant particulars, appears to come almost as near to perfection as can be expected in any human institutions. The owner of the soil is . . . vested with exactly the dominion and power of disposition overt it required for public good, and landed property in England is admirably made to answer all the purposes to which it is applicable.[21]

The Report also supported entail and primogeniture, noting that these 'bestow upon the present possessor of an estate the benefits of ownership, and secure the property to his posterity'. Accordingly, these are 'better adapted to the constitution and habits of this kingdom than the opposite Law of equal Partibility, which in a few generations, would break down the aristocracy of the country', and which will be 'unfavourable to agriculture and injurious to the best interests of the state'.[22] The reports recommended strengthening the existing landholders' management powers to fully exploit the benefits of security of tenure. The landholding class used the commission's findings and its immense clout in parliament to counter any momentum for the proponents of free trade in the land. It united to defend the 'core of the territorial system, the structure of landed estates'.[23] The free trade in land movement petered out by the 1850s because the 'programme rested on a paradox: measures designed to undermine the political and social power of the landed classes and substitute a different structure of ownership could scarcely be enacted until that power had previously been undermined by some other means'.[24]

In addition to the free traders who hoped to loosen the political and economic hold of the aristocratic landholders in England, two other movements attempted reforms involving landlord–tenant relationships and broader ownership of land. The former revolved around tenant rights, defined as the just claim to compensation for any unexhausted improvements made by a tenant that remained at the end of the tenancy.[25] Unlike the norm in Ireland, where the tenant undertook all the land improvements, the responsibility of investing in the supporting infrastructure for agriculture fell on the landlords in England. However, there were instances when the tenants did invest in the construction of fencing and drainage, which were permanent fixtures and thus had the potential for unexhausted value at the end of the lease. There was no legal mechanism in England to claim such compensation.

[21] 'First Report Made to His Majesty By the Commissioners Appointed to Inquire Into the Law of England Respecting Real Property' (House of Commons, May 20, 1829), 6, House of Commons Parliamentary Papers Online.

[22] 'First Report Made to His Majesty By the Commissioners Appointed to Inquire Into the Law of England Respecting Real Property', 6–7.

[23] F. M. L. Thompson, 'Land and Politics in England in the Nineteenth Century', *Transactions of the Royal Historical Society* 15 (December 1965): 33.

[24] Thompson, 39.

[25] Julian R. McQuiston, 'Tenant Right: Farmer against Landlord in Victorian England 1847–1883', *Agriculture History* 47, no. 2 (1973): 95–113. At this stage, this generic definition will suffice. The tenant right issue played a central role in the land reform movements across the British Empire and took various forms. These will be discussed in detail in the following chapters.

A tenant right movement was initiated in 1845 under the auspices of the London Farmers' Club and led by Philip Pusey, a Member of Parliament, landowner, and editor of the Royal Agricultural Society's journal. Pusey brought different versions of tenant right of compensation bills before parliament from 1847 to 1851,[26] which were all turned down on the pretext that such legislation impinged on the freedom of contract in landlord–tenant relationships.

There were also the Chartists, whose primary aim was parliamentary reform in the form of expanded suffrage and the abolition of property qualifications, among others, but who also took up the cause of broader land ownership in the 1840s.[27] This movement was influenced by the American National Reform Movement, which believed in the Jeffersonian idealism of an independent yeoman farmer being the 'most precious part of the state' and promoted 160-acre owner-cultivated farms.[28] The Chartists hoped to create peasant proprietors amongst the working class in England by settling them on four-acre cottage holdings. They created the Chartist Co-operative Land Company to purchase land for sale in the market that could be subsequently allotted to the working people through a lottery system. Unlike the American movement, which led to the successful Homestead Act of 1862 for the broad distribution of Federal land, the Chartists had limited success in England. There were both structural reasons in that there was not enough land that came up for sale in the market (unlike in America where the Federal Government owned large tracts of land which could be distributed), and socio-economic factors in England whereby '[a]griculture had been permanently biased against peasant proprietorship by an enclosure movement that sought to promote social distinctions as well as economies of scale'.[29] Moreover, while both the movements in England and America grew from the desirability of a 'landed lifestyle for working people', the former could not overcome the fact that 'landed independence for working people had become a much greater fixture in the American myth of the state than it had in the British one'.[30]

To sum up, England's landowners successfully resisted the multiple attempts by land reformers to weaken its influence during the first half of the nineteenth century.[31] The limited land reform that took place because of the recommendations of the Real Property Commission bolstered the landowners' security of

[26] The different versions had voluntary nature of compensation, compulsory compensation, role of arbitrators, etc. For details, see McQuiston.

[27] 'Chartism | British Working-Class Movement, Reforms & Demands | Britannica', accessed June 27, 2024, <https://www.britannica.com/event/Chartism-British-history>.

[28] Jamie Bronstein, 'The Homestead and the Garden Plot: Cultural Pressures on Land Reform in Nineteenth-Century Britain and the USA', *The European Legacy* 6, no. 2 (2001): 161.

[29] Bronstein, 166; Also see Jamie L. Bronstein, *Land Reform and Working-Class Experience in Britain and the United States, 1800–1862* (Stanford, CA: Stanford University Press, 1999).

[30] Bronstein, 'The Homestead and the Garden Plot: Cultural Pressures on Land Reform in Nineteenth-Century Britain and the USA', 171.

[31] The Land reform movement in England went through three phases: the first ran until the 1850s, with concurrent activities of the anti-corn Law League, proponents of free trade in land, the Chartists, and the tenant-right advocates. The landlords were, for the most part, able to resist substantive reforms in this phase. The following two phases, one from the 1870s to the 1880s and the other in the twentieth

tenure and inheritance rights. The landed interest survived the multiple land reform pressures, 'if not unscathed, then unbowed, and in the calm waters of the age of Palmerston once more exercised an easy and comparatively untroubled political dominance'.[32] Lord Palmerston (Prime Minister 1855–1858 and 1859–1865), for whom 'the sanctity of property was the bedrock of civilisation', felt confident to emphatically declare in parliament in 1865 that any tenant-right is landlord's wrong. He preserved the position of landlords at home and ensured that 'neither the Prince Edward Islanders nor the Irish tenants could obtain concessions of principle at the landlords' expense from the British government'.[33]

The English historian F. M. L. Thompson succinctly encapsulates the mechanism through which the landed class overcame the pressures of the land reformers:

> Opponents of the landed interest, whether they were discussing parliamentary reform, corn laws, the state of agriculture, or housing conditions, habitually reduced it to a set of landlords who possessed peculiar advantages for pursuing the normal human activity of furthering their own interests. Defenders and admirers of the landed interest in turn expanded it until it included the whole rural population, idealised as a happy harmonious community, but also every class and group which seemed to them to have pretence of serving causes above those of private interest and profit.[34]

By the 1860s, the landowning class in England felt comfortable with its position at home and confident in its belief that a robust aristocracy was essential for society's economic progress and stable political order. This ideology was further boosted by events in some of the Empire's colonies. The landowners in England blamed the political unrest in the colonies (for example, the Mutiny of 1857 British India and the Morant Bay rebellion of 1865 in Jamaica) on the ingratitude of the masses for not taking advantage of the policies implemented by the British in the form of peasant rights and emancipation. It also implicated liberal imperialism for disturbing the traditional hierarchies in colonial societies by weakening the landed class.[35]

On assuming power in 1868, William Gladstone faced competing pressures on colonial land tenures. His government, with its liberal leanings, saw the economic improvement of the mass of peasant cultivators through an assignment of proprietary rights (especially in the case of Ireland, for which the British government was

century were more successful. Thompson, *English Landed Society in the Nineteenth Century*. I discuss the two phases in Chapter 9.

[32] Thompson, 269.

[33] E. D. Steele, 'Ireland and the Empire in the 1860s. Imperial Precedents for Gladstone's First Irish Land Act', *The Historical Journal* 11, no. 1 (March 1968): 64.

[34] Thompson, *English Landed Society in the Nineteenth Century*, 3–4.

[35] Karuna Mantena, *Alibis of Empire: Henry Maine and the Ends of Liberal Imperialism* (Princeton, N.J.: Princeton University Press, 2010).

directly responsible) as critical to the material wellbeing of the colonies and the stability of the Empire.[36] The opposite view, supported by the English aristocratic class, attributed the political instability across the Empire to the introduction of liberal colonial institutions, which disturbed the traditional socio-political hierarchies,[37] and wanted a return to privileging the interests of landlords and a retreat from peasant proprietorship in the colonies.[38] The Gladstone government dealt with the land question across the Empire's three colonies (Punjab in British India, Ireland, and Prince Edward Island) during the 1868–1875 period under these circumstances. I briefly introduce the land question in each site during the time.[39]

The Three Colonial Sites

Out of the three colonial sites of interest,[40] Punjab was the last to come under colonial rule, being annexed by the East India Company in 1849. Given that it was part of the overall British India colonial administrative structure, its governance and land system post-annexation need to be understood in the context of broader institutions the East India Company put in place. The company gained a firm foothold in the eastern part of India after the Battle of Plassey in 1757, and soon after that, the Mughal emperor granted the right to collect land revenues in Bengal. The East India Company's activities in India were brought under the British government's oversight through a series of acts[41] to mitigate the company's excesses and enhance its accountability.[42]

[36] Ronald Hyam, *Britain's Imperial Century, 1815-1914: A Study of Imperial Expansion* (New York: Palgrave Macmillan, 2002).

[37] Karuna Mantena, 'The Crisis of Liberal Imperialism', in *Victorian Visions of Global Order: Empire and International Relations in Nineteenth-Century Political Thought*, ed. Duncan Bell (Cambridge, N.Y.: Cambridge University Press, 2007), 113–35; C. C. Eldridge, *British Imperialism in the Nineteenth Century* (London: Macmillan, 1984).

[38] Mantena, *Alibis of Empire*; Hyam, *Britain's Imperial Century, 1815–1914.*

[39] The objective here is to provide a basic comparison of the three sites of interest. A greater elaboration of each site is subsequently provided in the different chapters.

[40] In terms of terminology, this study considers a British 'colony' in a broad sense of being subject to British rule. Thus, although Punjab was a province in British India, rather than a separate colony, it is considered a distinct colonial site for the purpose of this study because a separate land law was being contemplated for Punjab which was quite different from some of the land tenure arrangements in other provinces of British India (India came under direct rule of the Crown in 1858). There are also different opinions about whether Ireland after the 1800 Act of Union should be considered a British colony. The approach taken in the current study is that it is also a site of British imperial control and thus can be considered another colonial site. 'Colonies' and 'colonial sites' are used interchangeably in the book.

[41] For example, the Regulating Act of 1773 and the Pitt's India Act of 1784. For details about early administration in India, see Mithi Mukherjee, *India in the Shadows of Empire: A Legal and Political History (1774–1950)* (New Delhi: Oxford University Press, 2009); H. H. Dodwell, ed., *The Cambridge History of India. Volume VI: The Indian Empire 1858–1918* (Cambridge: Cambridge University Press, 1932); Nicholas B. Dirks, *The Scandal of Empire: India and the Creation of Imperial Britain* (Cambridge, Mass: Belknap Press of Harvard University Press, 2006).

[42] Dirks, *The Scandal of Empire*; Jim Phillips, 'Parliament and Southern India, 1781–3: The Secret Committee of Inquiry and the Prosecution of Sir Thomas Rumbold', *Parliamentary History* 7, no. 1 (1988): 81–97.

The consolidation of England's political authority over large parts of India in the first half of the nineteenth century led to discussions about appropriate institutions to govern the colony. The debate revolved around whether the indirect rule in Bengal in the 1770s, which relied on the existing native institutions and administrative structures to govern the colony, should be continued. The alternative was a more direct rule entailing the anglicisation of the Indian administration through Western institutions and Western-trained bureaucracy.[43] The latter view became dominant in the early nineteenth century. William Bentinck, the Governor-General from 1828 to 1835, introduced reforms anchored in the ethical and moral considerations derived from liberal and utilitarian ideas taking shape during that time.[44] While transplanting of institutions from England for the sake of 'good government' in the colony overcame some of the 'precarious and illegitimate beginnings of empire in India',[45] these did not incorporate the fundamental prescriptions of political thought grounded in universal and democratic principles related to equal rights and liberties and representative government, aptly captured by Henry Maine's observation about British rule in India being a 'most extraordinary experiment involving the virtually despotic government of a dependency by a free people'.[46]

How was the partial compliance to universal principles of liberalism to be justified? This fell on political theorists such as J. S. Mill, who was instrumental in creating boundaries based on the racial inferiority of colonial subjects, and thus justifying their exclusion from benefits of liberty and representative government: 'Despotism is a legitimate mode of government in dealing with barbarians, provided the end be their improvement, and the means justified by actually effecting that end.'[47] The first half of the nineteenth century thus saw the dual strategies of introducing certain Western institutions in India under the guise of good government and the Empire's civilising mission, but at the same time providing ethical justifications of the Empire, primarily related to restricted participation of natives in some of these very institutions.

[43] The East India College in Haileybury, England, was established in 1806 to train young British administrators who joined the Bengal Civil Service and eventually the Indian Civil Service. For details about early administration of the East India Company and the ideological bases behind administrative reforms, see Eric Stokes, *The English Utilitarians and India* (Oxford: Oxford University Press, 1989); Dirks, *The Scandal of Empire*; Dodwell, *The Cambridge History of India. Volume VI: The Indian Empire 1858–1918*.

[44] Stokes, *The English Utilitarians and India*; Alan Ryan, *The Making of Modern Liberalism* (Princeton, NJ: Princeton University Press, 2012); Jennifer Pitts, *A Turn to Empire: The Rise of Imperial Liberalism in Britain and France* (Princeton, NJ: Princeton University Press, 2005).

[45] Duncan Bell, 'Victorian Visions of Global Order: An Introduction', in *Victorian Visions of Global Order: Empire and International Relations in Nineteenth-Century Political Thought*, ed. Duncan Bell (Cambridge: Cambridge University Press, 2007), 118.

[46] Quoted in Mantena, 'The Crisis of Liberal Imperialism', 114.

[47] John Stuart Mill et al., *Utilitarianism: And, On Liberty: Including Mill's Essay on Bentham, and Selections from the Writings of Jeremy Bentham and John Austin*, 2nd ed. (Malden, MA: Blackwell Publishing, 2003).

The land tenure system in India also evolved from the eighteenth to the nineteenth century. The initial system instituted in Bengal (the Permanent Settlement of 1793) privileged the landlords (*zamindars*), fixed their revenue obligations in perpetuity, and gave them almost a free hand in determining and collecting rent from the peasant cultivators.[48] The early nineteenth-century governance ideology of more direct rule necessitated significant contact with the mass of cultivators. Thus, the *ryotwari* system was introduced in the southern provinces, whereby the government assessed and collected revenue directly from the actual cultivators of the land. The objective of early land systems introduced by the East India Company was to maximise land revenues, which provided the primary source of income for the state under native rulers and the task of whose collection now fell on the British. The land tenure system and the associated proprietary rights supported the revenue collection. Since the state considered itself the ultimate landowner, these two systems acknowledged implicit proprietary rights to the entity on whom the land revenue was assessed and collected.[49]

When the British annexed Punjab in 1849, the East India Company introduced the prevalent system of administration under the East India Company in the province, and the initial land tenure settlement was a variant of the *ryotwari* model, with revenue settlement made with the entire village community rather than the individual cultivator. More importantly, the settlement recorded 'occupancy' rights of a large percentage of the tenants who had continuously held the land for twelve years, thus establishing proprietary rights for the actual cultivators of land.

The political environment changed a few years later, with the uprising against colonial rule in 1857 that spread throughout the country and threatened the survival of the Empire in India.[50] A significant structural change in the governance of India after the uprising was its formal transfer from the East India Company to the British Crown in 1858. The rebellion also raised 'troubling questions about how far the "blessings" of British rule, and liberal reform with it, were appreciated by those upon whom they were conferred'.[51] As pointed out by several historians, there was a 'conservative' turn in the governance ideology of the Empire, which manifested itself in a return to re-emphasising the traditional native socio-political hierarchies[52] and included the privileging of the landed a

[48] Ranajit Guha, *A Rule of Property for Bengal: An Essay on the Idea of Permanent Settlement* (Durham: Duke University Press Books, 1996).

[49] Tirthankar Roy and Anand V. Swamy, *Law and the Economy in Colonial India* (Chicago: The University of Chicago Press, 2016).

[50] For the psychological impact of the mutiny on the Empire and its persistence well into the twentieth century, see Kim Wagner, *Amritsar 1919: An Empire of Fear and the Making of a Massacre* (New Haven, CT: Yale University Press, 2019).

[51] Thomas R. Metcalf, *Ideologies of the Raj*, vol. 3, part 4 of *The New Cambridge History of India* (Cambridge: Cambridge University Press, 1995), 43.

[52] Mantena, *Alibis of Empire*; S. Gopal, *British Policy in India, 1858–1905* (Cambridge: Cambridge University Press, 1965); Hyam, *Britain's Imperial Century, 1815–1914: A Study of Imperial Expansion.*

ristocracy[53] at the expense of the peasant cultivators.[54] In the post-1857 political environment, there was a threat of retracting the occupancy rights of tenants in Punjab granted earlier.[55] The land question in Punjab in the 1860s entailed countering the pro-aristocratic bias prevalent in the rest of British India and preserving the proprietary rights of peasants established after its annexation.

Prince Edward Island (PEI) became part of the British Empire after France ceded it to England after the Seven Years' War and the 1763 Treaty of Paris.[56] However, unlike in Bengal, where the East India Company got the rights to collect revenue from land that was already in use and inherited a land tenure system of pre-existing relationships between landlords and cultivators, British rule on the island started with a clean slate as the Indigenous population had already been dispossessed of their land and most of the Acadian population expelled from the island.[57] The British divided the island into sixty-seven lots of 20,000 acres each, and sixty-six of these were distributed through a lottery in London on 23 July, 1767, to individuals or groups who were 'leading political or military figures, or merchants with already established interests in the region'.[58] The creation of landlords with significant holdings in the colony remained a source of political contestation for more than a hundred years.[59]

In contrast to British India, where much of the administrative structure for most of the nineteenth century consisted of colonial officials, Prince Edward Island's governance had included white settlers since its inception as a British colony. This participation took the form of appointed and elected councils and assemblies, whose legislative and executive powers grew over the years, especially after PEI was granted Responsible Government in 1851. However, any law passed by the local legislature related to property needed approval (Royal Assent) from the Colonial Office in London (consisting of the Secretary of State for the Colonies, advised by

[53] Thomas R. Metcalf, 'The Influence of the Mutiny of 1857 on Land Policy in India', *The Historical Journal* 4, no. 2 (1961): 152–63.

[54] Eric Stokes, *The Peasant and the Raj: Studies in Agrarian Society and Peasant Rebellion in Colonial India* (Cambridge: Cambridge University Press, 1978).

[55] The province of Oudh also saw a retraction of the occupancy rights after the 1857 rebellion. This is discussed in a little more detail in Chapter 4.

[56] D. H. Murdoch, 'Land Policy in the Eighteenth-Century British Empire: The Sale of Crown Lands in the Ceded Islands, 1763–1783', *The Historical Journal* 27, no. 3 (1984): 549–74.

[57] Philip Girard, Jim Phillips, and R. Blake Brown, *A History of Law in Canada* (Toronto; Buffalo; London: University of Toronto Press, 2019), chap. 13.

[58] Ian Ross Robertson, *The Tenant League of Prince Edward Island, 1864–1867: Leasehold Tenure in the New World* (Toronto: University of Toronto Press, 1996), 13.

[59] For a general political history of the island, see J. M. Bumsted, *Land, Settlement, and Politics on Eighteenth-Century Prince Edward Island* (Montreal: McGill-Queen's Press, 1987); Robertson, *The Tenant League of Prince Edward Island, 1864–1867;* Brendan O'Grady, *Exiles and Islanders: The Irish Settlers of Prince Edward Island* (Montreal: McGill-Queen's Press, 2004).

an appointed Council).[60] This system of governance implied that, on the one hand, PEI got greater political autonomy since it was composed of people with similar civilisations as that of England, and thus, according to J. S. Mill, were 'capable of, and ripe for, representative government'.[61] In practical terms, however, there were constraints to this political autonomy because the ultimate authority resided in the Crown-appointed governors and the London-based Secretary of State who was also part of the British cabinet. Thus, despite an 'egalitarian agrarian vision'[62] in the colony during the nineteenth century, the landlords were able to exercise their influence in England to thwart any abrogation of their rights to property.

Besides considerations around the political autonomy of the colony within the British Empire, a few local and regional aspects played salient roles in the land question. First, the socio-economic structure in the province by the middle of the nineteenth century was stratified along religious lines, especially with increased immigration from Ireland. In particular, while landlords were primarily Protestant, more and more tenant settlers were Roman Catholics.[63] The subsequent tenant rights movement in this polarised climate of Prince Edward Island paralleled events in Ireland during that time, where the Irish Catholic tenants were fighting for fixity of tenure, fair rents, and free sale from the Protestant Anglo-Irish landlords.[64] In addition to the influence of events in Ireland, there was pressure on PEI to resolve the land question in the 1860s in light of talks about the Confederation of British North American colonies, all of which had moved primarily towards freehold tenures.[65]

The nineteenth century land question in Ireland had its roots in the long and complex history of England's engagement with Ireland going back to the Middle Ages.[66] Through multiple waves of occupation, most of Ireland's land was confiscated and redistributed through grants to English and Scottish settlers, and the

[60] J. C. Beaglehole, 'The Colonial Office, 1782–1854', *Australian Historical Studies* 1, no. 3 (1941): 170–89; James A. Gibson, 'The Colonial Office View of Canadian Federation, 1856–1868', *The Canadian Historical Review* 35, no. 4 (1954): 279–313.

[61] Cited in Duncan Bell, *Reordering the World: Essays on Liberalism and Empire* (Princeton, New Jersey: Princeton University Press, 2016), 108.

[62] Rusty Bittermann and Margaret McCallum, 'When Private Rights Become Public Wrongs: Property and the State in Prince Edward Island in the 1830s', in *Despotic Dominion: Property Rights in British Settler Colonies*, ed. John McLaren, A. R. Buck, and Nancy E. Wright (Vancouver: UBC Press, 2005), 146.

[63] According to the 1871 census, about 40% of the island population consisted of Roman Catholics. See Abstracts of the Returns of the Population of Prince Edward Island, 1871 in 'Journal of the House of Assembly of Prince Edward Island, 1872' (Charlottetown: Thomas Reilly, 1872).

[64] Robertson sees parallels in the 'Tenant Leagues' of the 1860s in Ireland and Prince Edward Island. See Robertson, *The Tenant League of Prince Edward Island, 1864–1867*. There is also some suggestion that the Irish nationalist Fenian movement active in the United States and Ireland had influence in PEI. See Edward MacDonald, 'Who's Afraid of the Fenians? The Fenian Scare on Prince Edward Island, 1865–1867', *Acadiensis* 38, no. 1 (2009): 33–51.

[65] Bittermann and McCallum, 'The Pursuit of Gentility in an Age of Revolution'.

[66] For an extended discussion, see Chapter 4 of Daniel I. O'Neill, *Edmund Burke and the Conservative Logic of Empire* (Oakland, California: University of California Press, 2016).

Irish were forced to become tenants of the colonial proprietors.[67] In his influential book published in 1848, William Thornton aptly captured the conditions of the Irish:

> Ireland is one of the few countries in which there neither are, nor ever were, peasant properties. From the earliest appropriation of the soil, down to the present day, estates have always been of considerable size, and though these estates are now cut up into many small holdings, the actual occupiers of the soil, far from being landowners, are not even leaseholders, but are rackrented tenants at will. In this single phrase may be found a complete explanation of all evils of their condition, and all the defects of their character.[68]

Several historical and structural factors caused the peasantry to have poor economic conditions.[69] First, the dominance of England and the sectarian differences meant a religion-based class hierarchy, with most landlords being Anglo-Irish Protestants. At the same time, tenants were predominantly Roman Catholic, 'who, up to 1838, had to pay tithes for the Established Church of Ireland while their own clergy depended entirely on voluntary contributions'.[70] Second, unlike in England (and to some extent in the Ulster province in Northern Ireland, where tenant-right of compensation existed in practice if not in law), where landlords would invest in the improvement of the leased land, the onus of improvement, such as building wells, roads, and sheds, fell on the tenants. However, tenants did not have the security of tenure and no provisions for compensation for improvement at the end of their short leases. A third factor that exacerbated these conditions was the rapid increase of the Irish population. Increased population meant immense competition for leasehold land that strengthened the power of landlords but also had dire economic consequences from crop failure, such as the one experienced in 1846. The financial conditions of the Irish peasantry in the middle of the nineteenth

[67] For a broad overview of land tenure in Ireland over its long history, see William Ernest Montgomery, *The History of Land Tenure in Ireland* (Cambridge: At The University Press, 1889).

[68] William Thomas Thornton. *A Plea for Peasant Proprietors; with The Outlines of a Plan for Their Establishment in Ireland* (London: John Murray, Albermarle Street, 1848). Besides being a political economist, Thornton served in the East India Company in the early 1850s, advising the Governor General of India on infrastructure development. In 1858, he served as the first secretary in the newly formed India Office in London. Rack-rent is an extortionate or very high rent, the maximum that can be obtained. Tenants at will usually include yearly tenancies, or those which do not have any rights to continued occupation arising either from custom/status or contractual leases.

[69] Some of the reasons are captured in a tenant family's chronicles: 'We the Catholic majority in Ireland, had for years been treated as second class citizens by the authorities and sadly this was the case during most of my lifetime. This was most evident during the calamitous famine years when the government hardly lifted a finger to help our beleaguered Nation.' Terence Casey, *The Tenant's Tale: A Chronicle of Life in Rural Ireland during the 19th Century* (Berks, UK: Domlan Scott Ltd., 2013), 83.

[70] R. D. Collison Black, *Economic Thought and the Irish Question, 1817–1870* (Cambridge, UK: Cambridge University Press, 2015), 9.

century and the potential political fallout from their conditions, along with other Irish grievances (on matters such as political representation and religious issues), made agrarian reforms in Ireland of critical importance for the stability of colonial rule in Ireland.[71]

However, like the other two sites, any security of tenure for the peasants or tenants had to come at the expense of some property rights of the landlords. In the case of Ireland, the landlords were in a stronger position to resist encroachment on these rights. Punjab and Prince Edward Island fell on the opposite ends of the liberal imagination of the 'civilised' continuum,[72] reflected in the degree of political autonomy granted to each by the Empire. Ireland fell somewhere in between the two.[73] For example, J. S. Mill, who was closely involved in the mid-nineteenth-century land question in Ireland, was much more sympathetic to the plight of Irish peasants than those from India.[74] Yet the 'Irish still remained subordinate in [his] imperial topography; his sympathy did not translate into granting them civilisational equality'.[75] Thus, although Ireland had political representation in the British Parliament, which had the authority to pass laws for the colony, the vast majority of representatives came from the class of Anglo-Irish landlords rather than the peasantry.

The historical context of the Empire, as well as the three colonies during the period of interest, can be summarised as follows. The Liberal government of William Gladstone, with greater sympathies towards the peasants, was at the helm in England and was theoretically the final authority on any legislation across its colonies. In terms of land tenure, the common problem for the Empire in each of these sites was the need to institutionalise security of tenure for tenants/peasants, who were a large proportion of the total population in each colony and whose material wellbeing was perceived to have significant economic and political implications. However, tenants' security of tenure was to be balanced with the landlords' rights to property. While this conundrum was common in the three colonies, their differences along the following aspects influenced the land reform debates in each

[71] Matthew Kelly, 'Irish Nationalist Opinion and the British Empire in the 1850s and 1860s', *Past & Present*, no. 204 (2009): 127–54; Henry A. Brann, *Gladstone and Irish Grievance. An Essay* (New York: Benj. H. Tyrrel, 1881); E. D. Steele, 'Gladstone and Ireland', *Irish Historical Studies* 17, no. 65 (1970): 58–88; Black, *Economic Thought and the Irish Question, 1817–1870*.

[72] See J. S. Mill's views in India and settler colonies discussed above.

[73] Because of the majority Catholic population in Ireland as well as its poor economic conditions relative to the population in England, the Irish were considered to be an inferior race, 'not quite white'. For a fuller elaboration of this construction of racial inferiority of the Irish during the nineteenth century, see Kevin Kenny, 'Race, Violence, and Anti-Irish Sentiment in the Nineteenth Century', in *Making the Irish American: History and Heritage of the Irish in the United States*, ed. J. J. Lee and Marion R. Casey (New York: New York University Press, 2006), 364–80; Eagan, '"White," If "Not Quite"'.

[74] Pitts, *A Turn to Empire*.

[75] Bell, *Reordering the World*, 228.

colony: its perceived similarity with the metropole on the grounds of religion, race, or 'civilised continuum'; the degree of ambiguity about existing land-related property rights; and the power and influence of landlords in promoting their interests locally as well as in the metropole. These structural differences between the colonies eventually shaped the extent and form that security of tenure would take in each colony. A snapshot of some essential characteristics of the three colonies, which are directly relevant to land tenure, is provided in Tables 1.1 and 1.2.

Table 1.1 Some Relevant Characteristics of the Three Sites

	Punjab[a]	**Ireland**	**Prince Edward Island**[b]
Area	95768 square miles	32595 square miles	2185 square miles
Total population	17.6 million	5.4 million	94021
Cultivated area as a percentage of total land area	32%	27%[c]	43%
Land tenures (% of total acres)	Proprietors 61.6% Tenants 37.5% Other 0.9%[d]	97% of land cultivated by tenant farmers[e]	Freehold (fee simple) 67.8%[f] Leasehold 29.2% Other 3%
Other land tenure features	Average land holdings: Proprietors: 9.2 acres Tenants: 5.2 acres	50% of tenants held less than 15 acres; 44% between 15 and 100 acres	Length of leases: 999 years—83.5% 100–999 years—11.2% Less than 100 years—4.7%

[a] 'East India (Progress and Condition); Statement Exhibiting the Moral and Material Progress and Condition of India, During the Year 1867–68' (House of Commons, 1869), House of Commons Parliamentary Papers Online.

[b] 'Abstract of the Census of the Population and Other Statistical Returns of Prince Edward Island Taken in the Year 1871' (Reilly and Co., Charlottetown, 1871), Prince Edward Island Public Archives and Records Office.

[c] About 50% of the land area was for Grass and Pasture and 22% for Bog and Waste. See 'The Agriculture Statistics of Ireland for the Year 1868' (Dublin: Alexande Thom, 1869), House of Commons Parliamentary Papers Online.

[d] Government of India, Revenue and Agriculture Department, 'Punjab Revenue Report, 1880–1881. In Amendment of the Punjab Tenancy Act, XXVIII of 1868. Proceedings Nos. 21–22, January 1884', 1884, National Archives of India, NAI. 12.8 per cent was held by occupancy tenants and 24.7 by tenants-at-will. While it seems from the figures in Row 5 of this table that Punjab and PEI have similar proportion of freehold and leasehold tenures, in Punjab most of the proprietors cultivated their own land, which was not the case in PEI.

[e] Michael J. Winstanley, *Ireland and the Land Question 1800–1922* (London: Metheun & Co. Ltd., 1984). Fifty per cent of land owned by 750 families.

[f] The percentage of land under freehold increased from about 47% and leasehold decreased from 46% in 1861.

Table 1.2 Land Tenure Administration Characteristics

	Punjab	**Ireland**	**Prince Edward Island**
Antecedents to the land tenure system	Imperial creation of record of rights in the 1850s from those existing under Sikh rule	Mix of land grants after colonisation and precolonial customary tenures	Imperial allocation of property rights through land grants (1767)
Authority to make laws	Governor General of India through Council (no provincial authority)	British Parliament	Responsible Government of PEI
Possibility of local agency for land reforms	Low (no Indian members on Council)	Medium (through few elected MPs from Ireland in the British Parliament)	High (through elected legislature)
Land question in the 1860s	Preserving and expanding the occupancy rights of the tenants from the initial settlement	Legalising the tenant-right encompassing the 3Fs	Establishing tenant right of compensation in leasehold tenures and converting leasehold to freehold tenures

The Book's Arguments and Narrative Structure

Comparative analyses of the historical land tenure arrangements, the contestations during the enactment of the laws in the three colonial sites, and their interconnections reveal two crucial mechanisms which facilitated the institutionalisation of peasant proprietorship.[76] One was a fortuitous alignment of interests of the governing bodies in the three colonies whose interventions and agency were necessary to push the respective legislation on peasant rights. In the case of Punjab, it was the ideological orientation against landlordism and sympathy for the peasants of John Lawrence, the Governor General of India, and his followers who held

[76] I use a comparative method that analyses the context and content of the land tenure laws enacted in close temporal proximity across three diverse colonies of the British Empire. For some of the opportunities and challenges of this approach in dealing with the 'small-N' problem, see Anthony Musson and Chantal Stebbings, *Making Legal History: Approaches and Methodologies* (Cambridge, UK: Cambridge University Press, 2012); Oliver Moreteau, Anceto Masfesser, and Kjell A. Modeer, *Comparative Legal History* (Northampton, MA: Edward Elgar Publishing, 2019); James Mahoney and Dietrich Rueschemeyer, *Comparative Historical Analysis in the Social Sciences* (Cambridge, UK: Cambridge University Press, 2003); Mark Van Hoecke, 'Methodology of Comparative Legal Research', *Law and Method*, no. 12 (2015).

important administrative positions in India at the time. With the implicit support from the government in England, this 'Punjab School' stalled the momentum after the 1857 rebellion towards the restoration of land rights and associated privileges of the local aristocratic classes in British India. William Gladstone's agency was instrumental in legalising the rights of tenant cultivators in Ireland. Gladstone was neither ideologically driven as the 'Punjab School' nor in complete agreement with political economists regarding the fixity of tenure and peasant proprietorship. However, he understood the need to 'pacify Ireland' because of political expediency considerations arising from increased widespread unrest, the Fenian movement's activities,[77] and pressure from Irish leaders to resolve the land question. The long-standing land question in Prince Edward Island was resolved because of renewed efforts by the colony's legislature in the late 1860s to establish the rights of tenants and convert the leasehold tenures to freehold tenures considering the increased Fenian activities in North America and the ongoing discussions about joining the newly formed Dominion of Canada.

The book further shows that although the active involvement from the highest levels of the administrative hierarchy was necessary to promote the rights of the cultivators, it was not sufficient to overcome resistance from the aristocratic class in England, who saw any dilution of landowners' rights to property in the colonies as a threat to its position in the metropole. The second crucial mechanism that tempered its concerns and ultimately facilitated peasant rights was the redirection of the debate about how land reform in the colonies would impact the sanctity of English principles to one where these existing principles were deemed anomalous and thus inappropriate for the colonies. Extricating land tenure considerations in the colonies from the institutionalised practices in England allowed for inter-colony analogies and precedents to support the proprietary rights of peasant cultivators. The book identifies multiple analogies at work: the Punjab precedents of occupancy rights established in the 1868 Act and the prevalence of custom-based land relationships in the whole of British India helped legalise the Ulster and related customary tenures in Ireland in 1870; the tenant right in Ireland served as a model for Prince Edward Island Tenants' Compensation Act of 1872; and the land purchase clauses in the Irish Act and the norm of freehold tenures in British North America provided the impetus for the Island's Land Purchase Act of 1875.

Decoupling land tenure considerations in the colonies from England and using inter-colony analogies became the normative tools for successive British governments of all political stripes to expand peasant proprietorship across its colonies

[77] Fenianism was an Irish nationalist movement active in the 1860s, with the ultimate aim of Ireland's independence from British rule. It was quite active in Ireland and North America, and it often aligned its aims to land reforms favourable to Catholic tenants in Ireland and Prince Edward Island. MacDonald, 'Who's Afraid of the Fenians?'; Norman McCord, 'The Fenians and Public Opinion in Great Britain', *University Review* 4, no. 3 (1967): 227–40; John Newsinger, 'Fenianism Revisited: Pastime Or Revolutionary Movement?' *Saothar* 17 (1992): 46–52.

well into the twentieth century. *Empire and the Peasant Proprietor* demonstrates the importance of both reciprocal influences within the imperial system and the growing acceptance of the notion that policy expedients developed in one colony might be usefully considered and applied in others with similar problems, even though problematic in terms of contradicting the assumptions and rules of English law.

I develop these arguments within the context of the Empire's consolidation and evolution and the global and local challenges it experienced in the middle of the nineteenth century. Part I of the book (Chapters 1 and 2) provides the historical and theoretical contexts that informed the Empire's land question. Complementing the historical conditions outlined in this chapter are the theoretical arguments that informed the debates around land tenure across the Empire. Chapter 2 develops an analytical framework around three pillars of property rights, political economy, and political expediency. It identifies the various threads and evolving ideas amongst political theorists and political economists during the nineteenth century around the antecedents and implications of the assignment of rights of property and security of tenure in land tenure arrangements in the colonies and discusses the political concerns about the assignment of these rights to either the landowners or the peasants. The chapter shows that developing new thinking and re-evaluating existing ideas on property rights and political economy led to competing logics in the nineteenth century that could support the assignment to and/or recognition of rights of landlords or tenants. The Empire's challenge was finding ways to resolve or reconcile the competing arguments, considering its global objectives and local contingencies to address the land question.

The following parts examine land tenure contestations in the three colonies. The book dedicates two chapters to each site: the first outlines the historical antecedents to the land question of the 1860s, and the second delves into its resolution. The contestations are evaluated around the analytical framework articulated in Chapter 2.

Part II focuses on Punjab. Chapter 3 shows that the province occupied a special place in British India, reflected in its unique administrative structure and initial land tenure settlements favouring the peasant cultivators. The 1857 uprising shifted the momentum towards restoring the property rights and other privileges of the traditional aristocratic classes across British India. Consequently, it was expected that the rights of the *zamindars* (landlords) would be prioritised in Punjab during the reassessment of its initial land tenure settlements in the 1860s. Chapter 4 argues that the province could resist this conservative turn on land tenures because of the ascendancy of administrators in the colonial hierarchy with a strong affinity towards the peasants. Led by John Lawrence, the Governor General of India, the influence and agency of this 'Punjab School' was instrumental in ensuring the legalisation of substantial proprietary rights for many tenants in the 1868 Act.

Furthermore, the 'Punjab School' used the post-1857 emphasis on protecting local customs to its advantage by foregrounding customary land tenure rights before the advent of British rule. It received additional support from Henry Maine, a law member on the governing council of British India at the time, and his ideas on early institutions and communal property rights. The Punjab Act was thus a salient piece of legislation as it established peasant proprietorship (which incorporated the 'three Fs': fixity of tenure, fair rents, and freedom of sale) by overcoming strong opposition in India and England and foregrounding customary rights as a viable rationale to legalise peasants' security of tenure. The triumph of supporters of peasant rights in Punjab represented a turning point in the Empire's pursuit of institutionalising peasant proprietorship and expanding it across its colonies.

Part III examines Ireland's land question. The Irish Land Act of 1870 was the first substantial land tenure legislation after centuries of struggle that provided a modicum of security of tenure for the Irish tenants vis-à-vis their mostly Anglo-Irish landowners. To fully appreciate the challenges of establishing any proprietary rights for Irish tenants, Chapter 5 delves into the circumstances under which land tenure relationships were established during different waves of annexation, the subsequent struggles to improve the material conditions of the primarily Catholic tenants, the futile efforts of various commissions, and the numerous failed attempts to legislate in the first half of the nineteenth century through the British Parliament. The chapter shows that all efforts until the 1860s by Irish members of the British Parliament, writings of political economists such as William Thornton and J. S. Mill, and legislative actions of a few sympathetic British governments failed because of the influence of Anglo-Irish landlords and their supporters. They emphasised the English ideas of laissez faire economics, the sanctity of property rights, and the primacy of contracts in landlord-tenant relationships to deny any form of secure rights for the tenants.

Chapter 6 focuses on William Gladstone's attempts to resolve the Irish land question after leading the Liberal Party to power in 1868. Gladstone's involvement in the Irish land question coincided with two phenomena related to land tenure in India. First, the Punjab Tenancy Act, recently passed by the Governor-General of India's Council, was going to the Secretary of State for India, the Duke of Argyll. The simultaneous consideration of approving the substantial rights of tenants proposed in the Punjab Act and initiating discussions regarding appropriate rights in Ireland became intertwined. Second, a book by George Campbell, a colonial administrator in British India who closely aligned with the 'Punjab School', caught Gladstone's attention. In his book, Campbell brought attention to the historical similarities between custom-based land tenure in India and Ireland and, thus, the appropriateness of legalising such tenure for the Irish tenants. Public discussions about the Punjab Act and Campbell's book, along with new writings by Irish and English political economists, combined to change the narrative from India being an exception regarding customary rights of tenants to England being the exception in terms of contracts as the primary mechanism guiding landlord-tenant relations. The chapter suggests that this led to a theoretical shift whereby Irish land tenure issues were decoupled from existing English practices. The Gladstone government used these ideas to push the Irish Land Act through both Houses of Parliament in 1870.

Part IV describes the genesis of two land laws enacted in Prince Edward Island, the first (Tenants' Compensation Act of 1872) before and the second (Land Purchase Act of 1875) after it joined the Canadian Confederation. Approval of these laws was a culmination of a century-old struggle since France ceded the island to England in 1763 and the latter's decision in 1767 to grant large land parcels of land to a few 'persons deserving of the patronage of the Crown', most of whom remained absentee landlords. Chapter 7 outlines the implications of the initial land allocations in the colony and the various attempts by the local legislature to either get rid of the landlords or establish greater security of tenure for the tenants and the persistent push-back it received in England until the middle of the nineteenth century.

Chapter 8 evaluates the PEI legislature's attempts to resolve the land question in the late 1860s when it contemplated whether to join the Dominion of Canada, and there was a Liberal Government in England more favourably inclined towards the tenants. The chapter shows that in response to the colony's request, the Imperial Government hedged its bets by taking a two-track route in resolving the PEI land question, using inter-colony analogies, and decoupling the land question from England. From 1870 to 1872, it first used the Irish Land Act as a model to establish tenant rights in PEI when it was uncertain whether the colony would join the Dominion of Canada. Second, after PEI joined the Dominion in July 1873, the Imperial Government absolved itself from its land question on the pretext that the Dominion had the right to resolve land tenure issues based on local considerations under the new governance arrangement. In both cases, the Empire attempted to disconnect the PEI land tenure arrangements from those in England by linking it either to Ireland or British North America.

Chapter 9 in Part V reiterates the book's overall arguments and contributions. It suggests that although the Empire's overall goal was to establish some form of peasant proprietorship, it was attentive to local socio-political realities and adjusted its expectations for each colony. The different expectations explain the diversity in the extent of security of tenure and the form it took in the three colonies. The imperial approach did not necessarily involve transplanting laws from one colony to another. Instead, it used the broad logic of shared and relative rights and their implications for land improvement in the colonies to overcome the resistance of those who believed in landowners' absolute rights to property. Furthermore, by examining the implementations of the laws in each colony in the years following their enactment, this chapter shows that peasant proprietorship was either fully implemented (in the case of Prince Edward Island) or solidified (in both Punjab and Ireland) by the 1880s. More importantly, the subsequent expansion of the scope of multi-directional inter-colony analogies in assessing colonial land tenures led to further solidification of peasant proprietorship across the Empire and represented a salient institutional change that guided land reform well into the twentieth century.

The Book's Contributions

This book contributes to several bodies of literature by examining the institutionalisation of peasant proprietorship in the British Empire through a comparative approach that brings the experiences of a diverse set of colonies within a common analytical framework.

It adds to the growing corpus of research on the British Empire that exalts the virtue of 'sketching "connective" and "comparative" histories' to 'learn more about the complex and shifting nature of imperial relations as they evolved over centuries'.[78] As C. A. Bayly points out, comparative studies can help unpack questions of the Empire's global logic and the specificities of different colonial sites. One can learn 'even from the interconnections of histories . . . distant in space and cultural form' to forge a 'global social history'.[79] Similar calls are made to move towards 'imperial histories' with the 'Empire' as the unit of analysis rather than the more prevalent focus on individual colonies.[80]

The centrality of land in the formation and governance of colonial empires has generated a voluminous literature on land tenure systems, property rights, and tax revenue, among others. While much of this work falls within the domain of 'national' histories and examines multiple facets of agricultural systems and reforms in individual colonies,[81] a few recent studies have taken a comparative approach to identify various justificatory logics through which colonial empires dispossessed local populations of their lands and resources across the globe.[82] For

[78] Barry Crosbie, 'Networks of Empire: Linkage and Reciprocity in Nineteenth-Century Irish and Indian History', *History Compass* 7, no. 3 (May 1, 2009): 998. Also see C. A. Bayly, 'Ireland, India and the Empire: 1780–1914', *Transactions of the Royal Historical Society* 10 (2000): 377–97; S. B. Cook, *Imperial Affinities: Nineteenth Century Analogies and Exchanges between India and Ireland* (New Delhi: Sage Publications, 1993).

[79] Bayly, 'Ireland, India and the Empire', 377–78. Also see Annie Tindley, '"All the Arts of a Radical Agitation": Transnational Perspectives on British and Irish Landowners and Estates, 1800–1921', *Historical Research* 91, no. 254 (2018): 705–22.

[80] Steven Pincus, Tiraana Bains, and A. Zuercher Reichardt, 'Thinking the Empire Whole', *History Australia* 16, no. 4 (October 2, 2019): 610–37; Christian R. Burset, *An Empire of Laws: Legal Pluralism in British Colonial Policy* (New Haven, CT: Yale University Press, 2023).

[81] For example, see Rusty Bittermann and Margaret McCallum, *Lady Landlords of Prince Edward Island: Imperial Dreams and the Defence of Property* (Montreal: McGill-Queen's University Press, 2008); R. D. Collison Black, *Economic Thought and the Irish Question, 1817–1870* (Cambridge: Cambridge University Press, 2015); Guha, *A Rule of Property for Bengal*; Stokes, *The English Utilitarians and India*.

[82] Allan Greer, *Property and Dispossession: Natives, Empires and Land in Early Modern North America* (Cambridge, UK: Cambridge University Press, 2018); Brenna Bhandar, *Colonial Lives*

instance, Greer uses the concept of 'property formation' in the dispossession of Indigenous peoples in North America (Mexico, United States, and Canada) by the British, French, and Spanish empires during the sixteenth to eighteenth centuries to study the multiple processes through which they 'laid claim to the continent's resources, extended the reach of empire and established policies and jurisdictions for themselves'.[83] Bhandar examines the dispossession of land by the British in South Australia, British Columbia, and Palestine in the nineteenth and twentieth centuries. She argues that while colonial governments used a variety of strategies (use, improvement, propertied abstractions, status) and tools (surveying, registration, enclosures) to justify dispossessions, eventually, ideas about racial hierarchies were the common underlying narratives that took priority in this exercise around property rights in the various colonies.[84]

These comparative studies foreground how various colonial empires used law, 'regarded by the West as its most respected and cherished instrument of civilisation', as their 'vital and effective instrument of power during [their] genocidal conquest and colonisation of non-Western peoples'.[85] *Empire and the Peasant Proprietor* augments and extends this body of work by foregrounding the challenges of governing the land in the three colonies after the Empire claimed it through annexation or dispossession. These challenges included recognising pre-existing property rights, assigning new rights, and ensuring that assignees fulfil the political and economic expectations related to their land allocations. The book shows how some property rights and political economy logics (for example, 'improvement' and 'use') employed in acquiring the land often constrained imperial choices in establishing subsequent land tenure systems in its colonies. By paying close attention to how the colonial administrators reconciled some of the contradictions as the Empire transitioned from an expansion to a governance mode, this book provides a fuller picture of the Empire's legal approaches and practices in its different stages and across its diverse colonies.

A related body of research takes a comparative approach, but one based on analogies, transplants, and transfers.[86] Under the broad conceptual framing of

of Property: Law, Land, and Racial Regimes of Ownership (Durham: Duke University Press, 2018); John C. Weaver, *The Great Land Rush and the Making of the Modern World, 1650–1900* (Montreal & Kingston: McGill-Queen's University Press, 2003).

83 Greer, *Property and Dispossession*, 2.

84 These studies continue the tradition of John Weaver, who also took a comparative approach to understand the dispossession and allocation of land by various colonial powers. See John C. Weaver, *The Great Land Rush and the Making of the Modern World, 1650–1900* (Montreal: McGill-Queen's University Press, 2003).

85 Robert A. Williams, *The American Indian in Western Legal Thought: The Discourses of Conquest* (New York: Oxford University Press, 1990), 6.

86 Some influential works include Cook, *Imperial Affinities: Nineteenth Century Analogies and Exchanges Between India and Ireland*; Alan Lester, *Imperial Networks: Creating Identities in Nineteenth-Century South Africa and Britain*, 1st ed. (London: Routledge, 2001); Shaunnagh Dorsett and John McLaren, 'The Legal Histories of the British Empire: An Introduction', in *Legal Histories of the British Empire: Laws, Engagements and Legacies*, ed. Shaunnagh Dorsett and John McLaren (Abingdon,

'intra-imperial' analogies and precedents, this scholarship foregrounds how English laws and policies were transferred, transplanted, or transposed in different colonies. This book makes two contributions to this body of work. First, it examines the interconnections through the lens of 'inter-colony' analogies. Unlike 'intra-imperial' analogies, which functioned to justify the diffusion of policies based on Imperial or English principles across the Empire, I argue that 'inter-colony' analogies foregrounded the shared characteristics and experiences around land tenure relationships between the colonies and showed how these characteristics made English principles about property rights and improvement unsuited or inappropriate for the colonies. The use of inter-colony analogies, thus, led to a theoretical shift whereby existing English practices would no longer constrain subsequent land tenure questions. Second, the study uncovers multi-directional influences between the colonies in institutionalising peasant proprietorship well into the twentieth century, which include ideas originating in the 'lesser civilised' colonies influencing the 'more civilised' ones. It thus addresses the interrelated concerns identified in the literature, such as that the flows are unidirectional, with the predominant directionality being from the North to the South.[87] The reciprocal influences of colonies in facilitating land reform uncovered in this study augment the growing corpus of research that moves beyond the core/periphery model of legal transfers and transplants[88] and is attentive to the 'reverberations of actions and ideas in one colonial location across other colonial spheres'.[89]

Additionally, the book informs ongoing debates on the cohesiveness, consistency, and universality of the Empire's ideologies and institutions.[90] Several scholars have suggested that numerous events during the mid-Victorian period[91] led to a conservative backlash against the universality of liberalism and utilitarianism,

Oxon: Routledge, 2014), 1–11; John W. Cairns, *Codification, Transplants and History: Law Reform in Louisiana (1808) and Quebec (1866)* (Clark, New Jersey: Talbot Publishing, an imprint of The Lawbook Exchange, Ltd., 2015); Alison Games, *The Web of Empire: English Cosmopolitans in an Age of Expansion, 1560–1660* (Oxford: Oxford University Press, 2008); Alan Watson, 'Comparative Law and Legal Change', *The Cambridge Law Journal* 37, no. 2 (November 1978): 313–36; Toby S. Goldbach, 'Why Legal Transplants?', *Annual Review of Law and Social Science* 15, no. 1 (2019): 583–601.

[87] Goldbach, 'Why Legal Transplants?', 583–601.

[88] John McLaren, 'Chasing the Chimera: The Rule of Law in the British Empire and the Comparative Turn in Legal History', *Law in Context* 33, no. 1 (January 2015): 21–36; T. T. Arvind and Daithí Mac Síthigh, 'Constitutionalism in the Periphery: Revisiting the Roots of Self-Rule Movements in Ireland and India', *Northern Ireland Legal Quarterly* 71, no. 2 (2020): 211–37; Assaf Likhovski, 'Peripheral Vision', *Law and History Review* 36 no. 2 (2018): 235–66.

[89] Zoë Laidlaw, 'Breaking Britannia's Bounds? Law, Settlers, and Space in Britain's Imperial Historiography', *The Historical Journal* 55, no. 3 (September 2012): 830.

[90] David Armitage, *The Ideological Origins of the British Empire* (Cambridge: Cambridge University Press, 2000); Bell, *Reordering the World*; Pitts, *A Turn to Empire*; Uday Singh Mehta, *Liberalism and Empire: A Study in Nineteenth-Century British Liberal Thought* (Chicago: University of Chicago Press, 1999); Sartori, *Liberalism in Empire.*

[91] These include challenges to British rule in India (the rebellion of 1857, the Blue Mutiny in 1859), New Zealand (the Maori War in 1860), Jamaica (the Morant Bay rebellion in 1865), as well as in Ceylon and Hong Kong. Mantena, *Alibis of Empire*; Bell, 'Victorian Visions of Global Order: An Introduction'.

which, in turn, reinforced the ordering of the Empire based on a traditional/modern (or uncivilised/civilised) continuum of its various colonies.[92] According to this view, the 'culturalist' turn led to a retreat from Western ideas about property rights and political economy in the second half of the nineteenth century, with the implications for land tenure being that these ideas were now seen to be only appropriate for colonies perceived to be socio-culturally like the metropole ('civilised' and/or 'white'). In contrast, in others, traditions and customs needed to be foregrounded ('uncivilised and/or non-white). The three sites of interest in this book span the spectrum of the modernity and/or civilised continuum, and an evaluation of the debates around the pieces of legislation and their specific provisions allows for evaluating of the hypothesis (claim) regarding the disjuncture in the Empire's ideology about land tenure in the middle of the nineteenth century.

An argument probed in this book is that it was not the Western political economy and property rights theories per se that created problems for the Empire but how Western ideas about property rights could be accommodated within the various strands of political economy. The turn to 'customs' provided an additional tool to negotiate the sanctity of individual and absolute property rights questions head-on rather than indicate the abandonment of liberal principles. Foregrounding customs and customary rights during the debates on land tenure achieved dual objectives for proponents of peasant proprietorship. One, it helped promote the emerging perspective on shared or relative property rights and its implications for land improvement by landlords and tenants. Second, it allowed a decoupling of the land tenure issues from those prevalent in England and this decoupling tempered resistance in the metropole to subsequent land tenure legislation in the colonies. At least concerning land tenure, these findings support other scholars' viewpoint that resorting to customs is evidence of the Empire's adaptiveness to specific realities in its colonies.[93]

Scholarship on the British Empire is moving beyond the coloniser–colonised dichotomy within the confines of national histories and increasingly examining multi-directional flows of ideas and people across its global network. By examining specific laws related to landlord–tenant relationships across multiple colonial sites, this study attempts to contribute to the area of research that is attentive to shared legal histories arising from colonial connections.

[92] For example, see Richard Shannon, *The Crisis of Imperialism, 1865-1915* (London: Hart-Davis, MacGibbon, 1974); Karuna Mantena, 'The Crisis of Liberal Imperialism', in *Victorian Visions of Global Order: Empire and International Relations in Nineteenth-Century Political Thought*, ed. Duncan Bell (Cambridge: Cambridge University Press, 2007), 113–35; Bell, 'Victorian Visions of Global Order: An Introduction'; Bell, *Reordering the World*; Hyam, *Britain's Imperial Century, 1815–1914.*

[93] For example, Sartori, *Liberalism in Empire*; Onur Ulas Ince, *Colonial Capitalism and the Dilemmas of Liberalism* (Oxford, UK: Oxford University Press, 2018).

2

Concepts and Contestations

An Analytical Framework

Land tenure reforms in the nineteenth century were debated around the following questions: To whom are property rights in land currently allocated? To whom should they be assigned? Are there political implications depending upon whose rights are institutionalised (or not)? On the face of it, these questions were not new, as these issues informed debates on the origins, development, and implications of property rights in Western legal thought[1] and formed the basis for land occupation and appropriation by various colonial powers worldwide in the preceding centuries.[2] However, the growing consolidation of the British Empire during the nineteenth century and a shift from an 'expansion' to a 'governance' imperative necessitated thinking of property rights through the logic of reassignment and distribution rather than the previous logic of appropriation and possession.

Evolving intellectual and political currents provided the tools to rethink existing land tenure arrangements and explore new ones. First, political and legal thought shifted from the absolute sanctity of individual property rights towards concepts of relative or shared rights and distributive justice. Second, the ascendancy of the discipline of political economy provided new analytical tools to understand relationships between secure property rights and land improvement. Third, political developments created new anxieties about the stability and viability of the Empire.

These developments encompassing *property rights*, *political economy*, and *political expediency*, as well as their intersectionality, were crucial in the deliberations around the land question in the nineteenth century. The following sections foreground the contributions of political theorists, political economists, and colonial administrators in the evolution and institutionalisation of the underlying concepts

[1] J. M. Kelly, *A Short History of Western Legal Theory* (Oxford, New York: Oxford University Press, 1992); James Tully, *A Discourse on Property: John Locke and His Adversaries* (Cambridge, UK: Cambridge University Press, 1980); Alan Ryan, *Property and Political Theory* (Oxford, UK: B. Blackwell, 1984).

[2] Robert A. Williams, *The American Indian in Western Legal Thought: The Discourses of Conquest* (New York: Oxford University Press, 1990); Allan Greer, *Property and Dispossession: Natives, Empires and Land in Early Modern North America* (Cambridge, UK: Cambridge University Press, 2018); Brenna Bhandar, *Colonial Lives of Property: Law, Land, and Racial Regimes of Ownership* (Durham: Duke University Press, 2018); Andrew Fitzmaurice, *Sovereignty, Property and Empire, 1500–2000* (Cambridge, UK: Cambridge University Press, 2014); John C. Weaver, *The Great Land Rush and the Making of the Modern World, 1650–1900* (Montreal & Kingston: McGill-Queen's University Press, 2003).

Empire and the Peasant Proprietor. Preet S. Aulakh, Oxford University Press. © Preet S. Aulakh 2025.
DOI: 10.1093/9780198928270.003.0002

and ideas and various intellectual and political contestations. Some of these colonial protagonists not only provided intellectual ideas about land tenure but were also actively involved in the administration of the colonies in various capacities.[3] Wearing different hats often required tempering their intellectual positions to accommodate the practical necessities of governance.

In addition to questions about the appropriateness of secure tenurial rights for peasant cultivators given the landowners' property rights, there were also contestations around the meaning of tenants' security of tenure and the forms it could take. Furthermore, land tenures and landlord–tenant relationships in England during the middle of the nineteenth century cast a shadow on discussions on the land reforms being contemplated for the Empire's colonies. In particular, the debates revolved around the appropriateness of English principles and analogies on land tenure relationships in the colonies. The latter part of the chapter outlines the different forms of security of tenure and the salient features of English land tenures that informed land reforms in the three colonies of interest.

The methodological approach adopted in this study is a comparative historical and legal analysis entailing a 'systematic and contextualized comparison'[4] to understand the institutionalisation of peasant proprietorship during the second half of the nineteenth century in three diverse colonies of the British Empire. Such an approach necessitates an analytical framework around which the contexts and texts of the land tenure laws during the 1868–1875 period can be compared and contrasted.[5] This chapter articulates a framework (visualised in Figure 2.1) that incorporates and clarifies some of the foundational issues which resonate throughout the book.

Property Rights: Shifting Logics

A major challenge of land tenure for the Empire in the nineteenth century was the reassignment (or new recognition) of property rights. That is, colonial authorities were not operating from a *tabula rasa*. For instance, in the three colonies of interest, some form of land tenure arrangements existed by the middle of the nineteenth century: in the case of Punjab, the British inherited the pre-colonial land

[3] For instance, John Stuart Mill was employed by the East India Company and later served as a member of the British Parliament, Edmund Burke served in the British House of Commons for a long period and was actively involved in imperial policies about governing the empire, and Henry Maine played a crucial role as a law member of the Governor-General of India Council.

[4] James Mahoney and Dietrich Rueschemeyer, *Comparative Historical Analysis in the Social Sciences* (Cambridge, UK: Cambridge University Press, 2003), 10.

[5] David Ibbetson, 'Comparative Legal History: A Methodology', in *Making Legal History: Approaches and Methodologies*, ed. Anthony Musson and Chantal Stebbings (Cambridge, UK: Cambridge University Press, 2012), 131–45; Mahoney and Rueschemeyer, *Comparative Historical Analysis in the Social Sciences.*

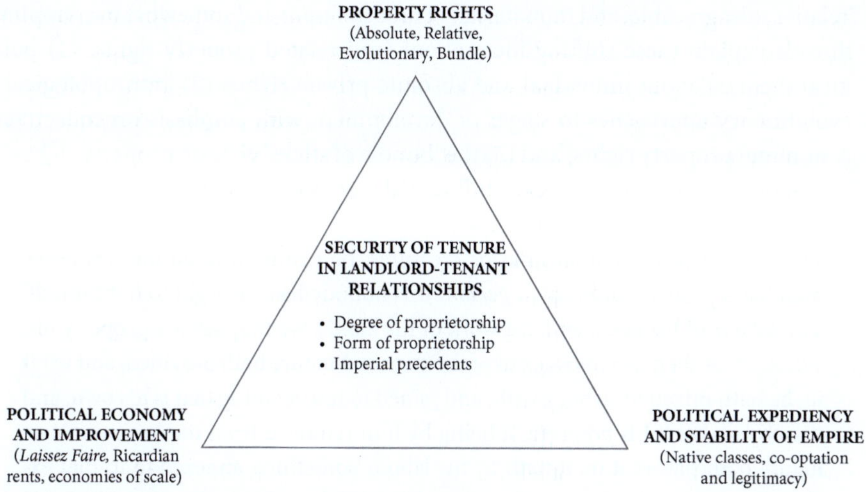

Figure 2.1 Land Tenure: An Analytical Framework

arrangements under Sikh rule; in Ireland, it was centuries-old land relationships between predominantly Protestant landowners and Catholic tenants or cultivators of the land; in Prince Edward Island, the land had been parcelled out to landlords through grants of large tracts in the eighteenth century. Thus, the Empire had to deal with some form of rights (legal or customary) residing in existing land relationships. The question was how to sift through these pre-existing arrangements to identify whose right would be prioritised and institutionalised in the proposed legislation. This entailed some form of reassignment, which caused the process of legislating the rights to become contentious in the three sites. On the fundamental question of who has which rights (in addition to who should have the rights from an economic or political perspective, which will be addressed in the subsequent sections), the various protagonists had a repertoire of theoretical justifications emanating from European political theory which they could tap into for promoting their respective positions. As suggested by Macpherson, '[p]roperty is controversial . . . because it subserves some more general purposes of a whole society, or the dominant classes of a society, and these purposes change over time: as they change, controversy springs up about what the institution of property is doing and what it ought to be doing'.[6] In particular, thinking about property rights oscillated between being seen as 'absolute, unitary, and physicalist' versus being

[6] C. B. Macpherson, ed., *Property, Mainstream and Critical Positions* (Toronto: University of Toronto Press, 1978), 11.

'relative, disagreeable, and immaterial'.[7] Three different and somewhat overlapping threads explain these shifting ideas about land-related property rights: (1) political theories about individual and absolute private rights; (2) anthropological/evolutionary approaches to stages of development with emphasis on collective/communal property rights; and (3) the 'bundle of sticks' view on property rights.

A good starting point is Locke's influential theory on property:

> Though the earth, and all inferior creatures, be common to all me, yet every man has a *property* in his own *person*: this nobody has any right to but himself. The *labour* of his body, and the work of his hands, we may say are properly his. Whatsoever then he removes out of the state that nature hath provided, and left it in, he hath mixed his labour with, and joined to it something that is his own, and thereby makes it his *property*. It being by him removed from the common state nature hath placed it in, it hath by his labour something annexed to it, that excludes the common right of other men: for this labour being the unquestionable property of the labourer, no man but he may have a right to what is once joined to, at least where there is enough, and as good, left in common for others.[8]

In summarising the prevalent discourses on property during the eighteenth century, Kelly argues that the 'philosophy of Locke on the origin and duties of property seemed perfectly satisfactory to the eighteenth century, and the century contains vigorous defences of private ownership, and the attribution of extra weight to the possession of wealth'.[9] Defenders include philosophers such as Emmanuel Kant, who expanded the ideas from ownership to possession and explained the inequity in possession of property in terms of inequalities in the distribution of human talents.[10] Additionally, they included political writers across both sides of the Atlantic. For instance, Edmund Burke, a conservative member of the House of Commons and an ardent defender of the aristocracy across the British Empire during the latter part of the eighteenth century,[11] argued that 'property, together with inequality in its distribution was both inherent in and a condition of civilisation;

[7] Faisal Chaudhry, 'A Rule of Proprietary Right for British India: From Revenue Settlement to Tenant Right in the Age of Classical Legal Thought', *Modern Asian Studies* 50, no. 1 (January 2016): 348.

[8] John Locke, *Two Treatises of Government* (Merchant Books, 1921), 134.

[9] Kelly, *A Short History of Western Legal Theory*, 293.

[10] Louis-Philippe Hodgson, 'Kant on Property Rights and the State', *Kantian Review* 15, no. 1 (March 2010): 57–87.

[11] For an excellent study of the life of Burke and in particular his justification of the empire and the need for the preservation of the local aristocracy, see Daniel I. O'Neill, *Edmund Burke and the Conservative Logic of Empire* (Oakland, California: University of California Press, 2016); For an comparison of conservative and liberal justifications of empire, see Uday Singh Mehta, *Liberalism and Empire: A Study in Nineteenth-Century British Liberal Thought* (Chicago: University of Chicago Press, 1999). For a discussion of Burke's 'universalism' and its implications for the empire, see Jennifer Pitts, *A Turn to Empire: The Rise of Imperial Liberalism in Britain and France* (Princeton, N.J.: Princeton University Press, 2005).

the confiscation of property was something totally unjustifiable, even under the pretext of a common good'.[12] Similarly, James Madison, writing in the Federalist Papers in 1787, wanted safeguards against 'a rage for paper money, for an abolition of debts, for an equal division of property, or for any improper or wicked project'.[13] Thus, at the end of the eighteenth century, Locke's theory of property, with its underlying 'principle of occupation as the origin of property was widely accepted in discussions of property in civil law and law of nations'.[14] In particular, the 'occupation–labour' combination provided the justification for dispossession of land from Indigenous populations in the New World Americas,[15] while the 'ownership' justification enshrined 'sanctity' to this absolute private property right which would constrain interference or reorganisation of this right once established as a natural right.[16]

While Rousseau, in his *Discourse on the Origins of Inequality among Men* (published in 1754), had initially raised the moral implications of inequality 'arising from the engrossment of property by individuals',[17] the intellectual currents in the early nineteenth century thoroughly explored the implications of the entrenched notions of property rights around Locke's theory and its variants. In particular, the influence of Jeremy Bentham and James Mill's utilitarianism in the early part of the century and its more radical version propounded by John Stuart Mill in the middle of the century are particularly useful in our context not only because they attempted to explore the linkages between property and distributive justice, but also because these ideas were instrumental in introducing various Western institutions (education, legal, judicial, etc.) across the British Empire in the nineteenth century.[18] On the face of it, utilitarianism's maxim that the ethical choice should

[12] Kelly, *A Short History of Western Legal Theory*, 293.

[13] Cited in Kelly, *A Short History of Western Legal Theory*, 293. For an expanded discussion of the relationship between different categories of rights, including private property, individual, and political, in early American political thought, see Jennifer Nedelsky, *Private Property and the Limits of American Constitutionalism* (Chicago and London: The University of Chicago Press, 1990).

[14] Fitzmaurice, *Sovereignty, Property and Empire, 1500–2000*, 127.

[15] Bhandar, *Colonial Lives of Property*.

[16] Locke's theory of property has had it critics, both his contemporaries and since then, who have questioned various aspects of his arguments. For details see Tully, *A Discourse on Property*; Fitzmaurice, *Sovereignty, Property and Empire, 1500–2000*. Some philosophers questioned the natural rights arguments of Locke, instead suggesting property to be either the creation of the sovereign (Hobbes) or some form of social contract (Hume). However, during much of the nineteenth century, Locke's theory (sometimes referred to as 'labour theory of property' or 'labour theory of occupation/appropriation') formed the baseline around which additional ideas of property were formulated by a few political theorists, some further supporting the sanctity of property while others questioning some of its implications for distributive justice. I engage with the relevant ideas in the following paragraphs.

[17] Kelly, *A Short History of Western Legal Theory*, 292.

[18] For information on the broader influence of utilitarianism on various aspects of the Empire, including its justification and governance, see Stokes, *The English Utilitarians and India*; Mehta, *Liberalism and Empire*; Andrew Sartori, *Liberalism in Empire: An Alternative History* (Oakland, California: University of California Press, 2014); Duncan Bell, 'John Stuart Mill on Colonies', *Political Theory* 38, no. 1 (February 1, 2010): 34–64; Bart Schultz and Georgios Varouxakis, eds., *Utilitarianism and Empire* (Lanham, MD: Lexington Books, 2005).

be one that will produce the greatest good for the greatest number (maximising overall utility) and Bentham's acknowledgement of diminishing marginal utility of wealth[19] suggest that equal distribution of goods (property) would have achieved the theory's objective of maximising overall societal utility. However, these utilitarians continued to be anxious about the implications of the distribution of property on the expectations of security from property rights (that is, how to balance equality with security).[20] For instance, in his Principles of the Civil Code (published in French in 1802 and English in 1830), Bentham identified four subordinate ends that the legislator should promote for the happiness of society: subsistence, abundance, equality, and security. He, however, acknowledged the need for trade-offs because of the impossibility of uniting these ends:

> It will sometimes happen that a measure suggested by one of these principles will be condemned by another. Equality, for example, might require a distribution of property which would be incompatible with security. When this contradiction exists between two of these ends, it is necessary to find some means of deciding the pre-eminence . . . At the first glance we see subsistence and security arising together to the same level; abundance and equality are manifestly of inferior importance . . . Equality ought not to be favoured except in the cases in which it does not interfere with security; in which it does not thwart the expectations which the law itself has produced, in which it does not derange the order already established.[21]

In essence, although the Benthamite utilitarianists accepted egalitarianism as one of the ends of political society and legislation, the primacy of security of property (that is, prioritising the 'disappointment-prevention principle' over 'the greatest happiness principle') did not allow the theory 'to bear out in its substance the promise offered by the form in which it was initially cast'.[22] The utilitarian ideas regarding political economy would play a more prominent role regarding land tenures, These are discussed in the following section.

[19] Jeremy Bentham et al., *Jeremy Bentham's Economic Writings: Critical Edition Based on His Printed Works and Unprinted Manuscripts* (London: Published for the Royal Economic Society by George Allen & Unwin, 1952).

[20] Ryan, *Property and Political Theory.*

[21] Reproduced in Macpherson, *Property, Mainstream and Critical Positions*, 41–43.

[22] D. G. Long, 'Bentham on Property', in *Theories of Property: Aristotle to Present*, ed. Anthony Parel and Thomas Flanagan (Waterloo, ON: Wilfrid Laurier University Press, 1979), 250; Critics have been puzzled with the inability of the early utilitarians to come to grips with the distributive implications of absolute property rights. Some have attributed this to the anxieties amongst British political theorists in the early part of the nineteenth century of the political implications of redistribution of land during the French revolution. Others highlight the continuing sympathies of a number of theorists to the institution of slavery as property. For details about these, see Schultz and Varouxakis, *Utilitarianism and Empire*; Ryan, *Property and Political Theory.*

Regarding property rights and distributive justice, it was John Stuart Mill who explored a more radical approach in the middle of the nineteenth century. Mill was uniquely positioned to refine ideas about property rights and land tenure in the colonies and shape some of the debates about land rights during the nineteenth century. He had imbibed ideas and limitations of earlier utilitarianism at a young age from his father, James Mill. He had engaged himself with the affairs of the Empire during his long career with the East India Company from 1823 to 1858 and as a Liberal member of the British Parliament from 1865 to 1868. Although John Stuart Mill continued to believe in the backwardness of colonised societies and the civilising mission of the British Empire articulated by his father and was unenthusiastic about introducing representative democracy in these colonies (or what is considered Mills' 'democratic partisanship' being at war with 'an elitist dread of majority tyranny'),[23] his ideas about property and peasant proprietorship were more progressive. I now turn to these.[24]

In his preface to John Stuart Mill's writings on property in *Principles of Political Economy*, Macpherson suggests that Mill viewed the 'gross inequity of the existing system ... [as being] due not to anything inherent in the principle of private property and market freedom of accumulation, but only to accidental historical features that had been built into the prevailing system and could be removed from it'.[25] To break away from the constraints of his utilitarian predecessors regarding balancing security with equality and furthering the cause of distributive justice in land relationships, Mill ('a sociologist with a conscience'[26]) probed the topic of property from multiple fronts.[27] One challenge was to address the sanctity of property rights. Here, he went back to Locke's labour theory of property but distinguished land from other forms of property:

> That a man should have absolute control over what his own labour and skill have created, and even over what he has received by gift or bequest from those who created it, is recommended by reasons of a very obvious character, and does not shock any natural feeling. Moveable property can be produced in indefinite quantity, and he who disposes of as he likes of anything which, it can fairly be

[23] J. N. Gray, 'John Stuart Mill on the Theory of Property', in *Theories of Property: Aristotle to Present*, ed. Anthony Parel and Thomas Flanagan (Waterloo, ON: Wilfrid Laurier University Press, 1979), 257.

[24] Because of his proximate position to Ireland and his stint as a member of the British parliament, John Stuart Mill was more involved with the problems of land tenure in Ireland. Here, I discuss his ideas applicable more broadly to property rights. His more specific interventions related to Ireland are discussed in more detail in Chapters 5 and 6. For his specific concerns about Ireland, see Bruce L. Kinzer, *England's Disgrace? J.S. Mill and the Irish Question* (Toronto: University of Toronto Press, 2001); J. S. Mill, *England and* Ireland, 2nd ed. (London: Longmans, Green, Reader, and Dyer, 1868).

[25] Macpherson, *Property, Mainstream and Critical Positions*, 75.

[26] Ryan, *Property and Political Theory*, 145.

[27] According to Kelly, Mill added two dimensions to the notion of utility which affirmed his commitment to promoting equality: altruism or concern for others and constructing the relationship between utility and justice. See Kelly, *A Short History of Western Legal Theory*, 215–20.

> argued, would not have existed but for him, does no worry to anyone. It is otherwise with regard to land, a thing which no man made, which exists in limited quantity, and which was the original inheritance of all mankind, and which whoever appropriates, keeps others out of its possession. Such appropriation, when there is not enough left for all, is at the first aspect, an usurpation on the rights of other people.[28]

Furthermore, he suggested that even if property in land is accepted as a principle, the nineteenth-century land tenure arrangements did not support the idea that the land's owner was contributing any value to the land through his labour: 'it is manifestly just that he who sows should be allowed to reap, this justice, which is the true moral foundation of property in land, avails little in favour of proprietors who reap but do not sow, and who assume the right of ejecting those who do'.[29] Having questioned both the labour theory of property as it applied to land and the contributions of existing proprietors to the value creation in the land through their own labour, Mill's next challenge was to justify the distributive goals, particularly that of 'peasant proprietorship'.[30] His immediate concerns were to alleviate the conditions of the peasants, motivated by his belief that the landed aristocracy was the 'concrete embodiment' of the 'sinister interests' of the British system, in which the 'nobility and squirearchy represented the dead weight of dogged obstructiveness . . . and were responsible for the degradation of the labourer'.[31] Here Mill flirted with Communism as a possible solution, writing in his *Principles*:

> If, therefore the choice were to be made between Communism with all its chances, and the present state of society with all its sufferings and injustices; if the institution of private property necessarily carried with it as a consequence, that the produce of labour should be apportioned as we now see it, almost in an inverse ratio to the labour . . . The remuneration dwindling as work grows harder and more disagreeable . . . ; if this or Communism were the alternative, all the difficulties, great or small, of Communism would be but as dust in the balance.[32]

However, he believed that some form of private ownership was necessary for the self-development and social welfare of the peasantry, and this could be accomplished through a 'national system for "raising a class of peasant-proprietors" which will provide a premium to prudence and economy affecting the whole labouring class'.[33] In this regard, Mill avoided suggesting expropriation from the

[28] Mill, *England and Ireland*, 2nd ed. (London: Longmans, Green, Reader, and Dyer, 1868), 10–11.
[29] Mill, 10–11.
[30] Leslie Stephen, *The English Utilitarians* (New York: London: G. Putnam; Duckworth, 1900).
[31] Stephen, *The English Utilitarians*, 192.
[32] John Stuart Mill and Jonathan Riley, *Principles of Political Economy: And Chapters on Socialism*, World's Classics (Oxford; New York: Oxford University Press, 1994), 14–15.
[33] Stephen, *The English Utilitarians*, 193.

landed aristocracy but instead promoted granting land to peasants from wastelands (at least in the context of Ireland).[34]

The preceding discussion revolved around the sanctity of private property related to individual and absolute ownership. I now turn to what is termed as the historical or the anthropological approach to property rights, which gained credence in the middle of the nineteenth century, with Henry Sumner Maine, a British legal theorist and long-serving (1862–1869) law member of the Governor-General of India Council, its main protagonist. Maine played a vital role in shaping ideas about property rights through his two books, Ancient Law (1861) and Village-Communities in the East and West (1871). He brought two aspects into discussions about land tenure: community and custom-based property rights.[35] In his review of Maine's *Village Communities*, John Stuart Mill wrote in 1871:

> [The book's] title indicates the double aspect of the important vein of thought which it has opened – the historical aspect, and the practical: the light which it throws on the ancient condition of mankind, and the intimate connection which it establishes between 'the early history of society' and 'modern ideas' . . . The question is opened whether the older or the later ideas are best suited to rule the future . . . A question of this nature in regard to property in land is raised by Mr. Maine's new work, which has clearly shown that the absolute ownership, which constitutes the idea of landed property as commonly conceived in England, is both modern as to time and partial as to place.[36]

The 'modern as to time and partial as to place' that Mill alludes to refers to two core ideas underlying Maine's writing on property. First, while acknowledging the natural law origins of occupation and property rights, Maine questioned the dominant notion that natural rights relate to 'individual' rights to property. Going back to the Roman law on property, he wrote in *Ancient Law* that 'there is a strong *a priori* improbability of our obtaining any clue to the early history of property if

[34] Lynn Zastoupil, 'Moral Government: J. S. Mill on Ireland', *The Historical Journal* 26, no. 3 (September 1983): 707–17.

[35] Maine's evolutionary anthropological approach on village communities in India has had its share of critics, with even fellow British colonial administrator, Baden-Powell, in his own book, *Village Communities of India*, questioning Maine's methodology and conclusions. Similarly, Bayly argues that the 'self-contained and ageless Indian village is another myth which appealed in a relatively sophisticated form to Maine and to the conservative nationalists . . . Maine's ideas and those of his followers were only historicist, not historical' (C. A. Bayly, 'Maine and Change in Nineteenth-Century India', in *The Victorian Achievement of Sir Henry Maine: A Centennial Reappraisal*, ed. Alan Diamond (New York: Cambridge University Press, 1991), 395–96). Irrespective of the veracity of Maine's claims about the village communities, what is important is that these ideas did enter into debates around land tenure at least in India and Ireland during the period of the study, and provided the justificatory logics for institutionalising particular land arrangements.

[36] John Stuart Mill, 'Maine on Village Communities', in *Collected Works of John Stuart Mill: Writings on India*, ed. John B. Robson, Martin Moir, and Zawahir Moir, vol. XXX (Toronto and Buffalo: University of Toronto Press, 1990), 215–16.

we confine our notice to the proprietary rights of individuals. It is more likely that joint-ownership, and not separate ownership, is the real archaic institution.'[37]

Having made a case for the origins of property in the form of communal ownership in primitive societies, the next challenge for Maine was to elaborate on the process by which the 'communal' transforms to 'individual'. Explaining this shift, according to him, was the 'great problem of legal history',[38] and he tried to do so through the logic of a natural process of progress whereby 'energetic and acquisitive members tended to rebel against communal authority, introducing an inequality that eroded the foundations of natural communism'.[39]

Although Maine did not provide a convincing rationale for the shift from communal to individual property, except through evolutionary progressivism from ancient to modern, his 'discovery of village communities' in India and elsewhere allowed him to make the second point, that of temporality in the development of the institutions of private property. Comparing the nineteenth-century village communities in India (and that of the Irish communities in the seventeenth century) with the ancient Roman communities and the medieval Teutonic communities in parts of Europe, Maine was able to 'question the viability and applicability of modern institutions (legal, political, and economic) in societies which have not reached the apposite state of social progress'.[40]

Maine's relativisation of private property (communal versus individual and the progress of society) had significant implications for colonial thinking on agrarian policy in the latter half of the nineteenth century.[41] One, it questioned the applicability of British ideas about property rights in the colonies at the early stages of progress, specifically those related to political economy and the efficacy of different types of land tenure.[42] Second, by foregrounding status (rather than contract) as the basis of land relationships, Maine brought customs and customary rights back into the discussions of land relationships.[43] As suggested by Mantena:

[37] Henry Sumner Maine, *Ancient Law: Its Connection with the Early History of Society and Its Relation to Modern Ideas* (London: John Murray, 1901), 271.

[38] Henry Sumner Maine, *Village-Communities in the East and West: Six Lectures Delivered at Oxford* (London: J. Murray, 1871), 131.

[39] Karuna Mantena, *Alibis of Empire: Henry Maine and the Ends of Liberal Imperialism* (Princeton, N.J.: Princeton University Press, 2010), 136–37. In addition, in the *Village Communities*, Maine attributes the shift from communal to individual property to the rise of feudalism whereby the original benefices of land from specific duties became hereditary, and passed from father to son (Maine, *Village-Communities in the East and West*, 132).

[40] Mantena, *Alibis of Empire*, 120.

[41] Clive Dewey, 'The Influence of Sir Henry Maine on Agrarian Policy in India', in *The Victorian Achievement of Sir Henry Maine: A Centennial Reappraisal*, ed. Alan Diamond (New York: Cambridge University Press, 1991), 353–75.

[42] I discuss these in more detail in the next section.

[43] The utilitarianism of Bentham and Mill loathed the idea of taking customs into consideration in introducing Western institutions in colonised societies and in achieving their goals of civilising the colonised (Andrew Sartori, 'The British Empire and Its Liberal Mission', *The Journal of Modern History* 78, no. 3 (2006): 623–42). For an expanded discussion about the linkages between customs and moral and political backwardness in the colonies by the proponents of utilitarianism and liberalism throughout the nineteenth century, see Pitts, *A Turn to Empire*; Mehta, *Liberalism and Empire*.

> The turn to custom would become more radical; anthropological and historical investigations such as Maine's would demonstrate the persistence of customary ideas and practices, themselves taken as signs of the resistance of traditional society to imposed modernisation. In India, a growing administrative deference to the imperatives of custom cemented the view that India (and Ireland) could no longer be viewed as a blank slate upon which one could recreate English institutions.[44]

While Maine's main objective was to draw a distinction between communal and individual property rights and justify the historical shift from the former to the latter in evolutionary progressivism, he also alluded to the possibility that property rights need not be unitary. In *Village Communities*, he wrote: 'The rights of property, are in the eyes of the jurist, a bundle of powers, capable of being mentally contemplated apart from one another and capable of being separately enjoyed.'[45] Maine's view of property as a bundle of rights aligned with the emerging ideas in the middle of the nineteenth century that questioned whether '"the" right to property constituted any single and distinct right at all.'[46]

There are two lines of thought around the 'bundle of rights' or 'bundle of sticks' view of property: property as a set of analytically distinct elements and its relational nature.[47] First, one could disaggregate an individual's absolute right of property into various components, such as claims, privileges, powers, and immunities,[48] or several basic elements, such as rights and duties.[49] For example, in his three-volume manual, *The Land-Systems of British India*, Baden-Powell, a colonial administrator, explained that the term 'proprietary right', which frequently appeared in revenue books of India in the middle of the nineteenth century, emanated from multiple claimants to the rights of property:

> I presume that the use of such a phrase is due to the feeling that we rarely acknowledge anything like a complete unfettered right vested in any one person ... It is true that, in many cases, only one person is called 'landlord' or 'actual proprietor,'

[44] Mantena, *Alibis of Empire*, 147.
[45] Maine, *Village-Communities in the East and West*, 158.
[46] Chaudhry, 'A Rule of Proprietary Right for British India', 348.
[47] Anna di Robilant, 'Property: A Bundle of Sticks or a Tree', *Vanderbilt Law Review* 66, no. 3 (2013): 869–932. The bundle of rights/sticks view is controversial, with some arguing that it undermines the very core of the sanctity of property rights by diluting the individual rights, while others critiquing it for continuing to emphasise the individual (having different types of rights) private rights and not paying more attention to the public or societal factors influencing these rights. See Myrl L. Duncan, 'Reconceiving the Bundle of Sticks: Land as a Community-Based Resource', *Environmental Law* 32, no. 4 (2002): 773–808.
[48] di Robilant, 'Property'.
[49] Oliver Wendell Holmes, 'The Arrangement of Law. Privity', *American Law Review* 7 (1872): 46–65; For an extended discussion on this, see Daniel H. Cole and Peter Z. Grossman, 'The Meaning of Property Rights: Law versus Economics?' *Land Economics* 78, no. 3 (2002): 317–30.

> but his right is limited; the rest of the right, so to speak, is in the hands of the other grades, even though they are called 'tenants,' or some vague title such as 'tenure-holders.' … The 'proprietary right' seems then a natural expression of the interest held by a landlord, when that interest is not the entire 'bundle of rights' (which in the aggregate make up an absolute or complete estate) but only *some* of them, the remainder enjoyed by other persons.[50]

Given the different components of and claimants to property rights, the role of the state becomes essential since it legitimises individual property rights and protects those rights (that is, 'property rights are state-backed entitlements rather than natural rights')[51] and can rearrange those rights to try to balance private rights with the public good.[52]

Second, there was a shift in seeing property in terms of a relationship between 'a person and a thing' to one of a relationship 'between persons' which bound the holder of property to 'other social actors'.[53] The relational and multiple-component views of property rights, in combination, challenged the unitary and absolute ideas that were the foundations of earlier political theories and allowed for the possibility of their malleability.[54]

The multiple and shifting ideas about property rights during the eighteenth and nineteenth centuries informed discussions and debates regarding the structuring of land relationships in the various colonies of the British Empire. Much of this discussion focused on some foundational principles underlying property rights: who has the rights, and whether these are absolute or relative, individual or collective, fixed or shifting?

Political Economy, Land Tenure, and Improvement

Along with being attentive to these questions, one must address another consideration: the economic implications of various combinations of land rights being

[50] B. H. Baden-Powell, *The Land Systems of British India, Volume I* (Oxford: Clarendon Press, 1892), 217–18.

[51] di Robilant, 'Property', 884.

[52] Margaret E. McCallum, 'The Sacred Rights of Property: Title, Entitlement, and the Land Question in Nineteenth-Century Prince Edward Island', in *Essays in the History of Canadian Law in Honour of R.C.B. Risk*, ed. G. Blaine Baker and Jim Phillips, vol. VIII (Toronto: University of Toronto Press, 1999), 358–97.

[53] Chaudhry, 'A Rule of Proprietary Right for British India', 371.

[54] For an extended discussion on the intellectual currents in the nineteenth century that exalted absolute rights to property as essential to society but at the same called for a rethinking of existing property relations based on the lived realities and actual practices across the colonies, see Greer, *Property and Dispossession*, chap. 11. The relational view is discussed at length in Shitong Qiao and Frank Upham, 'Evolution of Relational Property Rights: A Case of Chinese Rural Land Reform', *Iowa Law Review* 100, no. 6 (2015): 2479–2506.

contemplated. Colonial authorities could not be 'content merely to frame the agrarian structure (that is, establish and define landed property) in the hope of promoting commercial expansion and securing its revenue'. They had to think about mechanisms or policies that would promote the efficient use of land as part of 'broader social and economic strategies'.[55] Here, theoretical insights from the emerging discipline of political economy played a crucial role.

The economic motivation behind various empires' formation, expansion, and continuation necessitated coherent policies to achieve the desired objectives, and 'improvement' was the broad narrative under which colonial land policies were established. 'Improvement', as a mark of civilised society, was initially used to justify the dispossession of land from native societies and its appropriation for settlers.[56] From the previously discussed political theory perspectives on property rights, land not cultivated according to European notions of agriculture was considered 'no-one's land or *terra nullius*',[57] and a 'sign of cultural and intellectual inferiority'.[58] Accordingly, land used by '[n]omads, herdsmen, hunter-gatherers, or even peasants who moved frequently',[59] or for subsistence agriculture, was considered 'unimproved' and available for assignment to those who would bring it under acceptable cultivation methods.

However, once the land was settled and used through European ideas of cultivation, the objective was to improve (or develop) the settled lands. In this context, economic arguments regarding land tenure arrangements between landlords and tenants arose. As suggested by Weaver, '[i]mprovement and property rights have had a reciprocal association since the Enlightenment. People who improved land deserved property rights; property rights improved societies'.[60] From this perspective, one can differentiate how property rights and political economy discourses viewed improvement in the land. While political theory arguments discussed in the previous section relate to the first part (improvers get property rights), political economists were concerned with the effects of providing security of tenure (secure property rights lead to improvement) to the full exploitation/development of the land. Security of tenure benefits the occupiers of land through two mechanisms: first, it provides an *incentive* to make investments for improvement, with the

[55] Peter G. Robb, *Peasants, Political Economy, and Law* (New Delhi: Oxford University Press, 2007), 15. For an extended discussion on shifting conceptions of property in the nineteenth century, especially related to improvement or development, see Chapter II of Morton J. Horwitz, *The Transformation of American Law, 1780–1860* (Cambridge, MA: Harvard University Press, 1977).

[56] Greer, *Property and Dispossession*; John C. Weaver, 'Concepts of Economic Improvement and Social Construction of Property Rights: Highlights from the English-Speaking World', in *Despotic Dominion: Property Rights in British Settler Colonies*, ed. John McLaren, A. R. Buck, and Nancy E. Wright (Vancouver, B.C.: UBC Press, 2005), 79–102.

[57] C. A. Bayly, *The Birth of the Modern World 1780–1914* (Malden, MA: Blackwell Publishing, 2004), 299.

[58] Bhandar, *Colonial Lives of Property*.

[59] Bayly, *The Birth of the Modern World 1780–1914*, 299.

[60] Weaver, *The Great Land Rush and the Making of the Modern World, 1650–1900*, 28.

expectation that the fruit from the improvement flows to the occupiers. Second, security of tenure facilitates the *ability* to make investments for improvements through commodification or marketisation of their holdings and participating in credit (that is, use the land as collateral) and transfer markets (that is, the ability to sell or rent the land).[61]

Intellectual developments in political economy, especially related to laissez faire and rent theory principles, provided the economic foundations for formulating colonial land policies. However, like the property rights arguments discussed in the previous section, and maybe because of those, these principles within political economy also generated substantial differences of opinion amongst the proponents and colonial administrators. While there was agreement that secure property rights were the bedrock for improvement,[62] the fundamental debate revolved around who gets the security of tenure in land relationships: the landlord (the owner) or the tenant (the cultivator)? To elucidate the intersection of political theory and political economy on this security of tenure question, I briefly describe the case of land tenure in Bengal, which was the first part of India to come under the East India Company.[63]

The East India Company was responsible for land administration in India in 1765 when the Mughal emperor granted it the Diwani rights (that is, collection of land revenues directly from the people). The company paid an annual tribute to the emperor.[64] With minimal knowledge of the province and no experience in civil administration, the initial years of revenue collection were chaotic. Low revenue collections and the famine of 1770 brought the first attempt to systematise land revenue administration. The 'Farming System' introduced under the Governor-General, Warren Hastings, effectively expropriated all land from the landlords (*Zamindars*) and auctioned it to the highest bidders for up to five years' leases.

[61] Timothy Besley, 'Property Rights and Investment Incentives: Theory and Evidence from Ghana', *Journal of Political Economy* 103, no. 5 (1995): 903–37; Claire Priest, *Credit Nation: Property Laws and Legal Institutions in Early America* (Princeton: University Press, 2021); Michael Albertus, *Property without Rights: Origins and Consequences of the Property Rights Gap* (Cambridge, UK: Cambridge University Press, 2020).

[62] For a critical discussion, see Ross Levine, 'Law, Endowments and Property Rights', *Journal of Economic Perspectives* 19, no. 3 (September 2005): 61–88. Subsequent literature has identified three mechanisms through which secure property rights provide the incentives for improvement in land: freedom from expropriation, use of land for collateral, and ability to benefit from trade through sale. See Besley, 'Property Rights and Investment Incentives: Theory and Evidence from Ghana'; Timothy J. Besley, Konrad B. Burchardi, and Maitreesh Ghatak, 'Incentives and the De Soto Effect', *The Quarterly Journal of Economics* 127, no. 1 (February 1, 2012): 237–82. These mechanisms are closely related to two of three Fs (fixed tenure, and freedom of sale) demanded by tenant right proponents in Ireland (discussed in Chapter 5).

[63] For details about the institutionalisation of land tenure in Bengal, see the influential book by Ranajit Guha, *A Rule of Property for Bengal: An Essay on the Idea of Permanent Settlement* (Durham: Duke University Press Books, 1996); For a general description of land tenure in India see Chapters 3 and 4 of Tirthankar Roy and Anand V. Swamy, *Law and the Economy in Colonial India, Markets and Governments in Economic History* (Chicago, London: The University of Chicago Press, 2016).

[64] The local ruler of Bengal was defeated in the Battle of Plassey in 1757, and the agreement with the Mughal emperor led to the de facto rule of Bengal coming under the East India Company.

Edmund Burke, no friend of Hastings,[65] saw this expropriation and public auction as a gross subversion of private property rights that ripped 'apart the prescriptive inheritance passed on by their aristocratic forefathers in the form of ancient institutions and rights'.[66] Leaving aside criticisms around the sanctity of property rights, the system implemented did not solve the revenue collection problem, as the lease duration was too short to provide an incentive for the leaseholder to make any substantial improvements in the land.

After setting up a commission to probe the matter further, the East India Company put a new system called the Permanent Settlement in 1793, which would stay in place in one form or another until after India's independence in the second half of the twentieth century. The settlement restored land to the old landlords, made it inheritable, and fixed land revenue owed to the state in perpetuity. According to its promoters, the new system venerated private property, instituted security of tenure, and 'entrusted property to the care of a class of native entrepreneurs who had solid interest in the land and were politically reliable. This system alone could establish 'the permanence of dominion'.[67] These rationales aligned with the dominant eighteenth-century property (the sanctity of individual property rights) and political economy (laissez faire)[68] theories, which tilted in favour of the landlords and aristocrats. Although one of the proponents of permanent settlement had argued about the need for some form of secure tenure for the cultivators (*ryots*) way back in 1776,[69] the regulation that was adopted in 1793 reserved the right to consider this sometime in the future:

> The Governor-General in Council will, whenever he may deem it proper, enact such Regulations as he may think necessary for the protection and welfare of dependent talookdars, ryots, and other cultivators of the soil; and no zemindar, independent talookdar, or other actual proprietor of the land, shall be entitled,

[65] Burke prosecuted the impeachment trial of Hastings in the British Parliament. See Nicholas B. Dirks, *The Scandal of Empire: India and the Creation of Imperial Britain* (Cambridge, MA: Belknap Press of Harvard University Press, 2006).

[66] O'Neill, *Edmund Burke and the Conservative Logic of Empire*, 111.

[67] Guha, *A Rule of Property for Bengal*, 9.

[68] As discussed below, laissez faire theories/approaches saw minimal role of the state (through laws and policies) in coordinating economic activities.

[69] Minute of Philip Francis: Plan for a Settlement of the Revenues, January 22, 1776:

> 'Having thus taken ample care of the rights of the Zemindars, and given security to their property, the next step is to make similar provisions for their tenants. The land is the hereditary property of the Zemindar. He holds it by the law of the country. On the tenure of paying a certain contribution to Government. When this condition is complied with, he is master of the land to re-let it to whom he thinks proper; but when he has given a lease of any part of it to a Ryot, the condition of such lease should be invariably adhered to. In other words, the same security, which Government gives to the tenant in chief, should for the same reasons, descend to the undertenants in their several gradations; so that every rank of society and every member of it may have something to call own.' (Romesh C. Dutt, ed., Sir Philip Francis's Minutes of the Subject of a Permanent Settlement for Bengal, Behar and Orissa (Calcutta: S.C. Auddy and Co., Booksellers and Publishers, 1901), 55.)

> on this account, to make any objection to the discharge of the fixed assessment which they have respectively agreed to pay.[70]

Despite several attempts by colonial administrators to revisit the security of tenure for tenants in the first half of the nineteenth century, experiments with a form of peasant proprietorship in other parts of India, and persistent critiques from utilitarian and liberal political theorists of the permanent settlement for privileging landlord interests, it was not until 1859 that changes were made to land tenure in Bengal.[71] Multiple agrarian insurrections against the exploitative landlords in the 1830s and 1840s, the uprising of 1857, and the Indigo revolt in 1859[72] finally convinced the colonial government to enact some legislation to protect the tenants.[73] This took the form of the Bengal Rent Act of 1859, which, while reaffirming the property rights of landlords, created a category of privileged occupancy tenants whose tenures were secured in perpetuity, subject to paying a 'fair and equitable' rent. This fair and equitable rent became controversial in several high-profile legal challenges soon after its passage, drawing in theoretical debates about property rights and political economy.[74] The court challenges involved the ability of landlords to increase 'contract rents' (that is, the annual payments) when the value of the output from land increased. However, the legal arguments in the judgments were based on David Ricardo's 'economic rents', that is, what should be the proportionality of distribution of the gains between tenants and landlords.[75] The crux of the matter was determining whether land improvement was attributable to the landlord or the tenant. Furthermore, should a rent increase be apportioned according to the relative effort or be appropriated by the owner/proprietor, the landlord? Thus, the question of rights surfaced again, but this time, it was within the domain of political economy and revolved around laissez faire theories and Ricardian rents.[76]

[70] Reproduced in Roy and Swamy, *Law and the Economy in Colonial India*, 36.

[71] For details about the various regulations that further strengthened the hand of the landlords during this period, as well debates about furthering tenant rights, see Radharomon Mookerjee, *Occupancy Right, Its History and Incidents* (Calcutta: Calcutta University Press, 1919); Roy and Swamy, *Law and the Economy in Colonial India*.

[72] Indigo became a big export from India in the nineteenth century. Indigo production was done in large plantations owner by colonial merchants. The tenant-cultivators in these plantations were forced to grow indigo even when it was not economically viable for them. The tenants finally revolted in 1859, and their insubordination was violently crushed by the planters, with the support from the colonial government. For some of the political and legal aspects of the revolt, see Sartori, *Liberalism in Empire*. For cultural and political aspects, see Nandi Bhatia, *Acts of Authority, Acts of Resistance: Theater and Politics in Colonial and Postcolonial India* (Ann Arbor: University of Michigan Press, 2004).

[73] Robb, *Peasants, Political Economy, and Law*.

[74] For details about these cases, especially the 'Great Rent Case', see Chapters 3 and 4 of Sartori, *Liberalism in Empire*.

[75] The revenue demands by the state on the landlords were fixed in the Permanent Settlement. Any economic gains from the improvement in land (reflected in the chargeable rent) were theoretically for the landlord to appropriate.

[76] For details about political economy and land tenure in the three colonial sites of interest, see S. Ambirajan, *Classical Political Economy and British Policy in India* (Cambridge, UK: Cambridge

The discipline of political economy emerged in the eighteenth century.[77] It sought to develop principles that could 'advise the statesman on how he could best manage the economic affairs of the state so that the wants of the citizens could be met'.[78] The policy instruments were needed primarily to support the 'invisible hand' of the market to promote competitive behaviour between economic actors so that the initiatives of individuals are rewarded. Calling this a system of natural liberty, Adam Smith, in *Wealth of Nations*, identified only three duties of the state or sovereign to facilitate the functioning of this economic system: national defence, administration of justice, and providing public works and institutions related to infrastructure and education.[79] This doctrine of laissez faire, with minimal interference of the state in economic transactions, underlay the granting of unambiguous rights to the landowners, including the ability to choose the tenure of land for the tenants/cultivators and determine appropriate rent. As suggested by Thomas Metcalf:

> Those who accepted the theories of laissez faire . . . looked on tenancy legislation [that granted security of tenure to the cultivators] as a harmful and retrograde measure. By restricting the landlord, they argued, it would stifle capital investment and perpetuate uneconomic smallholdings. This faith in the landlord as the agent of agrarian progress reflected ultimately the success of large-scale capitalist farming in England.[80]

In contrast, while accepting the primacy of the market as the guiding economic principle, utilitarians such as Jeremy Bentham and John Stuart Mill nonetheless

University Press, 1978); R. D. Collison Black, *Economic Thought and the Irish Question 1817–1870*, Reprint edition (Cambridge, UK: Cambridge University Press, 2015); Rusty Bittermann and Margaret McCallum, 'When Private Rights Become Public Wrongs: Property and the State in Prince Edward Island in the 1830s', in *Despotic Dominion: Property Rights in British Settler Colonies*, ed. John McLaren, A. R. Buck, and Nancy E. Wright (Vancouver, B.C.: University of British Columbia Press, 2005), 144–68.

77 The foundational text of classical political economy is Adam Smith's *Wealth of Nations* published in 1776 (Adam Smith and D. D. Raphael, *The Wealth of Nations*, Everyman's Library 11 (New York: Knopf: Distributed by Random House, 1991)), and subsequently include writings of Jeremy Bentham (Jeremy Bentham et al., *Jeremy Bentham's Economic Writings: Critical Edition Based on His Printed Works and Unprinted Manuscripts* (London: Published for the Royal Economic Society by George Allen & Unwin, 1952)), David Ricardo (David Ricardo, *The Principles of Political Economy & Taxation*, Everyman's Library (London: New York: J.M. Dent & Sons, Ltd.; E. P. Dutton & Co, 1912)), and J. S. Mill, among others.

78 James A. Caporaso and David P. Levine, *Theories of Political Economy* (New York: Cambridge University Press, 1992), 1.

79 Smith and Raphael, *The Wealth of Nations*, 651. Smith also did not see an economic benefit of colonisation since imperial ventures necessarily encompassed monopolies and protectionism and thus 'interfered with the natural development of commercial economies . . . and injured the general welfare of society'. Pitts, *A Turn to Empire*, 54.

80 Thomas R. Metcalf, 'Laissez Faire and Tenant Right in Mid-Nineteenth Century India', *The Indian Economic & Social History Review* 1, no. 1 (1963): 75.

preferred a more expansive role of the state to promote some form of distributive justice. The economic rationale to achieve this objective, at least in the context of land tenure, was provided by the rent theory proposed by David Ricardo in 1817. Distinguishing contract rent from economic rent, he defined the latter as 'that portion of the produce of the earth which is paid to the landlord for the use of the original and indestructible powers of the soil'.[81] He suggested that the possibility of rent arose for the landlord due to two conditions: a limited quantity of land and the differential quality (fertility) across parcels of land,[82] and 'in the long run, as population and wealth increase, landlords would be able to appropriate a growing share of society's product. Landlords [thus] did not create rent, they merely appropriated it'.[83]

Ricardo's theory on the conditions for the emergence of rent in land and its appropriation by the landlords was adopted by those opposed to the political dominance of the landed aristocracy. In his own *Principles of Political Economy* published in 1848, John Stuart Mill used the logic of Ricardian rents to explain how the fruits of agricultural improvement went primarily to the landlords:

> The economical progress of a society constituted of landlords, capitalists, and labourers, tends to the progressive enrichment of the landlord class; while the cost of the labourer's subsistence tends on the whole to increase, and profits to fall. Agricultural improvements are a counteracting force to the last two effects; but the first, though a case is conceivable in which it would be temporarily checked, is ultimately in a high degree promoted by those improvements; and the increase of population tends to transfer all the benefits derived from agricultural improvement to the landlord alone.[84]

In his subsequent writings, Mill distinguished between two types of landlords: improving and sleeping. The increase in rent for the former was due to the 'exertion or expenditure of the owner' and thus could not be subject to any objection. On the other hand, the rent increase for the sleeping landlords was due to the 'general prosperity produced by the labour and outlay of other people'.[85] The possible alternatives to curb the appropriation of rent by the non-improving and absentee landlords included a tax on the landlord's rent (Ricardo's view that

[81] Ricardo, *The Principles of Political Economy & Taxation*, 33.

[82] He wrote: 'On the first settling of a country in which there is an abundance of rich and fertile land, a very small proportion of which is required to be cultivated for the support of the actual population, or indeed can be cultivated with the capital which the population can command, there will be no rent; for no one would pay for the use of the land when there was an abundant quantity not yet appropriated, and, therefore, at the disposal of whoever might choose to cultivate it' (Ricardo, 34).

[83] Avner Offer, 'Ricardo's Paradox and the Movement of Rents in England, c. 1870–1910', *The Economic History Review* 33, no. 2 (1980): 236.

[84] Mill and Riley, *Principles of Political Economy*, 99.

[85] J. S. Mill's address to the Land Tenure Reform Association in 1871, quoted in Offer, 'Ricardo's Paradox and the Movement of Rents in England, c. 1870–1910', 237–38.

'[g]round rents and the ordinary rent of land are, . . . perhaps, the species of revenue which can bear to have a peculiar tax imposed upon them')[86] and the more radical solution proposed by Marx and Engel's in the *Communist Manifesto* for 'the abolition of property in land and the application of all rents of land to public purposes.'[87]

As discussed before, political theorists such as Jeremy Bentham and John Stuart Mill were not ready to fully abrogate the principles of private property. However, from a political economy perspective, some form of state intervention to curb the parasitical landlord and improve the conditions of the cultivators could be justified. They supported legislation that established tenant rights in the form of security of tenure for the cultivators (that is, rewarding those making actual improvements in land) and restricting the ability of landlords to arbitrarily increase the rents (that is, ensuring equitable distribution from the gains from improvement).[88]

Political economists also explored improvement in relation to the size of landholdings as it had implications for the distributive objective of creating peasant proprietors. In his *Wealth of Nations*, Adam Smith had cautioned against large landholdings, arguing that it 'seldom happens . . . that a great proprietor is a great improver . . . To improve land with profit . . . requires exact attention to small savings and small gains, of which a man of great fortune . . . is very seldom capable.'[89] However, much of the economic thinking at the beginning of the nineteenth century was sceptical of small farms as engines of improvement on two grounds: one, the full potential of agriculture could be achieved only through large investments and economies of scale. Peasant proprietors did not have the means to invest in mechanisation and achieve the necessary scale.[90] Two, the thinking was that peasant proprietors lacked the incentive to improve because '[g]uaranteed against absolute poverty by their possession of a holding', they 'preferred leisure to economic maximisation.'[91] Critics of peasant proprietorship furthermore pointed to the large landholdings and capitalist farming prevalent in England as the model of agriculture progress. It was only in the nineteenth century that the benefits of small landholding gained currency as political economists used the success of small farms in a few European countries and the benefits of widely held freehold

86 Reproduced in Offer, 236–37.

87 Reproduced in Offer, 237.

88 For a detailed discussion on how liberalism was challenged in terms of its universal principles of liberty within the context of modern institutions and the empire, especially in relation to political economy, see Sartori, *Liberalism in Empire*; Sartori, 'The British Empire and Its Liberal Mission'.

89 Smith and Raphael, *The Wealth of Nations*, 225 Book III, Chapter II.

90 Clive J. Dewey, 'The Rehabilitation of the Peasant Proprietor in Nineteenth-Century Economic Thought', *History of Political Economy* 6, no. 1 (1974): 17–47; Ambirajan, *Classical Political Economy and British Policy in India*.

91 Dewey, 'The Rehabilitation of the Peasant Proprietor in Nineteenth-Century Economic Thought', 18.

tenures in North America to rehabilitate peasant proprietorship as a viable path for improvement.[92]

By the middle of the nineteenth century, principles from political economy could be used to justify land improvement by landowners and cultivators in large and small landholdings. These, along with the various interpretations of property rights, provided colonial administrators with enough theoretical tools to navigate the complexities of land tenure relationships and justify their respective views.[93] However, rights and economic benefits needed to be assessed within the political climate of the respective colony. Thus, questions about the political expediency and stability of the Empire became the third component in dealing with land tenure.

Political Expediency and Stability of the Empire

> Its chivalry was that of Robin Hood, who is said to have robbed the wealthy and to have given to the poor. Robin Hood, however, managed to secure the favour of those whom he gave his loot. We managed to make them as hostile as those we plundered.[94]
>
> ---- Lord Ellenborough, Governor General of India

This statement from the immediate aftermath of the 1857 Indian rebellion, lamenting the lack of support for the British by the peasants in the province of Oudh despite being granted secure tenure rights vis-à-vis the landed aristocracy in 1856, highlights colonial anxieties about the political ramifications of their land policies on the stability of the Empire. A vast majority of the population in the various colonies of the British Empire was economically dependent on land, and existing land relationships were closely tied to the local political and social structures. Any restructuring of land tenure necessarily impinged on existing hierarchies and had destabilising implications. Furthermore, political movements (with economic and social impact) across the Empire in the nineteenth century created anxieties due to their potential to make common cause with the landlords or peasants involved in the struggle over agrarian rights.[95] These considerations

[92] John Elliott Cairnes, 'Ireland in Transition: Peasant Proprietorship', *The Economist*, November 4, 1865.

[93] J. M. Currie, *The Economic Theory of Agricultural Land Tenure* (Cambridge, New York: Cambridge University Press, 1981).

[94] Reproduced in Thomas R. Metcalf, 'The Influence of the Mutiny of 1857 on Land Policy in India', *The Historical Journal* 4, no. 2 (1961): 155.

[95] The interests and objectives of political movements did not always have a symmetrical alignment with those of interests of either the landlords or the peasants. For instance, the 1857 Rebellion in India is considered by some historians as an elite insurrection to restore the Indian aristocracy to power (see Bipan Chandra, ed., *India's Struggle for Independence, 1857–1947* (New Delhi, India: Penguin Books,

brought the necessity of greater attentiveness to the political implications of reforms being contemplated in the various colonies.[96] Within the context of land tenure, political expediency required an assessment of the relative merits of promoting landlord or tenant interests to ensure the stability of colonial rule. Here again, there was disagreement regarding the value of the landed aristocracy in ensuring the Empire's stability, either by directly supporting colonial rule and/or by keeping the aspirations of the peasantry in check.[97]

On one side were those who considered the landed aristocracy in the colonies like the one in England regarding its socio-political standing and saw it as a guardian of a stable social order.[98] Landed estates 'held together by primogeniture and entail were supposed to maintain a beneficial political order'.[99] Edmund Burke, a major proponent of this view, critiqued British colonial rule in Ireland and India. He argued that the 'peculiarities of Ireland's conquest had warped and transmogrified Ireland's "natural aristocracy" and destroyed the appropriate relationship between landed wealth and political power that it should ideally embody'.[100] Burke was equally critical of the East India Company, calling company administrators 'destroyers of the nobility and gentry of a whole kingdom . . . [and] birds of prey and passage, with appetites continually renewing for a food that is continually wasting'.[101] The other side viewed the landed aristocracy as parasitical, tradition-bound, and a constraint on the moral and economic progress of the masses, as well as a 'heavy burden on agricultural productivity'.[102] According to John Stuart Mill, the British government had supported, in both Ireland and India, a 'rapacious nobility at the expense of wretched peasant populations'.[103]

1989)). Similarly, the struggle of the Irish home rule movement did not necessarily have land reforms as one of its primary objectives (see Matthew Kelly, 'Irish Nationalist Opinion and the British Empire in the 1850s and 1860s', *Past & Present*, no. 204 (2009): 127–54)), and the Escheat Movement and Tenant League in Prince Edward Island often had diverging interests (see Ian Ross Robertson, 'Political Realignment in Pre-Confederation Prince Edward Island, 1863–1870', *Acadiensis* 15, no. 1 (1985): 35–58). I will be exploring these aspects further in the individual chapters on each colonial site.

96 Duncan Bell, *Reordering the World: Essays on Liberalism and Empire* (Princeton, New Jersey: Princeton University Press, 2016); also see Sidney James Owen, 'The Stability of Our Indian Empire', *The Contemporary Review, 1866–1900; London* 31 (February 1878): 494–519.

97 From the perspective of the proponents of the aristocracy and those opposed to it, the alternative did not entail giving greater political rights to the masses, as both saw most of the colonised societies as inferior and in need of civilising before questions about political representation could be considered, see Mehta, *Liberalism and Empire*; O'Neill, *Edmund Burke and the Conservative Logic of Empire*; Pitts, *A Turn to Empire*. The settler colonies were seen somewhat differently regarding their readiness for limited self- government, see Bell, 'John Stuart Mill on Colonies'.

98 Pitts, *A Turn to Empire*.

99 Dewey, 'The Rehabilitation of the Peasant Proprietor in Nineteenth-Century Economic Thought', 17.

100 O'Neill, *Edmund Burke and the Conservative Logic of Empire*, 148.

101 Reproduced in O'Neill, 111–12.

102 Bayly, *The Birth of the Modern World 1780–1914*, 296.

103 Pitts, *A Turn to Empire*, 146.

Literature on non-democratic political regimes suggests that an essential determinant of their stability is the capacity to co-opt the 'strategically-relevant actors' who are 'persuaded not to exercise [their] power to obstruct'.[104] For colonial administrators with a greater affinity towards the aristocracy, the landed gentry in traditional and agriculture-based societies was the natural candidate for co-optation because of its structural similarity with social, political, and economic hierarchies in England. Through appropriate economic rewards,[105] inclusion in the civil and military governance of the colony,[106] and grant of certain privileges and perks via colonial honours[107] and rituals,[108] the aristocratic landlords could be the bulwark for countering popular discontent against colonial rule.

An alternative to this 'pyramid-shaped' hierarchical approach to maintain stability is more bottom-up. Built around notions of legitimacy, political stability is achieved by introducing just institutions that provide a moral right to rule.[109] Although just institutions typically include provisions for the political participation of the governed, in the context of colonial rule, legitimacy efforts may be restricted to economic considerations, that is, building legitimacy by placating the struggling masses through economic upliftment. Supporting the security of tenure and related proprietary rights of tenants could thus achieve two political objectives: legitimise colonial rule and, more importantly, quash any remnants of authority and influence of the traditional aristocracy.

Along with the relative importance of the aristocratic class versus the peasants in ensuring political stability in individual colonies, the Empire also had to be attentive to the political implications at home, from privileging one class over the other in pursuit of restructuring land relationships. Many British administrators across the colonies and cabinet members in the Imperial governments came from the landowning class. In addition, land grants in various colonies were based on socio-political connections at home and as rewards for military service towards the expansion and maintenance of the Empire.[110] The largest British and Irish landlords held estates in multiple colonies,[111] and 'their financial interests and

[104] Johannes Gerschewski, 'The Three Pillars of Stability: Legitimation, Repression, and Co-Optation in Autocratic Regimes', *Democratization* 20, no. 1 (2013): 22.

[105] Jennifer Gandhi and Adam Przeworski, 'Cooperation, Cooptation, and Rebellion under Dictatorships', *Economics and Politics* 18, no. 1 (2006): 1–26.

[106] Owen, 'The Stability of Our Indian Empire'.

[107] Bruce Knox, 'Democracy, Aristocracy and Empire: The Provision of Colonial Honours, 1818–1870', *Australian Historical Studies* 25, no. 99 (1992): 244–64.

[108] E. J. Hobsbawm and T. O. Ranger, eds., *The Invention of Tradition* (Cambridge, New York: Cambridge University Press, 2012).

[109] The concept of legitimacy has been a subject of interest to political theorists throughout history, and there is an extensive literature on this topic. For a review of this literature see Peter G. Stillman, 'The Concept of Legitimacy', *Polity* 7, no. 1 (September 1, 1974): 32–56; Roy Suddaby, Alex Bitektine, and Patrick Haack, 'Legitimacy', *Academy of Management Annals* 11, no. 1 (October 25, 2016): 451–78.

[110] Weaver, *The Great Land Rush and the Making of the Modern World, 1650–1900.*

[111] As discussed in Chapter 8, one of the largest proprietors in Prince Edward Island had made his fortune with the East India Company and was related to England's Prime Minister.

investments often ran through overseas and imperial channels'.[112] These landlords had the political capital at home and enough influence in the British parliament to thwart attempts by colonial governments to impinge on their rights to property. Thus, political expediency considerations necessitated a balancing act in each colony, which had to be performed to minimise any negative spillovers that could excite landowners and/or peasants at home in England.

The preceding sections, developed around the three pillars of property rights, political economy, and political expediency, identified the theoretical logics and historically anchored justifications that influenced considerations of land tenure relationships across the British Empire during the nineteenth century. The specific arguments made around these three and their relative importance varied across the colonies, and these will be discussed in the following chapters. A couple of clarifications are needed on this analytical framework.

First, while acknowledging interactions between and reciprocal influences amongst the three pillars, these are considered distinct in the proposed analytical framework. The contention is that each of these three pillars was sufficient to influence decisions about the principles behind the land tenure laws and their provisions. In addition, each pillar is based on different sets of assumptions. Thus, it is necessary to consider them as distinct and equally important to an understanding of the land tenure reforms of interest in this study.[113]

Second, a possible critique of this proposed analytical framework anchored around the three pillars is that it is not parsimonious. For instance, it could be argued that a liberal-minded colonial administrator involved in land tenure discussions would always support the position of relative property rights, political economy arguments for tenants' security of tenure, and hope to achieve political stability through the economic betterment of the tenants. Conversely, there should be alignment between absolute rights of property and the improving landlord, who would, in turn, be a natural political ally of colonial rule. If there is such correspondence, then there is redundancy in the framework, as one could come to the same conclusion by focusing on any one of the three pillars. There are two responses to this potential critique. First, the relative importance of each of the pillars could vary across administrators. In this case, the differential saliency provides an opportunity for negotiation and accommodation in instituting particular provisions in the law. A helpful example (which will be discussed in more detail

[112] Annie Tindley, '"All the Arts of a Radical Agitation": Transnational Perspectives on British and Irish Landowners and Estates, 1800–1921', *Historical Research* 91, no. 254 (2018): 717.

[113] For example, in the aftermath of the 1857 uprising in India, political expediency related to placating the local aristocracy took precedence in institutionalising land tenure, irrespective of whether a particular province in British India had established property rights for this class or whether this class was the most appropriate from political economy considerations regarding development/improvement of the land. In other instances, during the beginning of the nineteenth century, the sanctity of property rights was the one that took precedence over the other two pillars. Metcalf, 'The Influence of the Mutiny of 1857 on Land Policy in India'.

in Chapter 3) is the conflict between the Lawrence brothers, who were part of the Board of Administration in Punjab after it was annexed in 1849. Both wanted economic improvement of the peasantry. However, the mechanisms through which this was to be accomplished differed; one wanted to improve their economic conditions by granting them the security of tenure, while the other saw the improvement of peasants through the benevolence of the contented landlords.[114] Second, there is evidence that colonial administrators and theorists emphasised different logics across the various colonies. For instance, there was wide variance in the solutions proposed by John Stuart Mill to tenant difficulties in India, Ireland, and the settler colonies such as Australia and Canada.[115] In both examples, different combinations of logics across the three pillars are evident.

Security of Tenure

Land tenure is defined as the 'way land is held or owned by individuals and groups, or the set of relationships legally or customarily defined amongst people with respect to land'. Security of tenure is the 'degree of confidence that land users will not be arbitrarily deprived of the rights they enjoy over land and the economic benefits that flow from it' and 'the certainty that an individual's rights to land will be recognized by others and protected in cases of specific challenges'.[116] Thus, tenure includes land that is held or owned, implying that both landlords (owners) and tenants (users) can have it and possess the associated rights,[117] and the rights of both parties need protection. This, in turn, necessarily entails a vital role of the state that 'enforces property rights, facilitates private contracting, and applies the law fairly to all' but refrains from engaging in 'coercion and expropriation'.[118]

Much of the debate on land tenure during the nineteenth century concerned the relative rights of landlords and tenants and the state's role in assigning these rights and protecting the ones it assigned and recognised. Two approaches were considered to institutionalise tenants' security of tenure and, in the process, create

[114] Harold Lee, *Brothers in the Raj: The Lives of John and Henry Lawrence* (Oxford, UK: Oxford University Press, 2002).

[115] Bell, 'John Stuart Mill on Colonies'; Pitts, *A Turn to Empire.*

[116] UN-Habitat, 'Secure Land Rights for All' (Nairobi: United Nations Human Settlements Programme, 2008), 5.

[117] In his late nineteenth-century legal treatise, Holland noted that 'proprietary rights may be acquired which vary in extent from absolute ownership to a narrowly limited power of user . . . The owner of an object has . . . the right, unless he has expressly parted with it, to the possession of that object. But a person who is in possession . . . has also a right to continue in possession, and to be restored to possession, should he have been deprived of it; and this sometimes even as against the owner'. Thomas Holland, *The Elements of Jurisprudence*, 10th ed. (New York: Oxford University Press, 1906), 184–85.

[118] Levine, 'Law, Endowments and Property Rights', 61.

'peasant proprietors'.[119] First, security could be established by transferring ownership to tenants through state-assisted voluntary or compulsory land purchases from existing owners. The second approach involved the establishment and/or recognition of shared rights of landlords and tenants. The overall goal of peasant proprietorship[120] was to find remedies for the 'deadly evil of insecurity of tenure, and yet at the same time not shake the stability of property'.[121]

While there was general agreement about the causes and consequences of insecure tenure, how to rectify this (that is, create 'security') generated vast differences. Some suggested that fixity of tenure, compensation for improvements made by the tenant, and leases negotiated by mutual contracts were the modes through which security of tenure may be given to the tenants. However, only the leases did not impinge on the landowners' property rights.[122] For 'fixity of tenure' meant 'perpetuity', and 'perpetuity of tenure on the part of the occupier is virtually expropriation of the landlord, and . . . compensation would have to be paid to the landlord for the rights of which he would be deprived'.[123] On the other hand, proponents of tenant rights saw only the 'fixity of tenure' that would lead to a contented peasantry,[124] as it provided the requisite incentives for investments to improve the land and an adequate period to recoup the investments. In addition, fixity would protect the tenants from arbitrary evictions.[125]

Similarly, security of tenure through compensation for improvements also generated diverse opinions which were related less to the principles behind this form of security but more to the processes in implementing it (for example, what types of improvements could be claimed, within what time frame, whether these needed the consent of the landlord, who determines the value of the improvements, among others). Furthermore, there were questions as to whether a tenant in entitled to compensation for improvements if evicted by the landlord for non-payment of rent and whether a tenant can sell the unexhausted improvements made by him to the incoming tenant (that is, compensation for goodwill).[126]

119 Dewey, 'The Rehabilitation of the Peasant Proprietor in Nineteenth-Century Economic Thought'; Thornton, *A Plea for Peasant Proprietors*; John Elliott Cairnes, 'Ireland in Transition: Peasant Proprietorship', *The Economist*, November 4, 1865.

120 Peasant proprietorship is the broad umbrella term used which encompasses both the transfer of ownership to the tenant (full proprietor) and the recognition of shared rights between the landlord and tenant (co-proprietor).

121 'Irish Land Bill. Hansard Third Series CXCIX' (Hansard (3rd Series), 1870), 359.

122 James Caird, *The Irish Land Question* (London: Longmans, Green, Reader, and Dyer, 1869).

123 Gladstone, 'Irish Land Bill. Hansard Third Series CXCIX', 351.

124 Isaac Butt, *Land Tenure in Ireland: A Plea for the Celtic Race* (Third. Dublin: John Falconer 1866). It will become clear in the following chapters that the benefits of fixity of tenure would be debated under different names. While 'fixity' was one of the 3Fs demanded in Ireland, the term used in Punjab was 'occupancy rights', while in Prince Edward Island, the objective was to convert leasehold tenures to 'freeholds'.

125 In contemporary parlance, discussions in the nineteenth century encompassed both security of tenure *de jure* (that is fixed term, with right of eviction by the landlord in very specific conditions) and security of tenure *de facto* (that is, give better rights/conditions to the tenant in a way that it makes it difficult/costly for the landlord to evict).

126 George Campbell, *The Irish Land* (London: Trubner and Co., 1869); John Elliott Cairnes, 'Ireland in Transition: Land Tenure', *The Economist*, October 14, 1865; John Elliott Cairnes, 'Political

Underlying the discussions around both 'fixity' and 'compensation for improvements' as means to provide security of tenure to the tenants were questions about the rent payable by the tenants for cultivating the land. These included whether the right to determine the rent was the sole prerogative of the landlord, whether it needed to be controlled, and if so, by whom? Proponents of both fixity and compensation argued that security of tenure for the tenants could not be achieved without reining in the ability of the landlords to raise rents arbitrarily. The argument related to fixity was that if the tenants were guaranteed fixity of tenure subject to paying the rent, the landlord could increase the rent to a level that would lead to arrears on the part of the tenants, thus making fixity obsolete as the landlord could now evict for non-payment of rent. In the case of compensation for improvement, where there was high competition for land amongst the tenants, the landlord could increase the rent to a level that more than compensated for the payment due to the existing tenant for improvements. In both cases, the landlord could theoretically force an eviction of tenants by raising the rent. Accordingly, 'fair rents' became one of the three pillars (the other being 'fixity of tenure' and 'freedom of sale') in achieving security of tenure for the tenants.

Land Tenure in the Colonies and English Principles

On questions about land tenure across the British Empire, one of the salient points of discussion was the precedents from where land laws could be derived. A natural point of comparison was that of land tenure relationships prevalent in England. Differences emerged amongst colonial administrators and landlord and tenant groups across the colonies regarding the appropriateness of applying English principles and practices in the colonies. Some viewed the English land tenure system of the nineteenth century as embodying the sanctity of property rights and political economy ideas of laissez faire and capitalist farming. These features were seen as marks of an advanced society, and thus, the Empire should strive to transfer these very principles to the colonies. Others also acknowledged the superiority of English land tenure principles but used Maine's arguments about evolutionary historicism to question the appropriateness of these principles in less advanced societies.[127] Both viewpoints praised English land tenure principles; however, the question was whether transferring them to the colonies would facilitate the

Economy of Land (Originally Published in Fortnightly Review, January 1870)', in *Essays in Political Economy: Theoretical and Applied*, by John Elliott Cairnes (London: Macmillan and Co., 1873), 187–230. Some of these debates are elaborated upon in the following chapters.

[127] Mantena, *Alibis of Empire*, 120.

Empire's civilising mission or whether the colonies' uncivilised stage made them unfit to adopt these principles.

What English principles served as points of comparison in the debates about land tenure in the colonies?[128] The most salient principle that guided land tenure in England was the prevalence of 'contracts' (rather than 'status') in structuring landlord–tenant relationships: 'Great Britain is almost the only country in the world in which land-contract has been carried to the length of [the] threefold division of classes into superior capitalist owning the land . . . ; inferior capitalist cultivating under a definite contract; and the labourer working for hire.'[129] The contracts specified the 'money rents' payable by the tenants, the length of the leases, and other mutual obligations.[130] In addition, another structural characteristic that was prevalent in England was the 'custom according to which the landlord [undertook] all outlay of an important character needed for cultivation'.[131] That is, investments in 'improvement', which included farm houses and farm buildings, fences, gates, etc., were made by landlord, and the 'rent fixed with reference to the state of things'.[132]

Besides these structural characteristics of contract-based relationships, long leases, and landlords making investments for significant improvements, a few other features of land tenures in England were identified, which supposedly led to more amicable relationships between landlords and tenants, ones based on 'good understanding'[133] and 'good feeling'[134] rather than mutual hostility and suspicion. Even when a tenant invested in 'building upon the land on which he had no lease', he could trust the English landlord not to take 'advantage of so important an improvement'.[135] The relatively peaceful relationships between the two groups were

[128] Delving into the history of land tenures in England is beyond the scope of this study. Here, I summarise the main features of land tenures, especially the ones related to landlord-tenant relationships in the middle of the nineteenth century. It was these features that were contrasted in debates around the land laws in the three colonies of interest. For more extended treatment of land tenures in England, see: Finlason, *The History of Law of Tenures of Land in England and Ireland*; Mill, *England and Ireland*; Maine, *Ancient Law*; F. Seebohm, 'The Land Question: Part II. Feudal Tenures in England', *Fortnightly Review*, January 1870, 89–107; C. Wren Hoskyns, 'The Land-Laws in England', in *Systems of Land Tenure in Various Countries: A Series of Essays Published Under the Sanction of the Cobden Club* (London: Macmillan and Co., 1870), 92–144.

[129] Campbell, *The Irish Land*, 16.

[130] John Stuart Mill, 'Speech on Mr. Chichester Fortescue's Land Bill, House of Commons, May 17, 1866', in *Chapters and Speeches on the Irish Land Bill*, by John Stuart Mill (London: Longmans, Green, Reader, and Dyer, 1870), 99. Even the 'copyhold' tenure (a type of landholding based on the custom of the manor), which was initially held at the will of the lord grew into an occupancy right with fixed rent, first recognised by custom and subsequently by law. See Campbell, *The Irish Land*; Finlason, *The History of Law of Tenures of Land in England and Ireland*.

[131] Cairnes, 'Ireland in Transition: Land Tenure', 1239.

[132] 'Report from Her Majesty's Commissioners of Inquiry into the State of the Law and Practice in Respect of the Occupation to the Land in Ireland (Devon Commission)' (Dublin: Alexander Thom, 1845), 16.

[133] Hoskyns, 'The Land-Laws in England', 124.

[134] Cairnes, 'Ireland in Transition: Land Tenure', 1239.

[135] Smith and Raphael, *The Wealth of Nations*, bk. III, Chapter II.

attributed to the more active involvement of the landlords (that is, few absentee landlords) in their land and with their tenants, both groups being of the 'same mind in politics and in religion', and with few 'marks of conquest'.[136]

Navigating Competing Logics

If the objectives of land tenure laws were to find an ideal candidate who could be bestowed with the security of tenure, the discussion in the previous sections shows the complexity of making this choice across the British Empire in the nineteenth century. The ideal candidate needed to have justifiable claims to property, be willing to make the necessary investments to improve the land and be reliable in providing political support for colonial rule. The competing and often oppositional logics prevalent in colonial thinking concerning these three criteria exacerbated this complexity. How were the competing logics at multiple levels resolved and/or reconciled? Drawing from institutional theory and institutional logics literature, I identify some possible paths that could facilitate an understanding of how the different logics were adopted, reconciled and/or accommodated in the three colonies of interest.

Given their primacy as rules of the game in society and as structures of exchange between various societal actors, the study of institutions has attracted considerable scholarly interest in numerous disciplines.[137] One area of study is focused on scrutinising the process of institutional change, whether it is narrow or broad in scope, incremental or discontinuous, and exogenously or endogenously determined, among others. There is a general agreement among scholars that irrespective of the process, institutional change encompasses shifting rules of the game. The second area of inquiry, which is of interest here, is concerned with understanding how actors respond to the changes and negotiate between emerging and pre-existing rules of the game. Particularly useful in this regard is the conceptualisation around institutional logics, defined as organising principles through which various actors construct meaning to their social reality, and which constrain or enable behaviour by prescribing appropriate means and ends.[138] Institutional

[136] See speech by Gladstone, February 15, 1870. Reproduced in 'Irish Land Bill. Hansard Third Series CXCIX', col. 339.

[137] Peter A. Hall, 'Historical Institutionalism in Rationalist and Sociological Perspective', in *Explaining Institutional Change: Ambiguity, Agency, and Power*, ed. James Mahoney and Kathleen Thelen (Cambridge, UK: Cambridge University Press, 2009), 204–24; James Mahoney and Kathleen Ann Thelen, eds., *Explaining Institutional Change: Ambiguity, Agency, and Power* (Cambridge, UK: Cambridge University Press, 2010); Royston Greenwood et al., 'Institutional Complexity and Organizational Responses', *The Academy of Management Annals* 5, no. 1 (2011): 317–71.

[138] Patricia H. Thornton and William Ocasio, 'Institutional Logics', in *The SAGE Handbook of Organizational Institutionalism*, ed. Royston Greenwood et al. (London: SAGE Publications Ltd, 2008), 99–128; Roger Friedland and Robert R. Alford, 'Bringing Society Back In: Symbols, Practices, and Institutional Contradictions', in *The New Institutionalism in Organizational Analysis*, ed. Walter W. Powell and Paul J. DiMaggio (Chicago: University of Chicago Press, 1991), 232–63.

change often impinges on existing belief systems and taken-for-granted rules and thus introduces competing logics guiding the behaviour of various actors. Research has identified two mechanisms through which contested logics can be reconciled: agency and isomorphism.[139]

Enabling and constraining features of institutional logics allow individuals or groups active agency to either contest competing logics or accommodate them by finding some middle ground.[140] For example, it has been suggested that competition-based resolution of competing logics necessarily entails a period of flux when the two logics coexist but eventually leads to a 'winning logic' that is adopted in an organisational field.[141] Winning the competing logics battle depends on the relative power of the protagonists within the localised context or their ability to build powerful coalitions from both within and outside the local context. Actors may also collaborate to develop mechanisms that 'support the co-existence of competing logics'.[142] By breaking down the contested logics into their constituent parts and negotiating based on the centrality of the different parts to the conflicting logics, the actors are able to find a hybrid solution.[143] This body of research provides theoretical possibilities to understand the agency of various actors involved in resolving the conflicting logics identified in the previous sections.

Another possibility of managing competing logics is to mimic the solutions adopted by someone within one's social group.[144] That is, through the use of analogies,[145] isomorphism allows 'one unit to resemble other units that face the same set of environmental conditions'.[146] Reasons for isomorphism include gaining legitimacy by adopting practices of other entities on whom the focal unit may be dependent, reducing uncertainty by following the practices of a successful peer and internalising and implementing ideas of others that share the same worldviews or are similarly socialised.[147] While much of the research on isomorphism focuses

[139] William Ocasio, Patricia H. Thornton, and Michael Lounsbury, 'Advances to the Institutional Logics Perspective', in *The SAGE Handbook of Organizational Institutionalism*, ed. Royston Greenwood et al., 2nd ed. (London: SAGE Publications Ltd, 2017), 509–31.

[140] For instance, capitalism was historically associated with private business organisations operating through market-based economic transactions. However, in the last few years, public organisations owned by the state have also started to participate in the markets, thus leading to the emergence of a hybrid economic system, 'state capitalism' incorporating both market and state coordination. See Helen Wei Hu, Lin Cui, and Preet S. Aulakh, 'State Capitalism and Performance Persistence of Business Group-Affiliated Firms: A Comparative Study of China and India', *Journal of International Business Studies* 50, no. 2 (2019): 193–222.

[141] Trish Reay and C. R. Hinings, 'Managing the Rivalry of Competing Institutional Logics', *Organization Studies* 30, no. 6 (2009): 629–52.

[142] Reay and Hinings, 647.

[143] Ali Aslan Gümüsay, Michael Smets, and Timothy Morris, '"God at Work": Engaging Central and Incompatible Institutional Logics through Elastic Hybridity', *Academy of Management Journal* 63, no. 1 (2020): 124–54.

[144] Ocasio, Thornton, and Lounsbury, 'Advances to the Institutional Logics Perspective'.

[145] Julian S. Weitzenfeld, 'Valid Reasoning by Analogy', *Philosophy of Science* 51 (1984): 137–49.

[146] Paul J. DiMaggio and Walter W. Powell, 'The Iron Cage Revisited: Institutional Isomorphism and Collective Rationality in Organizational Fields', *American Sociological Review* 48, no. 2 (1983): 149.

[147] DiMaggio and Powell, 'The Iron Cage Revisited'.

on explaining institutional homogenisation and convergence, some emerging research sees the possibility of divergence in practices because of isomorphic pressures. This can happen in situations when a powerful actor supports divergence amongst the subordinate units,[148] or where peers are not seen as legitimate or successful.[149] One can build on these insights to see the possibilities of isomorphism to negotiate competing logics in the context of land tenure laws.

This chapter's framework will facilitate a comparison of the land tenure legislation in the three colonies. In the following chapters, I examine the debates leading to the enactment of various laws around the three pillars of property rights, political economy, and political expediency, and foreground how these intersected within each colonial site of interest. It will be shown that the nature of the debates on each of these pillars, their relative salience in the discussions, and the means through which oppositional logics were accommodated and/or contested differed in the three colonies due to their unique characteristics identified in Chapter 1. This heterogeneity ultimately explains the specificities of security of tenure institutionalised in the laws in the three colonies during the 1868–1875 period. I examine the sites chronologically based on the year the law was enacted, starting with the land question in Punjab and the Tenancy Act of 1868.

[148] As agued by Beckert, colonial regimes may 'not be interested in homogenization despite a unilateral distribution of power . . . These regimes developed institutional structures that were distinctly different from those in the 'motherland' – for instance, in terms of political rights of the colonial subjects. Here power preserves divergence' (Beckert, 'Institutional Isomorphism Revisited', 154).

[149] Beckert, 'Institutional Isomorphism Revisited'.

PART II
PUNJAB

3
Annexation of Punjab and Land Tenure

> [T]wo different schools of theorists on land tenures . . . have always existed amongst a portion of our English officials: the one in favour of a landed aristocracy, the other in support of peasant proprietorship; and according as supporters of either theory filled the highest places in Government, the views . . . of one or the other prevailed, and all powers of Government were put in force to give effect to them.[1]

The British annexed Punjab in 1849 and hurriedly carried out land tenure settlements that were to last fifteen years.[2] The initial settlements in the province followed the utilitarian approach prevalent in British India during the first half of the nineteenth century, one that prioritised proprietary rights of the peasant cultivators of land. When these settlements were revisited in the 1860s, the political climate in British India had dramatically changed. The 1857 uprising[3] created anxieties for the colonial rulers and led to a rethinking of the overall governance approach, which included a return to privileging the aristocratic class and restoring its property rights.[4] While the British restored the traditional sociopolitical hierarchies by rebalancing land tenure arrangements between landowners and peasants in several provinces, the approach was fiercely resisted in Punjab by a set of colonial administrators who emphasised the province's unique historical, geographical, and political position. This chapter foregrounds the role of this 'Punjab School' of administrators in the province's annexation, governance, and initial land tenure settlements, and the impact of their governance approach on the province's role during the rebellion against British rule in 1857.

[1] Minute of Sir Eskine Perry, member of the Secretary of State for India Council, 30 October 1869. In 'East India (Punjab Tenancy): Copies of the Despatch of the Secretary of State for India in Council Dates the 28th Day of October (No. 80) 1869, to the Governor General of India in Council, on the Subject of the India Act No. XXVIII. of 1868, (Punjab Tenancy Act)' (House of Commons, 1870), 6.

[2] 'Punjab' and 'Panjab' are both used in the literature. I use the former in this study and use the latter only when it is cited as such. Some colonial documents also spell it as 'Punjaub'.

[3] Various terms have been used including mutiny, rebellion, first war of independence, and revolt, among others. Some of these are used interchangeably in this chapter.

[4] Thomas R. Metcalf, 'The Influence of the Mutiny of 1857 on Land Policy in India', *The Historical Journal* 4, no. 2 (1961): 152–63; Thomas R. Metcalf, *The Aftermath of Revolt: India, 1857-1870* (Princeton, N.J.: Princeton University Press, 1964).

Empire and the Peasant Proprietor. Preet S. Aulakh, Oxford University Press. © Preet S. Aulakh 2025.
DOI: 10.1093/9780198928270.003.0003

These aspects combined to shape Punjab's land question that eventually led to the Tenancy Act of 1868.

*****

The period between 1799 and 1849 in Punjab is known as an era of Sikh Rule.[5] Ranjit Singh, who ruled from 1799 to 1839, consolidated various principalities under his rule, and it extended from just outside Delhi to Kashmir in the north and Peshawar in the West (see map in Figure 3.1).[6] Until the death of Ranjit Singh in 1839,[7] the British had a relationship of mutual respect with the Sikh ruler and saw the stability of his rule as a natural bulwark against any European threat to the British Empire in India from the West.[8] However, his heirs were not able to keep the state intact, and internecine struggles amongst the family members and chiefs led to the first Anglo-Sikh war in 1846, the establishment of a British residency in Lahore, and eventually the second Anglo-Sikh war in 1849, when the British fully annexed the province.[9]

From 1846 to 1858, the administration of Punjab went through three stages: (1) *Residency (1846–49)*, whereby a British resident, along with a council of eight native chieftains, assisted in the administration of the partially ceded territory; (2) *Board of Administration (1849–1853)*, consisting of three British administrators, each respectively in charge of political and military affairs, finance and land settlement, and judicial aspects of the newly annexed province; and (3) *Commissioner (1853–1858)*, whereby the Chief Commissioner was the overall in charge of the province, considered capital punishment appeals, and was assisted by Financial (revenue, land settlements) and Judicial (ultimate judge in all cases, civil and criminal) Commissioners. The British divided the province into four divisions, each headed by a commissioner (see Figure 3.1).[10] The divisions comprised a few districts, led by a deputy commissioner and supported by assistant commissioners

[5] J. S. Grewal, *The Sikhs of the Punjab* (Cambridge: Cambridge University Press, 1990).

[6] Within the territory between Delhi and Peshawar there were numerous native or princely states which had their own arrangements with the British. My focus in this chapter is the area under the Punjab province that was part of British India. The Native States had their own land tenure systems, which were subsequently integrated with either India or Pakistan after 1947. For details, see Fiona Groenhout, 'The History of the Indian Princely States: Bringing the Puppets Back onto Centre Stage,' *History Compass* 4, no. 4 (2006): 629–44.

[7] The British had gained some foothold in Punjab from 1805 to 1846, mainly through protection of smaller principalities. Details about the creeping political annexation is beyond the scope of this chapter. For details of this period, see Chapter 4 of Rajmohan Gandhi, *Punjab: A History from Aurangzeb to Mountbatten* (New Delhi: Aleph Book Company, 2013).

[8] Arthur D. Innes and Charles Gough, *Annexation of Punjab* (Delhi: National Book Shop, 1984); Gandhi, *Punjab: A History from Aurangzeb to Mountbatten.*

[9] N. M. Khilnani, *British Power in the Punjab, 1839-1858* (New York: Asia Pub. House, 1972); Yaduvansh Bahadur Mathur, *British Administration of Punjab, 1849-75* (Delhi: Surjeet Book Depot, 1973).

[10] Delhi was incorporated into Punjab as the fifth division after the 1857 Mutiny.

Figure 3.1 Map of Punjab Province

The non-shaded areas were part of British India; the shaded areas were the Princely States, with their own separate arrangements with the British.

Source: The Panjab, North-West Frontier Province, and Kashmir by Sir James McCrone Douie (Project Gutenberg, 2008). Available at <https://wiki.fibis.org/w/File:Punjab_district_map.jpg>.

(mainly European) and extra-assistant commissioners (European or Indian). Commissioners were superintendents of revenue and police and had the appellate powers of a civil judge and the criminal powers of a sessions judge. Deputy Commissioners exercised the powers of Magistrates, collected revenues in their districts and tried all civil suits over Rs 1,000. The British established a Chief Court in Punjab in 1866, consisting of two judges appointed by the Governor-General of India. It replaced the Judicial Commissioners' Court as the province's final appeals court for civil and criminal cases. However, the Financial Commissioner had the final power regarding land revenue settlement.[11]

Two salient features of early British rule in Punjab are essential in understanding the initial land settlements in the province: characteristics and ideologies of colonial administrators in the province and its 'non-regulation' system of administration.

[11] Herbert Cowell, *The History and Constitution of the Courts and Legislative Authorities in India* (Calcutta: Thacker, Spink and Co., 1884).

Competing Visions of the Lawrence Brothers

The Lawrence brothers dominated Punjab's early administration.[12] Henry Lawrence (1806–1857) served as the Resident Agent from 1846 to 1849 and headed the Board of Administration from 1849 to 1853. John Lawrence (1811–1879) served on the Board with his brother and was appointed the first Chief Commissioner of the province in 1853, the position which he held until 1859 when he was appointed its first Lieutenant Governor. After spending a few years in England (1859–1864), John Lawrence returned to India as Governor-General from 1864 to 1869. The brothers played important military roles during the annexation of Punjab (1846–1849) and marshalled the province's resources in defeating the rebellion of 1857. They came from a military family that served in British armies in India and elsewhere. Henry joined the East India Company as a military man, studying at the military academy and being commissioned in the Bengal Artillery. John entered it through the Indian Civil Service after studying at Haileybury College, the training ground for young colonial administrators.[13] These common familial but different educational backgrounds influenced their respective approaches to administration. Neeladri Bhattacharya, a historian of Punjab, succinctly points out the ideological bases of the two brothers, which essentially influenced the governance of the province in the following years:

> While the Lawrences accepted the ideas of personal rule, masculine paternalism, and a non-regulatory system, they interpreted them in distinct and at times divergent ways. Henry was inspired by a conservative romantic imagination, John by Utilitarianism . . . Romantic conservatives imagined village communities in which the aristocracy and the people, patrons and clients, were tied by natural and immemorial bonds. Traditional hierarchies were not to be radically disturbed . . . Utilitarians and Liberals detested the aristocracy and searched for industrious yeomen as the founding figures of their agrarian imagination.[14]

The strong paternalistic administration envisioned by the Lawrence brothers in the newly acquired province attracted several promising civil administrators to Punjab, imbibing either Henry's or John's approach to achieving the

[12] For details, see Harold Lee, *Brothers in the Raj: The Lives of John and Henry Lawrence* (Oxford: Oxford University Press, 2002); Frederick P. Gibbon, *The Lawrences of the Punjab* (London: J. M. Dent, 1908).

[13] Gibbon, *The Lawrences of the Punjab.*

[14] Neeladri Bhattacharya, *The Great Agrarian Conquest: The Colonial Reshaping of a Rural World* (New Delhi: Permanent Black, 2019), 40–44.

overall objectives of a firm but just colonial rule.[15] One of these administrators, Richard Temple (who would rise in the colonial hierarchy to eventually become the Governor of Bombay),[16] and a fan of John Lawrence,[17] described the lure of serving in Punjab in the early days after annexation because of its 'strategic position' and 'historical repute'.[18] While serving together (along with a third member) on the Board of Administration, the Lawrence brothers agreed on general principles of a paternalistic approach to governance. They put up a common front to counter outside criticisms of the Board.[19] However, their differences surfaced on questions about land tenure and revenue administration. John Lawrence had instituted a system of fixed land revenue payments in cash, while Henry preferred a more flexible payment system in kind and dependent on the market price of the crops. More importantly, their ideas diverged on handling the different classes dependent on agriculture, particularly the *jageerdars*, who held large land grants under Sikh rule as a reward for their loyalty and/or military service.[20] According to Charles Aitchison, a subordinate of the Lawrence brothers and future Lieutenant Governor of Punjab, John believed that a prosperous and contented peasantry would be 'a more solid foundation of our power than a landed aristocracy. This principle underlay all differences with his brother Henry in the early Punjab days. Large grants of land or money to the Native gentry seemed to him to be much taken from the people, with no corresponding advantage to the government'.[21] These differences eventually debilitated the functioning of the Board, and it was dissolved in 1853 by the Governor-General, Lord Dalhousie. Henry was appointed as a Resident Agent in the princely state of Rajputana. John Lawrence, whose ideology was more compatible with the Governor-General's utilitarian leanings, made the Chief Commissioner of Punjab. Henry's parting words to John were related to their different views on treating the native aristocrats, and he urged his brother to

15 Followers of John Lawrence's vision included Richard Temple, George Campbell, and E. L. Brandreth, while Edward Prinsep and D. H. McLeod were closer to Henry Lawrence's ideas. These were prominent figures during the debates on the Punjab Tenancy Act. Furthermore, most of the early administrators in Punjab had earned their spurs in the North-Western Provinces in the late 1830s under James Thomason, the Lieutenant Governor, and a follower of Benthamite utilitarianism. See Sir William Muir, *The Honourable James Thomason, Lieutenant-Governor N.-W. P., India, 1843-1853 A. D.* (Edinburgh: T. & T. Clark, 1897); Richard Temple, *The Story of My Life. In Two Volumes* (London, Paris, Melbourne: Cassell and Company, Limited, 1896).

16 Temple, *Story of My Life.*

17 Richard Temple in his biography of John Lawrence: 'He knew that an administrator shines, not only in what he does himself, but also in what he induces others to do, that his policy will in part be tested by the character of the men whom he raises up around him, that the master is recognized in his pupils, and that if his work is to live after him, he must have those already who will hand on the tradition, and will even take his place should he fall in the battle of life. His aim, then, was to establish a system and found a school' (Richard Temple, *Lord Lawrence* (London: MacMillan, 1890), 49).

18 Temple, *Story of My Life*, vol. 1, 35–36.

19 They put a common front against Charles Napier, the Commander-in-Chief, on military strategy and the overall non-regulation system of Punjab. See Lee, *Brothers in the Raj*, chap. 11.

20 Gibbon, *The Lawrences of the Punjab.*

21 Sir Charles Aitchison, *Rulers of India: Lord Lawrence* (Oxford: The Clarendon Press, 1892), 142.

treat them in 'kindly spirit . . . Because they are down, and because they and their hangers-on have still some influence as affecting public peace and contentment. I will do to them as I would be done'.[22] After Henry departed from Punjab, John Lawrence took complete control, and his views on land tenure took precedence amongst the settlement officers. However, as will be seen later in the chapter, some British officers did not forget Henry's pro-aristocratic leanings.[23]

The 'non-regulation' system of administration in Punjab, whereby the 'day-to-day operation was based upon an extremely flexible interpretation of basic administrative precepts contained in printed codes and circulars, rather than upon a strict observance of legislative regulations, as was the case elsewhere in British India',[24] facilitated the colonial administrators' ability to influence policy based on their ideological leanings. This system provided 'greater accessibility of officials to the people' because the 'union of all powers, executive, magisterial, and judicial' lay in the hands of the Deputy Commissioner.[25] Its success depended 'on the personal character, initiative, vigour and discretion of the local officers'.[26] On the one hand, the formalised non-regulation system and the discretion afforded to local colonial administrators allowed for quicker reforms than had been possible in other provinces. On the other hand, a lack of elaborate regulations and 'governance according to the essence of a rule rather than the letter'[27] allowed officers in different districts to use their interpretations to institutionalise the administrative apparatus. As noted by George Campbell in his autobiography:[28]

> It was in May 1846, when I was just twenty-two, that I . . . was gazetted to act as Deputy Commissioner . . . [in which role] I was magistrate,

[22] Reproduced in Bhattacharya, *The Great Agrarian Conquest*, 44.

[23] These included Edward Prinsep (Settlement Commissioner) and Donald McLeod (Lieutenant Governor).

[24] Andrew J. Major, *Return to Empire: Punjab under the Sikhs and British in the Mid-Nineteenth Century* (New Delhi: Sterling Publishers, 1996), 127.

[25] The paternalism is captured by Rudyard Kipling in his story, 'Head of a District'. In the story Yardley Orde, Deputy Commissioner of a fictitious district in Punjab, Kot-Kumharsen, is on his death bed, and even here he is worrying about his district. Addressing his assistant: 'the four Khusru Kheyl villages in our border want a one-third remittance this spring. That's fair; their crops are bad. See that they get it'. To the native subjects accompanying him, Orde extols: 'you must be good men, when I am not here. Such of you as live in our borders must pay your taxes quietly as before. I have spoken of the villages to be gently treated this year', Rudyard Kipling, 'The Head of the District,' in *Life's Handicap: Being Stories of My Own People* (Charleston, S.C.: BiblioBazaar, 2007), 173–74.; Also see Lee, *Brothers in the Raj*, 418–19.

[26] H. H. Dodwell, ed., *The Cambridge History of India. Volume VI: The Indian Empire 1858-1918* (Cambridge: Cambridge University Press, 1932), 87.

[27] Bhattacharya, *The Great Agrarian Conquest*, 46.

[28] Campbell (later Sir George Campbell) had a storied civil service career India with the East India Company and later the British administration. His understanding of tenant rights was published in the influential publication of the Cobden Club. George Campbell, 'The Tenure of Land in India,' in *Systems of Land Tenure in Various Countries: A Series of Essays Published under the Sanction of the Cobden Club* (London: Macmillan and Co., n.d.), 145–227. His book on Ireland written in 1869 would influence the 1870 Land Act in Ireland, and is discussed in detail in Chapter 6.

> collector and judge, for in these non-regulation provinces there were no separate judicial establishments . . . I was very nearly in the position of a benevolent despot . . . [W]e were told to follow the spirit of the regulations, but that was very elastic, and I did pretty much what I thought just and right.[29]

In particular, the initial land settlements and recording of rights in the districts often reflected the ideological leanings of settlement officers rather than being based on a uniform system. The disparity in details of the settlement reports from different districts during the 1850s later became a point of contention during the debates leading to the Punjab Tenancy Act of 1868. I now turn to the initial land tenure settlements in the province after it came under British rule. As argued by Bhattacharya, British power in rural Punjab 'was built through a new regime of categories. A vocabulary of terms was essential to comprehend reality, schematise knowledge, and classify social relations'. He further suggests that in developing these categories, often the 'logic of enquiry' (which necessitated looking for differences) conflicted with 'logic of classifications' (that demanded a search for similarities).[30] My objective here is not to evaluate the veracity of the various classifications, especially those related to land revenue settlements. Rather, it is to identify the record of rights of various classes of agriculturists identified by the colonial administrators. Eventually what mattered was how the colonial administrators defined the rights of the different groups, and the debates across colonial groups about their own choices.

It is helpful to briefly map out the province's socio-political characteristics during the period after annexation and identify how these may have influenced the British thinking about land tenure in Punjab. According to the census of 1868, the total population of Punjab was 17.59 million, which comprised Muslims (53%), Hindus (35%), and Sikhs (6%) as the three major religious groups.[31] On the annexation of Punjab, the British were sensitive to some of the communal tensions between the three communities, and the new administration responded to these problems

[29] Sir George Campbell, *Memories of My Indian Career*, ed. Sir Charles E. Bernard (London: Macmillan and Co., 1893), Vol I, 38, 56.

[30] Bhattacharya , *The Great Agrarian Conquest*. Given these ambiguities of categorization, we see a wide variety of terms used to define precolonial land tenures. For the different classifications of land tenure, and some of the difficulties encountered by colonial administrators in Punjab, see B. H. Baden-Powell, *The Land Systems of British India*, vol. II (Oxford: Clarendon Press, 1892); J. M. Douie, *Punjab Settlement Manual* (Delhi: Daya Publishing House, 1899); Edwin Arnold, *The Marquis of Dalhousie's Administration of British India, Volume the First, Containing the Acquisition and Administration of the Punjab* (London: Sauders, Otley, and Co., 1862).

[31] 'East India (Progress and Condition): Statement Exhibiting the Moral and Material Progress and Condition of India, During the Year 1867-68' (House of Commons, 1869), House of Commons Parliamentary Papers Online. Although these three groups were dispersed throughout Punjab, the Muslims were predominant in the area west and Hindus to the east of the river Indus. The Sikhs were concentrated in the centre, close to the political and religious base of the Sikh Empire (around Lahore and Amritsar).

by revoking some of the existing laws restricting certain religious practices and making public pronouncements about equal treatment of all sects by allowing each to 'practice its customs unless they infringed on the rights of the others'.[32] While the British were able to deal with the religious fault lines, their more significant challenge was to deal with occupational categories, some of which corresponded with specific religious affiliations. The census distinguished between two broad occupational groups, 'agriculturalists' making up about 54% of the population, and 'non-agriculturalists' making up the remaining 46%.[33] However, most soldiers in the Sikh army before annexation and the British army during and after the 1857 rebellion came from the 'agriculturalist group'. The British considered this group to be more critical in facilitating political stability and the economic betterment of the province. For example, the administration consistently identified the Jats (or agriculturalists) as the 'flower of the population. Essentially yeomen by lineage and habit . . . they display all their wonted aptitude for stirring war and peaceful agriculture'.[34] The colonial administration wanted to shift the loyalty of this group from their traditional local chiefs to the British. It made efforts in the land tenure settlements to improve the material wellbeing of the ordinary cultivators (which contributed the soldiers to its army), even if that entailed chipping away the privileges of the chieftains. This was especially the case for the soldiers in the 'Khalsa', the army consisting of Sikhs during the rule of Ranjit Singh. It fought the Anglo-Sikh wars in the 1840s, was disbanded after 1849, but then a large number of Sikh soldiers were integrated into the British army. These soldiers played an important role in helping defeat the 1857 rebellion. They were accordingly designated as a 'martial race' and the British administrations took various initiatives to placate this religious group through enactment of land tenure laws favourable to the peasantry, allocating them land in the new Canal colonies in the 1880s, and giving them other privileges relative to other religious groups.[35] Thus, in the initial years after annexation, the primary objective of the administration was to ensure allegiance of the agriculturalist class to the British.[36] It was under the above-described context that land settlements in Punjab were undertaken in the 1850s.

[32] N. Gerald Barrier, 'The Punjab Government and Communal Politics, 1870-1908', *The Journal of Asian Studies* 27, no. 3 (1968): 526.

[33] 'East India (Progress and Condition); Statement Exhibiting the Moral and Material Progress and Condition of India, During the Year 1867-68.'

[34] 'General Report on the Administration of the Punjab for the Years 1849-50 and 1850-51' (London: Printed for the Court of Directors of the East-India Company by J. and H. Cox, 1854), 4.

[35] For details, see Mark Condos, *The Insecurity State: Punjab and the Making of Colonial Power in British India* (Cambridge: Cambridge University Press, 2017); Grewal (n 5); Major (n 24).

[36] Religious tensions in Punjab resurfaced at the end of the nineteenth century because of indebtedness of the peasants (who were primarily Muslims and Sikhs) to the moneylenders (who were primarily urban Hindus and belonging to the non-agriculturalist class). The British were concerned about the alienation of land from the cultivators and passed an act to stem the tide. However, the new act created other problems that influenced the socio-political relationships. A more detailed discussion is beyond the scope of this chapter. For details, see Norman G. Barrier, 'The Formulation and Enactment of the Punjab Alienation of Land Bill', *The Indian Economic & Social History Review* 2, no. 2 (1965): 145–65; Judicial and Public Department, 'Act XIII of 1900, Punjab Alienation of Land Act 1900' (BL IOR

Initial Land Tenure Settlements

As described in Chapter 1, the East India Company gained a firm foothold in India in the middle of the eighteenth century after it was granted rights to collect land revenue in Bengal.[37] Land revenue was the primary source to cover the costs of governing the colony and generate returns for the Company's shareholders. For example, in Punjab, land tax contributed over 80% of the total revenue in 1849–50, the remaining 20% coming from excise and stamps, tributes, and the post-office.[38] Accordingly, great efforts were expended to develop an efficient land revenue system, which had various components such as the amount of revenue, the form it will take (cash or kind), from whom to collect (landlord or cultivator (ryot), individual or collective (e.g. village communities)), and assessment time period (fixed in perpetuity or reassessed after a few years), among others. Several land revenue systems, with different combinations of these components, were put in place as more provinces came under colonial rule in the nineteenth century.[39]

At its full annexation in 1849, Punjab's economy was primarily agricultural and land revenue the main source of government revenue.[40] The British inherited ambiguous land revenue and tenure systems in Punjab.[41] According to colonial interpretations, three categories of land tenures were discernible during the rule of Ranjit Singh: *talukdars* ('as a category of *zamindars* between the vassal chiefs on the one hand and the peasant proprietors on the other. They were known as . . . superior owners entitled to a species of head-rent under several designations'[42]),

J&P 2092, 1900), IOR J&P 2092, India Office Records, British Library; S. S. Thorburn, *Musalmans and Money-Lenders in the Punjab* (Edinburgh and London: William Blackwood & Sons, 1886).

[37] For an overview of the origins of land laws in British India, including the land revenue systems in various provinces, see Tirthankar Roy and Anand V. Swamy, *Law and the Economy in Colonial India*, ch. 3 (Chicago, London: The University of Chicago Press, 2016), 27–79.

[38] See Appendix B in 'General Report on the Administration of the Punjab for the Years 1849-50 and 1850-51' (London: Printed for the Court of Directors of the East-India Company by J and H. Cox, 1854), 112. This trend has continued in post-colonial India. See Roy and Swamy, *Law and the Economy in Colonial India*.

[39] For details, see Section V., 'The Beginning of British Land-Revenue Systems' in B. H. Baden-Powell, *The Land Systems of British India*, vol. I (Oxford: Clarendon Press, 1892), 281–323.

[40] This proportion of land revenue to total revenue declined substantially during the second half of the nineteenth century in Punjab as well as in the whole of British India both due to the diversification of the economy and the deliberate efforts by the provincial governments to lower the tax burden on the agricultural classes. This trend has continued in post-colonial India. See Roy and Swamy, *Law and the Economy in Colonial India*.

[41] For example, there was a wide variation on the mode of collecting the land revenue, in some cases it was collected by 'kardars' (the local or regional chiefs), in others by the heads of villages, and some directly by revenue officials. See 'General Report on the Administration of the Punjab for the Years 1849-50 and 1850-51', 56–67.

[42] Indu Banga, *Agrarian System of the Sikhs: Late Eighteenth and Early Nineteenth Century* (New Delhi: Manohar, 1978), 168–69. According to the author, '[b]y far the bulk of our information on land tenures in the Sikh dominions comes from early British administrators of the Punjab'. This has important implications about how 'customary rights' were discerned during the debates on the Tenancy Act. I revisit this issue later in the chapter. Also see Baden-Powell, *Land Systems of British India*, vol. III.

peasant proprietors (who owned and cultivated the bulk of the land), and tenants. While the centralised system of land revenue and somewhat structured land tenures worked well under Ranjit Singh, in the latter part of his reign, and especially under his successors, 'the regular system was allowed to fall into abeyance; [and] the governors [of the districts] . . . did what they pleased – farming the revenues . . . to contractors . . . getting as much (and paying as little to the Darbar treasury) as they could'.[43] Furthermore, rural elites during Sikh rule had been pacified through the grant of revenue assignments (*jageers*), revenue-free lands, and pensions.[44]

The Governor-General entrusted the newly formed Board of Administration of Punjab with stabilising the land revenues of the province. The directive stated that the *jageerdars* could only continue to hold rent-free land as a 'matter of grace' and a gift from the government rather than as a right. Furthermore, it mandated that the land revenue 'should be assessed upon each village or Tract which constitutes a separate Tenure, so that the *jageerdar* or other holder should not be allowed to rack-rent his Tenants or derive more from the Land than would be taken by the Government, whose Place he occupies'.[45] This policy had two objectives: chip away the privileges of the traditional land grant-holding *jageerdars* and ensure the wellbeing of the cultivators.[46] On the first goal, as mentioned earlier, there was a difference of opinion between Henry and John Lawrence, both members of the Board. While Henry believed that it would be politically expedient and 'morally just to uphold the full and in perpetuity the grants and powers [of *jageerdars*]', even for those who had opposed the British, John opposed such magnanimity both on the grounds of loss of revenues for the state and because he regarded them as 'parasites'.[47] The Governor-General agreed with John's view, thus drastically reducing the revenue-free land holdings and any other powers vested in the *jageerdars* during previous rule.[48]

The Board next turned to the broader land tenure settlement. It adopted the procedures introduced in North-Western Provinces, where the Lawrence brothers (and other administrators brought to Punjab) gained their previous experience. First, the land settlement in these provinces was based on the political economy theory of Ricardian rents promoted by the Benthamite utilitarians in the first half of the nineteenth century. In particular, a famous Minute in 1819 by Holt Mackenzie, a colonial administrator, 'equated the land revenue rights of the State with the right

[43] Baden-Powell, *Land Systems of British India*, vol. III, 541.

[44] Major, *Return to Empire*.

[45] 'Sir H. Elliott's Instructions to Board of Administration as to the Manner of Dealing with Landed Tenures in the Punjab, March 31, 1849', 1856, House of Lords Papers, Volume XIII, Paper Number 197.

[46] In its report for 1849 to 1851, the Punjab administration was proud of its achievement of reducing the land revenue demand from the cultivators, while still maintaining healthy revenue flows, which it attributed to taking away the land revenue previously alienated to the *jageers* (through rent-free grants). See 'General Report on the Administration of the Punjab for the Years 1849-50 and 1850-51', 110–11.

[47] Major, *Return to Empire*, 142–43.

[48] Mathur, *British Administration of Punjab, 1849-75.*

to enjoy the full economic rent', but warned 'against trespassing beyond this limit and trenching on the necessary profits of stock and wages of labour'.[49] The latter objective could be achieved by following the 'net produce criterion' in assessing land revenue, whereby revenue was assessed on gross produce minus the expenses of cultivation, wages, and the normal return of capital. Regulation VII of 1822, distributed to all settlement officers in the provinces, adopted this criterion and put forth the following principles to guide land settlements in the new provinces in British India: a moderate assessment ('being equally conducive to the true interests of Government and to the well-being of its subjects'); and a full inquiry into 'ascertaining, settling and recording the rights, interests, privileges, and properties of all persons and classes owning, occupying, managing or cultivating the land'.[50]

Second, the practicality of implementing these principles required very detailed information about the gross and net produce of land and the various types of rights that existed in the pre-colonial era. According to Richard Temple, a settlement officer in the Jullunder district from 1851 to 1856, the difficulty in determining revenue and recording of rights arose because of the mistrust of the native population to alien rule as well as the peasantry being unaccustomed to 'minute enquiries into their affairs under any system preceding British rule. Though their memories were long, and their traditions had been cherished, they were not careful to give us accurate information on countless particulars'.[51] However, the speed of establishing settlement records in the province was of urgent importance to John Lawrence (initially in charge of revenues in the Board of Administration and subsequently having full responsibility of the province as Commissioner), and settlement officers 'were expected to work at breakneck speed, expedition was the quality most prized in an executive officer, [and] an 'undue polish' was constantly decried'.[52] To expedite the settlement process but stay within the general principles of Regulation VII of 1822, revenue settlements were made with the village communities, who subsequently allocated the revenue demands to individual cultivators.[53] These initial settlements were created for fifteen to thirty years (depending on the conditions of different districts and villages), as cash settlements, and revenue demands were modest.[54] The period of settlement was fixed so that the government could

[49] Stokes, *The English Utilitarians and India*, 95.

[50] Bengal Regulations Vol. 5 1820 to 1825, 'Regulation VII of 1822,' 1822, BL IOR V.

[51] Temple, *Story of My Life*, 58–59.

[52] Clive Dewey, *The Settlement Literature of the Greater Punjab: A Handbook* (New Delhi: Manohar Publications, 1991), 23.

[53] Campbell, 'The Tenure of Land in India'; The basis of these settlements was Regulation VII of 1822 (mufassal settlement) where the revenue payable by the landlord was settled with him, and the revenue to be paid by the village community to the landlord was also settled, see Baden-Powell, *Land Systems of British India*, vol. III.

[54] Details about the land revenue settlements can be found in the following volumes: Baden-Powell, *Land Systems of British India*; Bhattacharya, *The Great Agrarian Conquest*; Mathur, *British Administration of Punjab, 1849-75*; Captain E. G. Wace, 'Report of the Land Revenue Settlement of the Hazara District of the Punjab 1868-74' (Lahore: Printed at the Central Jail Press, MDCCCLXXVI); Douie, *Punjab Settlement Manual*. My interest in this chapter is on recording of rights, especially in the

reassess the revenues and rents due with changing market and other economic conditions. The hope was that the recording of rights would be permanent; however, it was on these rights that the controversy erupted. There was a general satisfaction amongst the agricultural classes on the 'modest' revenue demands of the British.

Besides assessing the land revenue, framing the rights record was more important than the assessment, as its determination 'was permanent, and for all practical purposes final'.[55] The Board of Administration wanted clarity on the proprietary rights of the various agricultural groups with which the government had settled revenues. It thus gave leeway to the settlement officers to determine these rights.[56] The adjudication of disputed rights was taken away from Civil Courts and assigned to the settlement officers. Given the heavy burden placed on them, the settlement officers returned to the guidelines from the North-Western Provinces. Here, their guidance came from its Lieutenant Governor, James Thomason, a significant proponent of peasant-proprietorship, and his *Directions for Settlement Officers*.[57] In particular, Thomason gave great discretion to the government in assigning proprietary rights in situations where there was not enough clarity from existing practices. He argued that 'it rests with the Government to decide whether they will retain it in their own hands, confer it on any class of persons already connected with the Government, or grant it or sell it to strangers'.[58]

In determining the record of rights, the ambiguity arose in the case of tenants who had occupied the land for an extended period and often helped clear the land and settle the villages. For these tenants, the settlement officers in Punjab followed the directions of Thomason that tenants residing in the village who had occupied the land for twelve years and non-resident tenants who had occupied the land for twenty years should, without reference to any other considerations, be 'entered as cultivators having the right of permanent occupancy',[59] that is, twelve years of occupancy was considered as a 'prescriptive title to proprietary right'.[60]

context of landlord-tenant relationships. Although these were often tied to land revenue, I focus on the tenant rights in the rest of the chapter.

55 Douie, *Punjab Settlement Manual*, 52.

56 For a detailed study of the ideology behind and the process of recording the rights, see Richard Saumarez Smith, 'Rule-by-Records and Rule-by-Reports: Complementary Aspects of the British Imperial Rule of Law', *Contributions to Indian Sociology* 19, no. 1 (January 1, 1985): 153–76.

57 A major portion of these is reproduced in Chapter IX, 'The Land Settlement' in Richard Temple, *James Thomason* (Oxford: Clarendon Press, 1893).

58 Reproduced in Temple, *James Thomason*, 145–46.

59 Report by the Lahore Tenant Committee, 1865, reproduced in *Opinions of the Press in India*, 9.

60 G. R. G. Hambly, 'Richard Temple and the Punjab Tenancy Act of 1868', *The English Historical Review* 79, no. 310 (1964): 47–66. The 'twelve-year' rule became a default on questions of rights of occupancy. It came from practices in England. For details about the origins of the concept of 'occupancy rights', see Radharomon Mookerjee, *Occupancy Right, Its History and Incidents* (Calcutta: Calcutta University Press, 1919).

For the following fifteen years, these settlements were operative in the province, and there is no evidence of popular discontent with the initial settlements.[61] Furthermore, during the political upheaval around the 1857 rebellion in most parts of India, Punjab did not witness much hostile activity against British rule. Unlike in Oudh, where the peasants received similar proprietary rights but fought with the 'superior' *taluqdar* class against the British, they stayed neutral in Punjab.[62] Surprisingly, the old *jageerdars* and chieftains joined the British to quell the rebellion outside Punjab. The political strategy in the province after 1858 changed in two important aspects: first, permanent employment in the armed forces of people from the province which 'greatly contributed to the entrenchment of the military in rural Punjabi society. Second, the elites in rural Punjabi society were coaxed back into something like their old positions as intermediaries'.[63] Why did these classes of 'aristocrats', whose privileges were supposedly taken away by the initial settlement, stay loyal to the British even when there was an opportunity to join forces with similar 'superior classes' from other provinces? We can discern answers to this puzzle from the nature of property rights and the economic realities in Punjab before the British annexation.

One is that the 'State possessed a traditional claim to a share of the produce, known as the land revenue demand, and was in theory considered the ultimate owner'.[64] According to colonial estimates, the 'government share of the gross produce was assumed, as a matter of right, to be a clear half', and depending on the fertility of the soil, 'even more was taken'.[65] Thus, the landlords' and tenants' proprietary rights over land were not absolute but had more to do with a relative onus on the collection and contributions of the land revenues. Baden-Powell, in his voluminous treatise, suggests that although more apparent proprietary rights for landlords existed in other provinces, the political situation in Punjab during the more than a century preceding British rule did not allow the emergence of a landlord class. During the period just before its annexation, 'the Sikhs, caring only for revenue, treated all classes alike: the "proprietor" was no better than the "tenant"'.[66]

[61] A substantial percentage of tenants received occupancy rights. In the Lahore district, almost 50% of tenants were recorded as having rights of occupancy, in the Amritsar district, it was more than a third. Andrew J. Major, *Return to Empire: Punjab under the Sikhs and British in the Mid-Nineteenth Century* (New Delhi: Sterling Publishers, 1996).

[62] For official version of the role of Punjab in the Mutiny, see 'Papers "Relating to the Mutiny in the Punjab in 1857"' (House of Commons Parliamentary Papers, April 14, 1859).

[63] Major, *Return to Empire*, 227–28; Also see Rajit K. Mazumder, *The Indian Army and the Making of Punjab* (Delhi: Permanent Black, 2003).

[64] Thomas R. Metcalf, 'Laissez Faire and Tenant Right in Mid-Nineteenth Century India', *The Indian Economic & Social History Review* 1, no. 1 (1963): 74–81.

[65] 'General Report on the Administration of the Punjab for the Years 1849-50 and 1850-51: 56.

[66] Baden-Powell, *Land Systems of British India*, 618 vol. III, Pt. IV. CH. II. The low average size of landholdings of the proprietors supports this argument of a lack of large landholders, such as the *zamindars* of Bengal and *talooqdars* of Oudh who collectively had political clout and influence.

Another possibility is that by giving occupancy rights to one set of tenants, the initial settlement was a continuation of the 'customs' the British inherited in the aftermath of the Sikh rule. According to Banga, there were two categories of tenants during the Sikh rule, *muzarian-i-mustaquil* and *muzarian-i-ghair-mustaquil*,[67] with the former having greater security of tenure than the latter. However, if the proprietor wanted the land for his own use he could eject any tenant, irrespective of the length or the character of his tenancy. 'The formal distinction which the [British] administrators came to make between the occupancy tenant (*maurusi*, literally hereditary) and tenant-at-will (*ghair-maurusi*, literally non-hereditary) was their own creation, but it did have the informal precedent of the practice of the Sikh times.'[68]

Two economic reasons during the Sikh rule in Punjab may have also led to the acceptance of the twelve-year period for the grant of occupancy rights, including inherited rights, as well as the lack of resistance to the usurpation of landlords' proprietary rights: (1) the reality that 'labour being of greater value than land, the proprietor had every motive to retain and none to remove his tenant, who helped so materially in bearing all the heavy burdens of the State';[69] and (2) proprietorship (*wirasat* or *malikee*) would have been valuable only if anything was left from the proceeds of the land after paying the onerous revenues demanded by the state: 'the tendency became rather to abandon rights—symbols more of misery than of benefit—than to their exact definition and enjoyment'.[70]

In addition, the report of the Punjab Administration for the years 1856–1858 attributed the 'contentment of the agriculturalists' in Punjab to the light land tax and to 'tenures that had been fairly adjusted' because of which 'there was no class among landholders and cultivators ... who had suffered by British rule'.[71] The local administration was attentive to Punjab's agricultural conditions and gave periodic land revenue abatements depending upon the price fluctuations of agricultural produce in the market. It made up for the loss in land revenue through new taxes on drugs, opium, and salt.[72]

******

[67] '*Mustaquil*' literary means 'constant', while '*ghair-mutaquil*' means non-constant or changing.

[68] Banga, *Agrarian System of the Sikhs*, 180–81. For a discussion on the colonial institutionalization of these categories, and some push-back from administrators in certain districts, see Bhattacharya, *The Great Agrarian Conquest*, 166–70.

[69] W. G. Davies, *Tenant-Right in the Punjab, and the Punjab Tenancy Act* (Allahabad: Pioneer Press, 1882), 16.

[70] Davies, 10.

[71] 'A Copy of General Report on the Administration of the Punjab Territories, for the Years 1856-7 and 1857-8' (India Office, Ordered to be Printed by the House of Commons, April 11, 1859), 16, House of Commons Parliamentary Papers Online.

[72] The share of land revenue to total revenue came down from over 80% in 1850 to 75% in 1858, and to 66% in 1863. See 'A Copy of General Report on the Administration of the Punjab Territories, for the Years 1856-7 and 1857-8'; and 'Finance and Revenue Accounts of the Government of India 1862/63', 1864, House of Commons Parliamentary Papers Online.

Given the impending lapse of fifteen years to guide the initial settlements, by the early 1860s, it was time to revisit them. With land revenue demands becoming less onerous during the initial settlements, the significant contestation in the succeeding periods would be on the record of rights to the land rather than the amount of tax on the produce. The revisions were undertaken under new administrative arrangements in British India. Under the Act of 1858, India came under the Crown. The Secretary of State for India, who was a member of the British Parliament, and his Council governed British India from the India Office and in London. The Council was the final authority to approve all legislation initiated in the colony.[73] A Governor-General (also holding the title of Viceroy) was appointed to head the government in India with the help of its own Council. The core of the Council consisted of a five-member executive (all five were British: three administrators, one 'legal', and one 'financial'). Through the Indian Councils Act 1861 of the British Parliament, the Executive Council was akin to a cabinet with members having different portfolios. It also dealt with foreign policy and general administration of British India and vetted proposed bills coming from the provinces. An expanded Legislative Council with between six and twelve additional members considered Bills proposed by the various provinces that did not have their independent legislative councils (these included all provinces except Bengal, Bombay, and Madras).[74] Administratively, Punjab was put under a provincial government headed by a Lieutenant-Governor. However, the provincial administration did not get any legislative authority, which rested with the Governor-General of India and his Council.[75] The Council (often referred to as the 'Supreme Government') did not have any Indian members during this period. In terms of the overall governance ideology, this was a period of a conservative turn where the British were reconsidering the appropriateness of prioritizing peasant proprietorship in the colony.[76]

[73] For details on the new administration, post-1858, see Baden-Powell, *Land Systems of British India*, vol. I, Chapter III; Dodwell, *The Cambridge History of India. Volume VI*, chap. XI; Donovan Williams, 'The Council of India and the Relationship Between the Home and the Supreme Governments, 1858-1870', *The English Historical Review* 81, no. 318 (1966): 56–73.

[74] Punjab did not get its own Legislative Council until 1921.

[75] Only the provinces with full governorship (Bengal, Madras, and Bombay) could legislate for the respective province.

[76] Eric Stokes, *The Peasant and the Raj: Studies in Agrarian Society and Peasant Rebellion in Colonial India* (Cambridge: Cambridge University Press, 1978).

4

Resisting the Aristocratic Momentum

Punjab Tenancy Act of 1868

> The Punjab Tenancy Act [leads] us to hope that Sir John Lawrence is resolved to stamp the institutions of the country and leave his mark upon them . . . The prosperity of the yeomanry is more than a mere poet's theme; upon it depend, in a country like this, the stability of the public revenue, and the resistance to famine, and the greatest happiness of the greatest number—to protect them from rack-renting is a duty that we have inherited from our native predecessors, whom we ought at least to equal in humanity and wisdom.[1]

> Vaé Victis! [Woe to the conquered!] And so, the curtain falls on the last Act of a tragedy . . . The last Legislative Act of Sir John Lawrence has appropriately been his worst, and on the silent and deserted walls of the Council Chamber a ghostly hand in writing, in letters of fire. 'Mene, Mene, Tekel Upharsin' [God has doomed the Kingdom]. Thou art weighed in the balance and found wanting—Thy kingdom is divided.[2]

With the impending lapse of the initial land settlements after fifteen years, the provincial administration in Punjab commenced their reassessment in 1860, which took place in a changed political context after the 1857 uprising and the subsequent transfer of power from the East India Company to the British Crown.[3] These efforts culminated in the Punjab Tenancy Act of 1868 (that came into effect in 1869), which instituted security of tenure for many tenants by creating occupancy rights and including provisions that regulated the rents and allowed freedom of sale of

[1] Editorial in the *Pioneer*, 'Tenant Right', in *Opinions of the Press in India on (I) The Tenant Right Controversy in the Punjab. (II) The Action Taken by the Government of India. (III) The Legislative Measure Called 'The Punjab Tenancy Act', as Collected from the Newspapers, during the Years 1865 to 1869* (Lahore: Indian Public Opinion Press, 1869), 173.

[2] *Indian Public Opinion's* description of the debate on the Tenancy Act by the, in *Opinions of the Press in India*, 152. The full comment on the proceedings of the Council is written in the form of a scene from an Amphitheatre, see pages 146–52.

[3] Thomas R. Metcalf, *The Aftermath of Revolt: India, 1857–1870* (Princeton, N.J.: Princeton University Press, 1964).

Empire and the Peasant Proprietor. Preet S. Aulakh, Oxford University Press. © Preet S. Aulakh 2025.
DOI: 10.1093/9780198928270.003.0004

these rights.[4] The almost ten years it took to pass the first land law in the province and the theatrics in the various responses to the Act, reflected in the epigraphs, suggest that it was a controversial and hotly debated legislation. Opponents saw its institutionalisation of 'occupancy tenants' as an infringement of the property rights of landlords and characterised it as being 'socialist', 'mischievous',[5] and produced by 'immaculate conception',[6] among others.[7]

The Act of 1868 represented 'an important stage in the struggle between the rival revenue schools and administrative traditions which divided Indian officialdom in favour of either the peasant-proprietor or the landlord'.[8] These rival traditions refer to the two schools of thought: one, based on the utilitarian philosophy,[9] strove to give priority to tenant proprietorship because it 'was the machinery for moral and intellectual advancement among the masses';[10] and the other, influenced by absolute rights of property and laissez faire theory of political economy,[11] saw proprietary rights of the owners of the land as the foundation of social and political order, and extolled the framers of colonial laws to preserve the sanctity of private property.[12] The East India Company instituted land tenures based on these two schools of thought. After favouring the landlords in the Bengal permanent settlements of 1793, proprietary rights gradually shifted in favour of the tenants in the Southern

[4] 'ACT No. XVIII of 1868, The Punjab Tenancy Act, in A Collection of The Acts Passed by the Governor General of India in Council in the Year 1868: 180–197' (Calcutta: Office of the Superintendent of Government Printing, 1868).

[5] *Mischievous Legislation, Being a Series of Articles on Tenant Right in the Punjab. Reprinted from 'Indian Public Opinion', with Appendices* (Lahore: Indian Public Opinion Press, 1868), 1; Minute by Erskine Perry, in 'East India (Punjab Tenancy): Copies of the Despatch of the Secretary of State for India in Council Dates the 28th Day of October (No. 80) 1869, to the Governor General of India in Council, on the Subject of the India Act No. XXVIII. of 1868, (Punjab Tenancy Act)' (House of Commons, 1870), 5.

[6] Letter to the Editor of the Indian Public Opinion by an Administrator, in *Opinions of the Press in India*, 240–43.

[7] These invectives were hurled not just by the English press in India but also by members of the Secretary of State India Council in their various minutes of dissent to the approval of the Act in late 1869. See 'Papers and Letters Relating to the Punjab Tenancy Act, 8th Duke of Argyll Papers', 1869, BL OMF/IOR NEG 4231–4242.

[8] G. R. G. Hambly, 'Richard Temple and the Punjab Tenancy Act of 1868', *The English Historical Review* 79, no. 310 (1964): 65. Although the Act of 1868 was the first land legislation in Punjab, it has not garnered much scholarly attention. The only study dedicated to the Act is this article by Hambly, which foregrounds the role of one colonial administrator, Richard Temple, in the passage of the Act. Even book-length studies on land relationships in Punjab or extended studies on land tenures in British India make a cursory mention of this act. See Neeladri Bhattacharya, *The Great Agrarian Conquest: The Colonial Shaping of a Rural World* (New Delhi: Permanent Black, 2019); Tirthankar Roy and Anand V. Swamy, *Law and the Economy in Colonial India* (Chicago, London: The University of Chicago Press, 2016).

[9] Eric Stokes, *The English Utilitarians and India* (Oxford: Oxford University Press, 1989); S. Ambirajan, *Classical Political Economy and British Policy in India* (Cambridge: Cambridge University Press, 1978).

[10] Cited in Hambly, 'Richard Temple and the Punjab Tenancy Act of 1868', 48.

[11] Thomas R. Metcalf, 'Laissez Faire and Tenant Right in Mid-Nineteenth Century India', *The Indian Economic & Social History Review* 1, no. 1 (1963): 74–81.

[12] Daniel I. O'Neill, *Edmund Burke and the Conservative Logic of Empire* (Oakland, California: University of California Press, 2016).

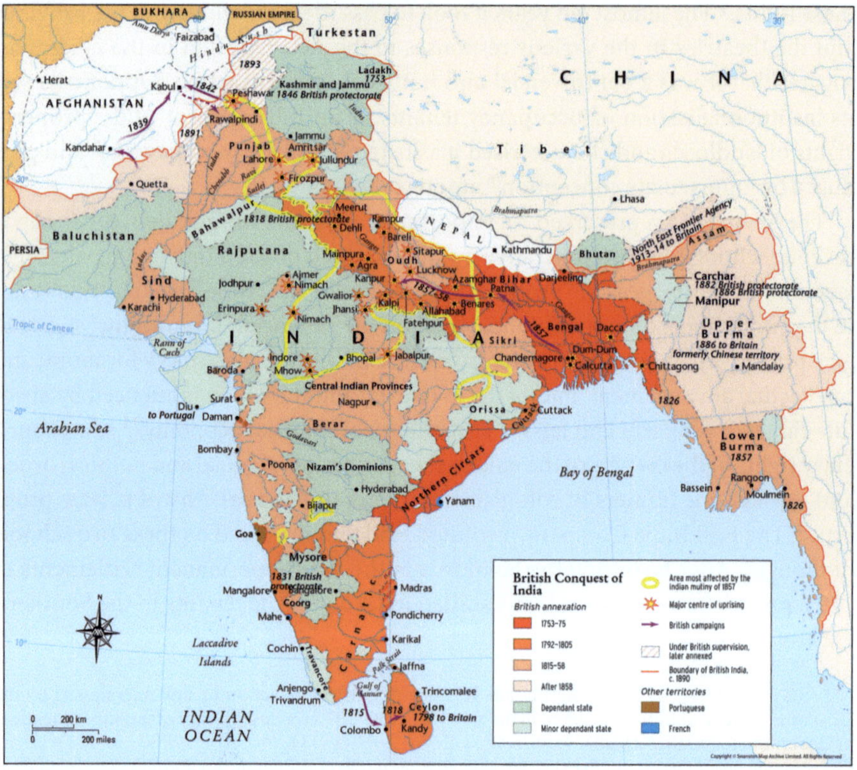

Figure 4.1 Map: British Conquest of India

Source: The Map Archive/Axiom Maps, Ax01147. **Copyright:** © 2025 The Map Archive/Axiom Maps. All rights reserved.

and Western provinces at the beginning of the nineteenth century. In the subsequently annexed territories of North-Western Provinces (1836), Punjab (1849), and Oudh (1856), the land tenure policies were based on peasant proprietorship models (see map of British India in Figure 4.1).[13]

In the aftermath of the 1857 rebellion, political expediency started taking precedence on questions of land tenure and 'opened the way for a new attitude to Indian society and a new *laissez-faire* landlord-oriented settlement policy'.[14] Restoring

[13] Michael Mann, 'A Permanent Settlement for the Ceded and Conquered Provinces: Revenue Administration in North India, 1801–1833', *Indian Economic & Social History Review* 32, no. 2 (1995): 245–69; Thomas R. Metcalf, *Land, Landlords, and the British Raj: Northern India in the Nineteenth Century* (Berkeley and Los Angeles: University of California Press, 1979); Abhijit Banerjee and Lakshmi Iyer, 'History, Institutions, and Economic Performance: The Legacy of Colonial Land Tenure Systems in India', *American Economic Review* 95, no. 4 (2005): 1190–1213.

[14] Thomas R. Metcalf, 'The Influence of the Mutiny of 1857 on Land Policy in India', *The Historical Journal* 4, no. 2 (1961): 155.

the proprietary rights of the landlords in Oudh was a direct result of the new thinking.[15] Thus, the 1860s reassessment of land tenure in Punjab occurred in the context of aristocratic ascendancy in British India. How could the supporters of tenant rights in Punjab resist the post-1857 currents favouring landlords and enshrine peasant proprietorship into law?

This chapter shows that an alignment of three factors—local conditions in Punjab, the emergence of a new discourse relating to the relativisation of property rights, and global concerns of the British Empire—was instrumental in achieving the objective of greater tenant rights in this piece of legislation.

First, the 'Punjab School' of administrators,[16] which included John Lawrence (who came back to India as Governor-General in 1864), ascended the governance hierarchy of British India in the 1860s. They emphasised Punjab's strategic location at the Empire's western frontier and its somewhat different political expediency considerations given the province's support of the British during the 1857 rebellion. The active agency of the 'Punjab School' during the re-assessment of land tenure was instrumental in preserving and strengthening proprietary rights of peasant cultivators in the province. As suggested by Hambly, the Punjab Tenancy Act of 1868 'so completely at variance with post-Mutiny trends, confirmed an impression already obvious during the first twenty years after annexation, that the administration of the Punjab province and the men who governed it tended to be a law onto themselves within the larger framework of British Indian government'.[17]

Second, customs and customary rights of property became important considerations during discussions about land tenure in Punjab because of Queen Victoria's proclamation on November 1, 1858, when India came under the British Crown. The proclamation promised to respect the 'feelings of attachment' of Indians to land and pledged to pay due regard to the prevailing ancient rights and customs 'in framing and administering the law'.[18] Supporters of both landlords and tenants seized on this proclamation and searched for customary rights prevalent in pre-colonial Punjab to promote their respective positions. A focus on customs shifted the debate from 'absolute' towards 'relative' rights of property and provided a theoretical justification for some form of proprietary rights for the tenants.[19]

[15] Thomas R. Metcalf, 'The Struggle Over Land Tenure in India, 1860–1868', *The Journal of Asian Studies* 21, no. 3 (1962): 295–307.

[16] P. H. M. Van den Dungen, *The Punjab Tradition: Influence and Authority in Nineteenth-Century India* (London: Allen & Unwin, 1972).

[17] Hambly, 'Richard Temple and the Punjab Tenancy Act of 1868', 66.

[18] 'East India (Punjab Tenancy)', 402.

[19] Faisal Chaudhry, 'A Rule of Proprietary Right for British India: From Revenue Settlement to Tenant Right in the Age of Classical Legal Thought', *Modern Asian Studies* 50, no. 1 (January 2016): 345–84; Karuna Mantena, *Alibis of Empire: Henry Maine and the Ends of Liberal Imperialism* (Princeton, N.J.: Princeton University Press, 2010).

An important point is that the debates around tenant rights in Punjab were primarily amongst the British administrators (or the different schools of European 'theoretical opinion'[20]) and the English language press affiliated with the respective groups.[21] The search for pre-colonial customary rights of landlords and tenants, which were difficult to discern, thus became a contestation between the two colonial groups regarding whose interpretation of these rights would hold sway.[22]

Third, proponents of peasant proprietorship in India had their way in the Punjab Tenancy Act because their ideology aligned with the new Liberal government of William Gladstone that came to power in England in 1868. Gladstone was very eager to settle the Irish land question, and his government was looking for templates across the Empire that would facilitate the improvement of the position of tenants in Ireland.[23] The current chapter shows that as the Punjab Tenancy Act moved to the Secretary of State for India Council in England, the implicit support of Gladstone allowed the Secretary of State, Argyll, to override the opposition from members of his Council to some of the Act's provisions which impinged upon landlords' absolute rights to property.[24]

Reassessing Tenurial Rights in the 1860s

To initiate the process of new settlements, primarily related to the recording of rights between landlords and tenants, the Financial Commissioner of Punjab proposed a Tenant Code to develop a uniform system.[25] According to the proposed code, the 'owner of the village is the party so recorded at Settlement, . . . if the

[20] See letter by Secretary of State for India dated October 28, 1869, in 'East India (Punjab Tenancy)', 2.

[21] During the period when the Act was being discussed, most of newspapers in British India, especially the English language ones, were run by the British in India, and often their ideological leanings were aligned with different groups of administrators. In the specific case of Punjab, the bill under discussion was going against the pro-landlord sympathies prevalent in the rest of British India. Thus, its pro-tenant leanings were opposed by most of the English press. The *Friend of India* (published from Calcutta) and *Indian Public Opinion* (published by the pro-landlord society from Lahore) were consistently hostile to the Act. On the other hand, the *Pioneer* (published from Allahabad) was more sympathetic to the cause of the peasants. Other newspapers cited here (such as the *Lahore Chronicle* and *Gazette of India*) were a bit more even handed in their overall coverage.

[22] Unlike in Ireland and Prince Edward Island, where active agency of local tenant- and landlord-rights groups was important in the discussion leading to the laws, in Punjab the struggle was amongst the British colonial groups for whom it was an ideological struggle rather than having any material impact on them.

[23] E. D. Steele, 'Gladstone and Ireland', *Irish Historical Studies* 17, no. 65 (1970): 58–88; C. A. Bayly, 'Ireland, India and the Empire: 1780–1914', *Transactions of the Royal Historical Society* 10 (2000): 377–97; John Stuart Mill, *England and Ireland*, 2nd ed. (London: Longmans, Green, Reader, and Dyer, 1868); George Campbell, *The Irish Land* (London: Trubner and Co., 1869).

[24] 'Gladstone Papers Vol. XVI. Correspondence with the Duke of Argyll. 1869–1870', n.d., British Library, Additional MS. 44.IOI.

[25] Letter from Robert Cust to the Government of Punjab, titled Proposed Tenant Code, October 15, 1860, reprinted in 'Selection from Records of the Government of Punjab, Papers Connected with the Question of Tenant Right in the Punjab' (Lahore: C.H. Voss, 1869, 1–16), 1.

owners are numerous, they are represented by their headmen', and these enjoy 'all manorial rights'.[26] The code identified four types of tenants,[27] but the one that was of importance was the category of 'occupancy' or 'hereditary' tenants, who were granted semi-proprietary rights (including rights of inheritance and transfer) and who were protected from ejection and arbitrary increase in rent by the proprietors. While proposing the code that would guide the new settlements and 'confident in the principles' of his positions, the Financial Commissioner nonetheless requested that the matter be 'ventilated' amongst the European and Native officers.[28]

Accordingly, the provincial colonial administration made extensive efforts to get the opinions of different segments of administrators, settlement officers, agriculturalists, and native gentry and officials.[29] However, responses from the District Commissioners of various districts diverged on questions related to the presence of occupancy or hereditary tenants and proprietors' rights in evicting these tenants, with some suggesting that 'occupancy tenants' were the creation of the British, while others finding different types of occupancy rights in existence before colonial rule. Similar differences of opinion were prevalent in responses from different classes of agriculturalists.[30] While proprietors believed that they had absolute rights over their land before British rule, including the right to evict tenants and increase their rents, tenants believed that prevailing customs did not allow arbitrary evictions (unless the land was to be used by the proprietor). Thus, some form of 'protected' and 'heritable' tenancy existed.

Native officials also provided contrasting responses.[31] Most agreed that before colonial rule, a separate category of 'hereditary cultivators' did not exist as a rule. However, certain tenants had more privileged positions than others. For instance, Kaim Alle, Extra Assistant Commissioner of Goordaspoor District, pointed out that 'where the proprietors were numerous, there was no need for cultivators – where they were few and weak, the village was mainly kept up by them. Such tenants could never be ejected . . . and [t]heir right was founded on the consideration that they had mainly supported the burden of the revenue, that they had borne loss with the proprietors, perhaps first cleared the land they held, left their own to come

[26] 'Selection from Records of the Government of Punjab, Papers Connected with the Question of Tenant Right in the Punjab', 9.

[27] Tenants on fixed and immutable rates for time of settlement, tenants with right of occupancy, tenants at will, and tenants on written lease.

[28] 'Selection from Records of the Government of Punjab, Papers Connected with the Question of Tenant Right in the Punjab', 8.

[29] See Landlord and Tenant Enquiry Papers and Appendices II-X (1863) in 'Selection from Records of the Government of Punjab, Papers Connected with the Question of Tenant Right in the Punjab', 17–213.

[30] Appendix III and Appendix IV in 'Selection from Records of the Government of Punjab, Papers Connected with the Question of Tenant Right in the Punjab', 65–99.

[31] The Extra Assistant Commissioner was the highest rank attainable by natives in the British bureaucratic hierarchy during that period. It is unclear as to whether the requirement was a certain level of social status or whether they needed to attain other qualifications.

to live in a half-ruined village'.[32] Other local officials, however, did not go as far regarding such rights and testified that proprietors could evict the privileged tenants, but such incidences were rare.[33]

The government commissioned the process of gathering opinions from various constituencies from 1860 to 1863 to clarify existing practices in land tenure relationships in the province before colonial rule and validate the Tenant Code proposed by the Financial Commissioner, which could form the basis of new settlements. However, fundamental differences in opinions, not only amongst colonial administrators but also between native officials and agriculturalists themselves, highlight the futility of this exercise. The new settlements were, thus, initiated with neither a uniform code to guide the process forward nor a uniform understanding of pre-colonial practices. A lack of clarity led to diverse approaches by settlement officers in recording the rights of different groups and created the need for some form of legislative action. The most controversial of the new settlements were the ones proposed by Edward Prinsep.[34]

The Aristocratic Turn

In 1863, Edward Prinsep, the Settlement Commissioner, initiated revisions to the existing system in all districts of Punjab, with Prinsep himself directly or indirectly in charge of six districts.[35] He doubted the accuracy of the initial settlement in his report on the Umritsar Division (consisting of three districts), especially regarding tenants granted occupancy rights versus those classified as tenants-at-will. For instance, in the initial settlement, 169,000 tenants (or ryots) were classified as tenants-at-will, while 60,000 were hereditary tenants with occupancy rights. However, only 15,547 of the 60,000 were given occupancy rights under the revised settlement. The rights of 29,588 were changed to long leases,[36] and the

32 'Selection from Records of the Government of Punjab, Papers Connected with the Question of Tenant Right in the Punjab', 69.

33 'Selection from Records of the Government of Punjab, Papers Connected with the Question of Tenant Right in the Punjab', 93.

34 Prinsep (Edward Augustus Prinsep) became a key player in the whole tenant rights controversy in Punjab because it was his revised settlement that raised doubts about the veracity of 'occupancy rights' in the initial settlement. His settlement report made him a cause celebre for the proponents of landlord rights (or the Aristocratic Tradition), with the *Lahore Chronicle* (July 8, 1865) calling him 'one of the most conscientious and ablest Revenue Officers that ever made that difficult branch of administration their special study . . . [and one who] is singularly free from bias or crochet . . . His name will become a household word . . . and his reputation will last long as a benefactor, after many are apparently brighter, but more ephemeral one, are lost in oblivion' ('Edward Augustus Prinsep Papers' (BL IOR/Mss Eur D488: 1848–1898, n.d.)).

35 For a sample district report, see Wace, 'Report of the Land Revenue Settlement of the Hazara District of the Punjab 1868–74'.

36 This was done at the discretion of the settlement officers, and primarily to appease the tenants whose heritable occupancy rights from the first settlement were being abrogated. As we shall see later, the Chief Court of Punjab took exception to this aspect.

remaining 12,592 were reduced to tenants-at-will.[37] In light of these reassessments of the record of rights of different groups of tenants, Prinsep, in his report to the Financial Commissioner, questioned (1) the practice of assigning hereditary rights based on twelve years of occupancy in the initial settlements, and (2) the assumption that landlords could not evict the tenants under any circumstance.[38] He further wrote that the 'subject of the relative position of landlord and tenant is one that must now come under consideration; any new principles that are to be laid out should receive the early attention of government . . . I beg I may be placed in receipt of full instructions and as early as possible'.[39] McLeod, being sympathetic towards the landlords,[40] agreed with Prinsep about the need to bring greater clarity to the new settlements, suggesting that the initial settlements were based on principles uncritically borrowed from other provinces and did not reflect the 'real feelings, wishes, and past usages of the people'.[41]

McLeod's suggestions were implemented soon after, once he was promoted to Lieutenant-Governor of Punjab in 1865, through the Lahore Tenant Committee. During the two sittings, the Committee heard from Edward Prinsep, who presented his findings from the settlement exercise in the Umritsur Division and the recorded responses from various constituents about land tenures in Punjab before British rule.[42] Based on his evaluation of 10,000 entries in his district, Prinsep provided the Committee with seven categories of tenants with varying rights. However, no category had rights close to the occupancy tenants identified during the first settlement and 'the general custom allowed the proprietor power of eviction, even for resident tenants with long-standing and inherited occupancy'.[43] He urged the Committee to institutionalise his schema of these categories and give settlement officers the power to amend the record of rights from the first settlement so that the government can 'rectify the errors it had made itself, remembering that so long as a great wrong remained unrighted, it was unworthy . . . to think of any other expediency than justice'.[44]

The Committee concurred with Prinsep that the settlement officer could amend the record of rights with the consent of both parties. However, it did not see it

[37] Notes by the Secretary to Government, 15th October 1866, in 'East India (Punjab Tenancy)', 152.

[38] In his recent book, Bhattacharya suggests that 'Prinsep's argument was ultimately internally contradictory. He used the rhetoric of custom but refused to see customary practice as the source of valid peasant rights. Against peasant claims to security, he was a Benthamite Utilitarian Positivist who saw in uncodified practice nothing but ambiguity and uncertainty . . . But this Benthamite scepticism disappeared in relation to the rights of the proprietors'. They were assumed to have 'an undoubted right to evict, even if they had never done so in the past'. Bhattacharya, *The Great Agrarian Conquest*, 172.

[39] Letter dated April 28, 1863, reproduced in 'East India (Punjab Tenancy)', 60–63.

[40] I will discuss his role in more detail later in the chapter.

[41] McLeod letter to Secretary to Government, Punjab dated October 14, 1864, reproduced in 'East India (Punjab Tenancy)', 40–41.

[42] Report of the Lahore Committee, reproduced in 'East India (Punjab Tenancy)', 20–35.

[43] Report of the Lahore Tenant Committee in 'East India (Punjab Tenancy)', 31.

[44] Report of Lahore Tenant Committee in 'East India (Punjab Tenancy)', 35.

reasonable to open every case and recommended that disputed cases could be brought up through regular suits. Furthermore, it did not agree with Prinsep's classification scheme of different tenants, stating that the proposed categories did not include all possible arrangements, thus making it difficult to 'lay out any rule or principle . . . and each case should be decided upon its merits'.[45]

Thus, the Lahore Committee did not bring much clarity to the tenant rights question and left it to individual settlement officers' discretion to determine the rights record in their respective jurisdictions. While the revised settlements from other districts also found discrepancies with the initial ones, the number of reclassified tenants was not as high as those identified by Prinsep. Furthermore, there was no consensus on his conclusions about the right to eviction. For instance, in responding to the question of eviction rights of the landlord, Colonel E. Lake, Financial Commissioner of Punjab, dissented because 'even if in theory the proprietor had this right, in practice in some cases he either did not exercise it, or was prevented from exercising it by the Government officer or *kardar*'.[46]

The revision of the initial settlements in Punjab was not going smoothly for the colonial government. First, it could not agree with a uniform code that would guide the settlement officers. Second, the discretion afforded to each settlement officer changed the records of rights for tenants and landlords in different districts, thus creating discontent in rural Punjab. Third, Prinsep's settlement, which restored the absolute rights of numerous landlords, raised their hopes of reasserting greater political, economic, and social power in the province. The landlords found a strong ally in the Anjuman-I-Punjab society and its newspaper, the *Indian Public Opinion*, in promoting their interests. Gottleib Wilhelm Leitner (1840–1899), a Hungarian-born linguist and Orientalist, founded the society. After being appointed the first principal of the Government College, Lahore, in 1864, he formed the 'Society for the Diffusion of Useful Knowledge' in 1865, which subsequently took the name Anjuman-I-Punjab.[47] The newly formed society wanted to promote the study of vernacular languages and literatures. While the overall aim of this society was to encourage orientalist education in Punjab, it became embroiled

[45] Copy of Letter regarding the Committee's Report addressed to the Financial Commissioner, May 5, 1865 reproduced in 'East India (Punjab Tenancy)', 19–20. The report also noted that it did not have time to consider the question of copyholds and hereditary tenants.

[46] Memorandum dated 8th March 1865, in 'East India (Punjab Tenancy)', 42.

[47] Jeffrey Price Perrill and Muḥammad Ikrām Cug̲h̲tā'ī, *Punjab Orientalism: The Anjuman-i-Punjab and Punjab University, 1865–1888* (Lahore: Pakistan Writers Cooperative Society, 2018). 'Leitner's vision markedly digressed from the education policy envisaged by Lord Macaulay . . . that Indian education should be remodeled in light of Western epistemic traditions' and instead advocated the promotion of local literary traditions. Tahir Kamran, 'An Orientalist of His Own Ilk: The Uncanny Genius of Leitner | Political Economy | Thenews.Com.Pk', May 1, 2016, <https://www.thenews.com.pk/tns/detail/560854-orientalist-ilk>. The society hoped to reform education policy in Punjab by establishing a university in the province, revive Arabic and Sanskrit learning, and introducing European science in the curriculum through the use of vernacular languages. Masood Akhtar Zahid, 'Orientalism's Last Battle in the 19th Century Punjab', *Journal of Pakistan Vision* 10, no. 1 (2009): 27–48.

in the tenancy question due to the nature of its membership. To achieve its goals, it tapped into the native-educated and influential community for membership and British administrators in the province. Members included D. H. McLeod and Edward Prinsep. The Anjuman, because of its orientalist ideological leanings or patronage from the native elite and through its newspaper edited by Leitner, took up the cause of the landlords.[48] McLeod supported its mission because he 'believed in the efficacy of rule through the use of Punjab's natural leaders'.[49]

Return of John Lawrence: Protecting His Legacy

When John Lawrence, back from England now as the Governor-General of India (January 1, 1864 to January 1, 1869), assumed his new role, he confronted the possible unravelling of the land tenure policies he had put in place in Punjab during the 1850s. Besides the controversies of the revised settlements in Punjab, two other notable changes in land tenure occurred during John Lawrence's absence from India. First, the Bengal Rent Act of 1859 institutionalised some occupancy rights for long-standing tenants and restricted arbitrary rent enhancement by landlords.[50] Second, during the post-Mutiny political anxieties, the occupancy rights granted to the Oudh tenants in 1856 were taken back, and full property rights were restored to the landlords (*Talookdars*), with Lord Canning, the Governor-General of India before John Lawrence, pronouncing:

> We must work downwards, through the landed aristocracy and the old hereditary chiefs. If we work upwards, elevating the village proprietors, whilst we thrust aside their heretofore arbitrary masters, . . . we shall succeed in nothing but in sowing dissension between the two classes of lords and cultivators of the soil, making discontented subjects of the first, and getting little gratitude from the second.[51]

As discussed in Chapter 2, the 'fair and equitable rent' issue in Bengal came under extensive judicial review in 1864–65.[52] Eventually, it resolved itself in favour

[48] For a compilation of the editorials related to the Punjab Tenancy Act, see *Mischievous Legislation, Being a Series of Articles on Tenant Right in the Punjab. Reprinted from 'Indian Public Opinion', with Appendices.*

[49] Perrill and Cug̲h̲tā'ī, *Punjab Orientalism*, 247.

[50] 'Act X. of 1859', *Calcutta Review*, 1864, 278–306. There was discussion in Lawrence's Governor-General Council and amongst other colonial administrators about the possibility of introducing the Bengal Rent Act in Punjab, but the idea was abandoned because of its weak protection of tenant rights. See Note by W. Muir, Secretary to Government of India, dated October 15, 1866 in 'East India (Punjab Tenancy)', 151–56. A discussion of the main provisions of this Act was provided earlier in Chapter 2.

[51] Reproduced in Lee, Harold. *Brothers in the Raj: The Lives of John and Henry Lawrence* (Oxford: Oxford University Press, 2002), 404.

[52] Andrew Sartori, *Liberalism in Empire: An Alternative History* (Oakland, CA: University of California Press, 2014).

of the tenant, thus not requiring Lawrence's intervention.[53] However, the restoration of landlord rights at the expense of the 'industrious and improving tenants' in Oudh was complete anathema to him, and he made concerted attempts to revert to a peasant-proprietor system during discussions on legalising Canning's system through a new Act in Oudh. He made a strong plea in his Minute in early 1866, arguing for legally restraining the power of landlords to arbitrarily increase rents of occupancy cultivators because the 'Government cannot trust to the personal interest of the landlord ensuring justice and moderation towards the cultivator'.[54]

Given the sympathies of most British administrators in Oudh towards the landlords, including the Chief Commissioner, Charles Wingfield,[55] the emergence of a strong lobby of provincial landlords, and an overall aristocratic turn of British policy in India, John Lawrence could not sway the tide towards his wishes. He ensured just a few protections against rent increases for the mostly tenants-at-will in the province.[56] His focus on land tenure shifted entirely towards ensuring the rights of tenants granted during his earlier stints in Punjab in various capacities.[57]

Since his return to India, John Lawrence had mainly followed the debates about the revised settlements in Punjab from the side lines. In a series of letters to the Lieutenant-Governor of Punjab in 1865, he requested the latter to do something about the tenant question: 'While we are considering it, Prinsep is going ahead upsetting the arrangements of the last letter, to a greater extent than seems to me to be desirable. The principle on which he acts is probably sound, but he carries it too far in my mind.'[58] However, as the revised settlement gained greater traction amongst the supporters of landlord rights, Lawrence became more involved in the debates surrounding tenant rights in the province.[59] Lawrence wrote directly to Prinsep and wished to 'see fair play to all parties' while acknowledging that, in the first settlement, tenants received favourable terms, as the British officers 'may have

53 Lee, *Brothers in the Raj*.

54 Minute by the Governor-General of India on Rights of Property and Occupancy in the Soil of the Province of Oudh, February 19, 1866, in 'Papers Regarding Tenant Rights in Oudh, Volume 6' (BL IOR/L/PS/6/548 Coll 40/6, 1867), British Library, India Office Records.

55 Charles Wingfield, a member of the colonial civil service in India (1840–1866), and later a Liberal member of the British Parliament (1868–1874), was a keen supporter of landlords' absolute rights of property. For his views on tenant rights, see Charles Wingfield, *Observations on Land Tenures and Tenant Right in India* (London: Wm. H. Allen and Co., 1869).

56 Delving into details about the extensive debates leading to the Oudh Rent Act of 1868 is beyond the scope of this chapter. For details see 'Papers Regarding Tenant Rights in Oudh, Volume 6'.

57 According to an editorial in the *Hindoo Patriot*, 'Sir John Lawrence has nearly evoked an agrarian insurrection in Oudh, but the good senses of his Masters in Victoria Hall, the firmness of the *Talookdars* themselves, and the strong public opinion of both India and England have saved that province from a threatened calamity. What he however could not accomplish in Oudh he now aims to do in the Punjab, his own Canaan'; 'Tenant Right in the Punjab (Reprint from Hindoo Patriot)' (*The Lahore Chronicle*, February 22, 1868).

58 Letter dated October 13, 1865, in 'John Lawrence Collection: Viceroy of India 1864–1869', n.d.

59 Richard Temple, who worked in various capacities in Punjab under John Lawrence, wrote that the latter's personal investment in land tenure of Punjab and the promotion of the security of tenure for the 'voiceless' millions of cultivators derived from a sense of justice 'towards a deserving and industrious class of British subjects' (Temple, *Lord Lawrence*, 1890, 105–6).

been misled as to the real state of things... because under Sikh rule there was practically very little distinction between the proprietors and cultivators, and between rent and revenue'.[60]

With Prinsep unwilling to entertain a tempering of his position and the reluctance of the Lieutenant-Governor of Punjab to rein him in from promoting his new settlements, John Lawrence finally decided to become more actively involved in the tenant rights question.[61] In his Note of August 30, 1866, he recorded his views: 'Inasmuch, then, as certain rights were accorded to cultivators of long residence and occupancy at last settlement, . . . it would be inexpedient to allow revenue officers conducting the revised settlements in this province, to make any great or radical change in the status of such tenants who were recorded as having a right of occupancy.' He was, however, willing to 'remove the evil and redress the injury sustained by the proprietary classes, provided that any redress now given is given in the spirit of fair play to the tenants who have, from the action of the Government, been recognised as hitherto entitled to protection'.[62]

Some members of his governing Council, including Henry Sumner Maine, the law member of the Council, supported Lawrence's position. Maine questioned the veracity of Prinsep's record of rights discovered through a 'roving commission under which he has assembled juries, if they may be so called, of the cultivating classes'. Responding to the new settlements and the Lieutenant-Governor of Punjab's Minute,[63] which supported these settlements, Maine further added:

> The truth appears to be that, when Mr. Prinsep proposes to redistribute these rights, he proposes to redistribute something which is exclusively the product of British rule in the Punjab. The rights are nothing without the enjoyment which they carry with them, and this enjoyment it is proposed to take away from somebody who now has it, and to give it to somebody else . . . [I]f the British rule created the property, I cannot see that it has very deeply sinned if it decided somewhat arbitrarily who was to have it. I should say that we should commit an injustice far more deeply felt if we took it away from those who have enjoyed it for 15 to 20 years.[64]

[60] Letter from Lawrence to Prinsep, dated June 4, 1866, reproduced in 'Edward Augustus Prinsep Papers'.

[61] Lawrence summoned Prinsep to Shimla in the middle of 1866 to discuss the settlements. Lawrence subsequently wrote to McLeod about his concerns about the proposed settlements. In a letter dated September 4, 1866, he wrote that although he agreed with Prinsep that the initial settlements were too favourable towards the tenants, he thought that Prinsep's settlements were going too much in the other direction as his 'arbitrators and assessors are all of the Landlord party apparently'. See 'John Lawrence Collection: Viceroy of India 1864–1869', n.d.

[62] Note by His Excellency the Right Honourable Sir John Lawrence, Viceroy and Governor-General of India; dated 30 August 1866, in 'East India (Punjab Tenancy)', 32.

[63] Minute by D. F. McLeod, September 15, 1866, reproduced in 'East India (Punjab Tenancy)', 34–39.

[64] Note by the Honourable H. S. Maine, Member of the Council of the Governor-General, reproduced in 'East India (Punjab Tenancy)', 157–58.

By the early part of 1867, thus, it was clear within both the Punjab administration and the Governor-General's Council of India that they needed some clarity on the validity of the revised settlements and a way forward to somehow reconcile the disparities in the rights of occupancy tenants between the two settlements. The Lieutenant-Governor of Punjab was more inclined towards the revised settlements, while the Governor-General of India was against any disruption in the occupancy rights given to tenants in the original settlements. To move the discussion further, the latter accepted the Punjab Government's classification of tenants into three classes:[65] quasi proprietors,[66] long resident tenants (twenty years or two generations), and tenants-at-will, but with the suggestion that there was not much to separate the first two categories.[67] However, Lawrence objected to the recommendations about the landlord's legal and customary rights of eviction of the first two categories of tenants: '[I]t is not necessary to search for *rights* which, needing a legal tribunal of their enforcement, cannot be supposed to have had any existence during a state of things when force was the only law; nor yet for traditional *customs*, regarding the precise nature of which the best informed authorities are often most at variance.'[68] He proposed a further consideration on matters of evictions so that there is 'no radical alteration in the relations between the two classes [and] subordination of one class and exaltation of another',[69] by following opinions of just one side of the debate:

> To enable the Government of India to accept recommendations on a point of such importance something more is needed than the expression of original opinions. If, again, bodies of native gentlemen are consulted, it will not be sufficient to accept their opinion when it is merely a selection (without reason assigned) of one or the other of two diametrically opposed opinions adduced. This

[65] In his Minute on Hereditary Tenants (dated September 15, 1866), and which was in response to John Lawrence's Minute of August 1866, the Lieutenant-Governor of Punjab again reiterated that there were three types of tenants in Punjab, 'inferior proprietors' or 'sub-proprietors', tenants who held their lands for long periods, or through several generations, and tenants-at-will. There was no concern about the first and third categories, as they either had full or no property rights, respectively. He was, however, against giving similar rights to the second group. He considered them like the English copyholds and pointed out to the law in England which laid down that 'when the enfranchisement of a portion of a copy-hold, would 'prejudicially affect in enjoyment or value the mansion house', arrangements are to be made, for the purchase by the latter of the tenant's interest in such portion'. 'Selection from Records of the Government of Punjab, Papers Connected with the Question of Tenant Right in the Punjab', 262–63.

[66] These included relatives of actual proprietors or those holding rent-free *jageers* from the State. Many of the latter were abolished after 1849, but a few remained, especially for the *jageerdars* who had shown loyalty to the British during the Mutiny.

[67] Minute by His Excellency the Right Honourable Sir J. Lawrence, Viceroy and Governor-General of India, dated 30th April 1867, in 'East India (Punjab Tenancy)', 160–63.

[68] Minute by His Excellency the Right Honourable Sir J. Lawrence, Viceroy and Governor-General of India, dated 30th April 1867, in 'East India (Punjab Tenancy)', 161.

[69] Minute by His Excellency the Right Honourable Sir J. Lawrence, Viceroy and Governor-General of India, dated 30th April 1867, in 'East India (Punjab Tenancy)', 161–62.

description applies to many of the conclusions which Mr. Prinsep's . . . Committee pronounced on the conflicting claims of the proprietors on the one hand, and the tenants on the other.[70]

Need for Legislation

The Punjab Government hence set up a committee to come up with a draft bill for 'amending and declaring the Law, relating to certain Matters connected with the Tenure of Land in the Punjab'[71] with objectives of defining occupancy rights of tenants, regulating rent, and the eviction of tenants, among others.[72] The Murree Committee prepared the initial draft.[73] It subsequently referred to another committee chaired by E. L. Brandreth and composed of ten additional members, which included Edward Prinsep and four native gentlemen. Brandreth sent his committee's report to the Lieutenant-Governor of Punjab for his consideration and dissemination in the public domain.[74]

The draft bill reaffirmed the occupancy rights granted to the tenants in the first regular assessment (and overriding the restrictive ones determined by Prinsep and other commissioners in the revised settlements). In particular, tenants who have 'continuously possessed proprietary rights in lands occupied by them, and have lost these rights otherwise [probably alluding to the revised settlement] than by operation of the law of treason, shall, in the absence of special agreement to the contrary, have a right of occupancy in such lands'.[75] The draft went further by giving occupancy rights to tenants who had held the land for twenty years before 1848, even if it was not recorded in the first settlement, unless it could be proven in court that either the tenant had voluntarily given up the right or the settlement record was erroneous.

The proposed Bill also protected both types of tenants (ones with occupancy rights and others at-will) from an arbitrary enhancement of rent. For the former, rent could only be raised by the revenue or settlement court, and for the latter, the landlord could increase the rent but only through an application via the relevant government agent (*Putwaree*).[76] Other sections provided for rent abatement when the area of the land or its productive power decreased, court-ordered rent

[70] Minute by His Excellency the Right Honourable Sir J. Lawrence, Viceroy and Governor-General of India, dated 30th April 1867, in 'East India (Punjab Tenancy)', 163.

[71] 'East India (Punjab Tenancy)', 164.

[72] Hambly, 'Richard Temple and the Punjab Tenancy Act of 1868'.

[73] For draft Bill, see 'East India (Punjab Tenancy): Copies of the Despatch of the Secretary of State for India in Council Dates the 28th Day of October (No. 80) 1869, to the Governor General of India in Council, on the Subject of the India Act No. XXVIII. of 1868 (Punjab Tenancy Act)', 166–69.

[74] For a draft of the Bill dated November 20, 1867, see 'East India (Punjab Tenancy)', 174–77.

[75] Right of Occupancy in the Bill of 20 November 1867, in 'East India (Punjab Tenancy)', 174.

[76] See items 9–12 under section 'Of the Enhancement of Rent' in 'East India (Punjab Tenancy)', 174–75.

remission and ejectment on rent arrears with adequate notice. Furthermore, the Bill allowed landowners to obtain a decree from the court to buy the right of cultivation from an occupancy tenant to support their families (22) and a tenant with occupancy right to sell or transfer his tenure after adequate payment to the landlord (23),[77] as well as accommodated tenants' rights to compensation from the landlord for any improvements made on the land (construction of wells, irrigations systems, etc.).

Most of the Committee approved the draft Bill. However, there was dissent on a few provisions and calls for more inquiries before moving forward. Not surprisingly, Prinsep was the most vocal dissenter on the overall principles of rights to occupancy as well the transfer of tenure by tenants, cautioning that approval of these provisions 'will lead to mischief and injustice of the most serious nature'.[78] Other members objected to the right of the landlord to buy off the occupancy tenant, arguing against the potential rights of the landlord over such tenants and the relatively low bar of making 'the landowner's need of the land as the sole condition on which the hereditary tenant may give way'.[79] Even the four native members of the Committee provided their dissent on various sections, including the amount of rent, transferability of rights, occupancy rights, compensation for improvements, etc.

While the Committee members differed on their evaluation of specific provisions of the proposed Bill, the Press was scathing in its attack on the draft Bill. Terming it 'Mischievous Legislation', *The Indian Public Opinion*, the newspaper of the pro-landlord Anjuman-I-Punjab society, wrote that on the 'question of rights in land, the mischief done would be wide-ranging and enduring, and the consequences impossible to foresee'.[80] Criticising the process that led to the introduction of the Bill (including the work of the Lahore Tenant Right Committee), its provisions of hereditary and transferable rights tenants, and lack of consideration for the customs and practices in the province, the newspaper suggested that Brandreth had 'forsaken practice for theory'. It produced 'this abortion as if it was the legitimate offspring of the united intelligence of the Punjab'.[81]

After giving another seven weeks to solicit responses, the Committee headed by Brandreth formalised the Bill into eight parts and forwarded it for consideration to the Governor-General of India Council on January 17, 1868.[82] In an editorial the

[77] See section 'Of Certain Incidents in the Tenure of Tenants Having a Right of Occupancy' in 'East India (Punjab Tenancy)', 176.

[78] Comments by E. A. Prinsep to some of the proposed sections in 'East India (Punjab Tenancy)', 178.

[79] Statement by C. U. Aitchison in 'East India (Punjab Tenancy)', 179.

[80] Published in the 'Indian Public Opinion' on December 24, 1867, in response to the Bill introduced in the Council, *Mischievous Legislation*, 1–2.

[81] *Mischievous Legislation*, 3.

[82] For the full Bill as introduced in the Council, see Appendix A in *Mischievous Legislation*, 39–48, For changes made by the Committee to the Bill introduced in Council, see 'East India (Punjab Tenancy)', 217–28.

following day, *The Gazette of India* questioned the occupancy rights and enhancement provisions of the Bill and lamented that the tenant who was 'once submissive to his landlord and on the best of terms with him . . . [h]as become independent and litigious and the most troublesome of neighbours, . . . and the proprietor [has] sunk to the position of a partner in an Agricultural company with limited liability of the most questionable kind'.[83] Further, the Press asked for more time before the Bill reached the Governor-General of India Council so that the opponents of the Bill could 'furbish up our armour and whet our swords, and summon our followers to the battle; allow us an opportunity of telling the Secretary of State and House of Commons that the men who swore to rule the Indian subjects of Her Majesty with impartiality and truth are with their own hands dragging down the scale of Justice'.[84] While most of the criticism of the proposed Bill was related to the 'abrogation of property rights' of the landowners by creating tenant sub-proprietors, it found support from some sections of the Press based on the 'improvement' logic. According to the *Lahore Chronicle*:

> The ryots in the Punjab derived very little assistance from their zemindars; on the contrary, the improvements of the land have all been owing to the capital and energy of the ryots themselves . . . [They] are now to be turned away out of their holdings at the bidding of their capricious lords, and we consider it would be the greatest injustice in their harsh treatment of the ryots.[85]

As the Bill moved to the Governor-General Council, it went through a few sittings, including in Select Committees of the Council before its passage on October 28, 1868. In the interim period, the leading proponent of the Bill, Brandreth, retired, and his mantle of shepherding it in the Council passed to Richard Temple.[86]

The Punjab Tenancy Act of 1868

In its first sitting to discuss the proposed Bill on January 17, 1868, where Mr Brandreth introduced its main provisions, the discussion mainly revolved around the process through which it was introduced in the Council.[87] Henry Durand, one of the members with greater sympathies for the landlords,[88] criticised 'the

[83] *Mischievous Legislation*, 8.
[84] *Mischievous Legislation*, 6–7.
[85] Editorial, *The Lahore Chronicle*, March 14, 1868.
[86] Hambly, 'Richard Temple and the Punjab Tenancy Act of 1868'.
[87] Authority of the Governor-General, 'Abstract of the Proceedings of the Council of Governor-General of India, Assembled for the Purpose of Making Laws and Regulations', 43–84.
[88] See eye-witness account of the debate in Council sent to the Friend of India, in *Opinions of the Press in India*, 153–60.

immature manner in which this Bill was introduced'.[89] In light of the various apprehensions about the proposed Bill, the Governor-General asked the members to consent to it being referred to a Select Committee and, while it deliberated, to get further opinions from the judiciary in Punjab and its Lieutenant-Governor.[90]

While the Select Committee was re-evaluating the Bill, Lawrence again made a plea to Punjab's Lieutenant-Governor to support the Bill in question, writing that since his tenure in India was coming to an end, he wanted to ensure that rights given to cultivators in the initial settlements were preserved. 'As a matter of policy', he wrote, '*it is wise to protect the cultivators. In a great agricultural Country like India, unless we do so, what is to become of them*'.[91] After deliberations by the Select Committee and incorporation of the findings from various reports from the provincial government, the final report on the Bill was moved for consideration by the Council on October 19, 1868.[92] The supporters of the Bill were heartened by the opinions received from the Chief Court of Punjab,[93] which endorsed the urgent need for legislative action, arguing that the 'confusion' into which land tenure had been thrown could not 'be remedied in any other way'.[94] More importantly, the Court questioned the legality of some aspects of the revised settlements done under the guidance of Edward Prinsep, especially the grant of long leases to tenants whose occupancy rights of the first settlement were rescinded. The Court opined that 'when the revision goes so far as to create a new tenure altogether, the settlement officers transcend their powers, and their orders on that account alone are invalid'.[95] Furthermore, the Lieutenant-Governor, McLeod, who was earlier in favour of the revised settlements and did not feel the need for legislation,[96] now supported the Select Committee's deliberations and the decision to move the Bill to the Governor-General in India Council.[97]

[89] Authority of the Governor-General, 'Abstract of the Proceedings of the Council of Governor-General of India, Assembled for the Purpose of Making Laws and Regulations', 57.

[90] Authority of the Governor-General, 78.

[91] Letter dated March 6, 1868 reproduced in 'John Lawrence Collection: Viceroy of India 1864–1869' (BL IOR/MSS.EUR./F.90/54, n.d.), British Library, India Office Records [italics mine].

[92] For the full proceedings of the discussion in Council on this sitting, see Authority of the Governor-General, 'Abstract of the Proceedings of the Council of Governor-General of India, Assembled for the Purpose of Making Laws and Regulations', 400–81.

[93] See Minute by the Chief Court on the Proposed Bill to define and Amend into Law Relating to the Tenancy of Land in the Punjab, 1868 sent on August 8, 1868, in 'East India (Punjab Tenancy)', 281–89.

[94] 'East India (Punjab Tenancy)', 287.

[95] Minute, signed by two judges of the Chief Court in Punjab, August 8, 1868, in 'East India (Punjab Tenancy)', 287. The creating of 'new tenure altogether' pertains to the granting of long leases to the tenants whose occupancy rights were rescinded.

[96] In his reply to Lawrence's letter of March 6, 1868, McLeod wrote in his letter to Lawrence (dated March 21, 1868) that he had no appetite for legislating tenant rights in Punjab, and thus would not want to personally participate in any discussions related to the bill. ('John Lawrence Collection: Viceroy of India 1864–1869' (BL IOR/MSS.EUR./F.90/52, n.d.), British Library, India Office Records.)

[97] Minute by the Lieutenant-Governor on the Report of the Committee appointed to consider the Provisions of the Punjab Tenancy Bill, as amended by the Select Committee of the Legislative Council, in 'East India (Punjab Tenancy)', 291.

With support from the Chief Court and the Lieutenant-Governor of Punjab, Richard Temple introduced the Bill to the Council for discussion and approval. Suggesting that the Bill had been attentive to the proprietary rights of tenants and landlords, he outlined the seven chapters and provided a brief rationale for the various sections. The main points of accommodation of the two groups around five key chapters are summarised in Table 4.1. The most critical part of the Bill was Chapter II (Of rights of occupancy) because it was around tenants having occupancy rights that the whole debate over land tenure in Punjab occurred.[98] These provisions created four categories of 'superior class of tenants' (Chapter II, Section 5, 1–4), and the fifth (Chapter II, Section 6) comprising those who had been recorded in the initial and revised settlements as occupancy tenants.[99] Essentially, anyone identified as a hereditary tenant in colonial records was now deemed to have the related proprietorship rights.

The Bill negated the revised settlements of Edward Prinsep by acknowledging tenant occupancy rights from either of the two settlements and putting an onerous burden on the landlords to overcome the presumption of these rights through the courts. Similarly, the Bill restricted landlords' ability to enhance rent or ejectment of tenants with occupancy rights while giving a freer hand in the case of tenants-at-will. Although some members offered a few minor amendments to different provisions (especially related to ejectment and compensation) during the discussions in Council and asked for more time for further debate and input, John Lawrence and Richard Temple, with active support from Maine, pushed the Bill tabled by the Select Committee. A six-to-three margin approved it. By affirming and strengthening the tenants' rights, the Punjab Tenancy Act of 1868 was a victory for the proponents of the peasant-proprietorship theory of land tenure, but against 'post-Mutiny trends . . . within the larger framework of British Indian Government'.[100]

Competing Perspectives in the Governor-General of India Council

The Council's discussions of the various provisions of the Bill foregrounded broader questions about the customary versus legal basis of proprietary rights in land tenure, the onus of improving agricultural land, and the importance of political expediency in post-1857 British India.

One of the main points of contention was the customs and customary rights that existed in land tenure in Punjab before British rule and how far these should be accommodated in institutionalising new tenure arrangements. The issue of

[98] See Appendix for the full text of the Act.

[99] Authority of the Governor-General, 'Abstract of the Proceedings of the Council of Governor-General of India, Assembled for the Purpose of Making Laws and Regulations', 402.

[100] Hambly, 'Richard Temple and the Punjab Tenancy Act of 1868', 66.

Table 4.1 Comparative Provisions in the Punjab Tenancy Act of 1868 in Favour of Tenants and Landlords

Regulation/Chapter	For Tenants[a]	For Landlords
Rights of Occupancy(Chapter II)	Occupancy status affirmed for tenants with any of the following: (1) with hereditary cultivation of land, (2) whose names with such rights recorded in the records of initial or revised settlements, (3) who have continuously occupied land as *jageerdar* for not less than 20 years; presumption of occupancy	Landlord can rebut presumption of occupancy right of the tenant through a regular suit if the latter has voluntarily attested to the contrary (that is, error in recording), or within the preceding 30 years, similar tenants have been ejected; non-acquisition of right of occupancy by mere lapse of time.
Rent (Chapter III)	Rent cannot be enhanced for any tenant unless by agreement or decree of Court; differential maximum rent enhancement for different classes of tenants defined in Chapter II	Power of enhancing rent for both occupancy tenants and tenants-at-will affirmed, but through decree of Court; limits the grounds for abatement of rent to decrease in size of land or decrease in land's productive powers
Ejectment (Chapter IV)	Occupancy tenants can only be ejected through a decree of Court for arrear in rent	Tenant-at-will can be ejected merely by notice
Leases, Alienation and Succession (Chapter V)	Occupancy tenant has the right to (1) sub-let (lease) the land in his occupancy, unless restricted in the agreement with the landlord; and (2) alienate the land, but the land for sale has to be offered first to the landlord at market value by most classes of tenants; Male lineal descendants or male collaterals have right of succession	Landlord's right of pre-emption in case of alienation of land by occupancy tenant
Compensation for Improvements (Chapter VI)	Grant of compensation for improvements made by both occupancy tenants and tenants-at-will on eviction	Right to terminate occupancy through payment of compensation

[a] The extent of tenants' rights granted in the Act was a function of their relationship to the land they cultivated. This included the length of occupancy, improvements made in the land, as well as the proximity of their residence to the land (that is, the Act made a distinction between resident and non-resident tenants of the villages associated with the land).

customs arose during discussions on the twelve-year rule applied in the initial settlement as a guiding principle to acknowledge the tenant's occupancy rights and in subsequent debates related to the inheritance of these rights and questions of ejectment. The Anjuman-I-Punjab Society, reflecting the viewpoints of the landlords, made a distinction between 'rights' and 'customs' to counter the argument made by the proponents of the Bill that tenants had 'acknowledged rights' of occupation:[101] '*Rights* can hardly even be understood, far less to be acknowledged, where there is neither law to define them, or an administration of justice, to protect it. *Custom*, on the other hand, can exist, for it depends not on a definition of law, but by the common consent of the people who practice it'. Similarly, *The Friend of India*, a newspaper, argued that '[t]his is not a country of large undivided estates or of non-resident landlords like Ireland; there is no competition among tenants, and no system of rack-rent. On the contrary, equitable customs everywhere prevail, which are morally binding both on landlord and tenant, and the infraction of which would leave social stigma on either party who broke them'.[102]

Thus, amongst the opponents of the legislation, its inability to accommodate the existing customs prevalent in Punjab was unacceptable, especially given the post-1858 guiding principle proclaimed by the Queen of paying due regard to ancient rights and customs of India in framing and administering law in the colony. However, which customs prevailed on land tenures were challenging to disentangle.[103] The debate in the Council on October 28, 1868, wrestled with this issue at length. The Governor-General argued that without written deeds or public records under the Sikh rule in Punjab, the settlement officers had to rely on oral testimony about prevailing customs, which differed not only across villages but even across sections of society within a single village.[104] Another member of the Council, William Mansfield, however, using opinions of the early-nineteenth century British officials, claimed that although occupancy rights of tenants were not customary, the ability of landlords to evict any tenant was prevalent in the province under the Sikh rule. Richard Temple opined that even though certain local customs on land tenure in Punjab can be traced, they are 'not provable, or not . . . absolutely ascertainable. If that were to be sole guide, the opinions of no two officers would agree: in no two districts would the result be similar'.[105]

[101] Report of the Law Committee of the ANJUMAN, sent to Edward Brandreth, i–xxi, in *Opinions of the Press in India*, v.

[102] *Opinions of the Press in India*, 125.

[103] For example, even to the broader distinction between occupancy tenants and tenants-at-will (*mouroosi* and *ghair-mouroosi*) was contested by the ANJUMAN, see *Opinions of the Press in India*, v.

[104] Authority of the Governor-General, 'Abstract of the Proceedings of the Council of Governor-General of India, Assembled for the Purpose of Making Laws and Regulations', 441–44.

[105] Authority of the Governor-General, 403.

Given the varied positions within the Council on identifying and isolating customs and customary rights in determining the security of tenure, H. S. Maine, with his legal background, cautioned members of the futility of basing their decisions on this issue alone:

> I observe . . . that in a great number of cases [during the Settlements], the persons under examination, whether landlords, tenants, or witnesses, were asked whether a particular class had a right to a particular thing . . . Now, everybody who has paid even a superficial attention to the subject is aware that there is no more ambiguous term than right, or some shade of it . . . *Prima facie* when you ask whether a class had rights of a particular kind, you mean legal rights; but legal rights imply a regular administration of fixed laws, and there was confessedly no such administration under Sikh rule . . . Perhaps . . . it may be said that rights about which enquiry was made were customary rights – rights arising under a custom. But here . . . I find myself in greater difficulties than ever . . . [f]or in papers relating to the Panjáb settlement, the word 'custom' is used in a sense certainly unknown to jurisprudence, and I believe also to popular usage . . . According to the understanding of lawyers, . . . the foundation of a Custom is habitual practice, a series of facts, a succession of instances, from whose constant recurrence a rule is inferred. But the writers of these papers perpetually talk of customs of eviction, or enhancement, or of rack-rent, and in the same breath admit the non-existence of any practice of the kind alleged.[106]

Questioning the custom-based rationale of determining occupancy and other rights in land tenure in both initial and revised settlements, Maine urged Council members to focus on the political expediency in institutionalising, through legislation, the tenure relationships that were put in place in post-annexation Punjab and the potential virtues of the peasant-proprietorship model. Considerations of political expediency were somewhat different in Punjab than in Oudh during that time. While the reversion of occupancy rights from the tenants to the landlords (*taluqdars*) in Oudh was based on the need to appease the 'superior class' and ensure their allegiance to the Empire in the post-1857 political environment, such compulsions were not present in Punjab since the landlord class had accepted (even if grudgingly) the initial settlements. However, Maine argued that given that land tenure arrangements had now existed for more than a decade, '[t]here could be no more dangerous precedent than the wholesale obliteration by the Government of vested rights [to the tenants] . . . merely on the ground that the Government made a mistake'.[107]

[106] Authority of the Governor-General, 419–20.
[107] Authority of the Governor-General, 421.

Furthermore, alluding to the earlier conditions in Punjab when land was cheap and in plentiful supply, but labour was scarce to clear the land, Maine posed rhetorical questions on the economic value of giving greater rights to the actual cultivators or tenants: 'Why should not the British government, under the peculiar circumstances of the Punjab, establish rights of occupancy in the tenants whom it found in the province at annexation? Who is it that has created in Punjab the rent of land and its value for sale or letting, which were practically unknown there under Native rule?'[108] This economic rationale was supported by another member, Noble Taylor, who was of the view that '[t]he hereditary cultivator is the real man of progress; as a rule, it is he and no other who puts his labour and his capital into the land, and it is upon his industry and frugality that all agricultural development depends'.[109] John Strachey also affirmed the beneficial relationship between security of tenure and economic progress suggesting that the 'class of tenants with a permanent interest in their holdings [is one] from which almost all real improvement of the land in India is derived'. He also went further by visualising how the proposed occupancy rights could influence land tenure in other parts of the Empire and may eventually reach the metropole: 'England is the only country in the civilised world in which any other doctrines are seriously held; but when we see what is going on in this regard to the position of the occupiers of land in Ireland, it seems hardly possible to doubt that great changes in the tenure of land may not be far distant even in our own country'.[110]

Much of the discussion of the Bill in the Governor-General in India Council, thus, revolved around the broader debates that had been festering amongst the peasant-proprietorship and landlord-proprietorship camps of colonial officials, supported by their respective backers in the Press.[111] No minds were changed during the discussion, and the Bill was passed and sent for assent to the office of Secretary of State for India. The next battle would have to be fought by influencing opinions in England.[112]

[108] Authority of the Governor-General, 414.

[109] Authority of the Governor-General, 426.

[110] Authority of the Governor-General, 432.

[111] One interesting suggestion was that like what had been done in Austria and Russia, the Punjab Tenancy Act should have gone further and given permanent leasehold to the tenant and compensation for the landlord to 'expressly extinguishing the double rights in the same property which the landlord and the ryot were said to possess.' See Authority of the Governor-General, 437–38.

[112] In a letter to Henry Maine dated January 1, 1869, John Stuart Mill expressed concerns about how the debates around the Act had foregrounded a 'reaction towards landlordism [in India] of the present English type, at the very time when in England opinion is, though slowly beginning to turn the contrary way . . . Until now the strong contrary convictions of Sir John Lawrence have moderated the mischief, but India has now got an Irish landlord [Lord Mayo] to rule over her & it is quite uncertain whether his official superior the Duke of Argyll will be any check upon his landlordism. In Francis E. Mineka and Dwight N. Lindley, eds., 'Letter from J.S. Mill to Henry Maine, January 1, 1869', in *The Later Letters of John Start Mill 1849–1873*, vol. XVII, Collected Works of John Stuart Mill (Toronto and Buffalo: University of Toronto Press, 1972), 1536–37.

The Bill Moves to England

As the Bill moved to England for consideration and approval in early 1869, there were further attempts to stall the passage of the legislation. A petition signed by over '200 chiefs, gentry, and landowners' was sent from Lahore to the Duke of Argyll, Secretary of State for India, in February 1869,[113] stating that although the motives of the Bill's proponents were to 'do justice between the landowners and tenants of this province; . . . the provisions of the Bill are not in accordance with the customs, usages, and wishes of the people', which the Queen, in Her Proclamation of the November 1, 1858, had promised in 'framing and administering the law'.[114] The petition requested a reconsideration of the Bill in light of the 'devotion' that the Punjab upper classes had shown to the British during the 1857 rebellion and their proven 'loyalty' to the Empire. The Lieutenant-Governor of Punjab endorsed the petition and, in his memorandum to the Secretary of State, requested due consideration to the landlords' petition and also wrote at length on the necessity of reconsideration of some of the sections of the Bill relating to the Chapters on occupancy rights, ejectment, alienation, and improvements.[115] In the meantime, the Earl of Mayo, an Irish landlord, had assumed the mantle of the Governor-General of India in January 1869, and he was keen on bringing closure to the long and contentious debate around land tenures in Punjab.[116] In his letter to the Duke of Argyll, Mayo acknowledged a significant difference in opinions about the provisions of the Bill and the way it was passed. However, he suggested that 'many of the arguments against the Bill are unsubstantiated and most of them exaggerated', and more importantly, there was no 'penchant for revisiting [it]'.[117]

The difficulty of dealing with diverse opinions is reflected in a series of letters sent by the Duke of Argyll to the British Prime Minister, William Gladstone. In one of his letters, he wrote about the 'violent feelings for and against it'. Although he was personally satisfied with its provisions, he was anxious that most of his Council would oppose them.[118] In subsequent letters, he lamented the opposition within his Council about his memo of not vetoing the Act. Still, he was heartened by the letters from the Governor-General of India, Lord Mayo, supporting his position.

[113] In the letter, it was mentioned that a similar petition was sent to the Governor-General of India in February 1868, see 'East India (Punjab Tenancy)', 402.

[114] Petition sent to the Duke of Agryll, Secretary of State for India in April 1869 to reconsider approval of the Punjab Tenancy Act, see 'East India (Punjab Tenancy)', 402.

[115] Memorandum on the Punjab Tenancy Act dated April 18, 1869 in 'East India (Punjab Tenancy)', 403–407.

[116] As argued by Metcalf, *The Aftermath of Revolt*, 200–202 although Mayo came from an aristocratic Anglo-Irish family, 'he was fully aware of the misery of the Irish cottier tenant, and [was] determined to avoid a repetition of "the Irish difficulty" in India'.

[117] Letter dated July 21, 1869 in 'Private Letters from the Earl of Mayo to the Duke of Argyll, with Enclosures, 1869–1870. In 8th Duke of Argyll Papers', 1870 1869, BL IOR/Neg 423–47.

[118] Letter dated August 23, 1869, in 'Gladstone Papers Vol. XVI. Correspondence with the Duke of Argyll. 1869–1870'.

to carry out loyally the orders of the Secretary of State and not to admit any fresh questions being raised on an act which is now fairly launched on its trial, and good, or bad, has best be carried through.'[132]

******

Questions about land tenure and tenant rights in Punjab in the mid-1860s, after the expiry of the initial settlements, generated tremendous amounts of debate and controversy in both India and England. The eventual Act was in line with the peasant proprietorship model as it gave generous occupancy rights to the tenants.

The controversy surrounding the passage of the Act foregrounded several important considerations for the British administration in the period after the 1857 rebellion and the 1858 transfer of power to the Crown. The peasant proprietorship model in the Punjab Act, with greater rights for the tenants vis-à-vis the landlords, and based on utilitarian principles of political economy, was hardly a new innovation under colonial rule as it had been implemented in the early part of the nineteenth century in southern and western provinces, and its variants had slowly crept their way up north by the middle of the century.[133] Despite its introduction in multiple provinces, the theoretical ideas behind peasant proprietorship could as easily be countered by those adhering to the principles of laissez faire and sanctity of property rights. The inability of the proponents of either school to win the debate on tenant rights with their respective principles of political economy forced them to look for alternative logics to further their respective cause.

The two groups attempted to use customs or customary rights as the overarching rationale on which land tenure rights needed to be determined and institutionalised. However, attentiveness to customs as a basis for the security of tenure posed a challenge because of the inability of colonial administrators to comprehend the local customs, given their limited experience in the province,[134] and the lack of clearly discernible customs on land tenure prevalent there.[135] In one sense,

[132] 'Edward Augustus Prinsep Papers'.

[133] D. A. Washbrook, 'Law, State and Agrarian Society in Colonial India', *Modern Asian Studies* 15, no. 3 (July 1981): 649–721; Tirthankar Roy and Anand V. Swamy, *Law and the Economy in Colonial India*, Markets and Governments in Economic History (Chicago; The University of Chicago Press, 2016).

[134] See dissent by Sir Erskine Perry to the Secretary of State for India's decision to approve the Act, in which he argued that '[c]ustoms which, though faint and obscure, and not easily traceable by an inexperienced English investigator, are still to be distinctly ascertained by a patient and impartial administrator'. In 'East India (Punjab Tenancy): Copies of the Despatch of the Secretary of State for India in Council Dates the 28th Day of October (No. 80) 1869, to the Governor General of India in Council, on the Subject of the India Act No. XXVIII. of 1868, (Punjab Tenancy Act)', 6, 10.

[135] Indu Banga, *Agrarian System of the Sikhs: Late Eighteenth and Early Nineteenth Century* (New Delhi: Manohar, 1978); Metcalf, 'Laissez Faire and Tenant Right in Mid-Nineteenth Century India'; C. L. Tupper, *Punjab Customary Law: Volume 1. A Selection from the Records of the Punjab Government*, vol. I (Calcutta: Office of the Superintendent of Government Printing, 1881); C. L. Tupper, *Punjab Customary Law: Volume II. Statements of Customary Laws in Different Districts*, vol. II (Calcutta: Office of the Superintendent of Government Printing, 1881); C. L. Tupper, *Punjab Customary Law: Volume III.*

the occupancy and related rights of tenants and landlords formalised in the Act would become the accepted customary rights in subsequent land tenure laws in Punjab.[136]

There was then a third rationale, that of political expediency, on which the proponents and opponents of tenants' occupancy rights could base their arguments. As discussed before, the landlords in Oudh, with the help of their colonial allies, were able to win back their property rights after 1858 on grounds of providing greater stability to the British rule in India. However, these political expediency arguments were not straightforward in Punjab. First, unlike other provinces, Punjab did not witness a widespread revolt against colonial rule in 1857, and the marshalling of its support by John Lawrence was crucial in suppressing the rebellion.[137] Second, John Lawrence was able to get political and military support from the traditional chieftains as well as the peasantry. While the former chieftains were placated after the revolt with honorary titles (such as Honorary Magistrates and *Zaildars*), the wellbeing of the peasantry needed to be accomplished through more tangible economic benefits, especially since 'Punjab became the nursery of the Indian army right through the end of the Raj. The British were grateful to the Punjabis for their role in suppressing the rebellion, particularly to the Sikhs, who had been conquered less than a decade earlier'.[138] Because of these factors, the political expediency arguments during the debates on the Punjab Tenancy Act did not feature the 'aristocracy versus peasantry' dichotomy prevalent in land tenure discussions in other provinces.[139] Rather, the political expediency argument was more to do with the political implications of taking away the hereditary occupancy rights granted to the vast number of tenants in the first settlements.

Questions on Tribal and Local Custom, vol. III (Calcutta: Office of the Superintendent of Government Printing, 1881).

[136] H. S. Maine's ideas about communal property rights reflected in the 'traditional village communities' which he proposed in his books (Henry Sumner Maine, *Ancient Law: Its Connection with the Early History of Society and Its Relation to Modern Ideas* (London: John Murray, 1901 and Henry Sumner Maine, *Village-Communities in the East and West: Six Lectures Delivered at Oxford* (London: J. Murray, 1871)) were not invoked by him during the various debates related to the Punjab Tenancy Act. It was only in the 1870s that elaborate efforts were made by some of Maine's followers in Punjab to codify customs in different districts. These are beyond the scope of this chapter, but this codification probably played an important part when the Act was revisited in the 1880s and found their way in the Punjab Tenancy Act of 1887. See Tupper, *Punjab Customary Law: Volume 1. A Selection from the Records of the Punjab Government*; Tupper, *Punjab Customary Law: Volume II. Statements of Customary Laws in Different Districts*; Tupper, *Punjab Customary Law: Volume III. Questions on Tribal and Local Custom;* India, *The Punjab Tenancy Act, XVI of 1887. With Introduction, Notes, Rules and Debates in Council by Madan Gopal... Second Edition. Revised and Annotated up to End of February 1899.* (Lahore: Gulab Singh & Sons, 1899).

[137] Major, *Return to Empire*; Gandhi, *Punjab: A History from Aurangzeb to Mountbatten.*

[138] Mazumder, *The Indian Army and the Making of Punjab*, 11. Punjab contributed 18.8% to the British India army in 1880, which had increased to 44.5% in 1919.

[139] Although the Petition signed by landlord groups (cited earlier) did try to make this case.

Eventually, active agency and relative power of the 'Punjab School', led by John Lawrence, in the colonial hierarchy were the crucial factors in stalling the post-mutiny aristocratic movement towards restoring the traditional social and economic hierarchies turn in British India.[140] Despite the controversy over the Act, it was a salient piece of legislation. The pro-peasant provisions of the Punjab Act and the process through which opposition to the Act were overcome in India and England were crucial in resolving the Empire's land question in the nineteenth century. The success in Punjab emboldened the Liberal government in England to reassess land tenure in other colonies, and thus shifted the momentum against landlordism across the British Empire. Furthermore, the foregrounding of customs and customary rights by both supporters and opponents of peasant proprietorship during the debates leading to the Punjab Act provided another analytical tool in resolving the competing logics around property rights and political economy for the Empire. The most immediate cause was the need for land reform in Ireland, to which I turn in the next two chapters.

[140] Several historians have used the restoration of landlord rights in Oudh to suggest an abandonment of the rights of peasant cultivators in British India after 1857. For example, see Karuna Mantena, *Alibis of Empire: Henry Maine and the Ends of Liberal Imperialism* (Princeton, N.J.: Princeton University Press, 2010); Ronald Hyam, *Britain's Imperial Century, 1815–1914: A Study of Imperial Expansion* (New York: Palgrave Macmillan, 2002), chap. 3. My chapter shows that the proponents of peasant rights did win the battle in an important province.

PART III
IRELAND

5
The Irish Land Question

The Irish land question, which preoccupied successive British governments for much of the nineteenth century, had its roots in the waves through which Ireland was occupied since the beginning of the twelfth century and the related legal regimes that evolved to govern the changing land relationships. Before the Norman conquest of Ireland in the latter part of the twelfth century, ancient Irish laws governed the land relationships (often referred to as 'Brehon Law' after the wandering lawyers/judges, or Brehons, who interpreted the written texts and applied them to the situation at hand).[1] A few distinct features of these laws are relevant here. First, the key unit in the land system was the clan or tribe, within which there existed a hierarchical order of property owners and their clients who performed various reciprocal services for each other. The overall structure in Ireland was decentralised, with more than one hundred clans, each ruled by a chief; these clans were grouped together, and each group paid homage to 'the lordship of some royal overlord'.[2] Second, the Irish law of succession (and the associated inheritance of land) was governed by unique features. *Tanistry* was a law of succession that decreed that the clan's chieftaincy and any property connected to it would pass on to the worthiest male ('*tanist*'), to be chosen by the clan during the tenure of the exiting chief. The *tanist* did not have to be the eldest son of the chief. Furthermore, under the *gavelkind* system, the chief of a clan would divide the land owned by a deceased clan member and distribute it to different households.[3] These features of the clan-based system and the possibilities for intergenerational redistribution of land made individual land ownership rights neither absolute nor inheritable.[4]

This traditional system of Irish land was disturbed by the Norman conquest of 1172 when Henry II of England invaded Ireland. Several Irish chiefs acknowledged him as their king. Henry II granted Irish land to Norman barons, 'who were to hold it, in return for feudal services, as tenants-in-chief of the King'.[5] These changes had

[1] William Ernest Montgomery, *The History of Land Tenure in Ireland* (Cambridge, UK: At The University Press, 1889); Henry Sumner Maine, *Ancient Law: Its Connection with the Early History of Society and Its Relation to Modern Ideas* (London: John Murray, 1901).

[2] J. C. W. Wylie, *Irish Land Law* (Abingdon, Oxon: Professional Books, 1986), 8.

[3] Wylie, *Irish Land Law*, 9.

[4] For more details of the different features of the Brehon Laws as it applied to land tenure, see Chapter II of Montgomery, *The History of Land Tenure in Ireland.*

[5] C. F. Kolbert and Timothy O'Brien, *Land Reform in Ireland: A Legal History of the Irish Land Problem and Its Settlement* (Cambridge, UK: University of Cambridge Department of Land Economy, 1975), 10.

Empire and the Peasant Proprietor. Preet S. Aulakh, Oxford University Press. © Preet S. Aulakh 2025.
DOI: 10.1093/9780198928270.003.0005

two crucial implications for land relationships: the introduction of a system of feudal tenure arrangements and the emergence of Anglo landlords in Ireland. Both results profoundly reshaped the land tenure relationships in the country. However, since only a small part of Ireland was conquered then, the feudal tenure system took shape in a limited area (the 'Pale'), where most of the superior tenants were probably settlers from England and Wales.[6] Other regions continued with the pre-existing Irish tenure system, and even some Anglo (or Anglo-Norman) landlords established relationships with their Irish tenants based on Brehon laws.[7]

The two systems continued to coexist until the beginning of the seventeenth century when two waves of conquests in a few decades led to England's fuller territorial control over most of Ireland and the imposition of English common law. In particular, the prevalent practices of *tanistry* and *gavelkind* were considered incompatible with English common law and were thus replaced by the feudal concept of succession, *primogeniture*. In terms of land confiscation and resettlement, a scheme to induce the chief Irish landowners to accept the English monarch as the king of Ireland after the Crown of Ireland Act of 1542 and to redefine their relationship with the English Crown according to feudal principles was well underway at the beginning of the seventeenth century.[8] The process was accelerated in 1607 when a failed rebellion by Irish chiefs in Northern Ireland led to the confiscation of their lands by the English Crown and the settlement of the Ulster plantation, where land was granted primarily to English and Scottish settlers, while the Irish were forced to become tenants.[9] The ensuing landlord–tenant relationship in the Ulster plantations took a unique form that would play an essential role in nineteenth-century efforts to resolve the Irish land question.[10]

Although Ulster plantation was considered relatively peaceful and prosperous, and there were attempts in the period immediately after 1607 by the Attorney General in Ireland, John Davies, to rectify the earlier wrongs of the land confiscation of native Irish people,[11] the rest of Ireland continued to see active resistance

[6] Wylie, *Irish Land Law*.

[7] Kolbert and O'Brien, *Land Reform in Ireland*; Montgomery, *The History of Land Tenure in Ireland*. The Anglo-Irish barons' adherence to the Brehon Laws was frowned upon by the English, as were intimate relations between the English and Irish, which were banned through the 1366 Statute of Kilkenny.

[8] Wylie, *Irish Land Law*.

[9] It is estimated that between 1603 and 1641, 70,000 English and 30,000 Scots migrated to Ireland, primarily to the province of Ulster (Terence Dooley, 'Land and The People' in *The Oxford Handbook of Modern Irish History*, edited by Alvin Jackson (Oxford: Oxford University Press, 2014) 107–25).

[10] Seebohm, F. "The Historical Claims of Tenant Right." *The Nineteenth Century: A Monthly Review* 9, no. 47 (January 1881): 19–36; . While the Protestant tenants in Ulster received similar tenancy conditions as existing in England, the Irish Catholic tenants in the province were also afforded better terms because of the high competition amongst landlords to secure suitable tenants for their land (Crawford, W. H. "Landlord-Tenant Relations in Ulster 1609–1820:" *Irish Economic and Social History* 2 (1975): 5–21). This is discussed later in the chapter.

[11] D. Alan Orr, 'Sir John Davies's Agrarian Law for Ireland', *Journal of the History of Ideas* 75, no. 1 (2014): 91–112; D. Alan Orr, 'From a View to a Discovery: Edmund Spenser, Sir John Davies, and the Defects of Law in the Realm of Ireland,' *Canadian Journal of History* XXXVIII (2003): 395–408. According to Davies, Ireland could only be peaceful and integrated with England through an equitable distribution of land and the adoption of English common law.

against English encroachment upon their land. A failed rebellion in 1641 led to the further forfeiture of Irish lands. This was followed by the expeditions of Oliver Cromwell from 1649 to 1652, which took a sectarian turn, led to the complete conquest of Ireland, the confiscation of rebels' lands, and the establishment of new settlements, and heralded the period of the 'Protestant Ascendancy', which would last into the nineteenth century.[12]

By the middle of the seventeenth century, England's occupation of Ireland was complete (see Figure 5.1). Most of the land was confiscated from the Irish and distributed to Protestant landlords, with some restitution granted through the transplantation of Irish landowners to the province of Connaught. Data show that before 1641, Irish Catholics owned nearly 60% of Ireland's land; this was reduced to 20% by 1665 and a mere 14% by the end of the century.[13] While the resettlement of land under Protestant Anglo-Irish landlords continued, there were difficulties with the efficacy of the English feudal tenure introduced to Ireland. In his essay 'Tenure of Land in Ireland,' published in 1870, M. Longfield, a judge of the Landed Estates Court in Ireland, analysed this challenge as follows:

> The laws which govern the relation between landlord and tenant are not very different in England and Ireland; but there are some differences in their pedigrees, and in some collateral circumstances, which have made them produce very different effects . . . In both countries the law is based upon the feudal system, which gave the landlord a certain superiority over his tenants. But the feudal relation, with its reciprocal rights and duties, never existed in Ireland. Here the landlord never led his tenants to battle; if they fought on the same field, it was on different sides . . . The relations that existed between them were hostile. According to the old feudal law, the lordship could not be transferred without the consent of the tenant, lest an enemy might be made his feudal superior; but in a great part of Ireland a sudden and violent transfer of the lordship was made to persons whom the tenants only know as their victorious enemies.[14]

Given the difficulty that feudal tenure arrangements faced in gaining traction in Ireland and the general trend away from such tenure arrangements even in England by the latter part of the seventeenth century, there was movement in Ireland towards leasehold tenure arrangements. Under these conditions, landlords granted tenants long leases, including those structured as 'three lives' or '999 years' tenure, among others. While these long leases created some level of security for the tenants, these beneficial aspects could be availed only by the Protestant tenants in

[12] John Cunningham, 'Oliver Cromwell and the "Cromwellian Settlement" of Ireland', *The Historical Journal* 53, no. 4 (2010): 919–37; Kolbert and O'Brien, *Land Reform in Ireland*.
[13] Wylie, *Irish Land Law*, 19.
[14] M. Longfield, 'Tenure of Land in Ireland', in *Systems of Land Tenure in Various Countries: A Series of Essays Published Under the Sanction of the Cobden Club* (London: Macmillan and Co., 1870), 1.

Ireland because the penal laws, such as the Irish Statute of 1703, debarred Catholics from purchasing land and limited the length of their leases to thirty-one years.[15] Thus, most Irish tenants were in a precarious position during the late seventeenth and eighteenth centuries because of short leases and a small acreage of their land holdings, which barely met the family's needs.

The absenteeism of a vast majority of the Anglo-Irish landlords further exacerbated the problem for Irish tenants. They preferred to live in England and let intermediaries manage their estates.[16] The preponderance of absentee landlords led to two difficulties: first, landlord–tenant relationships remained at arm's length and were often even hostile,[17] and second, the middlemen, who worked on commission, tried to extract the maximum rent from the tenants, accomplished through short-term leaseholds and subgrants. In addition to the land and penal laws that discriminated against Catholic tenants,[18] new commercial codes were implemented to protect England's industry by discouraging exports from Ireland. For instance, the export of Irish agricultural products, such as meat, butter, and cheese, was prohibited, and onerous import tariffs hampered a thriving linen industry in England.[19] The combined effect was that 'the English nation kept the Irish native race enthralled to the soil'.[20] At its union with Ireland in 1800, England thus inherited a disgruntled Irish population heavily dependent on agriculture but lacked adequate means to sustain itself.

Multiple and Multi-Level Attempts and Failures, 1801–1860

Following the Union with England in 1800, 'the English statesmen hoped that . . . everything would be changed in the country's political, social, and material

[15] The only respite they received was from the Act of 1793, which granted them 40-shilling franchise, whereby freehold tenants with such a franchise could vote for the Irish Parliament. Since tenants tended to vote for their respective landlords, it was in the latter's interest to have as many freehold 40-shilling tenants as possible. This act was withdrawn in 1829. R. Barry O'Brien, *The Parliamentary History of the Irish Land Question. From 1829 to 1869: And The Origin and Results of the Ulster Custom* (London: Sampson Low, Marston, Searle, and Rivington, 1880). The number of Catholic freehold tenants increased substantially during the operation of this Act (1795: 4,768; 1796: 64,752; 1803: 147,159; 1828: 191,732; 1830: 14,246). Montgomery, *The History of Land Tenure in Ireland*, 100.

[16] Wylie, *Irish Land Law*; R. D. Collison Black, *Economic Thought and the Irish Question 1817–1870*, Reprint edition (Cambridge, UK: Cambridge University Press, 2015), chap. III.

[17] There was also the question of whether the remittances of rent from Ireland were detrimental to Ireland because of capital outflows.

[18] For details, see W. N. Osborough, 'Catholics, Land and the Popery Acts of Anne', in *Endurance and Emergence: Catholics in Ireland in the Eighteenth Century*, ed. T.P. Power and Kevin Whelan (Dublin: Irish Academic Press, 1990), 21–56.

[19] Kolbert and O'Brien, *Land Reform in Ireland*. Some of the export restrictions of Irish products were reduced when Ireland joined the Union in 1801, but by that time the Irish industry was decimated, with only a few textile mills in the north of the country, and the main exports being reduced to raw materials for input in England's industry (Francis G. James, 'Irish Colonial Trade in the Eighteenth Century', *The William and Mary Quarterly* 20, no. 4 (1963): 574–84).

[20] Montgomery, *The History of Land Tenure in Ireland*, 84–85.

Figure 5.1 Map of Conquest and Settlements in Ireland (Seventeenth Century)

Source: Ward, Prothero, and Leathes, *The Cambridge Modern History Atlas* (New York, NY: The Macmillan Company, 1912). With permission from the Florida Center for Instructional Technology.

conditions. A new era of prosperity and contentment would it was said, now dawn upon Ireland'.[21] With the granting of direct representation of the Irish people at Westminster, the Irish Members of Parliament also hoped for a new beginning to alleviate the hardships emanating from existing religious, political, and economic conditions. However, any improvement for a vast majority of the Irish engaged in agriculture had to come by changing the tenurial relationships with their respective landlords, most of whom had Anglo origins and mainly resided in England or Scotland. Thus, while there was an opportunity for the Irish to voice their concerns in Westminster, the landlords also found natural allies in English landlords in parliament in resisting any pressure to enact laws that would undermine their position. More importantly, since discussions about land tenure were now occurring in the British Parliament, landlords' and tenants' relative rights and responsibilities in Ireland became intertwined with those in England. Consequently, any potential concessions by the Irish landlords were perceived to have implications for their brethren in England. The implicit collusion between landlords and their supporters was able to counter numerous efforts to address the land question in Ireland.[22] The only laws enacted were those that either helped the landlords during periods of crisis or reaffirmed their absolute rights vis-à-vis their tenants. In the following pages, I foreground the main issues underlying the debates at various levels. The main objective is to highlight the evolving and persistent ideas about relative rights in land relationships during this period, which led to a stalemate on the land question into the 1860s.[23]

During the first few years after the Union, Irish efforts at Westminster were focused on reducing some of the earlier religious and economic restrictions on the Catholic Irish, leading to the Catholic Relief Act of 1829, which allowed entry of Roman Catholics to parliament and to hold most public offices.[24] In the meantime, the economic conditions of the Irish people during the first two decades were 'still [full] of misery, wretchedness, and discontent. The relationship between the landlord and tenant remained unchanged; the poverty and hardships of the people

[21] O'Brien, *The Parliamentary History of the Irish Land Question*, 25.

[22] There were almost yearly efforts by private Members of Parliament to introduce bills that would give some rights to the tenants, as well as numerous other bills introduced by the government during this period. Since all of these met the same fate, I do not discuss all of them. These efforts have been detailed in Montgomery, *The History of Land Tenure in Ireland*; O'Brien, *The Parliamentary History of the Irish Land Question*; Wm. A. Dunning, 'Irish Land Legislation Since 1845. I', *Political Science Quarterly* 7, no. 1 (1892); Wm. A. Dunning, 'Irish Land Legislation Since 1845. II', *Political Science Quarterly* 7, no. 3 (1892).

[23] The debates and contestations around the land question in the nineteenth century did not happen in isolation, as they were part of the wider demands by the Irish for greater political and religious rights. Furthermore, while the legislative progress on the land question was somewhat slow, numerous laws were enacted to suppress some of the political activities, including coercive habeas corpus acts (which Black refers to as 'an uneasy vacillation between a policy of coercion and one of conciliation'; Black, *Economic Thought and the Irish Question 1817–1870*, 12). Also see Michael J. Winstanley, *Ireland and the Land Question 1800–1922* (London: Metheun & Co. Ltd., 1984); Dooley, 'Land and The People'.

[24] Wylie, *Irish Land Law*.

were unrelieved'.[25] The first of numerous select committees was appointed in 1819 to examine this situation. Its report identified two problems afflicting Ireland's agricultural economy: a lack of employment opportunities and the underdevelopment of the agriculture sector. The committee recommended significant efforts in reclaiming wasteland and increasing capital investment in the agricultural economy to improve its efficiency and productivity.[26] While no tangible legislative or policy changes ensued because of this report, its analyses and recommendations initiated meaningful conversations amongst political economists during that period regarding the mechanisms for improving agriculture (for instance, the efficiency of small versus large farms), as well as the role of the State in these efforts (laissez faire versus state intervention policies), both of which had relevance for landlord–tenant relationships in Ireland.

The orthodox viewpoint in the political economy of land during the first few decades of the nineteenth century held that capital investment in large farms, such as the English model, was the only way to improve the agricultural economy in Ireland. This viewpoint is aptly captured by the following letter to David Ricardo in 1822:

> [N]o permanent or substantial good can be done till all small farms and small tenancies are got rid of. They are the curse of Ireland. They are calculated to destroy that wholesome dependence of the lower upon the upper classes which is one of the master links of society; and to encourage habits of idleness, which are the bane of all moral feeling. I am aware, there would be difficulty in carrying this measure into execution, but the object is most important. The two deficiencies in Ireland are *want of capital* and *want of industry*. By destroying small tenancies, you obtain both.[27]

The withdrawal of the 40-shilling franchise in 1829 (which removed the incentive to have many tenants) and the Sub-Leasing Act of 1832 (which prohibited sub-letting by the tenants) aimed to facilitate the move towards larger farms.[28] However, the benefit of the consolidation of land into large farms was predicated on the assumption that the uprooted farmers (tenants) could be accommodated in other sectors of the economy. This remained a challenge because other sectors were not sufficiently developed to absorb the large number of farmers who would be displaced. Moreover, the population of Ireland increased rapidly during that period, going from 2.85 million in 1785 to 5.36 million in 1803 and 8.18 million in 1841.[29] Part of the population pressure was alleviated in the 1840s because of

[25] O'Brien, *The Parliamentary History of the Irish Land Question*, 25.

[26] For a detailed analysis of the report, see O'Brien, *The Parliamentary History of the Irish Land Question*, chap. II.

[27] Letter to David Ricardo in 1822, cited in Winstanley, *Ireland and the Land Question 1800–1922*, 32.

[28] O'Brien, *The Parliamentary History of the Irish Land Question*.

[29] Montgomery, *The History of Land Tenure in Ireland*.

emigration out of Ireland. However, most of the remaining population depended on agriculture, farming approximately eight acres under onerous tenancy relationships with their landlords or the latter's middlemen agents.[30]

Given the reality of small farms in Ireland and the devastation of the famine, a few political economists in the 1840s, using examples from some European countries with successful small-farm systems, started challenging the orthodox view of large-scale capitalist farming. For instance, G. Poulette Scrope, a political economist, suggested that the 'small farm system can in Ireland be made as conducive as it is in Belgium to the comfort of the population and the increase of production: but that the secret of this comfort and increased production ... lies in the possession by the cultivator of a durable and certain interest in the results of his labour'.[31] William Thomas Thornton[32] fully articulated this viewpoint in his book, *A Plea for Peasant Proprietors: With the Outlines of a Plan for their Establishment in Ireland*.[33] He made two primary arguments about small farms and peasant proprietors' benefits. Suggesting that '[e]ver since Adam Smith raised political economy to the dignity of a science, its British professors have been almost unanimously of the opinion that small farms are incompatible with the prosperity either of agriculture or agricultural labourers',[34] he presented data showing that the productivity of small farms in continental Europe (e.g. France and Belgium) was very similar to that of large farms in England. Thornton believed that farmers in Ireland with approximately eight acres could be incentivised to make the necessary improvements in the land while simultaneously earning a decent living. He further argued that small farms in Ireland are perceived to be 'defective' because they 'are wanting certain conditions, without which no farms, whether small or great, nor their occupiers, can be expected to flourish. There are no bounds to the tenant's liabilities, and no security against his ejection'.[35] Tenants could not make a better bargain with their landlords because they had no alternative other than to till the latter's land, and there were too many tenants chasing too few land options and thus agreeing to pay as much rent as was asked. Using the example of the province of Ulster, where the size of the holdings was like that in other Irish provinces, Thornton pointed out that the lower competition for land and the prosperity of the tenants were because the tenants there 'enjoyed something approaching a comfortable subsistence ... They are

[30] It was estimated that in 1845, approximately 10,000 landlords owned the bulk of the land, 50,000 to 100,000 were considered large tenants (cultivating between 50 and 80 acres), and more than 2.5 million tenants farmed on eight acres of land: Dooley, 'Land and The People'.

[31] Reproduced in Black, *Economic Thought and the Irish Question 1817–1870*, 30.

[32] Thornton was an economist and a civil servant. He worked in the India Office for more than twenty years and wrote a number of important works related to overpopulation and its remedies. G. Le G. Norgate and John Vint, *Thornton, William Thomas (1813–1880), Economist and Civil Servant* (Oxford, UK: Oxford University Press, 2004), <https://doi.org/10.1093/ref:odnb/27367>.

[33] William Thomas Thornton, *A Plea for Peasant Proprietors: With the Outlines of a Plan for Their Establishment in Ireland* (London: John Murray, Albermarle Street, 1848).

[34] Thornton, *A Plea for Peasant Proprietors*, 1.

[35] Thornton, *A Plea for Peasant Proprietors*, 187.

not mere tenants in the ordinary sense of the word but possess a proprietary right which limits that of the landlord, and restrains his power of raising the rent, or ejecting the actual occupant'.[36]

Thus, according to Thornton, the key to thriving agriculture in Ireland was not large-scale capitalist farming but rather small farms, with farmers having some security of tenure. However, since the existing landlords would not accept any security of tenure that constrained their property rights (including the ability to raise rents and eject tenants), the only way out was through the peasant proprietorship of wasteland, which the State could purchase from landlords and allocate to tenants. This would ease pressure on agricultural land and provide the necessary incentives for improvement and industry for farmers. John Stuart Mill supported Thornton's views in a series of articles published in 1848 in the *Morning Chronicle* and integrated into the first edition of his *Principles of Political Economy*.[37] Mill did not see value in introducing English capitalist farming in Ireland and disagreed with the Irish Repeal Association's call for fixity of tenure,[38] arguing that this 'would be a violent disturbance of legal rights, amounting to almost a social revolution'.[39] Instead, he saw the solution as the reclamation of wasteland as a public works project by the government and its subsequent distribution 'to the Irish peasantry, either through outright grants-in-deed or through permanent tenures under a quit-rent'.[40]

The debates among political economists centred around the pros and cons of large and small farms, with proponents of large farms arguing for laws that would consolidate farms and facilitate capitalist investment in them. At the same time, the Thornton–Mill scheme favoured the establishment of peasant proprietorship through state intervention and the purchase of wastelands from willing landlords in Ireland. According to the historian Collison Black, the 'general trend of ideas had long been in favour of the first approach . . . The Famine may have ruined many Irish landlords, but it did not shake the strength of the landed interest at Westminster. No measure that appeared to threaten 'the just rights of property' could have been carried out through the House of Lords at that time, and there can be no question that such schemes as those of Mill and Thornton fell into this

[36] Thornton, *A Plea for Peasant Proprietors*, 202.

[37] John Stuart Mill, 'Landed Tenure in Ireland', in *Newspaper Writings December 1847–July 1873, in Collected Works of John Stuart Mill, Volume XXV*, ed. Ann P. Robson and John B. Robson (Toronto and Buffalo: University of Toronto Press, 1986), 1112–15; Also see E. D. Steele, 'J.S. Mill and the Irish Question: The Principles of Political Economy, 1848–1865', *The Historical Journal* 13, no. 2 (June 1970): 216–36; Lynn Zastoupil, 'Moral Government: J. S. Mill on Ireland', *The Historical Journal* 26, no. 3 (September 1983): 707–17.

[38] I discuss this in the following paragraphs.

[39] Quoted in Zastoupil, 'Moral Government', 710.

[40] Zastoupil, 710. The scheme of Thornton and Mill differed from the tenants' land purchase option that was proposed and that led to the 1870 Act (referred to as the Bright Clause), for the former was a project for 'home colonization, with a proprietor status for the colonists, leaving the landlord–tenant relationship unaltered in the rest of the country but freed from the aberrations which had brought it into disrepute'. Black, *Economic Thought and the Irish Question 1817–1870*, 31. I discuss the 'Bright Clause' in Chapter 6.

category'.[41] Thus, until the 1860s, the government upheld the former view and facilitated the continuing viability of large-scale capitalist endeavours by enacting laws such as the Incumbered Estates Act of 1849. This Act authorised the sale of estates adversely impacted by the famine to be sold to new owners through the discharge of any incumbrances. The Act aimed to protect large landlords and inject fresh capital into larger farms.[42]

While debates among political economists regarding the appropriate size of land holdings and the viability of peasant proprietorship in Ireland as a pathway to the security of tenure were ongoing, two other initiatives, which were based on arguments around property rights, took shape intending to achieve security for tenants within their existing relationships with landlords. The underlying basis of these initiatives was the concept of 'tenant-right', which could take two forms: the 'tenant-right of occupancy' and the 'tenant-right of compensation for improvements'.[43] The former, which became popularly known as 'fixity of tenure',[44] was purportedly coined by a town clerk of Dublin, who defined it as the 'abolition of all tenancies at will . . . and in their stead that a fixed tenure in the land, for a given time, should be created by the statute law so that the farmer should have his land for that period free from ejectment, save for non-payment of rent'.[45] The tenant right of compensation, often referred to as the 'Ulster tenant-right', encompassed tenants' expectation of receiving compensation for the improvements they made to the land during their tenure.

The idea of fair rents in Ireland was championed by an Irish landlord, William Conner,[46] who promoted 'a valuation and a perpetuity' in landlord–tenant relationships whereby rents should be fixed by an independent valuation (rather than through market competition). Tenants should have an 'undisturbed occupation of the soil' if they pay the rent set by the valuation.[47] The underlying rationale for his

[41] Black, *Economic Thought and the Irish Question 1817–1870*, 34.

[42] Wylie, *Irish Land Law*; Montgomery, *The History of Land Tenure in Ireland.*

[43] Over the course of the nineteenth century, people interpreted 'tenant-right' in different ways, prompting it to be called 'a phantom that melts away under every attempt to define it and that, chameleon-like, appeared to assume a different aspect every time it presents itself'. William Dwyer Ferguson, *The Tenure and Improvement of Land in Ireland Considered with Reference to the Relation of Landlord and Tenant and Tenant-Right* (Dublin: E. J. Milliken, 1851); cited in William Edward Vaughan, *Landlords and Tenants in Mid-Victorian Ireland* (Oxford, UK: Clarendon Press, 1994), 67.

[44] This was very much akin, in principle, to the occupancy rights in the Bengal Rent Act of 1859 discussed in Chapter 2 and those institutionalised through the Punjab Tenancy Act of 1868 discussed in Chapter 4.

[45] Reproduced in Black, *Economic Thought and the Irish Question 1817–1870*, 26.

[46] Not much is known about Conner except information from an article published in 1922 on the centennial of his first pamphlet of 1822. The author of this article notes in reference to Conner that '[t]o have devoted the best part of one's manhood and the greater part of one's fortune to fighting the cause of a class not one's own, and to have been the pioneer in the advocacy of measures long afterwards adopted by the great agrarian reformers of modern times, must surely be allowed to constitute some slight title of remembrance, if not to gratitude'. George O'Brien, 'William Conner', *Studies: An Irish Quarterly Review* 12, no. 46 (1923): 279. Because of his fierce position against the exploitation of Irish farmers by landlords, Conner was charged and convicted for sedition in 1842.

[47] Black, *Economic Thought and the Irish Question 1817–1870*, 24.

prescriptions was that landlords could not be weaned away from rack-renting their tenants, given the great demand for limited land. Furthermore, his ideas echoed the labour theory of property: 'The labourer was entitled to the fruit of his labour and that the law should protect his property just as it protected the landlord's property.'[48] While not denouncing the institution of property, Conner pointed towards a goal of 'dual ownership' or co-proprietorship between landlords and their tenants, whereby the tenant also had a property right that went beyond contractual rights.[49]

The fixity of tenure and fair rents thus became two important pillars amongst the Irish in their quest to resolve the land question in the middle of the nineteenth century. To this was added the third 'F', that of 'freedom of sale', whereby tenants could sell their interests in the holdings to incoming tenants without their landlord's interference.[50] These principles underlay the demands of the Irish Repeal Association of the 1840s, which also had political goals of ending the Union, and of the Tenant League formed in 1850 under the guidance of William Sharman Crawford,[51] a Protestant landlord and two-term Member of Parliament, and Charles Gavan Duffy,[52] a Member of Parliament and the founder of the radical Irish newspaper, *Nation*.[53] These movements expected the Irish Members of Parliament to promote bills that would lead to the institutionalisation of tenants' security of tenure by writing the 'three Fs' into law. However, an ideological shift within the movement emanating from different priorities regarding Irish political and economic conditions weakened any collective efforts towards this goal.[54]

The Irish achieved a more favourable outlook for security of tenure via the tenant-right of compensation when, in 1843, the devastation of the famine in

[48] O'Brien, 'William Conner', 282.

[49] Black, *Economic Thought and the Irish Question 1817–1870.*

[50] 'Freedom of sale' connoted a tenant's right to 'dispose of his saleable interest to the highest bidder, subject to the landlord's approval of the purchaser'. The salable interest could include the value of the improvement's made by the tenant as well as the 'difference between the competitive market rent and the lower or "fair rent" he actually paid' (Lindsay Proudfoot, 'Tenant Right', in *The Oxford Companion to Irish History* (Oxford, UK: Oxford University Press, 2002). A tenant's saleable interest could be substantial, with one estimate saying that in the 1870s outgoing tenants 'received as much as twenty years' purchase of the rent of their holdings' (Vaughan, *Landlords and Tenants in Mid-Victorian Ireland*, 71).

[51] Sidney Lee and Alan O'Day, 'Crawford, William Sharman (1781–1861), Politician and Landlord in Ireland', *Dictionary of National Biography* (Ocford, UK: Oxford University Press, 2008).

[52] R. B. O'Brien and Brigitte Anton, 'Duffy, Sir Charles Gavan (1816–1903), Journalist and Politician', *Dictionary of National Biography* (Oxford, UK: Oxford University Press, 2008).

[53] Crawford continued his attempts to improve the land situation by introducing multiple private member's bills in parliament. Duffy conceived of a Freehold Land Society that would buy land from the landlords and resell it through instalments to small holders. Black, *Economic Thought and the Irish Question 1817–1870.* While this scheme was like the Thornton–Mill proposal, its implementation was hampered because of the land purchase financing. Furthermore, Duffy was charged with sedition because of his nationalistic views. These multiple frustrations forced him to emigrate to Australia in 1855, where he had a successful political career, including a stint as the prime minister of Victoria.

[54] Baron G. Eversley and Shaw-Lefevre. *Gladstone and Ireland: The Irish Policy of Parliament from 1850–1894* (London: Metheun, 1912).

Ireland and the persistence of Irish Members of Parliament prompted the government to appoint a royal commission to inquire into laws and practices regarding the occupation of land in Ireland. Headed by the Earl of Devon, the commission's five members (all landlords) examined a large body of official and unofficial literature, gathered testimonials from various quarters, and submitted their report to parliament in 1845.[55] One of the crucial contributions of the report was its clear articulation of the Ulster tenant-right:[56]

> [T]he mode in which occupiers hold their land, the most striking peculiarity is the custom prevalent in the northern counties, called the tenant-right. The origin of this custom . . . [is] a consequence from the manner in which property was generally granted and dealt with in that part of the country. Large tracts having become the property of public bodies, or of individuals resident at a distance, the landlords were well contented to let their farms to those who undertake the cultivation and entire management, reserving to themselves a rent, but making no expenditure, and exercising little interference with the land. Under these circumstances, it seems neither extraordinary nor unreasonable, that a tenant quitting a farm, either at his own desire or from any difference with his landlord, should obtain from his successor a sum of money, partly in renumeration of his expenditure, and partly as a price paid for the possession of the land . . . From this State of things a feeling of proprietorship appears to have grown up in the tenant, which continues in a great degree to the present day.[57]

This description of the origin of the tenant-right encompassed several aspects peculiar to Ulster (and, more importantly, in stark contrast to land tenure in England): absentee landlords, investments/improvements made by tenants rather than landlords, a sense of 'shared' proprietorship, and compensation for improvements and goodwill flowing from incoming tenants to outgoing tenants. The report further stated that the accepted custom placed 'the relation of landlord and tenant upon the footing most advantageous for both'. It could explain the relative prosperity of Ulster tenants and peace in the province.[58] The report then detailed

[55] 'Report from Her Majesty's Commissioners of Inquiry into the State of the Law and Practice in Respect of the Occupation to the Land in Ireland (Devon Commission)' (Dublin: Alexander Thom, 1845).

[56] As mentioned earlier, the origins and characteristics of the Ulster tenant-right have been interpreted in various ways. The Devon commission's interpretation became the officially accepted definition. For the various angles of the Ulster tenant-right, see Crawford, 'Landlord-Tenant Relations in Ulster 1609–1820'; Seebohm, 'The Historical Claims of Tenant Right'; Vaughan, *Landlords and Tenants in Mid-Victorian Ireland*, chap. 4; Montgomery, *The History of Land Tenure in Ireland*, chap. VIII.

[57] 'Report from Her Majesty's Commissioners of Inquiry into the State of the Law and Practice in Respect of the Occupation to the Land in Ireland (Devon Commission)', 14.

[58] 'Report from Her Majesty's Commissioners of Inquiry into the State of the Law and Practice in Respect of the Occupation to the Land in Ireland (Devon Commission)', 15.

how tenants' compensation for improvements (approved by their landlords), so prevalent in Ulster, could be legislated for the whole of Ireland.[59]

Ideas for using tenant compensation for improvements to address the grievances in Ireland's agricultural industry gained traction among successive mid-nineteenth-century British governments. Soon after the report was submitted, Lord Stanley, a cabinet member in Robert Peel's government, introduced a tenant compensation bill for Ireland in August 1845. In introducing the bill, he contrasted the landlord–tenant relationships in Ireland with those in England. He argued that given the inadequate involvement and investment in Ireland of absentee landlords and the precarious economic situation of their tenants with small landholdings, there was a need for legislating mechanisms to compensate the tenants upon the expiry of their lease.[60] In this regard, the bill provided for a government office headed by a commissioner that would determine the nature of improvements made by an outgoing tenant and the amount of the resulting compensation paid by the landlord. Stanley was emphatic in his speech that the bill would not interfere with landlords' discretion regarding whom to grant the lease, the period, or the rent to be charged. Nonetheless, the House of Lords did not receive the bill favourably, and it was eventually withdrawn. Similar bills introduced by different governments in the following years regarding compensation for improvements by tenants met with the same fate.[61] The tenant's proposed 'power of arbitrary improvement' threatened the landlord's interest in his land, and the 'good landlords as well as bad stood aghast at the results that would ensue, if every ignorant tenant . . . should have by law the right to work out his conception of 'improving' the holding and then to charge the landlord'.[62] Furthermore, the landlords considered the proposal of a commissioner determining compensation as interference with and confiscation of their property rights.[63]

Until the 1850s, all attempts to address the land question in Ireland and improve the conditions of a large proportion of the population dependent on agriculture through legislative action were defeated through the combined efforts of Anglo-Irish and English landlords in the British Parliament. While these landlords made common cause because any scheme that 'infringed [upon] the rights to property

[59] While much of the literature on the tenant-right in Ireland sees it in terms of promoting tenants' interests through some recognition of co-proprietorship, there is also an argument that tenant-right also benefitted the landlords as it served as 'a bond against nonpayment of rent and was part of a rational landlord's income-maximizing strategy'. Timothy W. Guinnane and Ronald I. Miller, 'Bonds without Bondsmen: Tenant-Right in Nineteenth-Century Ireland', *The Journal of Economic History* 56, no. 1 (1996): 113.

[60] Lord Stanley, 'Compensation of Tenants (Ireland) Bill,' Pub. L. No. Hansard Third Series, Volume 81, 211–35 (1845).

[61] For details about these numerous bills introduced by successive governments as well as others introduced by private members in both houses of parliament in the 1840s and 1850s, see O'Brien, *The Parliamentary History of the Irish Land Question*. Dunning, 'Irish Land Legislation Since 1845. I'.

[62] Dunning, 'Irish Land Legislation Since 1845. I', 64–65.

[63] O'Brien, *The Parliamentary History of the Irish Land Question*.

in Ireland might be held as a precedent for England',[64] the proponents of the three schemes (that is, peasant proprietorship through the purchase of wasteland, security of tenure through the 'three Fs', and the tenant-right of compensation for improvements) could not coalesce towards a united front to counter the political power of the landlords and the entrenched ideas about absolute rights to property and political economy.[65] Those advocating for the landlords felt confident enough to counter any possibility of the institutionalisation of the tenant right by passing an act in 1860 that deemed that '[t]he Relation of Landlord and Tenant shall be . . . founded on the express or implied Contract of the Parties, and not upon Tenure or Service'.[66]

Stalemate in the 1860s and Shifting Aspirations and Perspectives

The two land acts in 1860, one affirming landlord–tenant relationships based purely on contracts[67] and the second allowing limited sub-leasing and compensation for improvements by tenants, were legislated during a period when the Irish Tenant League's influence had waned. The landowners in Ireland were enjoying economic prosperity in the post-famine period due to the increased prices of agricultural products, the consolidation of large farms (more of which were devoted to pasture rather than tillage), and the decreased population pressure caused by mass emigration out of Ireland.[68] Accordingly, landlords in Ireland generally believed

[64] Black, *Economic Thought and the Irish Question 1817–1870*, 37.

[65] It should be noted that the Bengal Rent Act of 1859 (discussed in Chapter 2) was passed in the Indian province. This act was predicated on custom and tenure, and it granted perpetual inheritable tenancy and protection against rack-renting to the tenants with a certain number of years of occupancy. See Andrew Sartori, *Liberalism in Empire: An Alternative History* (Oakland, CA: University of California Press, 2014). It is interesting that until the 1860s, the various laws passed in India regarding land tenure did not figure in the discussions about land tenure in Ireland. See W. F. Finlason, *The History of Law of Tenures of Land in England and Ireland: With Particular Reference to Inheritable Tenancy; Leasehold Tenure; Tenancy at Will; and Tenant Right* (London: Stevens & Hayes, 1870). It was only in the late 1860s that some political economists pointed to Indian precedents as a way to tackle the Irish land question, and Campbell's book played an important role in this movement.

[66] 'Landlord and Tenant Law Amendment Act (Ireland), 1860. (Deasy Act), 23 and 24 Vic. c. 154' (1860), sec. III. Another act in 1860, the Tenure and Improvement of Land (Ireland) Act ('Cardwell's Act'), did legislate limited tenant-right of compensation for certain improvements carried out with the consent of the landowner. The two Acts, with emphasis on the importance of written contracts between landlords and tenants, took the recommendations of Neilson Hancock who undertook a follow-up report to the Devon Commission: W. Neilson Hancock, 'Report on the Landlord and Tenant Question in Ireland, from 1860 till 1866; with an Appendix Containing A Report on the Question from 1835 till 1859' (Dublin: Alexander Thom, 1866).

[67] For the antecedents to this law and its subsequent implications, see Alan Dowling, 'The Genesis of Deasy's Act Comments and Notes,' *Northern Ireland Legal Quarterly* 40, no. 1 (1989): 53–63.

[68] Black, *Economic Thought and the Irish Question 1817–1870*; Barbara Lewis Solow, 'A New Look at the Irish Land Question', *The Economic and Social Review* 12, no. 4 (1981): 301–14. The shift from tillage to pasture in Ireland was attributed primarily to the higher labour requirements for the growing of crops than for pasture, and the labour shortages due to famine and emigration in the 1840s and 1850s. For a detailed discussion, see Barbara Lewis Solow, *The Land Question and the Irish Economy, 1870–1903* (Cambridge, MA: Harvard University Press, 1971).

that the land question had resolved itself. They declared in parliament that 'no period was Ireland in a greater prosperity' than in the late 1850s and that at that time, it 'was one of the most tranquil countries in the world'.[69]

However, beneath this optimism of the Irish landlords and their supporters in England were simmering political tensions stemming from the bleak economic conditions facing much of the Irish population. Although, for a while, the optimists provided evidence of the health of Ireland's economy as reflected in nationally aggregated agricultural statistics,[70] 'the nationalist press assailed the executive and its policy, pointing to the continuing emigration of small tenants and the reduction of tillage as evidence of decay rather than prosperity'.[71] Weaker harvests during the first few years of the 1860s again led to calls for some security of tenure in terms of tenants' compensation for improvements. Still, these calls continued to be resisted by the government. The land question retook centre stage in the latter half of the 1860s because of the international revolutionary Fenian movement that originated in North America but had political, social, and economic goals for the Irish in Ireland. The strength of the campaign and its use of violent tactics worldwide to achieve its objectives brought it to the attention of governments and the public at large.[72] It generated two types of responses; one that aimed to suppress it through more stringent criminal laws that would facilitate the prosecution of acts detrimental to public order and another that sought to rethink once again the economic conditions of Ireland's large agricultural population, among which the Fenian movement was gaining a vast following.[73] The latter included revisiting the laws governing landlord–tenant relationships.

Accordingly, new legislative attempts were made to grant some concessions to the tenants. In 1866, the Secretary for Ireland, Chichester Fortescue, introduced a bill proposed by the Liberal Members of Parliament that would replace the 1860 Cardwell Act regarding compensation.[74] The bill divided the tenants into two groups: holding leases of thirty-one years or more and holding shorter leases. Any compensation for improvement in the first group was to be regulated through contracts between landlords and tenants. In contrast, tenants in the second group would receive compensation 'measured by the increase in letting value caused by such improvements, on determination of tenancy'.[75] In 1867,

[69] Cited in Norman McCord, 'The Fenians and Public Opinion in Great Britain', *University Review* 4, no. 3 (1967): 228.

[70] Hancock, 'Report on the Landlord and Tenant Question in Ireland, from 1860 till 1866'.

[71] Black, *Economic Thought and the Irish Question 1817–1870*, 44.

[72] Eversley, *Gladstone and Ireland: The Irish Policy of Parliament from 1850–1894*.

[73] Some representative sources fully explicating its history include John W. Boyle, 'Ireland and the First International', *Journal of British Studies* 11, no. 2 (1972): 44–62; McCord, 'The Fenians and Public Opinion in Great Britain'; O. Rafferty, *The Church, the State and the Fenian Threat 1861–75* (New York: Palgrave, 1999).

[74] Fortescue would play an important role in the 1870 Land Act. For a detailed discussion, see E. D. Steele, *Irish Land and British Politics: Tenant-Right and Nationality 1865–1870* (Cambridge, UK: Cambridge University Press, 1974).

[75] Black, *Economic Thought and the Irish Question 1817–1870*, 50.

Lord Naas[76] introduced a bill on behalf of the Conservative government that offered to advance public money to tenants for certain types of improvements that they could make without their landlord's consent.[77] Each of the two bills was attacked by both sides, with the landlords' supporters making the usual arguments that the new law would interfere with landlords' absolute rights to property. While acknowledging some positive movement in the tenant-right to compensation for improvements in the two bills, the other side was now not content with gains in only this aspect. They wanted action towards their greater demand of security of tenure, which included the 'three Fs'.

In this regard, the proponents of tenant rights were heartened by new writings from Irish nationalists, political economists, and even some landlords[78] that expanded the logic behind tenants' rights beyond just compensation for improvements. The solidification of fixity of tenure as the objective of the Irish nationalists in the late 1860s was likely influenced by the writings and activism of Isaac Butt (1813–1879), a professor of political economy at Trinity College Dublin in his early life and later a practising lawyer, Member of Parliament, and leader of the Irish Home Rule Movement.[79] Butt was sympathetic to the political, religious, and economic aspirations of the Irish people and defended several Irish charged with conspiracy during the Fenian movement in the 1860s. He was also closely associated with the Tenant League. He articulated his concerns about the economic conditions of Ireland in his book, *Land Tenure in Ireland: A Plea for the Celtic Race*, published in 1866. He attributed the rise of the Fenian movement to the dire economic conditions in Ireland, where the 'position of the occupiers of the soil [was that] of serfs, without any security for their tenure or the fruits of their industry. They are dependent for their very means of existence on the will of their landlord. In contrast, the amount of that which is called rent is regulated, not by any economic law, but the disposition of the landlord to extort, and their own ability to pay'.[80] Arguing against emigration as a remedy to ease pressure on the land, which he described as a 'flight not TO America but FROM Ireland',[81] he saw the only remedy to the Irish land question as coming from the elevation of the 'occupier from his position of serfdom, by giving him an interest in the soil' through fixity of tenure, and which could be accomplished by converting the short-term tenancies to a term of

[76] Naas took up the title of Lord Mayo and became the Governor General of India in 1868. Despite being an Irish landlord and having taken the landlord position with respect to Ireland, he supported the Punjab Tenancy Act of 1868 after succeeding John Lawrence in 1868. See Chapter 4.

[77] Dunning, 'Irish Land Legislation Since 1845. I'.

[78] For examples, see James Caird, *The Irish Land Question* (London: Longmans, Green, Reader, and Dyer, 1869); Lord Dufferin, *Irish Emigration and the Tenure of Land in Ireland* (London: Willis, Sotheran, and Co., 1867).

[79] Alan O'Day, 'Butt, Isaac (1813–1879), Politician and Lawyer' DNB (Oxford, UK: Oxford University Press, 2008), 22; Lawrence J. McCaffrey, 'Isaac Butt and the Home Rule Movement: A Study in Conservative Nationalism', *The Review of Politics* 22, no. 1 (1960): 72–95.

[80] Butt, *Land Tenure in Ireland*, 6.

[81] Butt, *Land Tenure in Ireland*, 100 [capitals in original source].

sixty-three years at a rent fixed at a fair letting value.[82] The landlords would continue to have the power to evict upon non-payment of rent.[83] Butt did not see his proposal as amounting to peasant proprietorship and made a forceful rebuttal, in 1867, to critics of his proposal by arguing that his proposed scheme would 'leave the "Protestant" proprietors in possession of their position and their estates' and 'would not diminish by a single unit the number of existing proprietors'.[84]

Butt's idea about the fixity of tenure as the most viable path for the economic upliftment of Irish tenants received backing from influential quarters in Ireland. John Gray, an Irish Member of Parliament and the owner of an influential newspaper, the *Freeman's Journal*,[85] promoted this scheme to his constituents. Gray's close association with the Roman Catholic clergy ensured its support.[86] Butt and another Irishman revived the Irish Tenant League in 1869 with the express objective of moving beyond just compensation for improvements and fighting for fixity of tenure. Irish nationalists maintained this position during the debates in parliament around the bill brought forward by Gladstone in February 1870.

While Irish nationalist thought on the land question had evolved from demanding 'compensation for improvements' to 'fixity of tenure' to uplift the peasantry economically, there was also a shift in the thinking of political economists in England on the Irish land question. In this regard, the writings of J. E. Cairnes and J. S. Mill were particularly noteworthy in placing the land question within appropriate legal, economic, and political frameworks that could justify the fixity of tenure. Cairnes,[87] an economist and friend of J. S. Mill, wrote four articles in 1865 for *The Economist* under the title 'Ireland in Transition'.[88] In these articles, he challenged the applicability of the accepted individual and absolute theory of private property as applied to land and the political economy arguments favouring large-scale capitalist farming working under free trade principles. Cairnes pleaded for acknowledging tenants' labour involved in improving the land (the tenant-right of compensation) and establishing the peasant proprietorship of small farms (that is, security of tenure). The importance of Cairnes' articles lay not in the novelty of his

[82] Butt, *Land Tenure in Ireland*, 6–7.

[83] Isaac Butt, *The Irish People and the Irish Land: A Letter to Lord Lifford; with Comments on the Publications of Lord Dufferin and Lord Rosse* (Dublin: John Falconer, 1867).

[84] Butt, *Land Tenure in Ireland*, 8.

[85] David Steele, Gray, Sir John (1816–1875), Newspaper Proprietor and Politician. *Dictionary of National Biography* (Oxford, UK: Oxford University Press, 2004).

[86] The influence of John Gray and his followers was strong enough that Lord Chancellor of Ireland warned Gladstone that 'the success or failure of the Land Bill depends on the *Freeman's Journal*; if it says, We accept this as fixity of tenure, every priest will say the same, and vice versa'. Cited in Black, *Economic Thought and the Irish Question 1817–1870*, 53.

[87] *R. D. Collison Black, 'Cairnes, John Elliot (1823–1875), Economist.' Dictionary of National Biography* (Oxford, UK: Oxford University Press, 2004).

[88] John Elliott Cairnes, 'Ireland in Transition: Land Tenure', *The Economist*, October 14, 1865; John Elliott Cairnes, 'Ireland in Transition: The Future of Irish Industry', *The Economist*, October 21, 1865; John Elliott Cairnes, 'Ireland in Transition: Tenant-Right', *The Economist*, October 28, 1865; John Elliott Cairnes, 'Ireland in Transition: Peasant Proprietorship', *The Economist*, November 4, 1865.

recommendations but in how he came to his conclusions by comparing the evolution of land tenure in Ireland and England. This comparative approach allowed him to argue that the demands by the supporters of Irish tenants could be accommodated through the principles of political economy and property rights, albeit in a somewhat different manner than how these principles worked in England. Accordingly, Englishmen should not 'persist in believing that laws under which agriculture has flourished with *them* must of necessity be suited for a people pervaded by ideas and habits very different from theirs'.[89]

Decoupling the land question in Ireland from the prevalent ideas in England was also taken up by J. S. Mill, whose own thinking evolved since the 1840s when he, along with Thornton, had proposed peasant proprietorship through the redistribution of wasteland. Mill was in a unique position, having engaged with the land question through his writings over thirty years and serving as an elected Liberal Member of Parliament during the mid-1860s, where he actively participated in debates around landlord–tenant relationships. In a speech during the discussion of the ill-fated tenant compensation bill introduced by Fortescue in 1866, Mill urged Members of Parliament to legislate on the land question for Ireland 'according to Irish exigencies, and no longer according to English routine'.[90] Highlighting the differences between the two countries in terms of the relative attachment of tenants and landlords to the soil, the onus of capital and labour outlays regarding improvements to the land, and trust between landlords and tenants, among other considerations, he suggested that 'Ireland is not an exceptional country, but England is. Irish circumstances and Irish ideas as to social and agricultural economy are the general ideas and circumstances of the human race; it is the English circumstances and English ideas that are peculiar'.[91]

Mill took a more radical approach to the Irish land question in his book *England and Ireland*, published in 1868.[92] In addition to reiterating the general ideas about property rights and political economy he had proposed in the various editions of the *Principles of Political Economy* (see Chapter 2), Mill approached the Irish land question in three new ways. First, he linked the rise of the Fenian movement in the 1860s and the ensuing violence to the failure of successive governments in England

[89] Cairnes, 'Ireland in Transition: Peasant Proprietorship', 1334.

[90] John Stuart Mill, 'Speech on Mr. Chichester Fortescue's Land Bill, House of Commons, May 17, 1866', in *Chapters and Speeches on the Irish Land Bill*, by John Stuart Mill (London: Longmans, Green, Reader, and Dyer, 1870), 97.

[91] Mill, 'Speech on Mr. Chichester Fortescue's Land Bill', 98. In particular, Mill pointed out that England was an anomaly because of the predominance of land tenure arrangements whereby rents are fixed by contract between landowners of great estates and capitalist farmers, and the latter have the wherewithal to take care of their interests. Furthermore, he argued that English landlords are more attached to their land and thus undertake the necessary investments for improvements.

[92] For the general analysis of Mill's book and its reception in various quarters in England and Ireland, see Bruce L. Kinzer, *England's Disgrace? J.S. Mill and the Irish Question* (Toronto: University of Toronto Press, 2001); E. D. Steele, 'J. S. Mill and the Irish Question: Reform, and the Integrity of the Empire, 1865–1870', *The Historical Journal* 13, no. 3 (September 1970): 419–50; Zastoupil, 'Moral Government'.

to address the various grievances of the Irish, including those related to the conditions of the peasantry. Highlighting the apathy the English upper and middle classes had towards Ireland, Mill stated that '[w]hat seems to them the causelessness of the Irish repugnance to our rule, is the proof that . . . they have allowed what was once indignation against particular wrongs, to harden into a passionate determination to be no longer ruled by any terms'.[93] He further argued that the Irish land question now had to be viewed through the lens of political expediency as well, for 'nothing which is not accepted by the Irish tenantry as a permanent solution of the land difficulty, will prevent Fenianism, or something equivalent to it, from being the standing torment of the English Government and people'.[94]

Second, in the 1840s, Mill proposed limited peasant proprietorship through the voluntary purchase and redistribution of wasteland from landlords to peasants. He did not support any legislation that impinged on property rights. However, he took a radical leap in the 1860s by recommending the 'permanent possession of land, subject to fixed burthens',[95] as the only path to resolving the land question. According to him, the fixity of tenure had become a necessity, because when 'the very hands farm the land of a country that till it, the social economy resulting is intolerable, unless either by law or custom the tenant is protected against arbitrary eviction or arbitrary increase of rent'.[96] He then proposed implementing his scheme through a commission determining a fixed rent.

Third, to assess whether England could implement this new land tenure regime based on the unique situation in Ireland, Mill invoked the example of a variety of land tenure systems instituted in India under the East India Company. He argued that this was proof that 'Englishmen are not always incapable of shaking off insular prejudices, and governing another country according to its wants, and not according to common English habits and notions'.[97] Given the similarities between the agricultural economies of Ireland and India, Mill argued that '[w]hat has been done for India has now to be done for Ireland; and as we should have deserved to be turned out of the one, had we not proved equal to the need, so shall we lose the other'.[98]

Through these three interventions on the Irish land question, on the one hand, Mill aligned his prescriptions around the fixity of tenure with those of Irish nationalists such as Butt and Gray. On the other hand, by bringing to attention the precedence of English land tenure ideas adapted to local conditions in India, Mill provided a path forward to settling the Irish land question without being

93 John Stuart Mill, *England and Ireland*, 2nd ed. (London: Longmans, Green, Reader, and Dyer, 1868), 7.
94 Mill, *England and Ireland*, 44.
95 Mill, *England and Ireland*, 21.
96 Mill, *England and Ireland*, 20.
97 Mill, *England and Ireland*, 22.
98 Mill, *England and Ireland*, 22–23.

constrained by their origins in England. As discussed in Chapter 6, this Indian analogy would play an essential role in the context of the approval of the Punjab Tenancy Act in 1869 and George Campbell's book published in the same year.[99]

During the last session of parliament in early 1868, the Irish land question was debated again under the Conservative government, and Mill elaborated on his proposals regarding the fixity of tenure. These were not favourably received even amongst other Liberal Members of Parliament, including Gladstone, who at that time had not given much independent thought to Irish land and was unwilling to go beyond what Fortescue had conceived in 1866 regarding compensation for improvements. Soon after, new elections resulted in a Liberal government headed by Gladstone, and his first effort was to take up the Irish church issue. It was not until the middle of 1869 that he returned to the land question.[100] John Stuart Mill lost his seat in parliament and did not directly contribute to the ensuing parliamentary debates under the new Liberal government. However, Gladstone continued to consult him privately, as evidenced by their correspondence.[101]

******

Despite numerous commissions set up by the British government since 1800 to find ways to assuage the concerns of the predominantly Roman Catholic Irish tenants vis-à-vis the Protestant Anglo-Irish landlords and multiple legislative attempts to alleviate the Irish grievances by granting some form of security to the tenants, the Irish land question remained unsettled in the late 1860s.[102] Competing logics emanating from different conceptions of property rights and political economy (as articulated in Chapter 2) were at play. Supporters of Irish landlords were able to coalesce around ideas about the absolute sanctity of ownership property rights, the contract between landlord and tenant as the guiding principle in land relationships, and large-scale capitalist farming as the only route to Ireland's prosperity. On the other hand, although the proponents of the Irish peasantry had similar perceptions about the causes behind the country's misery, the solutions they identified to alleviate the conditions were quite diverse and often conflicting (e.g., 'co-proprietorship' through occupancy rights, 'peasant proprietorship', and 'compensation for improvements'). The coalition of Irish and English landlords in parliament was able to thwart any legislation around these schemes because of three inter-related factors: (1) their united efforts in opposing any dilution of

[99] Campbells' expertise on land tenure in India was well accepted, and he was commissioned by the Cobden Club in 1868 to write an essay for a collection it was putting together. See Cobden Club (London, England) et al., *Systems of Land Tenure in Various Countries* (London: Macmillan, 1870).

[100] Black, *Economic Thought and the Irish Question 1817–1870*; Steele, *Irish Land and British Politics*.

[101] H.C.G. Matthew, *The Gladstone Diaries With Cabinet Minutes and Prime-Ministerial Correspondence: Volume Seven, January 1869–June 1871* (Oxford: Oxford University Press, 1982).

[102] Dunning, 'Irish Land Legislation Since 1845. I': 57–79; Dunning, 'Irish Land Legislation Since 1845. II': 500–521; O'Brien, *The Parliamentary History of the Irish Land Question*.

their shared perceptions about absolute rights to property; (2) the widely accepted viewpoint that Irish land tenure was similar to or a close extension of the guiding principles of English land tenure, especially concerning the 'contract' between landlord and tenant, and that any change in this guiding principle for Ireland would adversely impact English landlords; and (3) the unwillingness of successive governments in England to aggressively push for a solution to the Irish land question due to the political power and influence of the landlords relative to that of nascent Irish movements such as the Irish Tenant League. The historian Bruce Kinzer aptly captures the roadblocks to the institutionalisation of security of tenure for tenants for much of the nineteenth century:

> Such concepts as 'fair rent,' 'fixity of tenure,' and 'free sale' of an occupant's holding could not be reconciled with the thoroughly predominant English understanding of property rights and freedom of contract. This does not mean that the Irish farmers enamoured of tenant-right rejected the principle of private property; they considered tenant-right as a species of private property. The problem faced by any reformer who aspired to promote tenurial security for Irish tenants was that orthodox political opinion refused to concede such status to tenant-right, whose essence was deemed incontrovertibly alien to the conception of property regnant in England.[103]

[103] Kinzer, *England's Disgrace?* 95.

6
The Decoupling
Landlord and Tenant Act (Ireland) 1870

William Gladstone became Prime Minister of England for the first time in December 1868. Upon taking the helm of the Liberal government, his mission was to pacify Ireland, which was reeling from religious, political, and economic discontent. Gladstone 'believed that if the Irish were shown the Westminster Parliament addressing their grievances by spectacular acts of legislation, then this would encourage their adherence to the existing political structure'.[1] Accordingly, his first legislative effort regarding Ireland resulted in the Irish Church Disestablishment Act of 1869, whereby the Church of Ireland would no longer be the official church sanctioned by England and lose its privileges, such as seats in parliament and economic endowments. Severing the connection between the Protestant Church of Ireland and the State was expected to remove 'every vestige of grievance on the part of the great majority' of Catholics concerning 'the inequality of treatment of religious bodies'.[2] Soon after, Gladstone turned his attention to the land question, which caused intense discontent among a large part of the Irish population (see a political cartoon in Figure 6.1). He had to find ways to balance landlords' traditional and persistent arguments on political economy and property rights with the expanding demands for legal rights of Irish tenants, which were also now anchored within these frameworks.

Starting his engagement with the study of the land question in August 1869, Gladstone spent the next few months discussing his ideas about a legislative solution with his cabinet. These discussions led to a bill in the British Parliament in February 1870. After a series of amendments in the House of Commons and House of Lords, the Landlord and Tenant (Ireland) Act became law in August 1870.[3] The Act legalised the tenant-right custom,[4] provided tenants compensation for

[1] Matthew, Introduction to the Volume, in H. C. G. Matthew, *The Gladstone Diaries with Cabinet Minutes and Prime-Ministerial Correspondence: Volume Seven, January 1869–June 1871* (Oxford, UK: Oxford University Press, 1982), liii.

[2] Baron G. Shaw-Lefevre Eversley, *Gladstone and Ireland: The Irish Policy of Parliament from 1850–1894* (London: Metheun, 1912), 29.

[3] 'Landlord and Tenant Act (Ireland) 1870' (1870).

[4] The Ulster custom was understood to entail some security of tenure through compensation for improvements and goodwill. This was quite distinct from the 'three Fs'. For a book-length study of

Empire and the Peasant Proprietor. Preet S. Aulakh, Oxford University Press. © Preet S. Aulakh 2025.
DOI: 10.1093/9780198928270.003.0006

improvements and disturbance, and allowed a pathway to peasant proprietorship through the state-facilitated voluntary land purchase from landowners. Although these provisions did not fully incorporate any of the 'three Fs', the Act was nonetheless seen as an achievement. Even the pro-tenant Irish newspaper, *The Freeman's Journal*, gave tempered support to the Act by recognising 'the benefits conferred by the measure, incomplete though it be' as a significant advance 'towards the complete settlement of the Irish Land Question'.[5]

This chapter probes why and how this Act made headway in legislating some security for Irish tenants, given the multiple previous failures spanning almost seventy years since the 1800 Act of Union. Historians have attributed the agency of William Gladstone in shepherding the landlord–tenant bill through the British Parliament to his desire to bring peace and prosperity to Ireland in light of the historical Irish discontent and contemporaneous Fenian movement that was beginning to impact British public and political opinion.[6] Gladstone believed that the threat of Feniansim could be minimised by drawing a 'line between the Fenians & the people of Ireland, & to make the people of Ireland indisposed to cross it',[7] and saw the church and land bills for Ireland as possible ways to counter the growing influence of the movement. In contemplating the land tenure question in 1869, Gladstone was aided by the recent writings of political economists who were peeling away the entrenched virtues of laissez faire policies and large-scale capitalist farming by considering precedents from other parts of Europe where state intervention to create small-scale farming had been successful.[8] Furthermore, to overcome the hurdle from advocates of the sanctity of landlord property rights and of 'contract' as the basis of land tenure relationships, Gladstone relied on the Empire's experiences in India to justify the legalisation of the tenant-right in Ireland based on customary status as the guiding principle influencing the relative or shared rights of landlords and tenants. In this regard, the 'little book . . . on

the origin and practice of the Ulster tenant-right custom, see Martin W. Dowling, *Tenant Right and Agrarian Society in Ulster 1600–1870* (Dublin: Irish Academic Press, 1999).

[5] Editorial on the Passing of the Irish land bill 'The Land Bill', *The Freeman's Journal*, August 3, 1870, sec. Editorial.

[6] For example, see E. D. Steele, 'Gladstone and Ireland', *Irish Historical Studies* 17, no. 65 (1970): 58–88; Eversley, *Gladstone and Ireland*.

[7] Letter from Gladstone to General C. Grey, 28 March 1869. Add MSS 44536, f. 134. Reproduced in Matthew, *The Gladstone Diaries*, 45.

[8] R. D. Collison Black, *Economic Thought and the Irish Question 1817–1870*, Reprint edition (Cambridge, UK: Cambridge University Press, 2015); Barbara Lewis Solow, *The Land Question and the Irish Economy, 1870–1903* (Cambridge, MA: Harvard University Press, 1971); Joel M. Guttman, 'The Economics of Tenant Rights in Nineteenth Century Irish Agriculture', *Economic Inquiry; Oxford* 18, no. 3 (July 1, 1980): 408–24; Timothy W. Guinnane and Ronald I. Miller, 'The Limits to Land Reform: The Land Acts in Ireland, 1870–1909', *Economic Development and Cultural Change* 45, no. 3 (1997): 591–612.

Indian tenures as applied to Ireland' by George Campbell, a prominent civil servant in British India, played a central role in inspiring 'the thought underlying the Irish land Act of 1870'.[9]

Picking up on the influence of George Campbell's book on the Irish land question identified by his contemporaries and later historians, this chapter further probes how the Indian precedents regarding land tenure, including the ones articulated by Campbell, influenced conversations about the tenant-right issue in Ireland as well as the ultimate provisions that found their way in the final Act. My main argument is that Gladstone's involvement in the Irish land question at the beginning of August 1869 coincided with two phenomena related to land tenure in India. First, the Punjab Tenancy Act of 1868, recently passed by the Governor-General of India's Council, was making its way to the Secretary of State for India, the Duke of Argyll. Despite intense opposition from proponents of landlords' property rights in India and England, the Act institutionalised substantial tenure security for tenants. During this period, the correspondence between Gladstone and Argyll shows that the simultaneous consideration of approving the substantial rights of tenants proposed in the Punjab Act and initiating discussions regarding appropriate rights in Ireland were becoming intertwined. However, the precedent of custom-based tenure (as well as the rationale behind the efficiency of small farms based on European experience) was not considered enough of a justification for establishing rights of tenants in Ireland because of the dominant perspective in England that Irish land tenure was to be guided by English landlord–tenant relationships with their contractual elements. Ireland was perceived to be like England (or even an extension of England). Thus, Irish land tenure had to be legislated on English principles of absolute property rights, laissez faire policies, and contractual freedom within landlord–tenant relationships.

There had to be a conceptual leap from these perspectives for any headway to be made regarding the land question in Ireland. Here, the second phenomenon related to India's land tenure came into play: the circulation of Campbell's book in the middle of 1869, which caught Gladstone's attention as he began to put serious thought into solving the Irish land question. The specific recommendations Campbell propounded for Ireland were not novel per se, as similar suggestions had been made in various writings and reports in the preceding decades. The value of Campbell's book in influencing the ongoing discussions was that its reception in multiple circles and the public discussion of his ideas helped change the narrative from India being an exception to the question of customary rights of tenants

[9] This statement has been attributed to Gladstone's biographer, John Morley. Cited in S. B. Cook, *Imperial Affinities: Nineteenth Century Analogies and Exchanges Between India and Ireland* (New Delhi: Sage Publications, 1993), 56.

to England being the exception in terms of contracts as the primary mechanism guiding landlord–tenant relationships.

The acceptance or critique of Campbell's principles regarding the applicability of Indian precedents to the Irish situation solidified a theoretical shift whereby Irish land tenure issues were decoupled from historical English practices. With this shift, the political economy rationale for peasant proprietorship of smallholdings from other European countries and property rights implications of co-proprietorship from Indian examples could be used to rethink Ireland's land tenure and legislate respective rights in landlord–tenant relationships. Of course, the proximity of Ireland to England and the complex nature of Irish landlords' economic interests and political influence would affect the extent of the rights tenants could secure relative to the rights legislated in Punjab. Nonetheless, the Irish Land Act of 1870 was a significant turning point that became a springboard for subsequent legislation across the British Empire.

Figure 6.1 Gladstone Tackles the Irish Land Question in a Cartoon from the Punch, February 1870

Credit: Pictorial Press Ltd / Alamy Stock Photo.

Gladstone's Engagement with Irish Land in the Shadows of India's Land Tenure

Gladstone started giving his full attention to the Irish land question in the middle of 1869[10] after legislating the Irish Church Disestablishment Act, writing to his cabinet colleague, John Bright, that '[i]f we succeed with the Church, & fail with the land, we shall have done less than half our work'.[11] In his subsequent correspondence with various cabinet members, he acknowledged the complexity of the Irish land question, stating that the 'literature of the subject is large, larger than I can muster: but I feel the benefit of continuing reading upon it. We have before us a crisis, & a great crisis, for us all, . . . and I do not mean to fail through want of perseverance'.[12] The debates in parliament in the previous years and the new writings were coalescing towards two approaches to deal with the Irish land question. The first, related to tenant compensation for improvements as a form of security, and with antecedents in the Ulster tenant-right custom foregrounded by the Devon commission report in 1845, had gained some currency even amongst proponents of landlord rights. However, the form it would take and the administrative processes involved in implementing any legislation were still very much contested.[13] The second, which was gaining currency among Irish nationalists and was backed by writings of Mill and Cairnes, among others, wanted security for tenants through fixity of tenure and some constraints on rents. Complementing these two approaches was the idea of security through peasant proprietorship established via land purchase and distribution. However, this idea had gone somewhat out of favour, it still had its adherents, including John Bright, Secretary of the Board of Trade in the Gladstone ministry.[14] Thus, when Gladstone started educating himself on Irish land, there was a vast amount of literature (much of it 'trashy', according to his letters) that he needed to master to navigate the specific proposals

[10] My objective in the section is to probe how George Campbell's book and Indian analogies related to the Punjab Tenancy Act influenced Gladstone and his cabinet as they finalised the land bill that would be introduced in parliament. The broader literature on this is large and has been thoroughly analysed by E. D. Steele, *Irish Land and British Politics: Tenant-Right and Nationality 1865–1870* (Cambridge, England: Cambridge University Press, 1974). His book, however, does not fully explore the Indian precedents, particularly the Punjab Tenancy Act. Accordingly, my analysis builds on the work of Steele and other historians by adding another layer of thought that led to the passage of the first meaningful land act for the Irish.

[11] Gladstone letter to J. Bright, 22 May 1869, Add MS 43385, f. 30. Reproduced in Matthew, *The Gladstone Diaries*, 72–73.

[12] Letter to Duke of Argyll 29 November 1869, Add MS 44538, f. 6. Reproduced in Matthew, *The Gladstone Diaries*, 182. As pointed out by Eversley, 'the subject of Irish land tenure was new to [Gladstone]. He had never previously taken part in the debates on Irish Tenant Right Bills. It did not call into play his great genius for finance. It bristled rather with difficulties of great complexity and subtlety'. Eversley, *Gladstone and Ireland*, 41.

[13] For a broader discussion of the multiple concerns regarding compensation, especially from the perspective of landlords, see Hancock, 'Report on the Landlord and Tenant Question in Ireland, from 1860 till 1866; with an Appendix Containing A Report on the Question from 1835 till 1859'; Dufferin, *Irish Emigration and the Tenure of Land in Ireland*; James Caird, *The Irish Land Question*.

[14] Black, *Economic Thought and the Irish Question 1817–1870*.

that had garnered support within influential quarters. Two works caught his attention from the vast literature, *The Irish Land* by George Campbell and *The Land Difficulty of Ireland With an Effort to Solve It* by Gerald Fitzgibbon, both published in 1869. Gladstone recommended these books to his cabinet colleagues.[15] While he engaged with these works and the broader literature and started discussions within his cabinet about an Irish land bill in the fall of 1869, he first had to deal with another land tenure issue that came to him indirectly through the Secretary of State for India, the Duke of Argyll, and related to the Punjab Tenancy Act of 1868.

As discussed in previous chapters, the controversy around the Punjab Tenancy Act of 1868 revolved around tenants' security of tenure. Under the guiding principle of 'status', tenants were granted occupancy rights and compensation for improvements; thus, this controversy was akin to the ongoing 'fixity of tenure' and 'tenant-right' discussions in Ireland. The Act had gone further by removing landlords' ability to arbitrarily increase rent and making it possible for occupancy tenants to sub-lease and alienate the land.[16] These two provisions made the Punjab Act very similar to the 'three Fs' aspirations of the Irish. The debates about the Act in Punjab revolved around the very principles of the sanctity of property rights and the political economy that were contested in Ireland. The Act came to the Secretary of State for India, the Duke of Argyll, for final approval. After casting his tie-breaking vote in his council in favour of approving the Punjab Act, Argyll sent the complete documents, along with the decision letter he had drafted, to Gladstone for his opinion and pointed out that there were '[v]ery violent feelings for and against' the Act.[17] Gladstone supported Argyll's decision to approve the Punjab Act with all the provisions for tenants' security of tenure:

> I think your papers on the Punjaub [sic] Tenancy Act presuppose a more close knowledge of the subject than I possess. My impression would have been that the Prinsep process [denying occupancy rights to a large group of tenants] was radically questionable, unless an express title for the readjustment of all rights had been reserved: & that if this had been reserved, it must have been very rashly exercised to make it right then to go back upon it. But as far as I can judge from the papers, I should think the conclusion of your draft despatch the right one.[18]

The affirmation of the Punjab Act showed that both Gladstone and Argyll were not ideologically opposed to the principle of 'fixity of tenure' emanating from 'status'

[15] For numerous references to these pamphlets, including the days when he read them, see the letters to his colleagues and entries in his daily diaries reproduced in Matthew, *The Gladstone Diaries*.

[16] The main sections of the act are summarised in Table 3.1, Chapter 4.

[17] Letter dated August 22, 1869. Reproduced in 'Gladstone Papers Vol. XVI. Correspondence with the Duke of Argyll. 1869–1870', n.d., British Library, Additional MS. 44. IOI Add Ms 44101, F. 55, IOR, British Library. The main points of the said Despatch are summarised in Chapter 4.

[18] Letter dated August 30, 1869. Add MS 44537, f. 42. Reproduced in Matthew, *The Gladstone Diaries*, 122.

and occupancy rights that amounted to the co-proprietorship of the landlord and tenant.[19] On the contrary, both saw the Act as an appropriate way to structure land tenure relationships without concerns about its implications for the absolute rights of property. The shepherding of the Act in the Governor-General of India's Council by John Lawrence and the Secretary of State of India Council by the Duke of Argyll, despite intense opposition from the proponents of landlords' absolute property rights, also showed that active agency could swing the balance towards the rights of tenants and the associated security of tenure. The experience of the Punjab Tenancy Act, both in terms of its provisions and the process through which it was enacted, thus provided ample precedent for Gladstone in dealing with the Irish land question in 1869.[20] Whether and how he would use it would depend on his determination about the suitability of a precedent set in one of the empire's colonies for use in another. On this front, George Campbell's book played a salient role by facilitating the decoupling of the Irish land question from English principles and coupling it with those of another British colony.

The possibility of the Punjab Act serving as a precedent for the Irish land question was not confined to official discussions but was also taken up by several newspapers. For example, the *Pall Mall Gazette*, a moderately conservative newspaper, published a series of articles in August 1869 about lessons that could be learned from Indian precedents, especially from the Punjab Tenancy Act and its precursor, the Bengal Rent Act of 1859.[21] The paper suggested that Indian legislation could be used to enforce somewhat of a compromise between landlords and tenants in Ireland related to rent increases, and the customary Ulster tenant-right 'could be converted to positive law . . . by proceedings not altogether unlike those of an Indian settlement in principle'.[22]

An editorial of the more conservative newspaper, *The Times*, also discussed the potential applicability of Indian precedents to the Irish land question but wanted to ward off any possibility of customary tenures and occupancy rights in the Punjab

[19] Lord Mayo, who, as an Irish landlord and cabinet member in the conservative government, had opposed any substantive rights for the Irish tenants in 1867, was fully supportive of the Punjab Act upon taking over as the Governor General of India in 1868. Argyll, himself a Scottish landlord, wrote to Mayo on November 1, 1869: 'My opinion on the general principle of the Act is favourable, but I must direct attention to one part respecting which I entertain the gravest doubts. I refer to the power given to all occupancy tenants to sublet their holdings wither in whole or in part. I need not point out to an Irish landlord the dangers which are connected with such power', 'Letter from Argyll to Mayo, November 1, 1869', n.d., BL IOR Mss Eur Photo Eur 466, f141.

[20] Several British officials who had served in India in the 1860s also pointed to numerous similarities between India and Ireland on land tenure and wrote about the possibilities and challenges of using the Indian precedents to address the Irish land question. For example, see 'Iddesleigh Papers, Letter John Lawrence to Stafford Northcote', July 7, 1868, IOR BL Add. MSS. 50226. Northcote's comments during a session of the 1869 meeting of the Association for the Promotion of the Social Sciences. Charles Wingfield, *Observations on Land Tenures and Tenant Right in India* (London: Wm. H. Allen and Co., 1869), 3; Edwin Pears, ed., *Transactions of the National Association for the Promotion of Social Science, Bristol Meeting 1869* (London: Longmans, Green, Reader, and Dyer, 1870), 166–71.

[21] 'India and Ireland', *The Pall Mall Gazette*, August 16, 1869, sec. Editorial, 625.

[22] 'Outlines of the Irish Land Question', *The Pall Mall Gazette*, August 4, 1869, sec. Editorial, 465.

Act finding a place in the land law being discussed by the cabinet. It cautioned that the 'creation of occupancy rights in the Punjab is wholly inapplicable to Ireland now, however applicable it may have been in the days of . . . JAMES I. We are no longer dealing with people deriving their notions of land tenure from Brehon Law . . . [T]he Irish landlord is a very different being from the native landlord of the Punjab, . . . and is far more necessary part of the land system, apart from his legal or moral rights'.[23]

These examples show that substantive discussions were occurring in official and non-official circles about the possibility of seeing the Irish land question through other angles that went beyond English notions of property rights, political economy, and land tenure. However, not everyone was enthusiastic about the appropriateness of Indian precedents on Irish land relationships, and it was the circulation of George Campbell's book that influenced these sceptics. Campbell wrote his book in two parts based on the evidence he had gathered during two trips to Ireland while on furlough from the British Indian civil service in 1869. He began *The Irish Land* by professing that he had no personal connection to Ireland and that his authority arose because he had spent his life in 'intimate relations with the land in different countries, and in various stages of society'.[24]

Campbell saw the problem of any landlord–tenant relationship emanating from the fact that there were 'two claimants to the right to occupy the land', with the result that 'you cannot satisfy both: you can only compromise between them'.[25] In Ireland, this inherent adversarial relationship was compounded by the different religious affiliations of landlords and tenants and the clash of two sets of laws governing land relationships, one based on English laws and the other on the laws or customs of Ireland. The problem could be solved by finding a way in 'which the law of the land and the custom having the force of law may be brought into harmony and made to work together'.[26] In this regard, Campbell did not see any reason to disturb existing land tenure relationships in Ireland based on the English principles of 'contract', which were institutionalised by Deasy's Act of 1860. Instead, legislative efforts should focus on relationships perceived by the tenants to be

[23] 'Editorial', *The Times*, February 15, 1870, sec. Editorial.

[24] George Campbell, *The Irish Land* (London: Trubner and Co., 1869), 3–4. One must be cautious about Campbell's claim of an impartial observer. For, throughout his career as an administrator in British India, Campbell was always associated with the 'peasant proprietorship' group amongst the British Indian administrators. He was an early follower of John Lawrence's 'Punjab School' in the 1840s, being one of the officers who institutionalised occupancy rights in the North-Western Provinces and Punjab during the initial land settlements (see Chapter 3). Later, as the Commissioner of the Province of Oudh, he led the resistance against the usurpation of the tenants' rights during the post-1857 mutiny. Furthermore, during his furlough in 1868, he had considered contesting the elections to the British Parliament as a strong Radical on the Liberal Party ticket. From Campbell's political leanings in politics and persistent sympathies towards the peasants in various Indian provinces over an extended period, it was clear what direction he would lean on the Irish land question. See Sir George Campbell, *Memories of My Indian Career*, ed. Sir Charles E. Bernard, 2 vols. (London: Macmillan and Co., 1893).

[25] Campbell, *The Irish Land*, 5.

[26] Campbell, *The Irish Land*, 7.

guided by customs, and 'definite customs should be confirmed by law'.[27] Much of the book's first part was then devoted to describing the settlement of Irish land in the seventeenth century and the origin and persistence of customary tenure arrangements, with their underlying tenant-right implication.

Campbell saw parallels between the settlement of land by the British in various Indian provinces and Sir John Davies's settlement in the north of Ireland during the rule of James I at the beginning of the seventeenth century. He even suggested that if the 'names were changed in [Davies's account, it] might be taken almost word for word as the report of an administrator of an Indian province',[28] with the chiefs and tanists in Ireland being the equivalent of Indian 'Zameendars and Talookdars'. In both places, individual and absolute rights were sparse, and the relationships between landowners and cultivators were based on customary practices, which included a sense of 'co-proprietorship'. However, while the prevailing customs were recorded in India and tenants' rights 'were secured not only in theory but by [an] effective record of rights',[29] the legalisation of customs was not attempted in Ireland.[30] Even after the abolition of Brehon law and the introduction of common law, Campbell argued that customary practices continued side by side in Ireland. Like the situation in India, there was more competition for tenants than for land, and thus Anglo-Irish landlords continued to allow customary practices to retain their tenants.[31] Only when an increase in population in the eighteenth century led to a greater demand for land did the landlords gain the upper hand. With this power, the landlords increasingly evoked English common law in their land relationships with the tenants. The solution to the land question thus lay in the legalisation of customs that the Irish believed were the basis of their relationships with the landlords.

Having laid the case for the need to give legal sanctions to customs prevalent in different parts of Ireland, Campbell next approached the interconnected concepts of the tenant-right, fixity of tenure, and compensation for improvements as

[27] Black, *Economic Thought and the Irish Question 1817–1870*, 55.

[28] Campbell, *The Irish Land*, 25. Campbell also alludes to Henry Maine's ideas about the prevalence of village communities in Ireland, like those in India, where concepts of individual and absolute property rights had not yet taken hold.

[29] Campbell, *The Irish Land*, 29.

[30] Another economic historian, Fredric Seebohm, supported Campbell's argument in a series of articles published in the *Fortnightly Review* in 1869. Like Campbell, he saw no problem with the 'tenant farmers' whose relationships with landlords were guided by contracts. However, he thought that the real difficulty came for those tenants 'who are creatures of tenure, who hold their holdings to the circumstances that their ancestors . . . were found upon the land when Irish tenures were abolished, and feudal tenures substituted for them'. In essence, status tenure was recognised under the feudal system in England but not in Ireland. Seebohm, 'The Land Question: Part I. English Tenures in Ireland', 626. See the reference to Campbell's book on page 107 in F. Seebohm, 'The Land Question: Part II. Feudal Tenures in England', *Fortnightly Review*, January 1870, 89–107.

[31] 'The landlords were rather Asiatic zemeendars than English landlords, and the occupiers were not English tenants, but rather ryots holding very small tenures according to the custom, managing the land in their own way, transmitting it to their descendants under their own laws, and paying to the landlord his customary dues'. Campbell, *The Irish Land*, 37.

components of prevailing customs that must be formally institutionalised. Here, Campbell outlined practices in England and Ireland regarding the relative responsibilities of making necessary land improvements, reaffirming the Devon Commission findings in 1845 that the onus of these fell on the tenants. Tenants' investments in these improvements and the subsequent increase in the value of the land in the open market (referred to as 'goodwill') constituted the tenant-right. He argued that such a tenant-right existed in Ulster (as pointed out by the Devon Commission) and in other parts of Ireland. The real difficulties lay in determining where in Ireland such a right to compensation existed and how to determine the compensation for improvements because of the various intangibles involved, such as retrospective versus prospective compensation, the degree of approval needed from the landlord, and the valuation of goodwill. Given these difficulties, Campbell argued that 'you can never satisfy the people by any scheme of compensation for improvement except one which runs into and really becomes in practice identical with "fixity of tenure"'.[32]

Campbell devoted the final few pages of Part I of his book to outlining his plan for passing and implementing the relevant legislation. Here, he was emphatic that any bill must go much further than the previous bills introduced in parliament and critiqued many of the contemporaneous schemes in the public domain (such as those proposed by Butt, Mill, Bright, and others discussed above) for not being bold enough.[33] He then offered his plan as follows:

> Considering the question historically . . . an obvious suggestion would be to do what has been done on India and Prussia and Russia – to recognise the occupiers as in some sense co-proprietors of the soil. A law similar to Indian law might be passed, giving to the classes of tenants who may have supposed to hold rather by status than by contract . . . a definite right of occupancy – fixity of tenure in fact. Provision might be made for the right to sell, subject to reasonable veto of the landlord . . . [34] The rent would be subject to revaluation from time to time . . . It might well be said that all this would only be giving to people by law what in practice they already have.[35]

Realising the radical nature of his proposal to settle the Irish land question through fixity of tenure, Campbell wondered whether the landlords, with their considerable influence in both houses of parliament, would accede to such 'a one-sided compromise', noting that the 'plan is one which a strong and impartial foreign Power might perhaps adopt – which we might adopt if Ireland were in

[32] Campbell, *The Irish Land*, 72.
[33] Campbell, *The Irish Land*, 74–84.
[34] Campbell is probably referring to the Punjab Tenancy Act of 1868.
[35] Campbell, *The Irish Land*, 85–86.

India'.[36] However, he insisted that the legalisation of customs for the protection of tenants was critical and recommended the establishment of a commission, along with courts of conciliation and arbitration, to oversee the enactment and implementation of the law.

The analytical approach used by Campbell to build his arguments involved decoupling the land question in Ireland from the entrenched ideas prevalent in England and shifting the comparator to land tenures in India. Accordingly, throughout the first part of his book, Campbell foregrounded the similarities in the difficulties England faced in dealing with land tenure in India and Ireland and viewed the solutions to the Irish land question through the Empire's experience with land settlements in India, particularly those that had institutionalised a form of peasant proprietorship through fixity of tenure, the most recent being the Punjab Tenancy Act of 1868.

Gladstone read the first part of the book in early August 1869 and was impressed enough with Campbell's arguments to request that copies be sent to several of his cabinet colleagues.[37] It is unclear whether Gladstone read the second part of Campbell's book, completed in the latter part of October 1869, as the notes in Gladstone's diaries refer only to the first part. In any case, the second part of Campbell's book did not fundamentally alter his analysis of the situation or the thrust of his recommendations. Instead, he provided additional details and clarifications to address some of the critical feedback he had received from some readers of the first part.[38] In addition to receiving the attention of Gladstone and his cabinet colleagues, Campbell's book garnered much attention in various other quarters. Discussions around his ideas augmented the shift away from seeing the Irish land question purely through English ideas and practices[39] and towards incorporating precedents from other parts of the world, especially India.

John Stuart Mill enthusiastically endorsed Campbell's use of Indian analogies and precedents through numerous letters, which the two exchanged after Mill read the draft of the book's first part.[40] Mill thanked Campbell for sharing the draft

[36] Campbell, *The Irish Land*, 86–87.

[37] Matthew, *The Gladstone Diaries*.

[38] Some of the substantive issues discussed in Part II pertained to the mechanism through which rent would be determined, how to resolve the situations in parts of Ireland where contracts were not prevalent but there was also ambiguity surrounding the relevant customs, and how to improve the conditions of a large number of Irish who were neither landlords nor tenants but worked on the land as labourers. Since these issues are not germane to my arguments, I do not elaborate on Part II of the book.

[39] Addressing the concerns about negative spill overs on English land tenure from the institutionalisation of substantive rights for Irish tenants, Campbell emphasised in Part II of his book that 'we should put aside altogether the bugbear of the dreadful things which may happen to England if the Irish are satisfied in their own way – that the question should be considered as an Irish question, regarding only the principles of right and justice, as applicable to the state of things existing in Ireland'. Campbell, *The Irish Land*, 111.

[40] Although Mill was favourably disposed towards Campbell's idea, he did caution him about the usefulness of a commission proposed by Campbell to adjudicate some of the thornier issues because he believed that it will end up as a Landlords' Commission as '[a]ll Englishmen of the higher ranks who have not learnt better things in Ireland or India, have their prepossessions strongly on the

and agreed with the principles around which the latter had analysed the Irish land question and the details of his recommendations. Mill noted that 'Englishmen who know India are the men who can understand and interpret Ireland's social ideas and economic relations. They are not the slaves of English technicalities, and they know that the English form of property in land is neither a law of the universe nor an immutable principle of morality'.[41] After reading the second part of the book, where Campbell provided a more fine-grained explanation of his previous analysis, Mill was even more laudatory and wished the book could be put in the hands of everyone involved in the Irish land question, noting that he had not read anything 'that comes near it in fullness and clearance of knowledge it communicates of the real 'situation' in Ireland', and wondered 'how long it will take the English people to find out, that the Indian service is their best, or rather their only, good school for administrators; and to make the use they might make of that service for difficult works in other parts of the empire'.[42] J. E. Cairnes, whose ideological leanings were similar to Mill's, also praised Campbell in an article published in an influential magazine, the *Fortnightly Review*. He noted that the proposed scheme would be 'at the cost of minimum disturbance to the actual machinery of Irish society'.[43]

The ideas put forth by Campbell regarding co-proprietorship and fixity of tenure as ways to resolve the land question were enthusiastically welcomed in Ireland. *The Freeman's Journal* published the transcript of a lecture by a prominent Irish Member of Parliament at a town hall in Brighton. In this lecture, Professor Fawcett emphasised the virtue of Indian land tenure in settling the Irish land question. He noted that Campbell's work was particularly valuable because 'he looks upon the question from a different point of view than that from which English politicians look at it. In all their schemes of land settlement [in India] they recognise this fact – that the land is the joint property of the proprietor and those who cultivate it'.[44] In another editorial, the more radical Irish newspaper and mouthpiece of the Irish Tenant League, *The Nation*, commended Campbell 'for recognising the occupiers as in some sense co-proprietors of the soil and for giving tenants who have come in without special contract, and have invested their own capital in the soil, or who have paid the previous holders for the privilege of occupancy, a definite

side of landlordism'. Letter from J. S. Mill to George Campbell, dated January 4, 1870. Reproduced in John M. Robson, Michael Laine, and Marion Filipiuk, eds., *Additional Letters of John Stuart Mill* (Toronto: University of Toronto Press, 1991), 215–16.

[41] Letter from J. S. Mill to George Campbell, July 9, 1869, reproduced in Robson, Laine, and Filipiuk, 209.

[42] Letter from J. S. Mill to George Campbell, December 31, 1869, reproduced in Robson, Laine, and Filipiuk, 214–15.

[43] John Elliott Cairnes, 'Political Economy of Land (Originally Published in Fortnightly Review, January 1870)', in *Essays in Political Economy: Theoretical and Applied*, by John Elliott Cairnes (London: Macmillan and Co., 1873), 220.

[44] 'Professor Fawcett, M.P., on the Land Question', *The Freeman's Journal*, October 23, 1869, sec. Report, 4.4.

right of occupancy, fixity of tenure, in fact with due provision for sale and inheritance under fair conditions, and for periodic re-valuation'. The editorial, while not agreeing with Campbell's proposal of a commission determining who had these rights, nonetheless concluded that since 'an Imperial Indian Land Commissioner has publicly made the suggestion, ... [it] is a most encouraging sign of the times'.[45]

The Tablet, a Catholic newspaper published from London, printed a series of editorials in 1869 and 1870 regarding the Irish land question in which it critically evaluated Campbell's book and the applicability of his ideas based on the suitability of the Indian precedent for the situation in Ireland. While appreciating Campbell's 'proposition that in Ireland landlords and tenants are, in point of fact, joint proprietors of lands',[46] and calling the ideas presented in the book 'the best and most interesting attempts we have seen to elucidate the whole matter',[47] the editorials particularly emphasised the contrast made between the land situation in England and Ireland, noting that 'in England land is an appendage to the great man's State, an adjunct to the wealthy man's importance: land in Ireland is the poor man's only source of livelihood. In England, therefore, land may be let and relet in the open market to the highest bidder without more danger to the common weal than any other article of commerce'.[48]

Campbell's book also caught the attention of more mainstream newspapers in India and England. An editorial titled 'An Indian Remedy for Irish Discontent' in *Friend of India*, a pro-landlord paper published in Calcutta, espoused the belief that when Gladstone unfolded 'his plan for satisfying the landed interests of Ireland, it will be found that Mr. George Campbell's little book, *The Irish Land*, has had considerable influence on the measure ... because the suggested application of Indian precedents to Irish tenures and customs give to this work a peculiar value'.[49] The *Times of India*, published in Bombay, called Campbell's application of his experience to the case of Irish tenants 'one of the clearest and soundest of recent contributions to the literature on this question'.[50] Similarly, the editorial of the London-based *The Economist*, titled 'The Last Opinions Upon Irish Land', discussed the pros and cons of Campbell's proposals and concluded that these 'must be considered most heedfully; for of all great plans – of all plans which promise to do much – it certainly is by far the best'.[51] Even the conservative newspaper, the *Saturday Review*, in its editorial titled 'The Use and Abuse of Indian Precedents', saw possible value in Campbell's comparative framing of the Indian and Irish conditions, stating that '[i]t is not to be denied that there are some curious resemblances

[45] 'George Campbell', *Nation*, August 28, 1869, sec. Editorial, 9.
[46] 'Irish Land and Mr. George Campbell', *The Tablet*, November 27, 1869, sec. Editorial, 813.
[47] 'Mr. G. Campbell on Ireland', *The Tablet*, November 27, 1869, sec. Review, 819.
[48] 'The Irish Land Question', *The Tablet*, January 22, 1870, sec. Editorial, 99.
[49] 'An Indian Remedy for Irish Discontent', *The Friend of India*, January 13, 1870, sec. Editorial, 33.
[50] 'An Important Witness', *Times of India*, December 29, 1869, sec. Editorial, 3.
[51] 'The Last Opinions Upon Irish Land', *The Economist*, January 22, 1870, 95.

between Ireland and India . . . the fact that in both countries the people live almost exclusively on the produce of a soil barely sufficient to sustain their numbers'.[52]

The favourable reception of Campbell's recommendations and underlying rationale to resolve the Irish land question across a spectrum of prominent decision-makers and influencers in England suggests that the conditions were finally ripe to enact meaningful legislation on the Irish land question, with the potential for improving the economic conditions of a significant portion of its population dependent on agriculture. The pertinent question in the middle of 1869 thus revolved around the extent to which Gladstone was willing and able to implement the 'radical' ideas proposed by Campbell and others, the public dissemination of which had raised the expectations of the Irish.

The Irish Land Act of 1870

In gleaning through Gladstone's diaries and correspondence, it seems that his ideas about what constituted an appropriate land bill started to take shape in the middle of August 1869. By this time, he had read and internalised Campbell's ideas.[53] The other pamphlet that had caught Gladstone's attention was the one written by Fitzgibbon. Whereas Campbell developed his proposals by contrasting the history of land tenure in Ireland and England and proposing solutions to the Irish land question based on Indian precedents, Fitzgibbon based his arguments on the theoretical concepts of 'property rights' and 'improvements' as they applied to land:

> The capacity of improvement, no doubt, is an incident inherent in the land, and belongs to the owner. But this word 'BELONGS', when used in relation to land, has a meaning essentially different from its import, when applied to a chattel. . . . [W]hen a man says land belongs to him, he means nothing more than the fact, that the State, of which he is a subject, protects his exclusive possession of it. This protection imports . . . an obligation . . . to use it as the common interest of society, and of a rational owner would dictate.[54]

Fitzgibbon proposed that the tenant should have the liberty to make improvements in the land and that these improvements be protected through the grant of parliamentary leases 'of a term, on the old rent, and of duration proportional to

[52] 'The Use and Abuse of Indian Precedents', *The Saturday Review*, November 27, 1869, sec. Editorial, 692.

[53] See letters to the civil servant Trevelyan (dated August 13) reproduced on page 115, and J. Lambert (dated August 24) reproduced on page 120 of Matthew, *The Gladstone Diaries*. The tone of the letters suggest that he was favourably disposed towards the ideas and solutions proposed by Campbell, and he urged both to read and disseminate his pamphlet.

[54] Gerald Fitzgibbon, *The Land Difficulty of Ireland with an Effort to Solve It* (London: Longmans, Green, Reader, and Dyer, 1869), 40.

the magnitude of his addition to the permanent agricultural value of his farm'.[55] He further suggested that this scheme for determining the extent of improvements and the lease duration would be implemented by appointing 'impartial' public officers. Interestingly, Fitzgibbon's scheme of compulsory leases was also endorsed by George Campbell in Part II of his book. However, instead of relying on the discretion of these public officers, whom the landlords might influence, Campbell suggested that the scheme could be implemented by indenting 'on the India Office for a few good settlement officers – they are to be had in great abundance at present, and so many Indian settlements are approaching completion, – and the thing is done'.[56]

For Gladstone, these proposals were important for two reasons. First, Fitzgibbon was aiming towards some form of 'fixity' in tenure and rent, which was in line with the aspirations of the Irish. Second, and equally important, was that these ideas about the security of tenure were proposed by a conservative economist who had been a critic of Gladstone and who, as late as 1868, had 'declared . . . that there was no need for exceptional legislation on Irish land tenures'.[57] In his correspondence with a number of his cabinet colleagues, Gladstone urged them to read Fitzgibbon's pamphlet, emphasising that it was a 'very important sign of the times'.[58]

In proposing an Irish land bill, Gladstone considered the issue to be 'how far between the minimum and the maximum approach' the government should follow.[59] Given the previous reception of bills proposed in 1866 and 1867 (especially Fortescue's bill of 1866 discussed above), the minimum approach entailed some form of compensation for improvements made by a tenant. Most Members of Parliament had accepted this principle, but its implementation courted controversy. The maximum approach involved granting security to tenants through fixity of tenure, fair rents, and freedom of sale: the 'three Fs'.[60] Although in his correspondence with various people in August and September of 1869, Gladstone had emphasised that he was studying the land question with an open mind and had not committed to any specific proposal, the tone of the letters and entries in his diaries suggest that he was leaning more towards the 'maximum' approach, particularly regarding the 'fixity of tenure'.[61] This can be seen by his references to pages 68–73 of Campbell's book,[62] where the author elaborated on improvements

[55] Fitzgibbon, 41.

[56] 'Irish Land and Mr. George Campbell', 188.

[57] Black, *Economic Thought and the Irish Question 1817–1870*, 63.

[58] Gladstone Letter to Fortescue, the Irish Secretary, dated September 15, 1869. Carlingford MSS CP1/60, Reproduced in Matthew, *The Gladstone Diaries*, 129–30.

[59] Roy Jenkins, *Gladstone* (London: Macmillan, 1995), 316.

[60] Jenkins, *Gladstone*; John Morley, *The Life of William Ewart Gladstone: 1859–1880*, vol. 2, 3 vols. (Toronto: George N. Morang & Company, Limited, 1903).

[61] See Gladstone memo of December 11, 1869, in Gladstone Papers Volume DCLXXII. Additional MS. 44,7758. British Museum.

[62] See Gladstone letter to Fortescue, December 2, 1869, in which he noted that he was 'much struck with Campbell's argument pp. 68–71' Carlingford MSS CP1/72, reproduced in Matthew, *The Gladstone Diaries*, 186.

and compensation and concluded that 'fixity of tenure, compensation for improvements, . . . and [the] tenant-right . . . to sell, are all nearly one and the same thing'. Gladstone conveyed to some of his cabinet colleagues information about Fitzgibbon's proposal for granting long leases to tenants as compensation for improvements, suggesting that this was a sign of '[c]oncession from among the landlord & Conservative class'.[63] He believed that ideas coming from liberal (Cairnes, Campbell, and Mill) and conservative (Fitzgibbon) viewpoints regarding the fixity of tenure and their favourable public reception indicated by the narratives in the press suggested that the time was right to enact bold legislation that would come close to the expectations of the Irish. Convinced by the arguments of Mill and Campbell that Irish land tenure had to be re-thought in light of practices in other parts of the world, especially the experience in India, rather than those prevalent in England, Gladstone composed a comparative table highlighting the differences between England and Ireland on the historical antecedents and established practices related to land tenure (see Table 6.1). He probably expected that foregrounding these differences would help convince those in England who viewed the Irish land tenure as an extension of English principles.

Having studied the broader literature on Irish land and holding his own ideas about how to proceed, Gladstone asked the Irish Secretary, C. S. P. Fortescue, to begin drafting a land bill for the 1870 parliamentary session and start engaging the cabinet to back the proposed legislation. These discussions continued for several months, with the cabinet approving the bill to be presented to parliament on January 25, 1870. Gladstone noted in his diary that the '*great* difficulties of the [Irish Land] Bill *there* are now over – Thank God'.[64] The 'great' difficulties referred to the cabinet's complex and sustained discussions regarding the proposed bill's principles, scope, and provisions.[65] During his correspondence with cabinet members and in following members' pronouncements in their public speeches and lectures,[66] Gladstone realised that his goal of achieving legislation close to the 'maximum' option (that is, fixity of tenure) would be challenging. Moreover, there were fundamental differences even amongst cabinet members who were favourably inclined towards the aspirations of the Irish. For instance, John Bright, a proponent of peasant proprietorship, insisted on the land purchase scheme. At the same time, Fortescue believed that an elaborate compensation scheme for tenants' improvement would give the necessary security of tenure but also had 'grave misgivings about the wisdom of Gladstone's scheme to make custom the essential basis

[63] Gladstone letter to E. Cardwell, War Secretary, Dated September 21, 1869. Reproduced in Matthew, 135. Cardwell was in the pro-landlord camp within the cabinet.

[64] Matthew, *The Gladstone Diaries*, 228.

[65] Going into detail of these discussions is beyond the scope of this chapter. Steele discussed these in minute detail in his book-length study. See Steele, *Irish Land and British Politics*. Here, I provide a general description of the various camps within the cabinet and their positions.

[66] For a discussion of speeches made by three of his cabinet members in September 1869, see Steele, 127–36.

Table 6.1 Comparing Land Tenure in Ireland and England in Gladstone's Diary Entry from September 17, 1869[a]

Land Tenures in Ireland	*Land Tenures in England*
Tradition & marks of conquest, & of forfeiture still subsist	They do not subsist
Landlord does not find capital for improvement	Landlord finds capital for improvement
Landlord frequently absentee	Landlord rarely absentee
Landlords extensively object to leases	Landlord rarely objects to leases
In the parts of Ireland not under Tenant-Right, the law which gives tenants improvements to landlord is rigidly construed & applied	The law which gives the tenants improvements to landlord is mitigated, and even in some cases reversed, by local custom
Landlord commonly (in the said parts of Ireland) differs from tenant in religion and politics	Landlord commonly agrees with tenant in religion and politics
Administration of justice, & local discharge of other public duties, not extensively entrusted to landlords, & not conducive to good relations with tenants	Administration of justice & local discharge of other public duties, generally entrusted to landlords, and highly conducive to good relations with tenants
Ireland occupier (yearly) holds by custom	England. By contract

[a] From Add MS 44661, f. 50, National Archives. Reproduced in Matthew, *The Gladstone Diaries*, 130–31.

of the legislation'.[67] Gladstone also had to contend with cabinet members who were squarely on the side of the Irish landlords[68] and saw any concessions to tenants beyond some rudimentary compensation for prospective improvements as an impingement on their property rights.[69]

[67] Black, *Economic Thought and the Irish Question 1817–1870*, 67.

[68] Argyll coaxed Gladstone to somehow involve Lord Dufferin in the cabinet discussions to bolster the landlords' viewpoints within the cabinet. See Argyll Letter to Gladstone, October 13, 1869 in 'Gladstone Papers Vol. XVI. Correspondence with the Duke of Argyll. 1869–1870'. Dufferin considered himself a benevolent landlord in the north of Ireland and had written extensively on various schemes that had been proposed to solve the Irish land question. See Dufferin, *Irish Emigration and the Tenure of Land in Ireland*. Gladstone accommodated Dufferin in the cabinet discussions, and Dufferin ended up furthering Gladstone's ideas. Lord Dufferin was appointed Governor-General of Canada in 1872, where he played an important role in the land legislation of Prince Edward Island, which is discussed in Chapter 8.

[69] The cabinet ministers opposed to substantive concessions to the Irish included the Duke of Argyll (Secretary of State for India), Robert Lowe (Chancellor of the Exchequer), Earl of Clarendon (Foreign Secretary), and Edward Cardwell (Secretary for State for War). For details about their individual positions and correspondence with Gladstone regarding the Irish land bill, see Steele, *Irish Land and British Politics*, chaps. 4, 5, and 6.

Gladstone's detailed correspondence with the Duke of Argyll illustrates the former's difficulty with these cabinet members. As discussed before, Argyll, as the Secretary of State for India, approved the Punjab Tenancy Act in August 1869, which legalised the status-based occupancy rights of tenants. Furthermore, he urged Gladstone to take India as a model on how compensation for improvements was to be determined in Ireland, offering 'to have the clauses dealing with compensation in the Punjaub [sic] Act printed separately for the cabinet'.[70] However, Argyll was less willing to use the Punjab precedent to grant the Irish tenants security of tenure. He wrote to Gladstone that while he understood the theoretical justification for the security of tenure as a motivator for investments, he believed that Irish tenants who had such security might adopt 'the habit of hoarding profits, instead of reinvesting them in the land'.[71] Argyll was also sceptical about the political expediency of arguments of atonement for England's historical wrongs in Ireland:

> It is true no doubt, that Ireland formerly has been ill-used and ill-governed; and it is true also that the diseased condition of the country is due in some measure to those old sins of England. But for the last two generations at least there has been a general disposition to deal justly with Ireland, and not only a disposition, but a steady progress in legislative reform. I feel quite sure that the language of self reproach and humiliation may be easily overdone in the present State of Ireland, and this is entirely thrown away on the spirit of Fenianism, and I think it tends to make men, already excited, expect sweeping changes, corresponding in importance to the depth of the repentance we express.[72]

Opposition from some of his prominent cabinet members led Gladstone to abandon his goal of 'fixity of tenure'. He had already rejected the idea of 'fixity of rent' because he thought that the government 'could not . . . convert the landlords into [mere] stipendiaries'.[73] Gladstone understood that rejecting two essential elements related to the security of tenure expected by the Irish would not be well received by their representatives. He tried to engage with several of them,

[70] Duke of Argyll Letter to Gladstone, October 13, 1869 in 'Gladstone Papers Vol. XVI. Correspondence with the Duke of Argyll. 1869–1870'. In another letter dated December 2, he again uses the precedents of the Punjab Act regarding specific clauses to be included to address improvements: 'I send you my re-print of the Chapter in the last Punjaub Tenancy Act, which relates to tenants' improvements. The government in India being in the position practically of landowner has rights of law and usage which the government has not in Europe. Yet even there these clauses provide that improvement which are to be compensated must be of specific classes. [encloses Chapter VI of the PTA]'. Duke of Argyll Letter to Gladstone, December 2, 1869 in 'Gladstone Papers Vol. XVI. Correspondence with the Duke of Argyll. 1869–1870'.

[71] Argyll Letter to Gladstone, December 2, 1869 in 'Gladstone Papers Vol. XVI. Correspondence with the Duke of Argyll. 1869–1870'.

[72] Argyll to Gladstone, November 29, 1869, in 'Gladstone Papers Vol. XVI. Correspondence with the Duke of Argyll. 1869–1870'.

[73] Gladstone letter to John Gray, November 28, 1869. Add MS 44423, f.233, Reproduced in Matthew, *The Gladstone Diaries*, 181.

including two Irish Members of Parliament, John Gray and J. F. Maguire, and H. E. Manning, the Catholic Archbishop, by proposing alternative paths to achieve security of tenure. However, he did not receive encouraging responses from any of them.[74] Gladstone next leaned on the Irish secretary, Fortescue, and both agreed to find a solution that did not equate to the minimum of mere compensation for improvements.[75] To this end, the ideas revolved around legalising the Ulster custom (which had been promoted by George Campbell as well) for the whole of Ireland and expanding compensation in the case of a tenant's eviction from merely that for 'improvements' to also include some for 'disturbance'. Fortescue wrote in a memo to Gladstone that a bill incorporating these elements may not go 'to the extent of the popular demand in the way of fixity of tenure and rents fixed by public valuation' but could possibly 'make up in *breadth* for what it may want in *length*'.[76]

Gladstone and Fortescue obtained a majority consensus around their two pillars of 'custom' and 'disturbance',[77] which formed the basis of Bill 29 introduced in the House of Commons on February 15, 1870.[78] Section 4 of the bill addressed the 'minimum' expectations regarding compensation for improvements, which had stalled during multiple legislation attempts prior to 1870. The proposed legislation presumed that all improvements were made by tenants and granted retroactive compensation at the termination of the tenancy for past (within the last twenty years) and future improvements to any leasehold of fewer than thirty-one years.

The trickier part in moving beyond the minimum was to find ways to make it difficult and costly for a landlord to evict an existing tenant. The Devon Commission of 1845 and other writings since then had recognised the security of tenure implicit in the Ulster tenant-right, whereby the tenant not only was entitled to compensation for eviction but also for the goodwill arising from the increase in the value of land because of his or her improvements.[79] Gladstone hoped that the Ulster custom could be extended to the whole of Ireland in line with the wishes of the Irish nationalists, but fierce resistance from various segments within his cabinet

[74] See the extensive exchange of letters from September to December 1869 in Matthew, *The Gladstone Diaries*.

[75] Gladstone warned Fortescue that 'the proposition, that more than compensation to tenants for their improvements will be necessary in order to settle the Irish land laws, will be unpalatable or new, to several of these [cabinet members]'. Gladstone Letter September 27, 1869, Add. MSS 44121, British Library.

[76] Chichester Fortescue, 'Memorandum on the Irish Land Bill to Gladstone', September 13, 1869, British Library Add. MSS 44121.

[77] 'Compensation for disturbance' was highly contested by several cabinet members on the grounds that this would seriously constrain the landlords' discretion in choosing the right tenant. Lord Dufferin was a bit more sympathetic to this clause, although he preferred the term 'compensation for anticipated profits'. For details on this, see Steele, *Irish Land and British Politics*, chaps. 5 and 6.

[78] William Gladstone, Chichester Fortescue, and John Bright, 'Irish Land: A Bill to Amend the Law Relating to the Occupation and Ownership of Land in Ireland', Pub. L. No. 29 (1870).

[79] George Campbell also saw the value of this custom, arguing that 'fixity of tenure would be sufficiently secured by any rule of compensation which would make it ordinarily unprofitable to landlords to buy out tenants'. Campbell, *The Irish Land*, 73. This is one of conclusions that appealed to Gladstone.

led to a retraction of that objective. Instead, the bill divided all tenure agreements not subject to the provisions of a contract into three categories.[80] The first category (Section 1) comprised land tenure agreements in the province of Ulster, and the tenant-right custom in usage in the province was legalised.[81] In forming the second category (Section 2), the bill recognised that there might be customs in use outside Ulster that involved compensation being given to an evicted tenant. In such cases, a tenant could claim compensation for disturbance from the court, though with certain restrictions related to arrears in rent, subletting, and the length of the lease. The first two categories legalised the customary tenant-right where it could be shown to be in usage. The third category (Section 3) included all other tenants not covered by either customs or contracts. A tenant in this category, if 'disturbed in his holding by the act of the landlord', was entitled to compensation for disturbance, the amount of which would be determined by the court on a sliding scale.[82] This provision was qualified (Section 8), whereby ejectment for non-payment of rent would not be 'deemed disturbance of the tenant by act of the landlord [and thus would be ineligible for compensation], unless the Court decided [otherwise] . . . on special grounds'. The overall principle behind 'compensation for disturbance' had been vehemently opposed during the earlier cabinet meetings by those arguing for 'freedom of contract', who were particularly loath to give any compensation to tenants who were being evicted for non-payment of rent. This issue was prominent in debates about the bill in both houses of parliament, particularly in articulating the scope of the 'special grounds'. The House of Commons preferred that the charging of 'excessive rents' by the landlord be a special condition whereby the court could award compensation to an evicted tenant for non-payment of rent. At the same time, the House of Lords was inclined towards the phrase 'exorbitant rent'. The latter was eventually inserted into the final bill. In addition to these provisions regarding compensation for improvements and disturbances, which were based on the ideas of two of the bill's promoters, Gladstone and Fortescue, the bill also accommodated the wishes of the third promoter, John Bright. The bill (Part II) encouraged the voluntary sale of land to tenants by landlords, and tenants willing

[80] The proposed bill recognised the existence of 'status/custom'- and 'contract'-based land tenures in Ireland, and the provisions of the bill applied to only those tenures that were not bound by a contract (including instances where a landlord may have purchased the tenant-right from the tenant). This approach was in line with that suggested by George Campbell.

[81] Under the Ulster tenant-right custom, a tenant was entitled to make claims for improvements as well as for goodwill.

[82] Compensation was determined based on the value of holdings: Less than 10 pounds – seven years rent; between 10 and 50 pounds – five years rent; between 50 and 100 pounds – three years rent; above 100 pounds – two years rent. Like the provisions related to compensation for improvement, the tenant could not claim compensation for leases greater that thirty-one years. Instead, Section 16 provided an option for the landlord to grant a lease of at least thirty-one years in lieu of compensation. This was in line with the suggestions Fitzgibbon put forth in his book. However, this section was contested during the subsequent debates in parliament on various grounds, including the appropriate length of the lease, and the clause was eventually excluded from the final bill.

to make such purchases from amenable landlords could borrow up to two-thirds of the cost from Commissioners of Public Works with an annual interest of 5% to be paid back over thirty-five years.

The Irish Land Bill was introduced in the House of Commons on February 15, 1870. In presenting the bill, Gladstone made a long speech that alluded to the various legislative attempts since the Union in 1800 to settle the land question in Ireland and the causes of their failures. He attributed these failures to a lack of understanding of the fundamental differences between England and Ireland in the way that land tenure and landlord–tenant relationships had evolved and become institutionalised, thus necessitating 'special legislation on the subject of the occupation of land in Ireland' based on its specific needs.[83] He referred to the findings of the Devon Commission Report of 1845, which pointed out that 'insecurity of tenure is the great mischief' that had to be faced. In keeping with the consideration of the vast differences between the supporters of landlords and tenants in Ireland and England as to the remedy to this 'insecurity', Gladstone gave an elaborate justification of how these differences would be dealt with in the proposed bill:

> Sometimes we hear the remedy described by perpetuity, sometimes by fixity, sometimes by security, sometimes by certainty, and sometimes by stability of tenure. All these five words express in different forms the different shapes which it is desired the remedy should assume. As among these, I shall regard the word 'fixity' as meaning perpetuity, and I shall consider stability, certainty, and security as mutually corresponding, . . . and express the idea of a tenure which would enable a man to pursue his industry without fear of loss from any change that may happen to him on the part of the landlord; they do not express the transference to him of the essential right of property in the soil.[84]

He then reiterated that fixity or perpetuity of tenure contravened the rights of property. Thus, his government was not willing to 'entertain or propose' such options as a 'mode or form of remedy' to the Irish land question.[85] Instead, he argued that the tenant-right custom in Ulster, which the proposed bill wished to sanction by law, showed that it was 'possible to find a remedy for this deadly evil of insecurity of tenure, and yet at the same time not shake the stability of property'.[86] After explaining the overall principle of the bill around the 'security' or 'stability' of tenure, Gladstone then outlined its specific provisions.[87]

[83] 'Irish Land Bill. Hansard Third Series CXCIX' (Hansard (3rd Series), 1870), col. 340.

[84] 'Irish Land Bill. Hansard Third Series CXCIX' col. 350.

[85] 'Irish Land Bill. Hansard Third Series CXCIX', col. 354.

[86] 'Irish Land Bill. Hansard Third Series CXCIX', col. 359.

[87] Gladstone was cautiously optimistic about the reception of the Bill in the House of Commons, writing to Argyll the day after (February 16, 1870) that 'thus far the reception of it has been so favourable as almost to make me tremble. The Irish popular party are disposed (at present) to accept it: our immediate friends decidedly approve: none I believe are better pleased than the Conservatives, their

Given the overwhelming vote of approval for the bill in the House of Commons, Gladstone seemed to be on a path to pushing through the first substantive piece of legislation favourable to Irish tenants. The main resistance in the House of Commons did not come from the opposition but from some of the Liberal Members of Parliament, particularly Sir Roundel Palmer, who strongly objected to the principle of 'compensation for disturbance'.[88] George Campbell, following the House of Commons proceedings from the outside, wrote about his impressions of the proposed bill on April 20, 1870. He was pleased that Gladstone had done him 'an honour' in alluding to his book during his speech. He wrote that while he did not feel the 'most gratified by the first announcement of the Bill' because 'it was not quite in the lines' of his proposals, on reflection, he 'could not but confess that . . . the great principle of the measure . . . appeared to go much nearer to satisfying both parties'.[89]

However, the proponents of Irish tenants both within[90] and outside parliament[91] were less than enthused by the bill because it rejected fixity of tenure, despite Gladstone's explanation in a letter to Archbishop Manning that 'oftentimes the circuitous road is really the only one practicable, & is to be much preferred to scaling and descending precipices'.[92] The bill faced greater scrutiny in the House of Lords, where proponents of landlord rights were much more entrenched. However, the landlords in Gladstone's cabinet, Dufferin and Argyll, strongly defended the need to legalise tenant-right customs and provide some semblance of security of tenure for tenants. Various amendments were proposed related to adjusting the sliding scale regarding compensation for disturbance for the third category of tenants and 'special provisions' in case of evictions for non-payment of rent mentioned above. Some of these were accommodated in the revised bill; however, the government fended off any changes proposed in the House of Lords that would have radically changed the bill's essential character.[93] The Landlord and Tenant Act (Ireland)

pleasure partaking largely of the character of relief'. Gladstone Letter to Argyll, February 16, 1870, Add MS 44538, f. 76, reproduced in Matthew, *The Gladstone Diaries*, 237–38.

[88] See 'Irish Land Bill. Hansard Third Series CXCIX'; Palmer's objections are nicely summarised by Black, *Economic Thought and the Irish Question 1817–1870*, 68–69. The other objection concerned whether the claim of disturbance of the third category should expire at thirty-one or twenty-one years.

[89] George Campbell, *The Progress of The Land Bill* (London: Trubner and Co., 1870), 3.

[90] See the speeches by two Irish Members of Parliament, John Gray and J. F. Maguire (both of whom Gladstone had tried to engage during the deliberations in the cabinet before the bill was introduced) in 'Irish Land Bill. Hansard Third Series CXCIX'. While Maguire was at least appreciative of the government's initiative in bringing the bill forward, Gray continued to have misgivings about the bills' inadequacy in providing security of tenure.

[91] See the extensive correspondence between Gladstone and Archbishop Manning of the Roman Catholic Church regarding the latter's disappointment with the bill's limited attention to Irish expectations regarding the 'three Fs' in Matthew, *The Gladstone Diaries*.

[92] Private Letter from Gladstone to Manning, February 16, 1870. Add MS 44538, f. 77, reproduced in Matthew, *The Gladstone Diaries*, 238.

[93] For a more extended analysis of the specific amendments proposed in the House of Lords, see Wm. A. Dunning, 'Irish Land Legislation Since 1845. I', *Political Science Quarterly* 7, no. 1 (1892): 57–79; Steele, *Irish Land and British Politics*; Campbell, *The Progress of The Land Bill*.

1870 was passed and became law on August 1, 1870,[94] and with it, Gladstone was able to achieve two goals that he had set for himself in 1868 during his attempts to 'pacify' Ireland: church and land bills. However, he was forced to include the Coercion Bill with the Land Bill. Fenian activity in Ireland had led to pressure on the government to give special powers to courts and police through the Coercion Bill to deal with the associated increase in crime in Ireland.[95]

******

> [The main purpose of the Irish Land Bill] was to endeavour to establish harmony between Great Britain and the sister island that had not been effectually attained. By the aid of the … Parliament we have been … enabled … to lay the foundation … of relations between the principal classes of the community in an agricultural country … which will give promise of greater contentment, greater wealth, … and above all a nearer approach to that union of heart and sentiment.
>
> —Speech by William Gladstone, August 1, 1870[96]

> We are now done with the 'Irish Land Bill' but assuredly not with the Irish Land Question.
>
> —Editorial, *Nation*, August 6, 1870[97]

These two responses to the Irish Land Act of 1870, after it received royal assent and became law, capture the distinct perceptions of its value in easing the volatile political situation and fulfilling the aspirations of the Irish peasantry. Critics saw it as a sincere but weak attempt by the government to address the land question—one that did not go far enough to provide the necessary security of tenure.[98] An observation neatly captures this view that through this Act, the 'government had reached the point where the Irish agitation had been eighteen years before … British concession had got as far as the Ulster tenant-right; Irish demand was far away at "the three Fs"'.[99] It would take another eleven years and a second Gladstone ministry for the Irish to achieve their objective of the 'three Fs' through the Irish Land Act of 1881.[100]

94 Landlord and Tenant Act (Ireland) 1870.

95 See Jenkins, *Gladstone*.

96 From Gladstone's speech at a banquet after the Irish Land Act had received royal assent. Reproduced in 'Irish Land Bill', *The Cork Examiner*, August 3, 1870, sec. Editorial.

97 'Irish Land Bill', *Nation*, August 6, 1870, sec. Editorial.

98 Some historians also see the 1870 Act as having gone too far. For example, at the end of his exhaustive study, Steele concludes that '[i]n the Land Act of 1870 Parliament sacrificed on the altar of Anglo-Irish union the notion that the individual's rights of property were indefeasible, and with that cherished notion the concomitant freedom of contract'. Steele, *Irish Land and British Politics*, 315.

99 Dunning, 'Irish Land Legislation Since 1845. I', 72.

100 Chapter 9 discusses the aftermath of the 1870 Act and its implications for the 1881 Act in more detail.

However, despite its inability to fully resolve the land question in Ireland, the Act of 1870 was a critical milestone in the British Empire's attempts to establish equitable land tenure relationships in Ireland and its other colonies. For Ireland, the Act was beneficial because it 'was the first measure placed on the Statute Book to recognise that the occupier, as well as the owner, had a right in the land; the first measure, in other words, which reversed the trend towards an insistence on "free contract" as the basis of landlord–tenant relations, and was based, partially at least, on the concepts of status and custom'.[101] No doubt, legalising the tenant right through this Act, even if only partially satisfactory to the Irish at the time, encouraged Irish nationalists to push for their demands and the British government to consent to these efforts in future legislation.

The legislative efforts regarding Irish land resulting from Gladstone's active involvement and agency were facilitated by disseminating new ideas in the 1860s from various sources that attributed the success of small farms in other parts of Europe to the security of tenure granted to cultivators. These sources countered the entrenched political economy arguments of the capitalist farming system operating within a laissez faire policy framework because Irish land tenure agreements and their underlying characteristics were more akin to those of other countries than to English practices. The economic betterment of Irish agriculture as a whole and that of the large population of peasant cultivators could thus be accomplished within the existing structure of small-scale farming if proper incentives could be provided through legislation that granted security of tenure.

There was still the hurdle of countering the view of absolute ownership of property rights, which had been effectively used to thwart any institutionalisation of security of tenure for Irish tenants. Here, the Indian precedents from the recently approved Punjab Tenancy Act and the public dissemination of the writings of George Campbell, an administrator with long experience in land settlements across various provinces of India, allowed the concept of co-proprietorship in custom or status-based tenurial relationships to become an effective counter to the absolute rights of landlords in contract-based relationships. Thus, the combined effect of active agency and the use of isomorphic precedents from Europe and India allowed a way forward, overcoming the entrenched logics that had opposed the legalisation of the rights of tenants in Ireland for such a long time.

One final note on the influence of Campbell's book on the Irish Land Act of 1870 and beyond is warranted. While his work has been credited for influencing Gladstone by bringing to attention the historical similarities between custom-based land tenure in India and that in Ireland and thus the appropriateness of legalising such tenure in the proposed bill for Ireland, there is some debate amongst

[101] Black, *Economic Thought and the Irish Question 1817–1870*, 69; Also see William Ernest Montgomery, *The History of Land Tenure in Ireland* (Cambridge, UK: At The University Press, 1889); Jenkins, *Gladstone*; Campbell, *Memories of My Indian Career.*

historians about the enduring contributions of Campbell's ideas. At one end is the observation by Eric Stokes in his influential book *English Utilitarians and India* that in dealing with the Irish agrarian problem, 'it was Liberals with Indian experience, like . . . Sir George Campbell, who first taught their party that the State might justly lay hands on the sacred institution of private landed property'.[102] On the other hand, E. D. Steele, who has probably written the most on the Irish Land Act of 1870, concludes that Campbell's influence was, in the end, insignificant because his book did not 'point to a single course of action by the state on the Irish problem',[103] and none of his specific recommendations made it into the act that was eventually passed. This chapter shows that Campbell's influence was neither radical nor insignificant, as argued by these historians; instead, Campbell's work was more influential in showing an alternative way to view colonial land tenure. His ideas facilitated a fundamental shift whereby the land question would, from then onwards, no longer be solely tied to the property rights and political economy principles prevalent in England. Instead, the Empire could use analogies and precedents from across its various colonies rather than being constrained by English principles.

The usefulness of this approach of inter-colony analogies to the Empire would be tested soon after the passage of the Irish Act in 1870 in dealing with landlord–tenant relationships in another part of the British empire. Like Ireland, Prince Edward Island had a longstanding unresolved land question.

[102] Eric Stokes, *The English Utilitarians and India* (Oxford: Oxford University Press, 1989), 122.
[103] E. D. Steele, 'Ireland and the Empire in the 1860s. Imperial Precedents for Gladstone's First Irish Land Act, *The Historical Journal* 11, no. 1 (March 1968): 64.

PART IV

PRINCE EDWARD ISLAND

7

Prince Edward Island's Land Question

France ceded Prince Edward Island (PEI) to England in 1763. On taking possession, the first order of business for the new colonial ruler was to set up a process of settling the land and establishing an appropriate government to run its affairs. The Imperial Government considered several proposals[1] as to how and to whom it would allocate the land, and after surveying the island, decided to grant the sixty-six lots in 1767 'directly and separately to persons deserving the patronage of the Crown'.[2] It reserved two lots for a group of petitioners who had already established trading and fishing enterprises on the Island since 1764 and allotted the remaining sixty-four lots (each of about 20,000 acres) based on a lottery to people selected from a list of 166 petitioners who had applied for the land grants (See Figure 7.1).[3] The land grants were made on the conditions that each was to be settled within ten years with one Protestant settler per hundred acres, and the landholder pay an annual quit rent[4] (calculated based on the surveyors' assessment of the value of the land) directly to the Colonial Office in London.[5]

Initially intended to be a part of Nova Scotia, a separate colony was established in 1769 following the petitions from its newly minted proprietors.[6] Walter Patterson, who, along with his brother, received a lot in the initial lottery, was appointed Prince Edward Island's first Governor, a post he held until 1786.[7] In the directions provided to him by the Privy Council in London, the Governor would

[1] For more details on the process leading to the initial distribution of the land in Prince Edward Island (PEI), see Bumsted, *Land, Settlement, and Politics on Eighteenth-Century Prince Edward Island* (Montreal: McGill-Queen's University Press, 1987); Errol Sharpe, *A People's History of Prince Edward Island* (Toronto: Rail Publishing, 1976); Francis W. P. Bolger, 'The Beginnings of Independence, 1767–1787', in *Canada's Smallest Province: A History of P.E.I.*, ed. Francis W. P. Bolger (Charlottetown, P.E.I.: Prince Edward Island 1973 Centennial Commission, 1973), 37–65; Andrew Hill Clark, *Three Centuries and the Island: A Historical Geography of Settlement and Agriculture in Prince Edward Island, Canada* (Toronto: University of Toronto Press, 1959).

[2] Bolger, 'The Beginnings of Independence', 37. This land allocation approach was like other settlements in North America and especially the one used in Nova Scotia, to which PEI was attached in the early years of British rule. Bumsted, *Land, Settlement, and Politics on Eighteenth-Century Prince Edward Island.*

[3] See Footnote 2 in Bolger, 'The Beginnings of Independence, 1767–1787', 356.

[4] Quit rent was a nominal rent payable by the land grantee to the state in lieu of performing any service for the latter.

[5] Sharpe, *A People's History of Prince Edward Island.*

[6] For details of the process of establishing the first government, and its subsequent evolution, see Frank MacKinnon, *The Government of Prince Edward Island* (Toronto: University of Toronto Press, 1951). The head of the government was changed from Governor to Lieutenant-Governor in 1784.

[7] Harry Baglole, 'Patterson, Walter'. *Dictionary of Canadian Biography*, Volume IV (1771–1800) (University of Toronto/Université Laval, 2003).

Empire and the Peasant Proprietor. Preet S. Aulakh, Oxford University Press. © Preet S. Aulakh 2025.
DOI: 10.1093/9780198928270.003.0007

head the government, assisted by a Council of twelve members consisting of a resident Lieutenant-Governor, Chief Justice and 'of such . . . persons, chosen by you from amongst the principal inhabitants and proprietors of land in our said Island'.[8] The instructions further required forming a House of Assembly or House of Representatives, whose scope should be carefully considered so that 'no colour or pretence is given for the assumptions or privileges . . . which have not been allowed to Assemblies in our other colonies'.[9] Besides the structure of the government, the instructions to the first Governor made it clear that 'no law or ordinance respecting private property be passed without a clause suspending its execution until our royal will and pleasure is known'.[10] The first Assembly in Prince Edward Island was constituted in 1773.

The Imperial Government expected that the functioning of the colony's government would not impose any financial burden on it as the quit rents collected from the grantees would pay for the local expenses. A few aspects of these land allocation and governance arrangements are noteworthy, as these undermined some of the assumptions made regarding the colony's political and economic viability. First, the Imperial Government allocated property rights to landlords based on their social rank, determined by their past services and expectations of future services to the Empire. Given the landholders' influence in military and civil matters across the various colonies, it would have been challenging to hold them strictly to the initial conditions of their grants.[11] Second, the structure of the government, and the discretion of the Governor (and later the Lieutenant-Governor) to appoint members of the advisory council, had the potential to create a governing body of friends and family who could collude to further their objectives but which might not be in the best interests of the colony as a whole. Third, the incorporation of a suspending clause regarding all legislation related to private property meant that the 'opportunities for Island-made solutions to the land question . . . were circumscribed by the colonial situation . . . Legislative initiatives to limit the power of landlords . . . ultimately, before they became law, had to pass the scrutiny of officials in the Colonial Office in London'.[12]

These initial arrangements in the governance of Prince Edward Island combined to create intractable conditions for dealing with land tenures over the next century. In the years following the formation of a government, landlords had not fulfilled the conditions of their land grants. For example, by 1779, most proprietors had not paid any quit rents, and forty-nine of the lots did not have a single

[8] Reproduced in Appendix B of MacKinnon, *The Government of Prince Edward Island*, 347–43.

[9] Reproduced in MacKinnon, 332–33.

[10] Reproduced in MacKinnon, 333.

[11] Bumsted, 'The Land Question on Prince Edward Island and the Quitrent Controversy of 1802–1806', *Acadiensis* 29, no. 2 (2000): 3–26.

[12] Rusty Bittermann and Margaret McCallum, 'Upholding the Land Legislation of a 'Communistic and Socialist Assembly: The Benefits of Confederation for Prince Edward Island', *The Canadian Historical Review* 81, no. 1–15 (2006): 31–56.

settler. This trend continued as twenty-three lots remained uninhabited in 1793.[13] By 1802, proprietors were in arrears of quit rents to the Imperial Government to the tune of 60,000 pounds sterling.[14] While failing to fulfil the conditions of their grants, many of the landlords had commoditised their holdings by selling to other landlords or land speculators from across the British Empire.[15] In 1817, only seven of the sixty-seven lots were owned by original grantees or their heirs, which decreased to 2.5 in 1823. The ownership became very concentrated, with forty-six lots owned by eleven landlords in 1823.[16]

The Escheat Movement

Soon after the colony's formation, it was clear that the land grantees had not fulfilled the conditions of their grants, both in terms of quit rents and settlements. This posed revenue problems for the local government, and it started a quest to rectify the situation by either forcing the landlords to fulfil the conditions of their grants or forfeiting their land, which could then be reallocated, including through the conversion of leaseholds to freeholds for the cultivators/settlers.[17] Thus, the idea of escheat took shape in the colony's early years and evolved into various forms until the 1840s.[18] While the Imperial Government was aware of the nonfulfilment of the conditions of the grants and the impact of this on the revenues for the colony, its development, and broader socio-political implications, it did not approve any of the numerous acts passed by the local legislature up until the middle of the nineteenth century that would adversely impact the rights of the proprietors.[19]

13 Clark, *Three Centuries and the Island*, 50.

14 Clark, *Three Centuries and the Island*, 81.

15 For a full list of original grantees of the lots, and their subsequent year of sale and new owners, see Appendix B in Clark, *Three Centuries and the Island*, 263–69. Also see Bolger, 'The Beginnings of Independence, 1767–1787', 31–42.

16 Sharpe, *A People's History of Prince Edward Island*, 63.

17 An Ordinance was passed in 1771 under which the local government could use a judicial procedure to distraint land with quit rent arrears and sell it off. This process was different from escheat, where the land went back to the Crown for these arrears. The Imperial Government did not recognise this particular Ordinance. See Bumsted, 'The Origins of the Land Question on Prince Edward Island, 1767–1805'. *Acadiensis* 11, no. 1 (1981): 43–56.

18 Rusty Bittermann, *Rural Protest on Prince Edward Island: From British Colonization to the Escheat Movement* (Toronto: University of Toronto Press, 2006). Escheat involved the revoking of proprietorial land grants because of non-fulfilment of their conditions, and subsequently redistributing the land to other settlers.

19 For details of the various legislative acts passed regarding the land question, see Bolger, 'The Beginnings of Independence, 1767–1787'; Francis W. P. Bolger, 'The Demise of Quit Rents and Escheat, 1824–1842', in *Canada's Smallest Province*, 95–114; Bittermann, *Rural Protest on Prince Edward Island*; Rusty Bittermann and Margaret McCallum, 'When Private Rights Become Public Wrongs: Property and the State in Prince Edward Island in the 1830s', in *Despotic Dominion: Property Rights in British Settler Colonies*, ed. John McLaren, A. R. Buck, and Nancy E. Wright (Vancouver, B.C.: University of British Columbia Press, 2005); Matthew George Hatvany, 'Tenant, Landlord, and the New Middle Class: Settlement, Society, and Economy in Early Prince Edward Island, 1798–1848' (ProQuest Dissertations Publishing, 1996).

Figure 7.1 Map of Prince Edward Island (with townships/lots) 1775

Source: Holland, Samuel, and Andrew Dury. A plan of the island of St. John with the divisions of the counties, parishes, & the lots as granted by government, likewise the soundings round the coast and harbours. [London: Printed & sold by A. Dury, 1775] Map. <https://www.loc.gov/item/74694755/>.

An examination of the reasons for the persistence of the land question during the 1764–1851 period and the Colonial and Imperial Governments' unwillingness and/or inability to resolve the land question emanating from the non-fulfilment of the land grant conditions reveal some broad themes. An important factor influencing the Imperial Government's affinity towards the landlords across the Empire was the aristocratic tradition in England, which manifested itself in land allocation in its newer colonies to 'well-connected individuals who had performed special service'.[20] Thus, retracting these grants for not fulfilling the conditions was politically inexpedient. Furthermore, many Prince Edward Island proprietors resided in London and continued to exert influence in the imperial political circles to protect their property rights. In addition, during the period under discussion, Britain was involved in two wars (against America and France). The arrears in landlords' quit rents were excused because of their 'great sacrifices' in the Empire's war efforts. Consequently, the Imperial Government reduced those arrears from approximately 60,000 to less than 19,000 pounds sterling in 1802.[21] The grantees' inability to fulfil the condition of settling a certain number of cultivators was attributed to the onerous requirement that settlers be Protestants and the unavailability of enough of them willing to move to the geographically hostile terrain of PEI.[22]

The propensity of different Imperial Governments in the eighteenth and early nineteenth centuries to protect landed interests was facilitated in the case of Prince Edward Island by the emerging political factions and their activities within the colony. The 'documentable rapacity of the Island's officials vis-à-vis the proprietors', which included illegal land grabs of absentee proprietors by members of the Executive Council and its allocation to friends and family, was a vital factor behind the unwillingness of the Empire to penalise the proprietors.[23] The roots of the initial political conflict in the colony were the various attempts by resident proprietors, which included the first Governor Patterson and his appointees on the Legislative Council, to distrain the land of the absentee landlords. As a result, Patterson increased his landholdings from the initial allocation of one lot to three (consisting of 60,000 acres) by the end of his term.[24] However, differences amongst the colony's elite led to two factions, with one insisting on holding the absentee landlords to the original conditions. The other, referred to as the 'cabal' or 'Family Compact', wanted to challenge the resident landlords and thus aligned itself with

[20] John C. Weaver, *The Great Land Rush and the Making of the Modern World, 1650–1900* (Montreal & Kingston: McGill-Queen's University Press, 2003), 202.

[21] Bumsted, 'The Land Question on Prince Edward Island and the Quitrent Controversy of 1802–1806'.

[22] The population of the Island grew from approximately 7000 in 1805 to 23,000 in 1827, and further to 47,000. See Clark, *Three Centuries and the Island*, 66. Many settlers came from Scotland and Ireland and tended to be Catholics. See Bumsted, *Land, Settlement, and Politics on Eighteenth-Century Prince Edward Island.*

[23] Bumsted, 'The Origins of the Land Question on Prince Edward Island, 1767–1805', 47.

[24] Sharpe, *A People's History of Prince Edward Island.*

the absentee or non-resident landlords.[25] The intra-colony feud between the elites (consisting of resident landlords, Lieutenant-Governors, cronies, government officials, and land agents) continued into the nineteenth century. The Imperial Governments recalled the first three Lieutenant-Governors, and they had to make embarrassing exits from their positions because of accusations of corruption and mismanagement.[26] In the first few decades after 1767, 'the land question was not really a popular issue at all, but one created by contending factions of elites . . . for their own political, economic, and social advantage'. Since there were 'more place seekers than places . . . political conflict and factionalisation [were] bound to be not only inevitable but fierce'.[27]

The voice of the tenants on the Prince Edward Island land question began to take shape at the beginning of the nineteenth century when the goal of the agitation for non-fulfilment of original conditions became the redistribution of the escheated land to the tenant cultivators rather than the aggrandisement of the colony's elite of the earlier years. This shift occurred because of the dissemination of fresh ideas on land tenure introduced by newcomers to the colony and their immersion in local politics. Some prominent people included Joseph Robinson, William Cooper, and George Dalrymple. Robinson, a Loyalist who had settled in the Colony after the American Revolutionary War by leasing land from an absentee landlord, wrote a short manifesto titled 'To the Farmers in the Island of St. John, in the Gulf of St. Lawrence', that was widely circulated. It highlighted the difficulties of the tenant cultivators and recommended a court of escheat that would direct the land to small cultivators 'in direct proportion to the strength and number of their families', and these cultivators would pay quit rents directly to the Crown.[28] Cooper settled in Prince Edward Island from England in 1818 as a resident farmer and, for a few years, acted as a land agent to an absentee landlord. After being fired as the land agent, he took the tenants' cause, got elected to the Assembly in 1831, and led the escheat movement until the 1840s. Anchoring his ideas on the labour theory of value, he justified the expropriation of land from the landlords through escheat as a form of just allocation of property rights to those who add value.[29] Dalrymple came to Prince Edward Island in the early 1820s and became a businessman. He was a 'strong proponent of the use of state resources to facilitate economic development' and saw the dismantling of the hold of the landlords and having broader land ownership as key to the colony's development.[30]

[25] For details of the extended influence of the Family Compact, see Francis W. P. Bolger, 'Prince Edward Island Rejects Confederation, 1864–1867', in *Canada's Smallest Province*, 156–84; Bolger, 'The Beginnings of Independence, 1767–1787'; Bumsted, *Land, Settlement, and Politics on Eighteenth-Century Prince Edward Island*; Sharpe, *A People's History of Prince Edward Island*.

[26] Bolger, 'Prince Edward Island Rejects Confederation, 1864–1867'; Bumsted, *Land, Settlement, and Politics on Eighteenth-Century Prince Edward Island*.

[27] Bumsted, 'The Origins of the Land Question on Prince Edward Island, 1767–1805', 45–46.

[28] Cited in Francis W. P. Bolger, 'Land and Politics, 1787–1824', in *Canada's Smallest Province*, 69.

[29] Bittermann and McCallum, 'When Private Rights Become Public Wrongs', 144–68.

[30] Bittermann and McCallum, 'When Private Rights Become Public Wrongs', 149.

The enfranchisement of Catholics (who constituted about a third of the population and a large part of the tenantry)[31] in Prince Edward Island in 1830 'induced a greater democratisation of colonial politics', which provided weight behind reforming the land tenure system through legislation proposed by the elected Assembly.[32] Proponents of land reform in Prince Edward Island won sizeable majorities in the legislature in the 1830s and passed several acts prescribing escheat and increasing local revenues through a land tax.[33] Most of these initiatives were disallowed by the Imperial governments, including the one through a personal visit by an elected member of Prince Edward Island's assembly to England in 1839 to make the case for a Court of Escheat directly with the Secretary of the State for the Colonies.[34] As pointed out by Clark, '[n]early every year of the [eighteen] twenties and thirties brought some action by the current Governor or the Assembly; the ingenuity of various devices proposed was only matched by the unbroken record of failure to move either the proprietors or the home government'.[35]

While land reform through escheat did not make any headway, and the associated movement fizzled out by the early 1840s, its proponents got some support from unexpected quarters. The new Lieutenant-Governor in 1837, Charles A. FitzRoy, initially seemed more sympathetic to the cultivators and wanted the proprietors to grant concessions to the tenants to wean them away from demands of escheat. In a letter to the Secretary of State for the Colonies, he pointed out that a tenant would be willing to pay a fair rent for occupied land if he can get a 'tenure of sufficient endurance to ensure to his family the profits of his industry'. To improve the conditions of the tenants, he recommended long leases at fair rents, pathways for tenants to purchase the property, and compensation for their improvements at the end of their leases.[36] Furthermore, in his report of 1839 on Britain's North American colonies, Lord Durham, entrusted by the Imperial Government to probe the sources of political unrest in North America,[37] was also critical of the way the land was allocated in Prince Edward Island in the first place, as well as the inability of the Imperial Government to enforce the conditions of the grants. He noted that the 'political history of Prince Edward's Island is contained in the system

[31] This followed Catholic emancipation in England in 1829.

[32] Bittermann, *Rural Protest on Prince Edward Island*, 58.

[33] Bittermann, *Rural Protest on Prince Edward Island*; Bittermann and McCallum, 'When Private Rights Become Public Wrongs'; Bolger, 'The Demise of Quit Rents and Escheat, 1824–1842'; Hatvany, 'Tenant, Landlord, and the New Middle Class'.

[34] The Secretary of the State for the Colonies refused to meet Cooper, and instead wrote directly to the then Lieutenant-Governor of PEI categorically rejecting the Court of Escheat. See Bolger, 'The Demise of Quit Rents and Escheat, 1824–1842', 110–12.

[35] Clark, *Three Centuries and the Island*, 81.

[36] Quoted and summarized in Bolger, 'The Demise of Quit Rents and Escheat, 1824–1842', 108–9.

[37] For details, see Sir Charles Lucas, ed., *Report on the Affairs of British North America from the Earl of Durham, February 11, 1839*, 3 vols. (New York: August M. Kelley, 1912); Ged Martin, 'Lambton, John George [Nicknamed Radical Jack], First Earl of Durham (1792–1840), Politician', *Oxford Dictionary of National Biography*.

pursued with regard to its settlement, and the appropriation of its lands . . . and its past and present disorders are but the sad result of that fatal error which stifled its prosperity in the very cradle of its existence, by giving up the whole Island to a handful of distant proprietors'.[38] He further opined that the distant proprietors did not contribute to improving the land, and held the land 'as sort of a reversionary interest, which requires no present attention, but may become valuable some day or other through the wants of the inhabitants'.[39] As an immediate remedy, Durham recommended approval of the Land Assessment Act that the Prince Edward Island Assembly had passed. This act proposed a tax on the colony's land, which would be used to develop it and make it financially self-sufficient. The Imperial Government accepted these recommendations. The Act abolished the quit rents related to the initial land grant conditions and payable to the Crown and instead instituted a local tax that the local legislature would control.[40]

Much of the struggle on the land question until the 1840s revolved around quit rents and settlement conditions of the original grants, with escheat as the primary remedy. The disallowance of escheat by the Imperial Government as a solution to the land question required a search for alternative pathways. By the 1850s, there were beginnings amongst the various constituents of the colony to see the land question through more nuanced arguments around property rights and political economy,[41] with some of these ideas originating from similar debates about land tenure in other British colonies, including Ireland. These new ideas and the possibility of achieving responsible government were the altered conditions under which the next phase of Prince Edward Island's land question was contested after 1851. Before analysing the new contestations on the land question during the 1850s and 1860s, it is instructive to point out some essential facts. First, as shown in Figures 7.2 and 7.3, there was a consistent increase in freehold tenure (both in terms of the number of people holding freehold tenure and the area of land covered by such tenure) from the period after 1840, despite the lack of any legislation facilitating the land market. Second, the PEI legislature's efforts after 1851 did not have escheat as the primary objective (see Table 7.1). Instead, there were parallel efforts 'to soften the workings of the leasehold systems' by establishing some proprietary rights for the tenants and attempting to abolish leasehold tenures through

[38] Lucas, vol. 2, 198.

[39] Lucas, vol.2, 242.

[40] Bolger, 'The Demise of Quit Rents and Escheat, 1824–1842'.

[41] In particular, the two groups amongst the reformers of the 1830s and 1840s (that is, the pro-development one led by Dalrymple, and the other led by Cooper promoting justice) evoked the ideas of laissez faire, distributive justice, and improvement in their discussions about land tenure, which were quite like the ones shaping the debate in Europe. For details, see Bittermann and McCallum, 'When Private Rights Become Public Wrongs'.

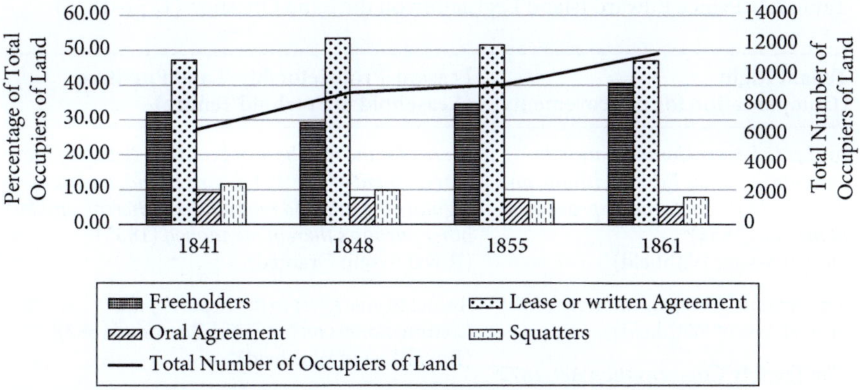

Figure 7.2 Land Tenure in Prince Edward Island: Number of Occupiers

Sources: Drawn by the author from data of Clarke, 1859 (Table III, page 95). In addition, freeholders in 1841 were 32% of the total holders of the land but held 41% of the total land. In 1861, they were 40% and held 50% of the land.

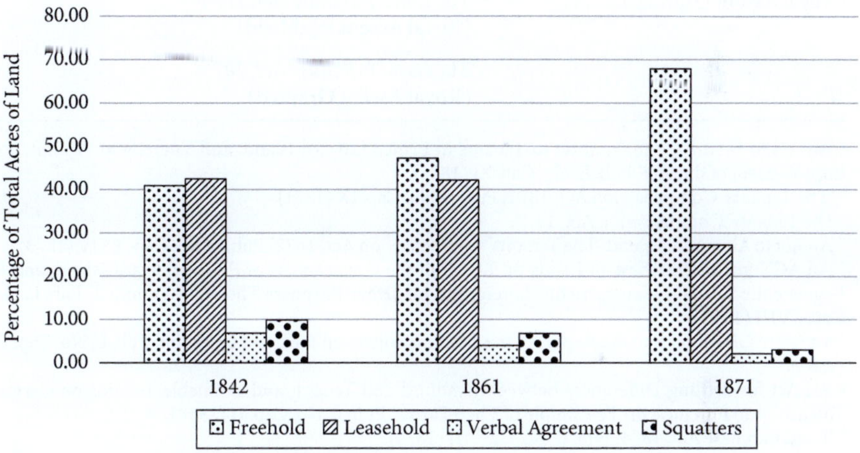

Figure 7.3 Land Tenure in Prince Edward Island: Acres of Land

Sources: Computed by the author from Abstracts of the Census of the Population and other Statistical Returns of Prince Edward Island (1842, 1861, 1871).

purchasing and redistributing proprietary estates.[42] Much of the literature has focused on the abolition of freehold tenure rather than the other objective of expanding tenants' rights.[43] The following section evaluates the debates around both these objectives.

[42] Robertson, Ian Ross. 'Introduction', in *The Prince Edward Land Commission of 1860*, ed. Ian Ross Robertson (Fredericton, NB: Acadiensis Press, 1988), ix–xxx.

[43] For a review of the literature, see Matthew G. Hatvany, 'Tenant, Landlord and Historian: A Thematic Review of the "Polarization" Process in the Writing of 19th-Century Prince Edward Island History', *Acadiensis* 27, no. 1 (1997): 109–32.

Table 7.1 Prince Edward Island Legislation on the Land Question (1851–1875)

Tenant Right (Compensation for Improvements)	**Peasant-Proprietorship/Land Purchase (Leasehold to Freehold Tenure)**
An Act to Secure Compensation to Tenants in Prince Edward Island, and Thereby to Promote the Improvement of the Soil (1855)[a] (Royal Assent Withheld)	*An Act for the Purchase of Lands on Behalf of the Government of Prince Edward Island, and to regulate the sale and management thereof, and for other purposes therein mentioned* (1853)[e] (Royal Assent Granted)
The Tenants' Compensation Act, 1871[b] (Royal Assent Withheld)	*An Act to give effect to the Report of the Commissioners on the Land Question* (1862)[f] (Royal Assent Withheld)
The Tenants' Compensation Act, 1872[c] (Royal Assent Withheld subject to an Amending Act)	*An Act for settling differences between Landlord and Tenant, and to enable Tenants on certain Townships to purchase fee simple of their Farms* (1864)[g] (Royal Assent Granted)
An Act to Alter and Amend 'The Tenants' Compensation Act, 1872' (1873)[d] (Royal Assent Granted)	*The Land Purchase Act, 1874*[h] (Royal Assent Withheld)
	The Land Purchase Act, 1875[i] (Royal Assent Granted)

[a] 'An Act to Secure Compensation to Tenants in Prince Edward Island, and Thereby to Promote the Improvement of the Soil', Pub. L. No. Cap. XI (1855).
[b] 'The Tenants' Compensation Act, 1871', Pub. L. No. Cap. IX (1871).
[c] The Tenants' Compensation Act, 1872.
[d] 'An Act to Alter and Amend 'The Tenants' Compensation Act, 1872', Pub. L. No. Cap. XXIV (1873).
[e] 'An ACT for the Purchase of Lands on Behalf of the Government of Prince Edward Island, and to Regulate the Sale and Management Thereof, and for Other Purposes Therein Mentioned', Pub. L. No. Cap. XVIII (1853).
[f] 'An Act to Give Effects to the Report of the Commissioners on the Land Question', Pub. L. No. Cap. IV (1862).
[g] 'An Act for Settling Differences between Landlord and Tenant, and to Enable Tenants on Certain Townships to Purchase the Fee Simple of Their Farms', Pub. L. No. Cap. II (1864).
[h] 'Land Purchase Act, 1874', Pub. L. No. Cap. III (1874).
[i] Land Purchase Act, 1875.

Land Reforms Under Responsible Government, 1851–1867

One of the Durham Report recommendations of 1839 was to consider responsible government in British North America,[44] which was actualised in the following years, with Nova Scotia getting it in 1848, New Brunswick and Upper and Lower

[44] Lucas, *Report on the Affairs of British North America from the Earl of Durham, February 11, 1839*, Volume 1, 137–152.

Canada in 1849, and Prince Edward Island in 1851.[45] The new political arrangement meant that the head of the government would be the locally elected leader, the Premier, of the majority party.[46] The two main limitations of Imperial authorities were that 'responsible government did not extend to political relations with foreign countries or to attempted settlement of the land question through infringing on property rights'.[47] The latter constraint meant that the ultimate authority to approve any legislation on the land question remained with the Imperial Government in London through the Colonial Office. Soon after, the elections led to the formation of the government of George Coles, head of the Liberal Party that had been a significant supporter of the escheat movement.[48] In the following years, this party alternated in forming governments with the Conservative Party that grew out of the Family Compact and was more sympathetic to the landlords. Over time, the two parties also took a sectarian character, with the Liberal Party supported by Catholic residents of Prince Edward Island and the Conservative Party by Protestants.[49]

Anticipating the re-emergence of the land question after attaining responsible Government in Prince Edward Island, the Imperial Government made its position clear on the property rights of landowners in the colony. In a strongly worded letter to Prince Edward Island's new Lieutenant-Governor, the Secretary of State for the Colonies wrote:

> On your proceeding to assume the Government of Prince Edward Island, I am particularly anxious to direct your attention to a question . . . of the Landed Tenures . . . [R]epeated applications have been made . . . to consent to measure to deprive Proprietors under the original grants of their Estates . . . Her Majesty's Government feel themselves bound to adhere to the decisions so repeatedly adopted by my predecessors in this matter, and . . . both on grounds of justice to the Landed Proprietors, and of the permanent interests of the community of Prince Edward Island, they regard such a measure as impractical.[50]

[45] For details of the circumstances of PEI's road to responsible government, see W.S. MacNUTT, 'Political Advance and Social Reform, 1842–1861', in *Canada's Smallest Province*, 115–34; Sharpe, *A People's History of Prince Edward Island*; MacKinnon, *The Government of Prince Edward Island*; Philip Girard, Jim Phillips, and R. Blake Brown, *A History of Law in Canada*, (Toronto, Buffalo, London: Published for The Osgoode Society for Canadian Legal History by University of Toronto Press, 2019), chap. 27.

[46] The powers of the Lieutenant-Governor were drastically curtailed, and some of them appointed after 1851 were reluctant to accept the new political reality. See MacKinnon, *The Government of Prince Edward Island.*

[47] MacKinnon, *The Government of Prince Edward Island*, 94.

[48] Ian Ross Robertson, 'Coles, George', *Dictionary of Canadian Biography*, Volume X (1871–1880) (University of Toronto/Université Laval, 2003).

[49] Robertson, 'Political Realignment in Pre-Confederation Prince Edward Island, 1863–1870', *Acadiensis* 15, no. 1 (1985): 35–58. The Catholic residents included the increasing number of immigrants from Ireland.

[50] Letter from Secretary of State for the Colonies, the 3rd Earl of Grey (Henry Grey) to the Lieutenant-Governor of PEI, Sir Alexander Bannerman, dated February 12, 1851. Reproduced in 'Appendix to the

Although a few proponents of the escheat movement were elected to the legislative assembly and continued to promote it in debates around various land bills, successive governments after 1851 took a cue from the Imperial Government to search for alternative pathways that did not entail penalising landholders for non-fulfilment of their original land grant conditions. One such path was through the purchase of lands by the government from willing landholders,[51] which was seen as more palatable to the Imperial Government because it overcame the two perceived flaws of the escheat doctrine, the compulsory nature of the appropriation and lack of compensation.[52] Accordingly, the first of the Land Purchase Acts was passed in 1853 and received the Royal Assent.[53]

Intending to improve the prosperity of the tenants through the conversion of their 'leasehold tenures into freehold estates, at an easy rate, and on fair terms',[54] the Act instituted the Commissioner of Public Lands, who would invite public tenders from landowners for sale of their parcels of land (with a minimum of 1,000 acres) to the government, with the aggregate price of cultivated and uncultivated land for sale not to exceed seven shillings and sixpence per acre. Purchased land would then be offered to the current tenants and occupiers of that land. They could get the fee simple by producing evidence of occupancy and paying 20% of the purchase price within six months. The Act entrusted the PEI treasury to take a loan of up to 30,000 pounds from the market ('Bodies Corporate or Politic') to facilitate the process. Three estates were purchased under the Act from 1854 to 1859 (81,303 acres of the Worrell Estate for 24,100 pounds sterling[55] and smaller portions of the Selkirk and Stansfield estates for about 8,500 pounds sterling).[56]

The 1853 Act did lead to the purchase of some land from landlords with significant holdings and their conversion to small freeholds. However, the future

Journal of the House of Assembly', 1850, Appendix Y. The need to move beyond holding proprietors to the initial grant conditions of 1767 was further reiterated in 1855 by the next Secretary of State for The Colonies, who wrote that 'whatever character may properly attach to the circumstances connected with the original grants, which have been often employed against the maintenance of the rights of the proprietors, they could not, with justice, be used to defeat the rights of the present owners who have acquired their property by inheritance, by family settlements, or for valuable consideration'. Letter from Labourchere dated December 21, 1855, reproduced in 'Journal of the House of Assembly of Prince Edward Island 1856', Appendix E.

[51] As discussed in the previous Chapters 4 and 5 on Ireland, the idea of peasant proprietorship through the allocation/sale of wastelands reclaimed by the State was taking shape in Britain, amongst its proponents being political economists such as William Thornton and John Stuart Mill, as well as members of the government such as John Bright. Voluntary sale of their lands by landlord proprietors was not considered an encroachment on their property rights.

[52] Robertson, 'Introduction'.

[53] An ACT for the purchase of Lands on behalf of the Government of Prince Edward Island, and to regulate the sale and management thereof, and for other purposes therein mentioned.

[54] Preamble, An ACT for the purchase of Lands on behalf of the Government of Prince Edward Island, and to regulate the sale and management thereof, and for other purposes mentioned therein.

[55] See Appendix H for the documents related to the sale of Worrell Estate in 'Journal of the House of Assembly of Prince Edward Island 1855', 1855.

[56] Clark, *Three Centuries and the Island*, 93.

success of this approach was in question for several reasons. First, the financial constraints faced by the Prince Edward Island Government in facilitating further purchases. It had used up the 30,000 pounds allowed by the Act and needed more money for future purchases. During the following years (to the end of the 1860s), it made numerous unsuccessful appeals for Imperial loan guarantees to implement land purchases. Second, the reluctance to provide loans to Prince Edward Island was partially due to the perceived mismanagement of the land purchase, especially the Worrell Estate.[57] It was alleged that the local representatives inflated the estate's price and skimmed 10,000 pounds for themselves, with the Worrell family receiving just over 14,000 pounds.[58] The exorbitant price for the land and its associated fraud undermined the programme's credibility. Third, Section XXVI of the 1853 Act deemed that where the tenants and occupiers of land purchased by the Commissioner of Public Lands did not come forward to buy that land, the Commissioner could sell that land 'in parcels not exceeding three hundred acres in any one Township to any one person'. In this situation, the existing tenants would continue their leaseholds but now pay rent to the new landlords (Section XXXVII). Based on these two sections, a person could purchase any amount of land in several townships and continue with the leasehold system with existing tenants. These two sections created a perception that the Act's objectives were to get rid of the large landlords (especially the non-resident or absentees) rather than abolish the leasehold system.[59] Furthermore, in subsequent attempts at land legislation in PEI, the landlords often alluded to how the 1853 Act enabled the 'authorities to sell and dispose of lands under the Land Purchase Bill to their numerous FRIENDS AND ADHERENTS'.[60] In essence, financial constraints and credibility problems slowed down further land purchases after the initial disposal of the three estates.

While the PEI legislature continued its attempts to get the Imperial Governments to underwrite future purchases through a grant of loans and coax more landlords to offer their lands for sale voluntarily, it also initiated legislation on greater rights of tenants. The government introduced a bill in the Assembly in 1855 to secure compensation for tenants' improvements.[61] After some discussion on its scope,[62]

[57] For details about the origin and eventual sales of this estate, see Rusty Bittermann and Margaret McCallum, 'The Pursuit of Gentility in an Age of Revolution: The Family of Jonathan Worrell', *Acadiensis* 43, no. 2 (2014): 31–56.

[58] For details of this so-called 'Worrell Job', see Robertson, 'Introduction', Sharpe, *A People's History of Prince Edward Island.*

[59] This aspect has been alluded to in Matthew G. Hatvany, 'The Proprietary Burden?, *The Island Magazine* 44 (1998): 3–7.

[60] See various petitions of the landlords and minutes of the Executive Council of August 27, 1855, in Appendix (E) of 'Journal of the House of Assembly of Prince Edward Island 1856'.

[61] 'An Act to Secure Compensation to Tenants in Prince Edward Island, and Thereby to Promote the Improvement of the Soil', Pub. L. No. CAP. XI (1855).

[62] Some members wanted that all tenants, irrespective of the length of their tenure, and circumstances of the end of their tenure, should be eligible for compensation for improvement. Although this was accommodated in the Preamble to the Act that was eventually passed, the specific provisions of compensation applied only to those tenants ejected because of non-payment of their rents. For details

the bill was approved by large majorities in both houses of the legislature, although two members noted their dissent in the Legislative Council.[63] The main provisions of the Act were: (1) a tenant ejected from land (which was in wilderness state at the time of occupancy) by the landlord because of non-payment of rent shall be entitled to receive compensation for improvements made during his occupancy; (2) the amount of compensation will be determined by three arbitrators, all being residents of the Island (one each appointed by the tenant and landlord, and the third chosen by the appointed arbitrators), who would take into consideration the increase in the value of the land because of the improvements, the amount of rent, and length of lease, etc. Either party could challenge the award amount in Court; and (3) the landlord could pay the compensation or forego the rent.

As expected, the landlords were up in arms and sent numerous petitions to the Colonial Office requesting that the Act be disallowed.[64] Some of their objections were related to the specific circumstances of land tenure in Prince Edward Island. The landlords pointed out that very low rents (about one shilling per acre) and long leases (usually 999 years) allowed the tenants to earn enough profits and recoup their investments in improving the land, thus making compensation for improvements unnecessary. The landlords had particular concerns about the fairness of three arbitrators (who had to be PEI residents) in determining compensation 'because in the Colony, ninety-nine persons out of every hundred have a direct fellow feeling and personal interest on behalf of the tenant, and quite the reverse towards a landlord'.[65] It was suggested that a more unbiased way to determine compensation 'would be by setting up the tenant's interest, subject . . . to the conditions of his lease, and the arrears in rent due . . . and then finding, by public sale, what such leasehold interest will bring'.[66] The proposed process of determining compensation was like the one practised in Ireland, where the willingness of the amount of rent paid by the incoming tenant (and comparison with existing rent) was an indicator of the value of the outgoing tenant's improvements. One significant difference, however, was that in Ireland, there was competition for limited land amongst many tenants, while in Prince Edward Island, there was competition

on the debates, see 'Debates and Proceedings of the House of Assembly of Prince Edward Island. First Session of the Twentieth General Assembly', 1855, Public Archives and Record Office of Prince Edward Island.

[63] These members questioned the need for such an act given the general cordial relationship between most landlords and tenants, and warned that the proposed 'class legislation' will 'create hostility between them'. 'Debates and Proceedings of the Legislative Council of Prince Edward Island for the Session of 1855' (Charlottetown, P.E.I.: F.W. Hughes, 1855), 57–58.

[64] These petitions are reproduced in Appendix (E) of the 'Journal of the House of Assembly of Prince Edward Island 1856'.

[65] Letter from R. F. Stewart to John Russell, May 19, 1855. Reproduced in 'Journal of the House of Assembly of Prince Edward Island 1856', Appendix E.

[66] Letter from proprietors to the Colonial Office, June 4, 1855. Reproduced in Appendix (E) of 'Journal of the House of Assembly of Prince Edward Island 1856'.

for tenants to improve large tracts of wilderness land. This difference was one of the reasons for low rents and long leases in PEI.

In their petitions, the proprietors also highlighted the political motivations behind the legislation. Citing a speech by the Premier in the Assembly on March 29, 1855, where he suggested that the purpose of the Compensation Act was to compel the proprietors 'to come in and offer their lands to the Government under the land purchase Bill', the proprietors questioned whether the bill was intended to further the interests of the tenants.[67]

Besides doubts about procedural fairness to the landlords under the prevailing conditions in Prince Edward Island, the correspondence also pointed out the various implications of the Act to broader principles regarding property rights. The underlying principle motivating the Compensation Act in Prince Edward Island was pushed by William Cooper in the 1830s: 'that the labour invested by settlers in clearing their land gave them titles naturally superior to the allegedly forfeited claims of absentee proprietors'.[68] However, while the escheators saw the need to transfer full property rights from landlords to the actual cultivators of land, compensation for tenants' improvement could be seen as an acknowledgement of co-proprietorship in the sense that both landlords and tenants shared the fruits of the increased value of the land.[69] The landlords' petitions did not question the value of the improvements made by the tenants, and they believed that the low rents and long leases allowed for recouping the investments. Instead, they saw the rewarding of the tenant for non-payment of rent as subverting the long-established legal norms governing contractual relationships between landlords and tenants by which 'payments of the rent reserved in such contracts have ever, by the law of England, been compelled to be made with rigour and strictness'. One of the petitions further pointed out that in the case 'the extraordinary power vested in the landlord [is] . . . abused, . . . the tenant of Prince Edward Island . . . has the same advantage given by the law of replevin, and may avail himself of any plea in bar . . . as fully as the tenant in England can'.[70] Most of the objections to the Compensation Act by landlords were based on comparing its principles and procedures with

[67] See letter signed by over thirty proprietors addressed to the Queen, June 19, 1855. Reproduced in Appendix (E) of 'Journal of the House of Assembly of Prince Edward Island 1856'; for the full text of the referenced speech, see pages 50–57 of 'Debates and Proceedings of the House of Assembly of Prince Edward Island. First Session of the Twentieth General Assembly'.

[68] Harry Baglole, 'Biography – COOPER, WILLIAM (d. 1867) – Volume IX (1861–1870) – Dictionary of Canadian Biography', accessed September 15, 2021, <http://www.biographi.ca/en/bio/cooper_william_1867_9E.html>; for a detailed discussion on the arguments made regarding the labour theory during various stages of the PEI land question, see Margaret E. McCallum, 'The Sacred Rights of Property: Title, Entitlement, and the Land Question in Nineteenth-Century Prince Edward Island', in *Essays in the History of Canadian Law in Honour of R.C.B. Risk*, ed. G. Blaine Baker and Jim Phillips, vol. VIII (Toronto: University of Toronto Press, 1999), 358–97.

[69] This was one of the rationales for compensation rights of tenants taking shape in the context of Ireland by the mid-1850s (see Chapter 5).

[70] Letter from numerous proprietors to the Queen regarding the Tenant Compensation Act, June 29, 1855. Reproduced in 'Journal of the House of Assembly of Prince Edward Island 1856', Appendix E.

those practised in England, and saw the proposed legislation as 'a monstrous innovation upon all those principles which . . . had been . . . consider[ed] fixed and established by justice and usage, in regard to such property'.[71]

The Lieutenant-Governor of Prince Edward Island, Dominick Daly, supported the Act on the grounds that the 'tenantry have long been anxious for this measure . . . and . . . it was desirable . . . that their reasonable expectations should not be disappointed', especially at a time when the PEI government was trying to resist the resurrection of escheat as a remedy for the land question by certain elected members of the assembly.[72] He further reiterated that in Great Britain, where real property is generally let in an improved state, 'public policy has pointed out that improving tenants should be sustained from loss', which makes it even more urgent to approve similar legislation in PEI 'to protect those whose lives must be spent in arduous task of reclaiming [land] from . . . state of primitive nature'.

The Imperial Government, more convinced by arguments made by the proprietors and their 'proprietary influence',[73] refused consent to the Compensation Act and reiterated that it could not recommend the Crown's assent to 'Colonial Acts which are variance with the principles of justice, and invade those rights of property which are the foundation of social organization'.[74] The Secretary of the State for the Colonies' letter to the Lieutenant-Governor of Prince Edward Island identified the specific concerns about the provisions of the proposed Act:

> This Bill provides that where a tenant is unable or unwilling to fulfill the contract between him and the landowner by which the tenant has agreed to pay to the landowner a fixed annual rent . . . the landlord must either forego the rent, and thus let the land pass practically to the tenant, or he must pay to the tenant a sum equal to 20 years' purchase of what is termed the 'annual profit to the landlord created by the tenant's or lessee's improvements on the soil'. . . . In the one case he would make over to the tenant the land itself: in the other case he would make over to the tenant sum which might even go beyond the value of the land. Such a measure of undisguised spoliation cannot be sanctioned by Her Majesty.[75]

[71] Letter from R. F. Stewart to John Russell, May 19, 1855. Reproduced in 'Journal of the House of Assembly of Prince Edward Island 1856', Appendix E.

[72] Letter from D. Daly to the Secretary of State for the Colonies, June 28, 1855. Reproduced in 'Papers on the Subject of Affording the IMPERIAL GUARANTEE to a LOAN for the Service of PRINCE EDWARD ISLAND' (House of Commons, April 16, 1858), 5–6.

[73] Robertson, 'Introduction', xvi.

[74] Letter from G. Grey, Colonial Office, to Lieutenant-Governor Daly regarding Bill Numbers 913 and 915 sent for Royal Assent in 1855. Reproduced in 'Colonial Bills: North America' (The House of Commons, July 26, 1864), 41–43, House of Commons Parliamentary Papers Online.

[75] Letter from Colonial Office to Lieutenant-Governor of Prince Edward Island, November 17, 1855, regarding 'An Act to Secure Compensation to Tenants in Prince Edward Island, and thereby to promote improvement if the soil'. Letter reproduced in 'Colonial Bills: North America', 42. In addition to this act, the letter also stated the refusal of Royal Assent to another land law, 'An Act to impose a Rate or Duty on the Rent rolls of the Proprietors of Certain Township Lands in Prince Edward Island, in order to defray the Expenses of any Armed Force which may be required for the withdrawal of the Troops and

The overall imperial reluctance to legalising tenants' rights, including through compensation, in the mid-1850s was due to similar concerns in Prince Edward Island and Ireland, that is, the impact it would have on the landowners in England. The British Prime Minister, Palmerston,[76] who had intervened in similar legislation in Ireland, also weighed in on the proposed tenant-right legislation in Prince Edward Island, writing to his Secretary of State for the Colonies on December 19, 1855, that we must not 'establish a principle of authorized spoliation even in a remote corner of the Queen's Dominions . . . [T]he owners have as good a right to their Property as you or I . . . have to our Estates; and it would be as unjust and of as bad example to *extinguish* the Rights of these owners, as it would be to *extinguish* our Rights and to fix the conditions on which we should be compelled to make over our Farms to the Tenants'.[77] This ended the aspirations embodied in the proposed Act to secure some rights for tenants related to their improvements. An editorial in the *Examiner*, a local paper leaning towards land reforms, aptly captured the sense of dejection in the colony: 'It was mortifying and humiliating to think that a Colony . . . with all the machinery of self-government, cannot be allowed to make such laws as are necessary to promote their own interests, without an irresponsible faction of land-owners --- most of them out of the country --- being allowed to interfere between the Crown and the colony.'[78]

Similar to the situation in Ireland in the 1850s, there was not much headway in terms of the rights of tenants within the existing land tenure system in Prince Edward Island, and soon after the disappointment regarding the 1855 Compensation Act, the focus of the legislature shifted again to the conversion of leasehold to freehold tenures. In this regard, encouragement was given by the new Secretary of State for the Colonies, Henry Labouchere. In his first correspondence with the Lieutenant-Governor of Prince Edward Island in December 1855,

for further Encouragement of Education'. The latter was disallowed because, according to the Colonial Office letter, it amounted to 'oppressive class legislation'.

[76] The Third Viscount Palmerston (British Prime Minister 1851–1858, 1859–1865) was himself a landlord having holdings in England and Ireland (David Steele, 'Temple, Henry John, Third Viscount Palmerston (1784–1865), Prime Minister' *Oxford Dictionary of National Biography* (Oxford, UK: Oxford University Press, May 2009). His sister Elizabeth was married to Laurence Sulivan, one of the large proprietors of Prince Edward Island. Their daughter, Charlotte, was amongst the last holdouts to the PEI Land Purchase Act of 1875 (discussed later in the chapter), see Kenneth Bourne, ed., *The Letters of the Third Viscount Palmerston to Laurence and Elizabeth Sulivan, 1804–1863* (London: Offices of the Royal Historical Society, University College London, 1979); Rusty Bittermann and Margaret McCallum, *Lady Landlords of Prince Edward Island: Imperial Dreams and the Defence of Property* (Montreal: McGill-Queen's University Press, 2008).

[77] Cited in E. D. Steele, *Irish Land and British Politics: Tenant-Right and Nationality 1865–1870* (Cambridge, UK: Cambridge University Press, 1974), 44–45.

[78] 'Rent Roll and Tenant Compensation Bills', *The Examiner*, December 10, 1855, sec. Editorial, 87; there were passionate debates in both houses of parliament lamenting the disallowance of the act, as well as on the petitions of the various proprietors that may have led to the decision. See 'The Parliamentary Reporter: Debates and Proceedings of the Legislative Council and House of Assembly of Prince Edward Island for the Session Ending 14 April 1856' (Charlottetown, P.E.I.: Examiner Office, 1856).

he agreed with his predecessor's decision in declining assent to the Compensation Act. He reiterated that the Imperial Government would not entertain any legislation related to escheat. However, he was willing to consider ways tenants could become proprietors provided that 'it be effected without injustice to the proprietors'.[79] He saw the voluntary sale of land by proprietors either directly to the tenants or to the state as a possibility. Still, he suggested that the cost of this would have to be borne by the Colonial Government. This encouragement led to the legislature's next phase to find ways to convince landowners to sell their holdings voluntarily.

In the decade following the disappointment from the disallowance of the Compensation Act, most of the efforts at legislative and political levels in Prince Edward Island were directed to expand the land purchase programme. The specific initiatives/activities included the establishment of a land commission, passing a few land acts (not all of which got the Royal Assent), and agitation of the Tenant League. Several studies have extensively documented attempts at land tenure reforms during this period,[80] so my purpose is to provide a brief outline of how things unfolded after 1855 and foreground the evolution of various rationales used by different stakeholders to promote or resist these reforms.

The inability of the PEI legislature to achieve its objective of either directly improving tenants' rights in existing leasehold tenures or forcing landlords to part with their land through the onerous demands of compensation in the disallowed Act led it to go back to the option of purchasing land from willing landlords. In the following years, from 1856 to 1859, the legislature attempted to resurrect the previous Land Purchase Act by requesting a loan of 100,000 pounds to be guaranteed by the Imperial Government.[81] Despite multiple pleas, the loan was not approved, and except for the purchase of a part of one estate in 1859, no more land was offered for sale from the proprietors. To get land tenure reforms moving again, Prince Edward Island requested the Imperial Government to appoint a commission to inquire into the existing relations between landlord and tenant and to negotiate with the proprietors to convert their leaseholds into freeholds.[82] After consulting

[79] Letter from Labourchere dated December 21, 1855, reproduced in 'Journal of the House of Assembly of Prince Edward Island 1856', Appendix E.

[80] Ian Ross Robertson, ed., 'Report of the Commissioners Appointed by the Queen to Inquire into the Differences Prevailing in Prince Edward Island to the Rights of Landowners and Tenants with a View to a Settlement of the Same on Fair and Equitable Principles, July 18, 1861', in *The Prince Edward Land Commission of 1860* (Fredericton, NB: Acadiensis Press, 1988), 183–208; Robertson, 'Political Realignment in Pre-Confederation Prince Edward Island, 1863–1870'; Ian Ross Robertson, *The Tenant League of Prince Edward Island, 1864–1867: Leasehold Tenure in the New World* (Toronto, Buffalo, London: University of Toronto Press, 1996); MacDonald, 'Who's Afraid of the Fenians?'; Bittermann and McCallum, 'Upholding the Land Legislation of a "Communistic and Socialist Assembly"'.

[81] See extensive correspondence between the Lieutenant-Governor and the Colonial Office, as well as the joint addresses of the PEI legislature to the Crown in 'Papers on the Subject of Affording the IMPERIAL GUARANTEE to a LOAN for the Service of PRINCE EDWARD ISLAND'.

[82] 'COPY of the ADDRESS to Her Majesty, Adopted by the House of Assembly of Prince Edward Island on the 9th Day of May 1859, Praying for the Appointment of A COMMISSION to Inquire into the Existing Relations of LANDLORD and TENANT in That Colony: And, COPY or EXTRACTS of

with some large landowners, including Sir S. Cunard,[83] who was one of the largest proprietors in Prince Edward Island, owning almost 212,000 acres, the Secretary of State for the Colonies gave the go-ahead for establishing a Commission consisting of three members, one each being appointed by the Imperial Government, the PEI Assembly, and the landlords. It was to have wide latitude in looking at the land tenure issues in totality, and it was expected that all parties would accept its decisions.[84]

The Commission submitted its report in July 1861. Its main recommendation was that the Imperial Government guarantee 100,000 pounds to continue the programme of voluntary sales under the Land Purchase Act of 1853, arguing that this amount should be able to buy 800,000 acres of land currently under leasehold tenures.[85] It further recommended that given the wide variation in the existing tenures and the land quality, the purchase price should be negotiated between individual landlords and tenants, and arbitration should be used in case they could not agree. The report further suggested that if the new initiative did not facilitate voluntary sales, a compulsory compromise would be needed to give most tenants the right to purchase the land currently occupied at a fair valuation. It then provided a detailed formula of how fair valuation could be determined.[86]

While the Prince Edward Island Government accepted the report and soon after passed legislation in 1862 that would give effect to the recommendations of the three commissioners,[87] the landlords did not find the report favourable for two reasons:[88] (1) the underlying principle whereby the 'award was giving the tenant's

the Subsequent CORRESPONDENCE of the Secretary of State for the Colonies with the Governor of Prince Edward Island and Landowners and Others of That Colony, Relating to the Same Subject' (House of Commons Parliamentary Papers, 1864).

[83] For details about Cunard, including his extensive role in discussions on land tenure and his influence with the Colonial Office, see Phyllis R. Blakely, 'Cunard, Sir Samuel', *Dictionary of Canadian Biography*, Volume IX (1861–1870) (University of Toronto/Université Laval, 2003).

[84] See letter from Secretary of State for the Colonies to the Lieutenant-Governor, March 21, 1860 in 'COPY of the ADDRESS to Her Majesty, Adopted by the House of Assembly of Prince Edward Island on the 9th Day of May 1859, Praying for the Appointment of A COMMISSION to Inquire into the Existing Relations of LANDLORD and TENANT in That Colony: And, COPY or EXTRACTS of the Subsequent CORRESPONDENCE of the Secretary of State for the Colonies with the Governor of Prince Edward Island and Landowners and Others of That Colony, Relating to the Same Subject'.

[85] For the full report of the commissioners, see Robertson, 'Report of the Commissioners Appointed by the Queen to Inquire into the Differences Prevailing in Prince Edward Island to the Rights of Landowners and Tenants with a View to a Settlement of the Same on Fair and Equitable Principles, July 18, 1861', 183–203.

[86] Besides the landlord–tenant relationships, the report also made comments and recommendations on other aspects related to quit rents, escheat, fishery reserves and Indian claims. A detailed discussion of these is beyond the scope of this chapter. For a summary of the report, see Sharpe, *A People's History of Prince Edward Island*, 106.

[87] An Act to give effects to the Report of the Commissioners on the Land Question.

[88] For numerous letters written by proprietors, see section 'Correspondence with Landowners and Others' in 'COPY of the ADDRESS to Her Majesty, Adopted by the House of Assembly of Prince Edward Island on the 9th Day of May 1859, Praying for the Appointment of A COMMISSION to Inquire into the Existing Relations of LANDLORD and TENANT in That Colony: And, COPY or EXTRACTS of

claim to freehold priority over proprietor's *legal* right to his property'; and (2) the practicality of selling their estates in small chunks to individual tenants, which would keep the administrative costs of estates constant while reducing the revenues.[89] The Imperial Government sided with the proprietors and declined assent to the Act on procedural grounds that the Commissioners were 'authorized by the proprietors to make an award themselves, but they were not authorized to transfer the duty of making that award to others'.[90] The Commission had exceeded its authority by recommending arbitrators to determine the awards.

With a comprehensive solution to the land question in Prince Edward Island expected from the Commission again proving elusive, the legislature passed a more limited Act in 1864, popularly known as the 'Fifteen-Year Purchase Bill'. It gave tenants with an unexpired term of more than forty years a right to purchase the lands at a price equivalent to fifteen years of rent.[91] The Act was supported by some proprietors and received the Royal Assent, although it led to the purchase of a mere 2,911 acres of land by forty-five tenants during the 1864–1868 period.[92] This period corresponded with the short-lived Tenant League activities, which used the strategy of resisting rent collection from tenants to force a change in the leasehold land tenure system.[93] In the meantime, the Colonial Government finalised the purchase of the sizeable Cunard estate in 1866 by taking a loan from the market and made a few additional acquisitions of smaller estates in the following years. By the end of 1871, the PEI Government had purchased more than 450,000 acres of land owned by the big landholders. However, over 380,000 acres were still owned by proprietors in significant holdings.[94]

Encouraged by the purchase of the large Cunard Estate in 1866, the PEI Government sent feelers to many proprietors in 1867 to assess a willingness to sell their land holdings under the provisions of the Land Purchase Act of 1853.

the Subsequent CORRESPONDENCE of the Secretary of State for the Colonies with the Governor of Prince Edward Island and Landowners and Others of That Colony, Relating to the Same Subject'.

[89] Robertson, 'Introduction', xxii.

[90] Copy of Despatch from His Grace the Duke of Newcastle to Lieutenant-Governor, August 9, 1862. Reproduced in 'COPY of the ADDRESS to Her Majesty, Adopted by the House of Assembly of Prince Edward Island on the 9th Day of May 1859, Praying for the Appointment of A COMMISSION to Inquire into the Existing Relations of LANDLORD and TENANT in That Colony: And, COPY or EXTRACTS of the Subsequent CORRESPONDENCE of the Secretary of State for the Colonies with the Governor of Prince Edward Island and Landowners and Others of That Colony, Relating to the Same Subject'.

[91] An Act for settling differences between Landlord and Tenant, and to enable Tenants on certain Townships to purchase the fee simple of their Farms.

[92] Robertson, 'Introduction', xxiv.

[93] For details about the origins and activities of the Tenant League including its shared ideology and tactics with a similar movement in Ireland, as well its contributions to the settling of the PEI land question, see Robertson, *The Tenant League of Prince Edward Island, 1864–1867*; for details about the concerns about the Fenian movement spilling over in the colony, see MacDonald, 'Who's Afraid of the Fenians?'

[94] Bittermann and McCallum, 'Upholding the Land Legislation of a "Communistic and Socialist Assembly"'.

Most of the proprietors were either unwilling to sell or wanted a purchase price well beyond that allowed by the Act.[95] Accordingly, in early 1868, the Executive Council requested the Lieutenant-Governor to forward its Minute to the Colonial Office, which pointed out that every effort had been expended to get the landlords to sell their estates voluntarily. Since the leasehold system no longer existed 'across the narrow strait which separates this Island from the Dominion of Canada', the Minute requested support for compulsory settlement to 'obliterate the last traces of the leasehold tenure in British North America'.[96] The Secretary of State for the Colonies, Richard Temple-Grenville, denied the plea as he saw no 'special reason in the minute of Council, which . . . would justify, on the ground of public policy, the proposed direct appropriation of private property'.[97]

******

During the contestations between the Colonial and Imperial Governments in the 1860s, several conceptual issues regarding property rights and their implications for the PEI land question came to the forefront, which played an important role during the final phase discussed in Chapter 8. Along with arguments that proprietors had foregone their rights to their land because of the non-fulfilment of the original grant conditions and the cultivators/tenants had earned some co-proprietorship due to their efforts in clearing the land and increasing its value, additional rationales were inserted into the discussion. One was a resurfacing of the idea of balancing private rights and public goods.[98] The Land Commission Report countered the sanctity of private property arguments of the landlords by emphasising that 'though the law has sacredly guarded the rights of property, whenever the possession or abuse of property becomes prejudicial to the public interests, the rights and prejudices of individuals can be constitutionally controlled for the public good'.[99] Similarly, in a legal opinion sought in England by the Secretary of State for the Colonies on the Commission's recommendations, two legal experts (who were also members of the British Parliament) opined that the

[95] See Letter from the Lieutenant-Governor to the Secretary of State for the Colonies, 11 January 1868. Reproduced in Appendix (CC) of 'Journal of the House of Assembly of Prince Edward Island 1868' (Charlottetown, P.E.I.: Frederick W. Hughes, 1868).

[96] Minute of the Executive Council, containing their views on Land Tenures, and submitting considerations on which they seek sanctions of the Imperial Government to the introduction in the Local Legislature of a measure compelling Proprietors to sell their interests in their Estates. Reproduced in 'Journal of the House of Assembly of Prince Edward Island 1868', Appendix CC.

[97] Letter from Secretary of State for the Colonies to the Lieutenant-Governor of Prince Edward Island, March 2, 1868. Reproduced in 'Journal of the House of Assembly of Prince Edward Island 1868', Appendix CC.

[98] This had been one of the arguments used by both factions within the escheat movement of the 1830 discussed earlier. See Bittermann and McCallum, 'When Private Rights Become Public Wrongs'.

[99] Robertson, 'Report of the Commissioners Appointed by the Queen to Inquire into the Differences Prevailing in Prince Edward Island to the Rights of Landowners and Tenants with a View to a Settlement of the Same on Fair and Equitable Principles, July 18, 1861', 191.

'Act . . . must be founded and justified . . . solely for reasons of public advantage . . . and for . . . the general good'.[100] In both these communications, examples of precedents cited from across the Empire around public good and private rights included the rights of copyholds in England, seigneurial tenures in Lower Canada,[101] slaveholders in the West Indies, and encumbered estates in Ireland, among others.

Second, proponents of land reforms in Prince Edward Island increasingly reiterated the colony's geographical location for their persistence for freehold tenures. For instance, the Commissioner's report noted that it was 'difficult for any European to understand why almost every man in America considers it a personal degradation to pay rent. In the British Islands leasehold tenure is the general rule, and freehold the exception. A wealthy man pays rent with no more sense of inferiority than he feels when he pays taxes. On this side of the Atlantic a very different sentiment grew . . . where every industrious man may own a freehold . . . The tenantry of Prince Edward Island share the common sentiment of the continent which surrounds them'.[102] The land question in the colony was emphasised to be a mixture of 'Old World issues and New World environment and expectations'.[103] It thus required approaches different from those adopted in other parts of the Empire.[104]

In dealing with continuing requests from the PEI legislature to find ways to resolve the land question in the second half of the 1860s, the Imperial Government also had to be cognisant of the changing political situation in North America, especially concerning the impeding dominion status for Canada under a Confederation of its colonies as well as the British Empire's economic and political relationship with America.[105] The political and economic fallout from the British role during the American Civil War led to a serious consideration of a federation

[100] Letter from W. Atherton and Roundell Palmer dated June 9, 1863. Reproduced in 'COPY of the ADDRESS to Her Majesty, Adopted by the House of Assembly of Prince Edward Island on the 9th Day of May 1859, Praying for the Appointment of A COMMISSION to Inquire into the Existing Relations of LANDLORD and TENANT in That Colony: And, COPY or EXTRACTS of the Subsequent CORRESPONDENCE of the Secretary of State for the Colonies with the Governor of Prince Edward Island and Landowners and Others of That Colony, Relating to the Same Subject'.

[101] Given the geographical and temporal proximity of the abolition of seigneurial tenures in Lower Canada and leasehold tenures, parallels are drawn between the two. For an understanding of the difference in the two types of tenure, as well the reasons for the abolition of the former in 1854, see Michael B Percy and Rick Szostak, 'The Political Economy of the Abolition of Seigneurial Tenure in Canada East', *Explorations in Economic History* 29, no. 1 (January 1, 1992): 51–68.

[102] Robertson, 'Report of the Commissioners Appointed by the Queen to Inquire into the Differences Prevailing in Prince Edward Island to the Rights of Landowners and Tenants with a View to a Settlement of the Same on Fair and Equitable Principles, July 18, 1861', 195.

[103] Robertson, *The Tenant League of Prince Edward Island, 1864–1867*, 7.

[104] This aspect was repeatedly emphasised in both legislative and public domains. See debates in the House of Assembly and Legislative Council after 1865 as well as editorials in the local newspapers such the *Examiner* and *The Herald*.

[105] Phillip A. Buckner, *Canada and the British Empire* (Oxford, UK: Oxford University Press, 2010); Joseph Howe, *Confederation Considered in Relation to the Interests of the Empire* (London: Edward Stanford, 1866); Bolger, *Prince Edward Island and Confederation, 1863–1873*.

in the 1860s.[106] Although Prince Edward Island hosted the conference in 1864 to discuss the union, there was not much local public support for joining the Confederation.[107] In the period leading to the eventual Confederation in 1867, the Imperial Government and the other North American colonies provided various sticks and carrots to coax Prince Edward Island to join it. The sticks included the threat by the Imperial Government to pass the costs of the Lieutenant-Governor's salary and the costs of maintaining law and order by getting troops from Nova Scotia during the Tenant League agitation to the local government. The carrot was the promise of an $800,000 loan from the Dominion of Canada to Prince Edward Island to buyout the large landlords. The PEI legislature rebuffed these.[108] The Island's Government continued to flirt with the Dominion of Canada after 1867 to get better terms for joining the Confederation and with America for possible deals related to stronger political and economic ties.[109]

When Prince Edward Island broached the land question again in 1868, the Imperial Government had to find ways to accommodate pressures from multiple directions. On one side, the PEI landlords had the support of the British governing class because of the 'inescapable mental linkage between land issues in Prince Edward Island and the United Kingdom . . . In a political system based on custom, precedent, and convention, only the foolhardy would overlook the danger of creating precedents which could be turned against them'.[110] On the other hand, there was convergence among the various political and religious factions in Prince Edward Island toward the common goal of eliminating the leasehold system.[111] These oppositional demands had to be considered in the context of the uncertainty about Prince Edward Island's decision to either become part of the Dominion of Canada or continue as a separate colony of the British Empire.

[106] This included the British support for the South in the war, the ending of the reciprocal trade agreements with the British colonies by America, and a general perception that America may have political designs over these colonies. Buckner, *Canada and the British Empire*.

[107] Some of the reasons behind the opposition were insularity of the population because of the colony's location, and loss of political and economic independence. For details, see Francis W. P. Bolger, 'Nation Building at Charlottetown, 1864', in *Canada's Smallest Province*, 135–55.

[108] For details, see Bolger, 'Prince Edward Island Rejects Confederation, 1864–1867'; Bolger, *Prince Edward Island and Confederation, 1863–1873*.

[109] Given PEI's close economic ties with America, the end of the reciprocity treaty hurt it economically, with exports to America as a percentage of total exports declining from 42% to 9%. See Sharpe, *A People's History of Prince Edward Island*, 114.

[110] Robertson, *The Tenant League of Prince Edward Island, 1864–1867*, 27.

[111] Robertson, 'Political Realignment in Pre-Confederation Prince Edward Island, 1863–1870'.

8

The Imperial Hedge

Tenant's Compensation Act of 1872 and Land Purchase Act of 1875

Parts II and III of this book have shown how the Empire used custom or status-based arguments and analogies between its colonies to legislate security of tenure for the actual cultivators of land in Punjab and Ireland. Security of tenure took various forms, including occupancy rights, customary tenant rights, compensation for improvement and disturbance, and, in a limited way, proprietorship through the purchase of land made available by willing landlords. The sanctity of the property rights of landlords was a central question in discussions around the security of tenure in both colonies. The imperial authorities walked a fine line in balancing the property rights of landlords and those cultivating their land while being attentive to the economic and political implications of allocating these rights.

As the Liberal Government of William Gladstone was institutionalising land tenure relationships in Punjab and Ireland, the Colonial Office had to deal with the land question in Prince Edward Island (PEI). Like Ireland, the land issue in Prince Edward Island had been simmering for almost a century. The two colonies also shared histories of land allocation 'by rank'[1] under British rule, a preponderance of well-connected absentee landlords, and persistent demands for the betterment of economically struggling tenants. In the context of the Empire's granting of Dominion status to Canada in 1867 and the ongoing political discussions in the colony about whether to join the Dominion,[2] the PEI's legislature prodded the Imperial Government[3] again to resolve the long-standing issues regarding land tenure.

[1] Weaver, *The Great Land Rush and the Making of the Modern World, 1650–1900* (Montreal & Kingston: McGill-Queen's University Press, 2003).

[2] Bolger, *Prince Edward Island and Confederation, 1863–1873* (Charlottetown: St. Dunstan's University Press, 1964).

[3] In much of the official correspondence regarding Prince Edward Island, the terms 'Imperial Government' and 'Colonial Government' are used to distinguish the government in England from the one in PEI. The former includes the Secretary of State for the Colonies, the Colonial Office, and other departments dealing with the colonies. 'Colonial Government' refers to the government set up on the island, which took many forms (these are discussed later in the chapter). I use this distinction throughout this chapter.

Empire and the Peasant Proprietor. Preet S. Aulakh, Oxford University Press. © Preet S. Aulakh 2025.
DOI: 10.1093/9780198928270.003.0008

After extensive correspondence between England, Prince Edward Island, and Ottawa, and with fierce resistance by the colony's landowners, the Imperial Government approved two Acts passed by the Prince Edward Island legislature: the Tenants' Compensation Act of 1872 and the Land Purchase Act of 1875. The former, modelled on the Irish Land Act of 1870, established a tenant's claim for compensation from the landlord for improvements made on the leased land at the 'expiration of his lease or upon the legal determination of his tenancy, by any act of himself or his landlord'.[4] The latter Act mandated the compulsory purchase of all landholdings over 500 acres. Compensation to the proprietors was to be determined by three commissioners, one each appointed by the Governor-General of Canada, the Colonial Government, and the individual proprietor. The government would sell the appropriated land to the tenants, thus converting their tenures from leasehold to freehold.[5] It is apparent from the letters written by the proprietors to the Imperial Government protesting each Act that they considered them a subversion of their rights to property:

> [B]y the [Tenants' Compensation] Act . . . it appears . . . that every axiom and rule, constitutional or prescriptive of the ancient common law and statute of Great Britain, with regard to real property and its rights . . . are at once to be swept away and annihilated.[6]

> There is no exaggeration in calling [the Land Purchase Act] . . . an Act of Confiscation. It is treatment that never yet has been inflicted on the unoffending owners of land in a peaceful Province. We have heard of wholesale confiscations of land in former times in our country, in Ireland, and in other countries; but it has always been under the pretense that the expelled owners were traitors, and had engaged in rebellion.[7]

The process of approving these laws and their specific clauses raises two questions. First, why did the Imperial Government encourage the use of the provisions of the Irish Land Act regarding compensation for improvements to provide security of tenure to the tenants, being fully aware that the long-standing objective of the Prince Edward Island legislature was to provide security through the conversion of leasehold to freehold tenures? Second, why did the Imperial Government sanction a more extreme form of abrogation of rights in Prince Edward Island in 1875, that

[4] 'The Tenants' Compensation Act, 1872', Pub. L. No. Cap. X (1872).

[5] 'Land Purchase Act, 1875', Pub. L. No. Cap. XXXII (1875).

[6] A letter signed by eighteen proprietors was sent to the Secretary of State for the Colonies requesting the withholding of the Royal Assent to the Tenants' Compensation Bill. Reproduced in 'Correspondence Relative to the Land Tenure Question in Prince Edward Island' (Presented to both Houses of Parliament by Command of Her Majesty, August 1875), 13, British Parliamentary Papers.

[7] Letter from Lady Georgina Fane, a proprietor in Prince Edward Island, to the Colonial Office, November 25, 1874, protesting the compulsory purchase of land legislation under consideration. Reproduced in 'Correspondence Relative to the Land Tenure Question in Prince Edward Island', 43–44.

is, the state-facilitated transfer of property rights of unwilling proprietors, given its reluctance to entertain the milder 'three Fs' (fixity of tenure, fair rent, and freedom of sale) that would have at most acknowledged co-proprietorship of landlords and tenants in Ireland a few years earlier? While the existing historiography has not addressed the first question,[8] the following arguments regarding the second question have been made in the literature.

The received view is that the colony's conversion from leasehold to freehold tenure followed North America's land tenure norms: 'Islanders breathed the air of North America, where freehold tenure was the norm. Rent-paying was anathema, identified with the Old World, and believed inconsistent with a spirit of independence.'[9] This natural propensity towards freehold tenures gained momentum by the end of the 1860s because of a political alignment in Prince Edward Island between political and sectarian groups, which provided a unified position against leasehold tenure.[10] In this regard, the colony's negotiations leading to and after joining the Dominion of Canada allowed the local government to use its 'legislative power to trump the "sacred rights" of property and break the concentrations of land ownership on the Island'[11] and also have the necessary financial wherewithal to buy out the landlords through the $800,000 loan provided as part of the Confederation agreement.[12] Accordingly, the 'settlement of the century-old land question was the greatest blessing that the Island received from the terms granted by the Dominion.'[13]

Legislative freedom from 'direct supervision of the British Government'[14] after joining the Confederation was also the rationale given by the Secretary of State for the Colonies[15] during a debate in the House of Lords regarding the approval

[8] Passing references are made about tenant Compensation Acts in a few studies, and it is generally assumed that these were fleeting attempts to deal with the land question on the way to complete conversion of leasehold to freehold tenures. For example, see Ian Ross Robertson, 'Introduction', in *The Prince Edward Land Commission of 1860*, ed. Ian Ross Robertson (Fredericton, N.B.: Acadiensis Press, 1988), ix–xxx; Margaret E. McCallum, 'The Sacred Rights of Property: Title, Entitlement, and the Land Question in Nineteenth-Century Prince Edward Island', in *Essays in the History of Canadian Law in Honour of R.C.B. Risk*, ed. G. Blaine Baker and Jim Phillips, vol. VIII (Toronto: University of Toronto Press, 1999), 358–97; Rusty Bittermann and Margaret McCallum, 'Upholding the Land Legislation of a "Communistic and Socialist Assembly": The Benefits of Confederation for Prince Edward Island', *The Canadian Historical Review* 81, no. 1–15 (2006): 31–56.

[9] Ian Ross Robertson, *The Tenant League of Prince Edward Island, 1864–1867: Leasehold Tenure in the New World* (Toronto; Buffalo; London: University of Toronto Press, 1996), 7.

[10] Ian Ross Robertson, 'Political Realignment in Pre-Confederation Prince Edward Island, 1863–1870', *Acadiensis* 15, no. 1 (1985): 35–58; Robertson, *The Tenant League of Prince Edward Island, 1864–1867*.

[11] Bittermann and McCallum, 'Upholding the Land Legislation of a "Communistic and Socialist Assembly"', 15.

[12] Bolger, *Prince Edward Island and Confederation, 1863–1873*, 292.

[13] Francis W. P. Bolger, 'Long Courted, Won at Last', in *Canada's Smallest Province: A History of P.E.I.*, ed. Francis W. P. Bolger (Charlottetown: Prince Edward Island 1973 Centennial Commission, 1973), 230.

[14] McCallum, 'The Sacred Rights of Property', 364–65.

[15] By the time this Act was approved, the Liberal government of Gladstone had been replaced by the Conservative government led by Disraeli, and it had appointed a new Secretary of State for the Colonies.

by the Imperial Government to the Land Purchase Act of 1875. He emphasised that the Act was 'passed by the Colonial Legislature of Prince Edward Island, and which consequently receives the sanction, not of the Crown through the Imperial Government at home, but the sanction of the Governor-General of Canada'.[16]

Numerous studies support the narrative of viewing the Prince Edward Island land question primarily from the perspective of the prevalent conditions in North America, both regarding the political situation related to the Dominion of Canada and the norm of freehold land tenures.[17] This chapter probes the two questions in tandem and through a wider lens. It suggests that from the viewpoint of the Empire, the land question in Prince Edward Island had components that were like those of its other colonies, even those beyond North America. It had to be mindful of the impact of any legislation sanctioned for Prince Edward Island on land tenures across its colonies and political implications at home. Thus, in considering the legislation involving tenant rights and peasant proprietorship initiated by the colony's legislature, the Imperial Government took a dual-track approach in resolving the PEI land question, both involving inter-colony analogies. From 1870 to 1872, it used the Irish Land Act as a model to establish tenant compensation in Prince Edward Island, a period when it was uncertain whether the colony would join the Dominion of Canada. After Prince Edward Island joined the Dominion in July 1873, the Imperial Government absolved itself of its land question on the pretext that the Dominion had the right to resolve land tenure issues based on local considerations under the new governance arrangement. In both cases, the Empire attempted to disconnect the PEI land question from conditions in England by linking it to either the one being considered for Ireland (tenant right) or the one that seemed to be the norm in North America (freehold tenure). Through this dual approach, based on inter-colony analogies rather than precedents from England, the Imperial Government hedged its bets and hoped that the new laws in Prince Edward Island would help in realising its overall objective of extending peasant proprietorship across the Empire while at the same time minimising any political fallout emanating from potential threats to aristocratic rights and privileges in England.

16 Response by the Secretary of State for the Colonies, the Earl of Carnavaron, to a question in the House of Lords, July 26, 1875, on concerns about and implications of the Land Purchase Act on the property rights of landowners in PEI. Reproduced in 'Correspondence Relative to the Land Tenure Question in Prince Edward Island', 49.

17 See, for example, John McLaren, A. R. Buck, and Nancy E. Wright, 'Property Rights in the Colonial Imagination and Experience', in *Despotic Dominion' Property Rights in British Settler Societies*, ed. John McLaren, A. R. Buck, and Nancy E. Wright (Vancouver, B.C.: University of British Columbia Press, 2005), 1–21. Bittermann and McCallum, 'Upholding the Land Legislation of a "Communistic and Socialist Assembly"'.

Irish Precedents for the Tenants' Compensation Act, 1872

Persistent efforts in Prince Edward Island to eliminate landlordism established under British rule in 1767 yielded no substantial results until the middle of the nineteenth century. For much of this period, the thinking on property rights and the political economy of land tenure amongst Imperial Governments was unitary, that is, absolute rights of the landowners and efficiency of large landholdings, and all attempts to establish any tenurial rights of the cultivators were resisted. With the formation of the Liberal Government in England under William Gladstone in 1868, the PEI Executive Council tried again with the new Secretary of State for the Colonies, the Earl of Granville. In its address, the Council argued that 'numerous precedents may be quoted, in which private property has been dealt with by law when its possession by individuals proved inimical to the public interests... If... the commutation of their leasehold tenures was conceded to the people of Lower Canada... as a matter of justice or policy, can a like privilege be refused to the loyal people of Prince Edward Island?'[18] In addition, the Council requested that the Imperial Government guarantee a loan of 100,000 to 150,000 pounds for purchasing wilderness lands on the Island. While conveying to the Colonial Government the low possibility of a loan guarantee, the thrust of Granville's response was meant to put subtle pressure on Prince Edward Island to join the Confederation:[19]

> Having regard to the evident uncertainty whether the Colony of Prince Edward Island will or will not soon unite itself to the Dominion of Canada, I am not prepared to enter on the consideration of a question with which, if such union were to ensue, the Imperial Government would probably cease to concern itself, the Land Question, therefore, should, in my opinion, be left as far as possible for the decision of those who, under the altered circumstances of the colony, would have to carry out the execution any measures connected with it.[20]

While the Prince Edward Island Government was pondering in early 1870 the course it would take on joining the Confederation, considering its negotiations with the Dominion and the local public opinion on the issue, an opportunity arose for it to make legislative headway on the question of compensation for tenants

[18] Minute or Address of the Executive Council of Prince Edward Island to the Secretary of State for the Colonies about Land Tenures, February 6, 1869. Reproduced in 'Journal of the House of Assembly of Prince Edward Island, 1866', Appendix S.

[19] The letter in which the Imperial Government stated its position that the land question in Prince Edward Island would not be under its purview if the colony joined the Dominion of Canada was cited by the PEI legislature on numerous occasions to push the compulsory land purchase legislation after 1873. This is discussed below.

[20] Letter from Secretary of State for the Colonies to the Lieutenant Governor of Prince Edward Island, March 13, 1869. Reproduced in 'Journal of the House of Assembly of Prince Edward Island, 1869', Appendix S.

which had been on the back burner since the last attempt in 1855. There was excitement in Prince Edward Island about the legislation being contemplated by Gladstone to institutionalise tenants' rights in Ireland.[21] Accordingly, an address was sent to the Queen in April 1870 stating that many tenants in Prince Edward Island held short-term leases and were therefore 'exposed to the grievous hardship and losing the hard-earned fruits of many years industry and economy' at their expiry. Having heard that 'Gladstone had introduced a Bill into the Commons house, which provides for the compensation of tenants in Ireland who may be evicted from their lands on which they may have made valuable improvements', the address prayed for a similar measure that could be sanctioned for the tenantry in Prince Edward Island.[22] The response from the Secretary of State for the Colonies, Granville (who was himself shepherding the Irish Land Act through the House of Lords during that time), was encouraging. He wrote that while he was 'not prepared to express any general opinion or to give fresh instructions to the Lieutenant-Governor respecting the settlement of this difficult question', he would give his best attention to any measure prepared in the legislature embracing the 'principal provisions of the Bill introduced in the Imperial Parliament' for Irish tenants.[23]

Encouraged by Granville's response, the Prince Edward Island Government introduced a Bill that passed unanimously in the PEI House of Assembly and the Legislative Council in April 1871.[24] The Tenants' Compensation Act[25] was sent to the Secretary of State for the Colonies for approval by the Imperial Government,[26] along with a Minute from the Executive Council of Prince Edward Island providing a rationale for the bill and a petition by several proprietors requesting its disallowance.[27]

[21] For details, see 'The Parliamentary Reporter! Or Debates and Proceedings of the House of Assembly of Prince Edward Island for the Year 1870' (Charlottetown: Patriot Book and Job Printing Rooms, 1870); 'Debates and Proceedings of the Legislative Council of Prince Edward Island for the Session of 1870' (Charlottetown: F. W. Hughes, 1870); 'Journal of the House of Assembly of Prince Edward Island, 1870' (Charlottetown: Thomas Reilly, 1870).

[22] Address to Her Majesty the Queen by the Legislative Council of Prince Edward Island, April 18, 1870. Reproduced in 'Debates and Proceedings of the Legislative Council of Prince Edward Island for the Session of 1870', 1870, 123–34.

[23] Letter from Granville to Government of PEI, July 10, 1870. Reproduced in 'Correspondence Relative to the Land Tenure Question in Prince Edward Island', 3.

[24] For debates and discussions around the provisions of the bill in the House of Assembly and the Legislative Council, see 'Debates and Proceedings of the Legislative Council of Prince Edward Island for the Session of 1870', 'The Parliamentary Reporter! Or Debates and Proceedings of the House of Assembly of Prince Edward Island for the Year 1870' (Charlottetown: Patriot Book and Job Printing Rooms, 1870). The primary thrust of the debates was the inclusion of appropriate provisions that would be acceptable to the Imperial Government given that the previous attempt to legislate compensation for tenants in 1855 was disallowed.

[25] The Tenants' Compensation Act, 1871, PUB. L. No. Cap. IX (1871).

[26] In his letter to the Secretary of the State for the Colonies dated April 17, 1871, the Lieutenant-Governor gave his provisional assent to the bill, but at the same conveyed his concerns about the 'Act as an improper interference with the rights of property and opposed to the general principles of the law of contracts'. Letter from Robinson to Kimberley, April 17, 1871. Reproduced in 'Correspondence Relative to the Land Tenure Question in Prince Edward Island'.

[27] The minutes and petitions are reproduced in 'Correspondence Relative to the Land Tenure Question in Prince Edward Island', 5–10.

The main provisions of the Act were: (1) compensation for permanent improvements at the end of the lease for 'any tenant occupying lands under a lease or agreement, verbal or in writing, or any memorandum of agreement whereby any term or estate is reserved to the landlord, which lands shall have been in a wilderness or unimproved state when the possession was given'; (2) tenant applies to Supreme Court who appoints three arbitrators to determine the compensation for improvements (which could include clearing the land, new buildings, works to increase the productive power of the land, etc.). The award could be appealed to the Supreme Court by either party; (3) the landlord to have fourteen days to decide after the award is made as to whether he will pay the compensation, or instead grant a lease of 999 years to the tenant at the last year's rent; (4) compensation can only be claimed by the original tenant who made the improvements; and (5) there was to be no entitlement for tenants where tenancy had been forfeited for non-payment of rent or breach of other conditions. In the explanatory minute accompanying the Act, the Executive Council acknowledged that most of the leases on the Island were for 999 years, and the 'grievances intended to be redressed are those whose lands have been granted to tenants on lease for short terms'. These twenty- to forty-year leases were insufficient to clear the wilderness land and recoup the investments made to make the land productive (unlike in the mother country where tenants cultivated more developed land). It further suggested that tenants on short leases could not avail of the purchase opportunity given in the Fifteen Years' Purchase Act of 1864.

The landlords' petition to the Imperial Government reiterated the same points that were made in their opposition to the 1855 Act (that is, the prevalence of long leases in Prince Edward Island, and low rent paid by the tenants), and in addition, highlighted that it was the landowners who invested in roads, bridges, etc. It was these investments that increased the value of the land.[28] The Secretary of State for the Colonies, the Earl of Kimberley,[29] who succeeded Granville in July 1870, declined assent not because of the landlords' objections, but because the Act went far beyond the one passed by the British Parliament for Ireland and identified specific provisions that needed to be brought in line with the Irish Act.[30] His first primary concern was regarding the options available to the landlord: pay compensation or give a lease for 999 years. '[T]he provision by which the only alternative left to the landlord . . . is open to the gravest objection. It would compel the landlord to

[28] Memorial and Petition of Mr. Stewart and others to the Earl of Kimberley, June 10, 1871. Reproduced in 'Correspondence Relative to the Land Tenure Question in Prince Edward Island', 7–10.

[29] Kimberley had served as the Lord Lieutenant of Ireland in the 1860s and had been actively involved in assisting Gladstone in the Disestablishment of the Church of Ireland. See 'Wodehouse, John, First Earl of Kimberley (1826–1902), Politician', *Oxford Dictionary of National Biography* (Oxford, UK: Oxford University Press).

[30] Letter from the Earl of Kimberley to Lieutenant Governor Robinson, sated September 2, 1871. Reproduced in 'Correspondence Relative to the Land Tenure Question in Prince Edward Island', 10–11.

transfer the ownership of the land to the tenant in every case where he might be unable or unwilling to purchase the tenant's improvements.' He cited section 21 of the Irish Land Act of 1870, whereby a tenant 'who may be decided by the Court to be entitled to compensation by the landlord cannot be compelled by process of law to quit his holding until the amount of compensation due to him has been paid to him or deposited; but, on the other hand, under that Act, the landlord retains his right to re-enter upon the land at any time, subject to the condition of compensating the tenant for his improvements'. He further cited the Irish Land Act of 1870 regarding time limits within which improvements were made, compulsory arbitration in the PEI Act 1853, especially by people who may be impartial towards the landlords, and more precise rules of determining improvements.

Kimberley concluded that while many of the 'provisions of the Irish Act are inapplicable to Prince Edward Island', especially ones related to customary tenant rights, 'those sections which relate to improvements seem . . . to afford the basis upon which, with the necessary alterations, a measure might be framed with advantage to the Colony', and to which he might advise the Queen Majesty to give her assent. Such an act 'would give reasonable satisfaction to the tenants' claims without depriving the landlords of their rights'.

Despite the disappointment of the fate of the 1871 Act, the PEI legislature was encouraged by the tone of the letter communicating the disallowance, with one member noting that it 'was of a much milder nature' than they had ever seen from the Colonial Office upon the Land Question.[31] Another member pointed out that Granville's letter reflected that 'the views and intentions of the British Government are changing on that subject. They now concede the injustice of the way in which the Island was granted away'.[32] The PEI Government proposed another bill, the Tenants' Compensation Act of 1872, which was approved unanimously by the House and Legislative Council. This Act embodied Kimberley's suggestions, and its overall principles and specific provisions were mostly similar to those of the relevant sections (that is, those involving landlord-tenant relationships based on contracts) of the Irish Land Act.[33] In particular, the new Act removed the requirement of a 999-year lease instead of compensation, formalised the presumption that the tenants made improvements, and allowed the deduction of rent arrears from

[31] 'Debates and Proceedings of the Legislative Council of Prince Edward Island for the Session of 1872' (Charlottetown: Henry Cooper, 1872) June 14, 1872: 78.

[32] 'Debates and Proceedings of the Legislative Council of Prince Edward Island for the Session of 1872', June 14, 1872: 82.

[33] For a section-by-section comparison of the PEI and Irish Acts, see a letter written by the Solicitor-General of PEI, Louis H. Davies, to the President of the PEI Executive Council, dated November 21, 1872. Reproduced in 'Correspondence Relative to the Land Tenure Question in Prince Edward Island', 21–23 The letter was written in response to a petition by several proprietors (see pages 12–15) who argued that the proposed act had diverged from the instructions of the Secretary of State for the Colonies.

the compensation for improvement. It further clarified the role of the Supreme Court and arbitrators in determining the compensation amounts.

The Secretary of State for the Colonies and the Lieutenant-Governor of Prince Edward Island received numerous petitions from proprietors, either individually or in groups, arguing for the disallowance of the Act.[34] After another iteration of two amendments/additions,[35] the Secretary of State transmitted to the Governor-General of Canada that the two acts had received the Royal Assent. Since the PEI legislature passed the main Act of 1872 before the colony joined the Dominion of Canada on July 1, 1873, the final approval for the Act and its amendment lay with the Colonial Office.[36]

Thus, during the period of uncertainty about whether Prince Edward Island would join the Dominion, the Imperial Government encouraged and consented to a piece of legislation granting some security for the tenants because of the improvements made by them on the land they occupied.[37] The provisions of the Tenants' Compensation Act of 1872 closely followed the Irish Land Act of 1870. Since the Imperial Government instructed the local legislature to use the Irish precedent to craft the tenants' Compensation Bill for PEI, questions about the appropriateness of inter-colonial analogies arose during the debates around the Bill in the legislature and subsequent memorials from proprietors. The proprietors argued that the land tenure conditions in Prince Edward Island were very different from those in Ireland given the excess of land available relative to its demand in PEI, thus 'enabling the tenant to make his own terms with the landlord', including that of long leases and low rents, while in Ireland 'the population being in excess of the area to be occupied, causes the tenantry to outbid one another in their offers of rent'.[38] Further, they pointed out that the primary rationale behind the Irish Act was to

[34] See Inclosures 1, 3, and in No. 6 (pages 12–26) and Inclosures 1 and 2 in No. 7 (pages 29–31), in 'Correspondence Relative to the Land Tenure Question in Prince Edward Island'.

[35] An Act to alter and amend 'The Tenants' Compensation Act, 1872'.

[36] For the relative responsibility of the Colonial Office and the Governor General of Canada in approving the PEI legislation before and after it joined the Dominion, see the exchange of letters between Kimberley and Dufferin in the latter part of 1873. Reproduced in 'Correspondence Relative to the Land Tenure Question in Prince Edward Island', 33–35.

[37] This period also coincided with the Red River Rebellion to the west of the Dominion, which also involved a resistance to Imperial land tenures and trading rights established in the seventeenth century. For more details comparing the two movements (in PEI and the Red River settlement), see J. M. Bumsted, 'Island Resistance: Two Popular Movements for Political Change in the Era of Confederation', *Acadiensis* 27, no. 2 (1998): 135–41. However, from the archives it is not clear whether the Imperial Government perceived any connections between the two movements.

[38] The Memorial and Petition by sixteen proprietors addressed to the Secretary of State for the Colonies regarding the Tenants' Compensation Act, 1872. Reproduced in 'Correspondence Relative to the Land Tenure Question in Prince Edward Island', 12–15; The more favourable conditions of tenure enjoyed by the tenants in PEI compared to those in Ireland was also noted by John Francis Maguire, a Member of Parliament in the British Parliament from Ireland in the book that he published after a visit to North America in 1867. In particular, he identified the extremely low rents and long leases prevalent in PEI. For details see Chapter II of John Francis Maguire, *Irish in America* (New York: D&J Sadlier, 1873).

give tenants a fixity of tenure, which already existed for tenants in Prince Edward Island under the norm of longer leases.[39]

On the other hand, discussions in the PEI legislature foregrounded similarities between tenants' conditions in the two colonies. For instance, in response to the proprietors' petitions, the Executive Council of Prince Edward Island noted that '[i]nsecurity of tenure produce[d] the same effects in Prince Edward Island which are observed in Ireland and elsewhere, and demand[ed] the same remedy – a Tenants' Compensation Bill'. It further reiterated that they were 'not demanding for the tenants of Prince Edward Island any greater privileges than the tenants of land in Ireland enjoy, though if the extent of such privileges depended on the relative difficulties and hardships which have been surmounted, as Mr. Gladstone seems to intimate, then the tenants of this island . . . would be entitled to the more complete freedom of tenure'.[40]

In essence, unlike the 1855 Act, where discussions took place around the differences and similarities between Prince Edward Island and Britain concerning landlord–tenant relationships, the 1872 Act invoked a comparison between Prince Edward Island and Ireland. Thus, Ireland came into the discussions more centrally. The landlords continued to emphasise that any form of compensation for tenants needed to be evaluated based on universally accepted property rights (those prevalent in England), and the Irish land law was to be considered an exception. On the other hand, the PEI legislature and the Colonial Office saw similarities between land tenure arrangements for tenants in Prince Edward Island and Ireland. Hence, the appropriateness of the Irish Land Act as a relevant precedent for the 1872 Act.

Shadow of the Dominion and the Land Purchase Act of 1875

While the Imperial Government contemplated approving the Compensation Acts, Prince Edward Island decided to join the Dominion of Canada on July 1, 1873.[41] Any Act passed by the colonial legislature under the new political arrangement would have to go for approval from the Governor-General of Canada on the advice of the Dominion government. Prince Edward Island's decision to join the Dominion in 1873 had more to do with economic necessity than public support,

[39] Letter from Georgina Fane to the Earl of Kimberley, March 29, 1873, protesting the injustice of the 1872 Compensation Act. Reproduced in 'Correspondence Relative to the Land Tenure Question in Prince Edward Island', 29–30.

[40] Extract from the Minutes of the Executive Council of Prince Edward Island addressed to the Lieutenant-Governor, December 28, 1872. Reproduced in 'Correspondence Relative to the Land Tenure Question in Prince Edward Island', 23–24.

[41] Bolger, 'Prince Edward Island Rejects Confederation, 1864–1867', in *Canada's Smallest Province*, 156–84; Bolger, 'Long Courted, Won at Last'; Bolger, *Prince Edward Island and Confederation, 1863–1873*; MacKinnon, *The Government of Prince Edward Island*.

as the 'great majority of the people . . . did not take up the question *cum amore*, and when the day arrived that the union was a *fait accompli*, they did not have a cheer to give'.[42] The immediate financial crisis was the massive debt the PEI Government had taken to build an elaborate railways network on the Island in 1871. The costs of building the network by 1872 far exceeded the initial projections. The local government saw no way out other than to reconsider the offer on the table from the Dominion. The proposal included Canada assuming PEI's railway debt and finishing the project, starting a steamship service to connect the Island with the mainland, and guaranteeing a loan of $800,000 to convert the remaining land from leasehold to freehold tenures.[43]

With a loan guarantee to purchase the remaining land from proprietors and the assurance given by the Secretary of State for the Colonies, Granville, in 1869 that the Imperial Governments would take a hands-off approach to the land question once Prince Edward Island became part of Canada,[44] the island legislature went to work to resolve the land question. Following the approval of a Minute by the Executive Council of PEI on November 18, 1873, circulars were sent to the proprietors (or their agents) of large estates to 'ascertain . . . the lowest price per acre, in cash, at which [they] will be prepared to sell . . . [their] Township Lands in Prince Edward Island, including all arrears in rent due thereon'.[45] The responses from the proprietors were mixed; a few did not want to sell their estates, some were willing to entertain selling if the whole land could be sold at once at a reasonable price, and others wanted the government to make an offer. Some proprietors provided specific demands regarding the number of acres that could be sold and their price. Prices ranged from 16s per acre, $4 per acre, 1250 pounds sterling for 1000 acres, fifteen years' rent plus arrears, etc.

Refusal by the proprietors to voluntarily sell their land led to the passing of the Land Purchase Act, 1874, which made it mandatory for 'any proprietor owning or possessing five hundred acres of land, or upwards' to offer the land for sale. The government and the proprietor would each appoint a commissioner, who would then choose a third person to serve on the three-person panel. This panel will determine the purchase price based on several factors (for example, the cost of land

[42] Editorial in the Patriot, July 3, 1873. Cited in Bolger, 'Long Courted, Won at Last', 230 [italics in original].

[43] 'Minutes of Conference between the Committee of the Privy Council of Canada, and the Undersigned Delegates from the Colony of Prince Edward Island, on the Subject of the Union of That Province with the Dominion of Canada', *Royal Gazette*, March 17, 1873.

[44] This letter of Granville was invoked numerous times during the debates in Prince Edward Island's House of Assembly and Legislative Council leading up to the Land Purchase Act of 1874. See 'The Parliamentary Reporter! Or Debates and Proceedings of the House of Assembly of Prince Edward Island for the Year 1874' (Charlottetown: J. H. Fletcher, 1874); 'Debates and Proceedings of the Legislative Council of Prince Edward Island for the Session of 1874' (Charlottetown: Macgowan & Haszard, Printers, 1874).

[45] For correspondence with the various proprietors, see 'Journal of the House of Assembly of Prince Edward Island, 1875' (Charlottetown: Henry Cooper, 1875) Appendix I.

in the vicinity, the number of acres leased and the length of the leases, rents paid and arrears, etc.) to make the award to the proprietor.[46]

The proprietors were up in arms against the proposed legislation. They wrote numerous petitions to both the office of the Governor-General of Canada in Ottawa and the Colonial Office in London, characterising the Act as the 'most radical attack upon the rights of property', 'an outrage against modern civilization', and 'one . . . that could only emanate from a Communist or Socialist Assembly', among others.[47] The Earl of Dufferin was the Governor-General of Canada at the time, having been appointed to the office in the summer of 1872 by Gladstone. As proprietor of a large estate in Ireland, he was sympathetic to the landlords and had reluctantly supported the Irish Land Act in 1870.[48] However, with the fall of the Gladstone government in England in early 1874, the new Conservative government appointed Henry Herbert, the Fourth Earl of Carnarvon, as the Secretary of State for the Colonies. Carnarvon was well versed with the Empire's North American colonies, having served in the same capacity from 1864 to 1867 during the negotiations around the Confederation.[49] After consulting with the Dominion government[50] and Carnarvon,[51] Dufferin declined assent to the Land Purchase Act of 1874 because it did not 'provide for an impartial arbitration, in which the proprietors would have a representation, for deciding on the nature of rights, and the value of the property involved, and also for securing a speedy determination

[46] Land Purchase Act, 1874; For debates on the specific provisions of the Act, including whether the compulsory purchase should be lands over 500 or 1,000 acres, see 'The Parliamentary Reporter! Or Debates and Proceedings of the House of Assembly of Prince Edward Island for the Year 1874'; 'Debates and Proceedings of the Legislative Council of Prince Edward Island for the Session of 1872'.

[47] For a collection of these petitions to both offices, see 'Correspondence Relative to the Land Tenure Question in Prince Edward Island'; Appendix (E) 'Journal of the House of Assembly of Prince Edward Island, 1875'.

[48] For the role played by Dufferin on the PEI land question, his overall approach to land tenure issues across the Empire, as well ideas on the governance of the colonies, see Annie Tindley, *Lord Dufferin, Ireland and the British Empire, c. 1820–1900: Rule by the Best?* (London: Routledge, 2021); Bittermann and McCallum, 'Upholding the Land Legislation of a "Communistic and Socialist Assembly"'; Richard Davenport-Hines, 'Blackwood, Frederick Temple Hamilton-Temple-, First Marquess of Dufferin and Ava (1826–1902), Diplomatist', *Oxford Dictionary of National Biography* (Oxford, UK: Oxford University Press, 2008); Andrew Gailey, *The Lost Imperialist: Lord Dufferin, Memory and Mythmaking in an Age of Celebrity* (London: John Murray Press, 2015).

[49] For details, see Peter Gordon, 'Herbert, Henry Howard Molyneux, Fourth Earl of Carnarvon (1831–1890), Politician', *Oxford Dictionary of National Biography* (Oxford, UK: Oxford University Press, 2008).

[50] See Memo from the Deputy Minister of Justice, dated December 23, 1874, evaluating the specific provisions of the Land Purchase Act, 1874 'Correspondence Relative to the Land Tenure Question in Prince Edward Island'. For more extensive opinions on the said Act within the Dominion government, see 'Sessional Papers. Second Session of the Third Parliament of the Dominion of Canada, Volume VIII', 1875.

[51] For the extensive correspondence between Dufferin and Carnarvon regarding the PEI land question as well as other aspects of governance in British North America, see C. W. De Kiewiet and Frank H. Underhill, eds., *Dufferin-Carnarvon Correspondence, 1874–1878* (Toronto: The Champlain Society, 1955).

and settlement of the matters in dispute'.[52] Objecting more to the procedure in determining the awards rather than the principle of compulsory purchase, Dufferin took the suggestion given by Carnarvon in a secret dispatch[53] and recommended that the third Commissioner (the other two being chosen by the PEI Government and the respective proprietor) should be appointed by the Governor-General.

Taking into consideration the objections raised by Dufferin on procedural aspects and those by the proprietors on the wording of the Preamble (which laid the blame on the landlords to come to a satisfactory solution to the land question in PEI),[54] the legislature passed another bill, the Land Purchase Act, 1875.[55] Dufferin gave this Act assent despite another round of petitions from the proprietors.[56] With the approval of the Act and the appointment of Commissioners, the task of finally forcing the large landholders to sell their property to the State was initiated.[57] Some landlords contested their awards in the Supreme Courts of PEI and Canada but without success.[58] The judgment of the Supreme Court of Canada to the final appeal from a proprietor reiterated the long-debated question in Prince Edward Island regarding the need to balance private property rights with the public good:

> The [Land Purchase Act] . . . ought . . . to be viewed . . . as the settling of an important question of great moment to the community, and in principle like the abolition of the Seigniorial tenure in Lower Canada, and the settling of the land question in Ireland. In carrying out measure as these, there may be cases where the law works harshly, where important rights may seem to be disregarded, and private interests are made to yield to the public good.[59]

[52] Letter from the office of the Governor General of Canada to the Lieutenant Governor of Prince Edward Island, December 19, 1874. Reproduced in Appendix (E) of 'Journal of the House of Assembly of Prince Edward Island, 1875'.

[53] Letter from Earl of Carnarvon to Earl of Dufferin, November 2, 1874. Reproduced in 'Correspondence Relative to the Land Tenure Question in Prince Edward Island'.

[54] The Preamble to the 1875 merely mentioned that the land purchase was being initiated because of the terms negotiated with respect to the colony joining the Confederation.

[55] Land Purchase Act, 1875.

[56] Letter from Dufferin to Carnarvon, May 14, 1875. Reproduced in 'Correspondence Relative to the Land Tenure Question in Prince Edward Island'.

[57] The implementation of the Act was the responsibility of the province and the Dominion, with no specific obligations of the Imperial Government. Much of the correspondence between the Governor-General of Canada and the Colonial Office after the former gave assent was more informational (especially regarding the happenings in the two courts) rather than with any substantive aspect. See 'Further Correspondence Relative to the Land Tenure Question in Prince Edward Island', April 1876, House of Commons Parliamentary Papers Online.

[58] The period after the passage of the Act, including the work of the Commissioners, the awards, and subsequent legal contestations, has been extensively examined in numerous studies. For some representative work, see Bittermann and McCallum, 'Upholding the Land Legislation of a "Communistic and Socialist Assembly"'; Bittermann and McCallum, *Lady Landlords of Prince Edward Island*; Rusty Bittermann, 'Lady Landlords and the Final Defence of Landlordism on Prince Edward Island: The Case of Charlotte Sulivan', *Histoire Sociale/Social History* 38, no. 76 (2005): 204–33.

[59] Canada Supreme Court judgment on the case involving the commissioners' award of land purchase of the Charlotte Sulivan. In *Judgment of the Supreme Court of Canada on the Appeal from the Judgment of the Supreme Court of Prince Edward Island Setting aside the Award of the Commissioners under the Land Purchase Act 1875, in the Case of Charlotte Antonia Sulivan* (Charlottetown: Henry Lawson, 1877), 17.

From the perspective of Prince Edward Island, the Land Purchase Act of 1875 finally resolved the more than a hundred-year contestation over the initial land grants and the creation of a class of large landlords. It brought its land tenure system closer to that which existed in North America. However, from the viewpoint of the Empire, the expropriation of land from unwilling proprietors, even if it entailed adequate compensation, went against preserving the sanctity of property rights that had been the bedrock of its land tenure policies at home and across its colonies. The Imperial Government had promoted an alternative way to resolve the land question in 1872 by acknowledging co-proprietorship through tenants' rights to compensation for improvements in case Prince Edward Island decided not to join the Dominion and continued as an independent colony. However, Prince Edward Island's decision to become part of the Dominion and the promise made by Granville of non-interference on the land question in 1869 in case the colony joined the union left the Imperial Government no choice but to consent to the Act in 1875. The main task for the Colonial Office and the Governor-General of Canada now was to minimise the impact of their acceding to the 'Communistic' piece of legislation in other colonies and answer questions at home about their commitment to protecting property rights. The Imperial Government (through the Colonial and the Governor-General of Canada's offices) took a multi-pronged approach to justify its decision and absolve itself from these potential repercussions.

It attributed its decision to the difficulties brought upon themselves by proprietors because of their reluctance to fulfil the obligations under the original grants. For example, while being challenged in the House of Lords on his decision to support the Land Act of 1875, Carnarvon blamed the PEI landlords for non-compliance to the conditions and their absenteeism, leading to a situation that 'property which was lightly won was lightly treated'.[60] Dufferin, on the other hand, attributed the land problems in Prince Edward Island to the different norms in North America, writing to the Colonial Office in 1874 that '[p]roprietorial rights, in the sense in which they exist in England, are very unsuitable to the atmosphere of this country, and I imagine a perpetual agitation will prevail in this island until its land tenures are assimilated to those of neighbouring provinces'.[61]

To soften the blow of compulsory land purchase on the proprietors, the Imperial Government attempted to ensure procedural fairness in their dealings with the Commissioners and the Prince Edward Island Land Commission, which oversaw the post-award formalities. The insistence on having the Governor-General's appointee as one of the three commissioners was meant to protect the landlords' interest. Dufferin chose Hugh Childers, a respected member of the British Parliament, as his nominee. In his request to Childers to take on the task, Dufferin

[60] Response by the Earl of Carnarvon in the House of Lords, July 26, 1875, to a question from a member. Reproduced in 'Correspondence Relative to the Land Tenure Question in Prince Edward Island', 47–49.

[61] Letter from Dufferin to Holland in the Colonial Office, June 9, 1874. Cited in Tindley, *Lord Dufferin, Ireland and the British Empire, c. 1820–1900*, 128.

emphasised the importance of his appointment to the perceived fairness of the process to all parties because Childers' role in passing the Irish land bill in 1870 rendered him 'acceptable to the Anti-Landlord party, while the proprietors themselves would feel that, inasmuch as something has to be done, they would probably never be likely to find themselves in safer hands'.[62]

Furthermore, the Imperial Government tried to distance itself from the compulsory land legislation by emphasising that because of the new political arrangements with the Dominion of Canada, it had no authority to interfere with its internal matters. The standard response of the Colonial Office to the petitions coming from the proprietors on the Land Purchase Act was that 'the land question in Prince Edward Island is not one with which the Secretary of State is authorised to deal by the Constitution of Canada: but the decision in this matter rests with the Governor-General of Canada',[63] who takes advice from the Dominion Government.

Despite these attempts, Dufferin and Carnarvon could not escape the scrutiny in England on the impingement of property rights in the British Empire under their watch. As noted by the *Saturday Review*:

> The compulsory transfer of property in Prince Edward Island may perhaps have alarmed nervous English landowners who have become acquainted with the transaction by occasional conversations in Parliament. The precedents of which the Irish Land Act was the first are likely to accumulate with constantly diminishing regard for rules which were once deemed immutable. Every separate Act of interference with property is excused, and perhaps justified, by the special circumstances of the case; but the common principle that private right must yield to real or supposed public convenience acquires additional practical importance by each successive recognition of its validity ... Lord DUFFERIN and Lord CARNARVON may be acquitted of willingness to tamper with the foundations of property; but their authority will be hereafter invoked in favor of schemes for redistribution of land.[64]

****

Soon after establishing tenant rights in Punjab and Ireland, the Empire had to deal with the land question in another colony, Prince Edward Island. Like Ireland, the

[62] Letter from the Earl of Dufferin to Hugh Childers, February 23, 1875. Reproduced in Edmund Spencer Eardley Childers, *The Life and Correspondence of the Right Hon. Hugh C. E. Childers, 1827–1896* (London: J. Murray, 1901), 232.

[63] Letter dated June 26, 1875, from Colonial Office to F. C. Morgan, an MP in the House of Commons, who had forwarded a letter from one of the PEI proprietors regarding the land purchase bill. Reproduced in 'Correspondence Relative to the Land Tenure Question in Prince Edward Island', 46.

[64] 'Landed Property in Prince Edward Island', *The Saturday Review*, March 18, 1876, sec. Editorial, 355–56' [capitals in original].

land issue in Prince Edward Island had been simmering for almost a century. The two colonies also shared histories of land allocation by rank under British rule, a preponderance of well-connected absentee landlords, and persistent demands for the betterment of economically struggling tenants. The land question in Prince Edward Island, with origins in the way the whole Island was divided into 'townships' or 'lots', which were parcelled out to prominent people in 1767, was finally resolved in 1875 through an Act passed by the colonial legislature that made it compulsory for proprietors to part with their holdings that exceeded 500 acres. This chapter has probed the circumstances that led the Imperial Government to approve this extreme form of land tenure reform which entailed a forced transfer of proprietorship from landlords to tenants, especially given the opposition it had to overcome in contemplating granting tenants occupancy rights in Punjab and compensation for improvement/disturbance in Ireland, each of which entailed at most an acknowledgement of co-proprietorship of both landlords and their tenants. Most of the detailed historical accounts on the PEI land question have suggested that the Imperial Government had no other choice because of the norm of freehold tenure in the Empire's North American colonies. Finally, however, the grant of Dominion status to Canada in 1867 and the decision by PEI to become part of the Dominion in 1873 forced the Imperial Government to accede to the colony's demands, even if it meant abrogation of the property rights of landlords.

The prevailing historical accounts are based on two underlying assumptions. First, it is assumed that the Imperial Government was reacting to the evolving political situation in Prince Edward Island from the middle of the 1860s (i.e., political alignment of different political factions, all demanding an end to leasehold tenure, pressure from the Tenant League and the Fenian movement, and the new governance arrangements with the Dominion). It was politically expedient to let go of its defence of the proprietors after 1873. The second assumption is that the Empire's other colonies in North America had rid themselves of leasehold tenures. All that Prince Edward Island aspired to was to have its land tenure system compatible with these geographically proximate colonies.

In this chapter, I have attempted to unpack both assumptions. Regarding the second assumption, as shown in Figures 7.2 and 7.3 of the Chapter 7, the percentage of cultivators and acres of land under freehold tenures consistently rose in Prince Edward Island since the 1840s.[65] It could be argued that the trend in the colony was towards freehold tenures. In addition, as reported by Catharine Anne Wilson in her detailed studies on tenants in Canada, leasehold tenures persisted in

[65] The increase could be attributed to the natural commodification of land, with more and more cultivators having the wherewithal to purchase land from willing proprietors. For details on the emergence of a prosperous middle class in PEI both within the leasehold system and growing number of small freeholders, see Matthew G. Hatvany, 'Tenant, Landlord, and the New Middle Class: Settlement, Society, and Economy in Early Prince Edward Island, 1798–1848' (ProQuest Dissertations Publishing, 1996). In addition, the redistribution of land under the Land Purchase Act of 1853 had converted large acreage from leasehold to freehold.

all the colonies/provinces during the nineteenth century.[66] Progression towards freehold tenures in PEI until the end of the 1860s, and the fact that it was converging towards those in the proximate colonies, calls into question whether the primary objective in PEI was to convert leasehold to freeholds or whether it was merely to get rid of the big landlords, a large number of whom continued to be absentee landlords throughout this period.[67]

Regarding the first assumption that the Imperial Government played a reactive role, that of a gatekeeper to protect the proprietors as long as possible, this chapter has shown how it attempted to actively shape land tenure during the period of uncertainty (1867–1873) about whether PEI would continue with the existing arrangements as a separate colony of the British Empire or join the new governance arrangements as part of the Dominion of Canada. The decision of Prince Edward Island to choose the latter option probably explains the conclusion of existing scholarship that the Imperial Government's decision to consent to the provisions of the Land Purchase Act in 1875 was politically necessary and could be justified based on local analogies of freehold tenures. On the other hand, efforts on behalf of the Imperial Government by Granville and Kimberley, the two Secretaries of State for the Colonies, to shape legislation on tenants' security of tenure during the 1870–1873 period using the precedent of the Irish Land Act in case PEI remained a separate colony also shows the commitment of the Gladstone government towards its goal (similar to one in Punjab and Ireland) of institutionalising some proprietary rights of the peasant-cultivators and improve their economic wellbeing.

As was the case in Ireland, the imperial use of inter-colony analogies and precedents to push land tenure legislation in PEI also facilitated in overcoming some of the entrenched ideas about property rights and political economy that had been used to resist land tenure reforms entailing recognition of any proprietary rights of the tenants. The demands to get rid of the large landholdings in PEI started soon after the initial land grants in 1767 and continued during the next hundred years through various means (e.g., escheat, quit rents, land purchase) and agency (e.g., Escheat Movement, Tenant League), and under different local governments and governance arrangements with the Empire. For much of the period until the middle of the nineteenth century, the thinking on property rights and the political economy of land tenure amongst imperial governments was quite unitary, i.e., absolute rights of the landowners and efficiency of large landholdings, and any

[66] For example, in 1844/48, there were almost 43% farm tenants of all occupiers of rural land in Ontario, and 33.2% in Quebec. At that moment, there were 61% of farm tenants in PEI. The number of occupiers with leasehold tenure remained over 15% in Ontario until the end of the nineteenth century. See Table 3.1 in Catherine Anne Wilson, *Tenants in Time: Family Strategies, Land, and Liberalism in Upper Canada, 1799–1871* (Montreal and Kingston: McGill-Queen's University Press, 2009). Also see Catherine Anne Wilson, *New Lease on Life: Landlords, Tenants, and Immigrants in Ireland and Canada* (Montreal, CA: McGill-Queen's University Press, 1994).

[67] Matthew G. Hatvany, 'The Proprietary Burden?', *The Island Magazine* 44 (1998): 3–7.

attempts to acknowledge co-proprietorship or improvements by the cultivators were resisted across the Empire. Additionally, in the case of Prince Edward Island, supporters of landlords within the colony and wider imperial circles were able to effectively counter any attempts to infringe on the landlords' property rights because of a lack of coherent logic on property rights, shifting objectives of the land tenure reforms, and differences in the means through which land reform was to be accomplished.[68]

By the 1860s, there was a shift in thinking about property rights across the Empire, which, along with the political alignment between different groups with a coherent goal of getting rid of the leasehold system in Prince Edward Island,[69] led to pressures on successive imperial governments to rethink their approaches to land tenure on the Island. However, as seen in Ireland, while the Gladstone government was sympathetic to the aspirations of the tenantry, it had to overcome resistance from the proprietors and their supporters. In the case of Ireland, the resistance was overcome by shifting the comparator for Irish land tenures from England to India through recourse to general principles around customary rights of tenants. However, similar custom-based arguments could not be made in Prince Edward Island because the origins of landlords' proprietary rights were the least ambiguous, having been given by the Imperial Government itself in a single day in 1867. In proposing the Irish Land Act as a model, the government identified the specific provisions of the Irish Act that were relevant to the situation in Prince Edward Island.[70] This approach succeeded in shifting the discussion about tenant rights in the PEI legislature relative to those in Ireland. However, the proprietors' petitions continued to insist on comparing conditions in PEI with those in England.[71]

The eventual resolution of the land question in Prince Edward Island in the early 1870s was predicated on the colony's choice regarding its political future. The Imperial Government prepared itself for both possibilities. It hedged its bets by encouraging the Prince Edward Island Government to consider legislation that could be justified through Irish or North American analogies, depending on which political course was adopted.[72] Because it decided to join the Dominion, the Land Purchase Act of 1875 is remembered as converting the leasehold to freehold tenures in Prince Edward Island.

[68] McCallum, 'The Sacred Rights of Property'.

[69] Robertson, 'Political Realignment in Pre-Confederation Prince Edward Island, 1863–1870'.

[70] In the case of Ireland, the Imperial Government used the analogy from India regarding the 'principle' behind tenant rights (i.e., status and customs), although the actual provisions of the Irish act were quite different from the ones in the Punjab Act. For the PEI act, the analogy from Ireland was in the 'provisions' of the Act.

[71] James F. Montgomery, 'An Experiment in Communism and Its Results: A Letter to the Right Honorable the Earl of Carnarvon' (Charlottetown: Bremmer Brothers, 1875).

[72] It would be a matter of scholarly curiosity to imagine/conjecture how the leasehold tenure system would have fared in the colony if its government did not undertake the ambitious project of developing the railways and continued as a separate colony of the British Empire.

The establishment of peasant proprietorship during the 1868–1875 period through state-supported redistribution of property rights via voluntary purchase in Ireland and compulsory purchase in Prince Edward Island, and recognition of tenants' rights in the three colonies represented a significant disjuncture for the Empire in governing land tenure relationships. It was instrumental in furthering the rights of the peasants in numerous colonial contexts well into the next century.

PART V
CONCLUSION

9
The Institutionalisation of Peasant Proprietorship

Several land tenure laws were enacted across the British Empire during the mid-Victorian period which established some form of security of tenure for the actual cultivators of land by recognising co-proprietorship of tenants and landlords and/or transferring proprietorship from landlords to tenants. Co-proprietorship was established by acknowledging heritable rights of occupancy, along with regulated rents and freedom of sale of these rights in Punjab; legalisation of the tenant-right in customary tenures, and establishment of rights of compensation for improvement and disturbance in other tenures in Ireland; and extension of similar rights of compensation for leasehold tenures in Prince Edward Island (PEI). Voluntary land purchase from willing landlords in Ireland and compulsory purchase of landholdings greater than 500 acres in PEI, assisted by financial support from the State in both colonies, were the mechanisms used to transfer proprietorship (see Table 9.1 for a summary).

Placing its analysis within the context of evolving ideas during the nineteenth century about property rights and political economy and their political implications within and across the colonies, *Empire and the Peasant Proprietor* examined how proponents of peasant proprietorship were able to accomplish their objectives in each colony. An underlying theme is that all forms of security of tenure for the cultivators contemplated in the various laws in the three colonies were met with fierce resistance, primarily emanating from the logic of sanctity of property rights of landlords but also evoking political economy arguments of laissez faire and capitalist farming, as well as the value of this class for effective governance of the Empire and its stability. This study has probed how these competing logics were accommodated, reconciled, and contested.

One common element in overcoming resistance to peasant proprietorship in each colony was the steadfastness of their governing agents during the discussions leading to different pieces of legislation: John Lawrence's resolve as Governor-General of India to forcefully counter the pro-aristocratic leanings in British India after the 1857 Rebellion and preserve the occupancy rights of Punjab peasants which he had himself established as the first administrator of the province after its annexation; William Gladstone's determination to deal with Ireland's land question through security of tenure for the Irish tenants even if it meant taking on influential supporters of the landowning class in the British Parliament, which included

Empire and the Peasant Proprietor. Preet S. Aulakh, Oxford University Press. © Preet S. Aulakh 2025.
DOI: 10.1093/9780198928270.003.0009

members of his own party; PEI legislator's resilience in persisting in its objective of freehold tenures for the Island's farmers despite multiple failures and pushback from England for over a century.

The vital role of these governing agents in promoting tenants' rights, supported by the writings of political theorists and colonial administrators such as John Stuart Mill, Henry Maine, and George Campbell, among others, aligns with the findings of each colony's extensive historiography on land tenures. However, my study has extracted new aspects relevant to understanding the broader debates on land tenure that existing scholarship missed because of its focus on each colony in isolation. For instance, in the case of Punjab, the limited scholarship on the Tenancy Act of 1868 primarily evaluated the contestation between two rival schools of revenue administration, each promoting competing versions of property rights and political economy. The current study shows that a salient outcome of the various debates on the occupancy rights of tenants in Punjab was the foregrounding of customs and customary rights in landlord–tenant relationships. Although the eventual grant of substantial security of tenure for large numbers of tenants had more to do with the relative power of the proponents of peasant proprietorship in Punjab than with the definitive identification of pre-colonial customary rights, attentiveness to customs brought the legalisation of status tenures as a legitimate way to think about property rights in the relationships between landlords and tenants. Recognition of the customary rights of tenants played a crucial role in establishing security of tenure in Ireland through the 1870 Act.

Similarly, much of the existing scholarship on the Prince Edward Island land question has focused on various attempts to convert leasehold to freehold tenures for much of the nineteenth century, culminating in the Land Purchase Act of 1875. This scholarship has largely ignored parallel efforts from the 1850s to establish tenants' rights within the existing leasehold system of land tenures. By uncovering the debates around the establishment of tenant rights in the colony and the use of Irish precedents to institutionalise these in the Tenants' Compensation Act of 1872, the study provides a comprehensive picture of the land question and highlights the conundrums faced and strategies employed by the Imperial governments to deal with the land question considering its overall land tenure policies.

Probing these new connections between the colonies was instrumental in uncovering the second mechanism which played a critical role in overcoming resistance to establishing peasant proprietorship: the extrication of land tenure considerations in the colonies from institutionalised practices in England. It is clear from the multiple contestations discussed in the previous chapters that active agency by itself was not enough to overcome resistance from existing landholders because the proprietors in each of the colonies and their politically connected supporters across the Empire used the land tenure principles prevalent in England to resist encroachment on their rights embodied in the proposed laws. The resort to inter-colony analogies and precedents, which disengaged land tenures of the colonies from the existing principles guiding land relationships in England, eventually helped surmount the opposition.

The preceding chapters describe how security of tenure was established in very distant colonies between 1868 and 1875. However, there are remaining questions about whether this shift toward peasant proprietorship was sustained within the three colonies in subsequent years and its lasting impact on the governance of land tenure for the British Empire. This concluding chapter describes the evolution of land tenure arrangements in these colonies, their broader influence in other colonies and the metropole, and the institutionalisation of peasant proprietorship by the end of the nineteenth century. It outlines the implications of peasant proprietorship and the process through which it was institutionalised to scholarship on legal transfers and the governance of the Empire. The chapter closes with a few thoughts on the implications of the study's findings on contemporary discussions on property rights for marginalised groups.

Peasant Proprietorship in the Three Colonies and Beyond

Of the three colonies of interest in the study, the compulsory purchase of landholdings greater than 500 acres in Prince Edward Island was the most radical or extreme in terms of abrogation of property rights of proprietors, despite the Imperial Government's attempts to soften the blow for proprietors by ensuring they get a fair price for the land through the appointment of impartial commissioners.[1] For the most part, after the Supreme Court of Canada's decision in 1876 upholding the commissioner's awards in the case of one holdout proprietor, the Empire took a hands-off approach to any further questions on PEI's land tenures, arguing that these were domestic matters of the Dominion of Canada. One intervention came in early 1876 when the PEI legislature passed an amending act to the Land Purchase Act of 1875 to clarify some of the provisions because of the Supreme Court of PEI's decision to set aside the commissioners' awards for a few proprietors. On the advice of Canada's Minister of Justice, the Governor-General of Canada, Dufferin disallowed the Act. In his letter to the Secretary of State for the Colonies dated June 27, 1876, Dufferin reiterated that while the 'annulling or disannulling of this act becomes altogether a domestic question' (mainly because 'English proprietors are out of the running' as their claims have already been dealt with), he thought that it wouldn't be a 'bad thing to make these Provincial Parliaments understand that they will not be allowed to expropriate private property, unless they take pains to

[1] There is not much information in the archives regarding the working of the Tenants' Compensation Act of 1872. It could well be that its provisions were rendered moot immediately after the land purchase act given that almost 95% of the land was converted to freehold in the next few years.

Table 9.1 Peasant Proprietorship in the Three Colonial Sites

	Punjab	Ireland	Prince Edward Island
Acts	Punjab Tenancy Act of 1868	Landlord and Tenant (Ireland) Act of 1870	Tenants' Compensation Act, 1872 Land Purchase Act, 1875
Security of Tenure for Tenants/ Cultivators	*Co-proprietorship*: Rights of occupancy; Regulated rent; Right to alienate holdings	*Co-proprietorship*: Legalise customary tenant-right where existed (compensation and goodwill); Compensation for improvement and disturbance in other tenures *Proprietorship*: Voluntary purchase	*Co-proprietorship (1872 Act)*: Compensation for improvements in leasehold tenures *Proprietorship (1875 Act)*: Compulsory purchase of holdings greater than 500 acres
Agency	'Punjab School' of British Administrators led by John Lawrence	Gladstone led Liberal Government and Irish Members of Parliament	PEI Legislature
Analogies/ Precedents	Pre-1857 ryotwari system; Customary tenures in Pre-British Punjab and recorded during the first settlements (the 1850s)	Customary tenures of pre-colonial Ireland and those from India (including the ones in Punjab)	Irish Land Act of 1870; Norms of freehold tenures in British North America
Post-script	Strengthening of procedures and expansion of occupancy rights in the 1887 Tenancy Act (which continues till the present day in both West (Pakistan) and East (India) Punjab)	Security of tenure through the 3 Fs (fixity, fair rents, freedom of sale) established through the Act of 1881; Voluntary purchase legislation in the 1890s; Compulsory purchase legislation in the early part of the twentieth century	A preponderance of freehold tenures; continuing restrictions on the size of holdings for non-resident proprietors

have their bills properly drawn, and the interest of the persons affected as carefully guarded as may be compatible with the attainment of the object in view'.[2]

[2] See C. W. De Kiewiet and Frank H. Underhill, eds., *Dufferin-Carnarvon Correspondence, 1874–1878* (Toronto: The Champlain Society, 1955), 254.

The Land Purchase Act of 1875 successfully created smallholders by converting tenants' leaseholds to freehold tenures. According to PEI's Commissioner of Public Lands Report,[3] by 1880, the government had purchased 343,216 acres of land (of the remaining 380,000 leaseholds in 1873) from fifty-seven proprietors. Out of these, 193,847 acres were bought by 2781 tenants, with an average purchase of approximately 70 acres (77% of the tenants' purchases were for less than 100 acres).[4] As a result, in 1881, only 6.2% of the land in PEI was held as leasehold, which declined further to 5.5% in 1891 when the government purchased the last of the land. Interestingly, PEI surpassed the other British North American colonies regarding the percentage of land held as freehold tenures (the corresponding figures of leasehold tenures in 1881 were: Ontario 11.7%, Quebec 9%, New Brunswick 7.6%, and Nova Scotia 7%).[5] Besides the success in converting leasehold to freehold tenures, data also show the preponderance of small landholdings with an average farm size between 80 and 90 acres until the end of the nineteenth century.[6] Furthermore, the percentage of the total area occupied as farmland increased from 74% in 1871 to 87% in 1891. The ratio of the occupied area improved, and fit for cultivation increased from 43% in 1871 to 59% in 1891.[7]

The compulsory purchase achieved the twin objectives of redistribution and development in Prince Edward Island and brought the colony's land tenure system closer to the proximate provinces of Canada. More importantly, for the Empire, the implementation of compulsory purchase and its perceived success in fulfilling the political aspirations of the colony and economic aspirations of a vast majority of its people could subsequently be used as a precedent in other colonies.

*****

If the compulsory land purchase in Prince Edward Island was the most extreme in terms of appropriating property rights from one group and assigning them to another, the provisions of the Punjab Tenancy Act were the most comprehensive in granting rights of co-proprietorship for the tenants (that is, it embodied security

[3] Report of PEI Commissioner of Public Lands Addressed to the Lieutenant-Governor, dated November 4, 1880, in 'Prince Edward Island. Further Correspondence Relative to the Land Tenure Question. Presented to Both Houses of Parliament. February 1881' (London: Her Majesty's Stationary Office, 1881), 50–55, House of Commons Parliamentary Papers Online; also see Appendix in Rusty Bittermann and Margaret McCallum, *Lady Landlords of Prince Edward Island: Imperial Dreams and the Defence of Property* (Montreal: McGill-Queen's University Press, 2008), 151–54.

[4] 77% of the purchases made by the tenants were for less than 100 acres each, which was very similar to the land purchased (approximately 400,000 acres) through voluntary sales from 1854 to 1873.

[5] See Table 3.1, Appendix B in Catherine Anne Wilson, *Tenants in Time: Family Strategies, Land, and Liberalism in Upper Canada, 1799–1871* (Montreal and Kingston: McGill-Queen's University Press, 2009), 231.

[6] See Table IX, Farm Numbers and Sizes, 1861–1952 in Andrew Hill Clark, *Three Centuries and the Island: A Historical Geography of Settlement and Agriculture in Prince Edward Island, Canada* (Toronto: University of Toronto Press, 1959), 134.

[7] See Table XII in Clark, 152.

of tenure through the 'three Fs'). The Act liberally recognised the occupancy rights of large numbers of tenants (fixity of tenure), put constraints on the ability of landlords to raise rents arbitrarily (fair rent), and allowed tenants to alienate the land on which they had rights of occupancy, subject to landlords' rights of first refusal (freedom of sale). Even for tenants without occupancy rights (tenants at will), the Act provided similar security of tenure regarding rent enhancement and compensation for improvements.

Given the legalisation of extensive rights for the tenants and the goal of creating peasant proprietors, which were at odds with the trend in the rest of British India after 1857, what was the legacy of the Punjab Tenancy Act? As discussed in Chapter 4, the Punjab Act generated considerable debate between sets of British administrators in India and England. It was approved by the Secretary of State for India, the Duke of Argyll, using his tie-breaking vote in Council. However, there were concerns about whether the provisions of the Act would create hostility amongst the different classes of agriculturalists and lead to increased litigation (because the filing of regular suits was the primary mechanism for both landlords and tenants to exercise their rights provided in the Act). These concerns led the Duke of Argyll to caution the Governor-General of India that the 'exact effect of [the Punjab Tenancy Act] . . . cannot perhaps be certainly known until the provisions of the Act have been made the subject of judicial interpretation'. He instructed the latter that his administration should watch the operation of the Act 'with the closest care and . . . devise measures for affording every possible facility to all classes, whose rights are effected', to prove 'in a regular suit', but cheaply and easily, any errors which the First Settlement may have involved'.[8]

The Governor-General instructed the Punjab administration to provide monthly updates on the workings of the Act. Various reports submitted from the province affirmed satisfactory progress. For example, in the preamble to one of the reports in 1870, the Financial Commissioner of Punjab noted that '[n]o excitement whatsoever has occurred from the introduction of the Act in any class of people connected with the land'. Therefore, he did not see difficulty in its workings.[9] Satisfied with similar reports from the Punjab Government and the supporting data, the Governor-General of India wrote to the Secretary of State for India in 1871 that the Act was working smoothly: 'The tenants who lost status under the operation of the recent settlements have been very active in suing to recover the lost position; but the proprietors have been singularly apathetic, and the

[8] Letter from Secretary of State for India to the Governor-General of India, 28 October 1869. In 'East India (Punjab Tenancy): Copies of the Despatch of the Secretary of State for India in Council Dates the 28th Day of October (No. 80) 1869, to the Governor-General of India in Council, on the Subject of the India Act No. XXVIII. of 1868, (Punjab Tenancy Act)' (House of Commons, 1870), 5.

[9] Memorandum by the Financial Commissioner of Punjab on the Statement of Tenancy Cases, June 29, 1870. In Government of India, Foreign Department, 'Suits under the Punjab Tenancy Act from Date of Introduction to End of May 1870. No. 1. K.W. Proceedings, September, Nos. 17–23', 1870, National Archives of India, NAI.

Table 9.2 Working of the Punjab Tenancy Act of 1868: Number of Suits Filed During the 1870–1874 Period[a]

Year	Suits by Tenants for Rights of Occupancy (Section 5)	Suits by Landlords to Rebut Presumption of Occupancy Rights (Section 6)	Suits by Landlords for Enhancement of Rent (Section 10)
1870–71	1351	1454	109
1871–72	1451	838	638
1872–73	1725	423	555
1873–74	2272	192	461

[a] Government of India, Department of Revenue, Agriculture and Commerce, 'Land Revenue and Settlements: Working of the Punjab Tenancy Act. Proceedings - Nos. 13 to 16', December 1874, National Archives of India, NAI. In the Minute accompanying this report, the Lieutenant Governor expressed satisfaction with the working of the Act, noting that the apprehension during the passage of the Act that its provisions would lead to 'excessive litigation ... proved to have been groundless'. This report further showed that most of the landlords' suits (almost 90%) for ejectment were targeted towards tenants without rights of occupancy.

provisions enabling them to evict occupancy tenants on payment of compensation are most rarely put in force'.[10] Further data over the next few years assuaged the apprehensions of both the British Indian government and the India Office about any adverse socio-political implications (Table 9.2 summarises the Sections of the Act on which most of the suits were filed). Satisfied with the Act's workings, the Governor-General of India rescinded the Punjab government's monthly reporting requirements in 1874.

The Act of 1868 achieved its objectives of creating a large number of cultivators in Punjab as peasant proprietors. In his memorandum in August 1882, the Lieutenant Governor of Punjab noted that in 'other provinces vast tracts of land ... are the property of a few great zamindars, the mass of people being tenants. Here the mass of the people are themselves the proprietary body cultivating their own lands'. The land tenure data from 1882 shows that proprietors cultivated 62% of the land themselves, and 13% of the land was farmed by occupancy tenants. Thus, 75% of the cultivators had proprietary rights, the remaining 25% being tenants at will.[11]

However, a few difficulties were encountered during the ongoing revision of settlements in certain districts. These involved provisions regarding the period of occupancy and residency status of the cultivators that qualified them for

[10] Letter from Government of India to the Secretary of State for India, January 18, 1871. In Government of India, Foreign Department, Revenue A, 'Suits under the Punjab Tenancy Act from June to September 1870. K.W. Proceedings, Nos. 16–28', 1871, National Archives of India, NAI.

[11] 'Amendment of the Punjab Tenancy Act, Proceedings- Nos. 33 and 34' (Government of India Revenue and Agriculture Department, 1882), National Archives of India, NAI.

occupancy rights, as well as the landlords' use of proximate rates to increase their tenants' rents.[12] Some of these concerns about specific provisions of the 1868 Act and additional procedural issues identified during the compilation of new settlement reports in the 1870s and 1880s led to the Punjab Tenancy Act of 1887.[13] Although the new act replaced the Act of 1868, the 'principles of the tenant-right remain[ed] the same'.[14] These were further solidified and expanded for different categories of tenants with occupancy rights. New provisions were added to clarify fair rents and freedom of sale.[15]

The establishment of security of tenure for large numbers of tenants and the preponderance of proprietors who cultivated their land meant that the land tenure system in Punjab after 1868 provided appropriate incentives for investments in improving the land. Occupiers of land, both proprietors and occupancy tenants, could use their respective rights to access credit markets and appropriate gains by selling their rights in the market. Evidence points towards increased land alienation and borrowings from the credit market after the passage of the 1868 Act. The sale of land in Punjab almost quadrupled from 88,000 acres in 1874 to 371,000 acres in 1896, and the mortgaged land increased from 143,000 to 673,000 acres during the same period.[16] However, a negative consequence of the security of tenure to access the market was the increased indebtedness of Punjab's agricultural classes and the alienation of their holdings to urban moneylenders. This created tensions along the rural/urban and Hindu/Muslim divides that required state intervention in the form of the Punjab Land Alienation Bill of 1900, which put constraints on the market for land and access to credit.[17]

[12] In the Sirsa District, where the initial settlement in 1852 was done within the provisions of North-Western Provinces (to which it was associated at the time, it became part of Punjab after the Mutiny), during the revisions it was discovered that numerous tenants with earlier occupancy rights would be deemed as tenants at will according to the Punjab Act because they were not residing in the area and did not have continuous occupancy, although they had done most of the improvements and brought land under cultivable state. See J. Wilson, 'Final Report on the Revision of Settlement of the Sirsa District in the Punjab, 1879–83' (Calcutta: Calcutta Central Press Company, 1884). In another district, there was great demand for land leading to very high rents. Thus, landlords could always find a few tracts with high rents and use their precedents to increase rent of their tenants. See Part IV, Chapter II in B. H. Baden-Powell, *The Land Systems of British India, Volume III* (Oxford, UK: Clarendon Press, 1892).

[13] This Act was much more comprehensive than the 1868 Act, with 112 sections (compared to 45 sections in the previous Act). See 'The Punjab Tenancy Act, 1887. A Collection of the Acts Passed by the Governor General of India in Council in the Year 1887' (Calcutta: Superintendent of Government Printing, 1888).

[14] For a comparison of the main sections of the two acts, see Baden-Powell, *The Land Systems of British India, Volume III*, 712–13. Also see Neeladri Bhattacharya, *The Great Agrarian Conquest: The Colonial Shaping of a Rural World* (New Delhi: Permanent Black, 2019), 167.

[15] The Punjab Tenancy Act of 1887 continues to be operational in both West and East Punjab. Although it was revised numerous times both under British rule (1887–1947) and subsequently in India and Pakistan, the institutionalisation of shared proprietary rights of occupancy tenants along with the landowners can be traced to the Punjab Tenancy Act of 1868.

[16] See Appendix A in N. Gerald Barrier, *The Punjab Alienation of Land Bill of 1900* (Durham, N.C: 1966), 103.

[17] For an extended discussion on the socio-political implications of land alienation in Punjab at the end of the nineteenth century, see Norman G. Barrier, 'The Formulation and Enactment of the Punjab Alienation of Land Bill', *The Indian Economic & Social History Review* 2, no. 2 (1965): 145–65; Preet

Despite the unintended consequences of overusing secure property rights as collateral in the credit markets, akin to Prince Edward Island, the lasting result of the land tenure legislation in Punjab was the institutionalisation of peasant proprietorship in the province.[18]

*****

Unlike these two colonies, where the land laws established stable land tenure arrangements, the Irish Act of 1870 was perceived as a first step in resolving the land question in Ireland.

The Irish Land Act of 1870 recognised co-proprietorship between landlords and tenants by legalising customary tenant-right where it existed and establishing compensation for improvement and disturbance in other agreements. It also provided a pathway for complete proprietorship through the 'Bright Clause'. While the Act was acknowledged as one passed because of 'an earnest and sincere desire to protect the Irish tenant', it was considered 'imperfect and inadequate' soon after its passage because of a failure to incorporate the 'three Fs' expectations of the Irish.[19] Subsequent workings of the Act affirmed the perceived inadequacy of its provisions. Regarding the 'Bright Clause', there were few takers because tenants wishing to purchase the land required a down payment of 33% of the price, which proved to be a big hurdle and led to the creation of only about 700 new peasant proprietors by 1881.[20] The compensation clauses created multiple problems, which were documented in the report of the Bessborough Commission. This commission was appointed in 1880 to inquire into the workings of the 1870 Act in light of the declining agriculture conditions from 1876 onwards[21] and the political pressure arising from the growing Home Rule movement and the activities of the

S. Aulakh, 'Law, Identity and Imperial Logics of Exclusion: The Case of the Komagata Maru Passengers', *The Journal of Imperial and Commonwealth History* 45, no. 5 (2021): 866–98; S. S. Thorburn, *Musalmans and Money-Lenders in the Punjab* (Edinburgh and London: William Blackwood & Sons, 1886); Malcolm Lyall Darling, *The Punjab Peasant In Prosperity And Debt* (Oxford, UK: Oxford University Press, 1928); Pervaiz Nazir, 'Origins of Debt, Mortgage and Alienation of Land in Early Modern Punjab', *The Journal of Peasant Studies* 27, no. 3 (April 1, 2000): 55–91; Clive J. Dewey, 'The Official Mind and the Problem of Agrarian Indebtedness in India, 1870–1910' (Ph.D. Thesis, Cambridge, UK: University of Cambridge, 1972).

[18] For land tenures in Punjab after the 1880s (including new settlements in the Canal Colonies), see Imran Ali, 'The Punjab Canal Colonies' (Ph.D. Thesis, Canberra: The Australian National University, 1979); Imran Ali, *The Punjab Under Imperialism, 1885–1947* (Princeton, N.J.: Princeton University Press, 2014).

[19] Letter by Isaac Butt, cited in R. D. Collison Black, *Economic Thought and the Irish Question, 1817–1870* (Cambridge, UK: Cambridge University Press, 2015), 70.

[20] Daniel Patrick Moriarty, 'The Transformation of Rural Ireland: The Irish Land Purchase Policy of the Conservative Party in Britain, 1885–1923' (Ph.D., North Carolina, The University of North Carolina at Chapel Hill).

[21] Value of agriculture production fell from 72 million in 1876 to 55 million pounds a few years later. There were increased evictions of tenants because of the difficulty in paying rent. Moriarty, 19.

Land League in Ireland.[22] The 1870 Act provided two types of compensation: the unexhausted value of improvement made by a tenant that could be claimed from the landlord on leaving his holding; and loss suffered that could be claimed because of termination (disturbance) of a tenancy. In both cases, the Act provided for the court to determine whether the tenant-right custom and the amount of compensation covered a given tenancy.

Furthermore, the 1870 Act did not provide for the fixity of rent, which led to landlords increasing rent to force tenants to fall into arrears and initiate eviction proceedings. Given the competition for land for the cultivators, new tenants were willing to pay the higher rent, which more than covered the compensation for improvement or disturbance assigned by the court to the evicted tenant. The Irish Act of 1870, thus, 'suffered . . . from one fundamental weakness; it did not give Irish tenants the basic security of tenure they sought. They did not want compensation after the eviction; they wanted protection from eviction itself'.[23] The Bessborough Commission recommended that the Act be reformed to incorporate the principles of fixity of tenure, fair rents, and free sale.[24] Gladstone, who was back as Prime Minister for the second stint in 1880, accepted the recommendations of the Commission and introduced a Bill, which was enacted as the Land Law (Ireland) Act 1881.[25] In 1881, the institutionalised security of tenure for Irish tenants was similar to the one granted in the Punjab Tenancy Act of 1868 for 'occupancy' or 'hereditary' tenants. The Act 'gave a statutory basis to what amounted to a co-proprietorship in Irish agricultural land: landlords had the right to draw an income from land, but tenants had limited property rights in the same land'.[26]

While the Irish land acts of 1870 and 1881 represented an important movement for tenant rights related to the 'three Fs', their other provisions regarding the creation of peasant proprietors through state-facilitated land purchase from willing landowners were less successful because the tenants either did not have the requisite funds to make the purchases or did not feel the need to become full proprietors

22 The Home Rule movement was led by Isaac Butt and the Land League by Charles Stewart Parnell, both Irish nationalists, and elected Members of Parliament during the period. The 1879–1882 period is often referred to as one of 'Land Wars'. See Michael J. Winstanley, *Ireland and the Land Question 1800–1922* (London: Metheun & Co. Ltd., 1984), 27–31.

23 J. C. W. Wylie, *Irish Land Law*, 2nd ed. (Abingdon, Oxon: Professional Books, 1986), 29.

24 'Report of Her Majesty's Commissioners of Inquire into the Working of the Landlord and Tenant (Ireland) Act, 1870', Presented to Both Houses of Parliament (Dublin: Alex Thom & Co., 1881).

25 'The Irish Land Bill. Speech Delivered by the Rt. Hon. W. E. Gladstone, in the House of Commons, On His Motion Introducing the Land Law (Ireland) Bill, April 7th, 1881' (London: The National Press Agency, Limited, 1881); The Duke of Argyll, who had supported the Irish Land Act of 1870 now broke ranks with Gladstone on the more security of tenure being proposed in the 1881 Act. He subsequently resigned from the cabinet. See his speech in 'The Bessborough Commission. Speech Delivered by the Duke of Argyll, During the Debate in the House of Lords on July 1st, 1881' (London: P. S. King, Parliamentary Bookseller, 1881).

26 Timothy W. Guinnane and Ronald I. Miller, 'The Limits to Land Reform: The Land Acts in Ireland, 1870–1909', *Economic Development and Cultural Change* 45, no. 3 (1997): 595; also see Rachael Walsh and Lorna Fox O'Mahony, 'Land Law, Property Ideologies and the British–Irish Relationship', *Common Law World Review* 47, no. 1 (2018): 7–34.

given the generous conditions in their favour through co-proprietorship inherent in the newly legislated tenant rights. Under the provisions of the two acts, until 1885, only 80,000 acres of land had been purchased through 1608 loans taken from the government by the tenants.[27]

Numerous bills were passed in the British Parliament between 1888 and 1903, which provided additional funds for land purchase by tenants and eased the conditions for the tenants to repay the loans.[28] Interestingly, land purchase was facilitated by governments across the political spectrum. While support from the Liberal governments was expected, the initial support for the land purchase schemes from the Conservative governments was aimed at getting the best possible price for the landlords who were suffering economically in the 1880s.[29] However, by the end of the century, the conservatives also saw the political benefit of an economically prosperous peasantry.[30] As argued by Winstanley, land purchase was 'an eminently admirable outcome' to the Conservatives. 'Demoralised, impoverished landlords increasingly supported the idea of a rescue operation which involved utilising taxpayers' money to subsidise purchases by making loans available to tenants on favourable terms. The old landowning class could then retire gracefully on the proceeds while the new farming landowners in this property-owning democracy would, it was hoped, become defenders of the status quo, upholders of law and order and supporters of British rule'.[31] As a result of the additional incentives for land purchase, by 1913, almost half of the agricultural land exchanged hands.[32] This trend eventually culminated in the compulsory land purchase legislation by the Irish Free State in 1923.[33] Leaseholds were converted to freehold, and by the Second World War, 'landlords in Ireland were a memory'.[34]

With its roots in the Middle Ages, the Irish land question had made little progress until 1870. In the following decades, land tenures in Ireland evolved quickly through co-proprietorship arrangements between landlords and tenants because of the land acts of 1870 and 1881 and, subsequently, complete peasant proprietorship owing to

27 C. F. Bastable, 'The Irish Land Purchase Act of 1903', *The Quarterly Journal of Economics* 18, no. 1 (1903): 1–21.

28 Bastable; Winstanley, *Ireland and the Land Question 1800–1922.*

29 According to Solow, tenants did not have an incentive to purchase the land because the annual payment of the loan would be higher than the judicial rent given by the 1881 Act. 'It was the landlord class, squeezed between declining rent rolls and inflexible charges, who pressed for land purchase financed by government loans'. Barbara Lewis Solow, 'The Irish Land Question After 1870', *The Journal of Economic History* 27, no. 4 (December 1967): 620.

30 For an extended discussion, see Moriarty, 'The Transformation of Rural Ireland'.

31 Winstanley, *Ireland and the Land Question 1800–1922*, 39–40.

32 Guinnane and Miller, 'The Limits to Land Reform'.

33 For details on the eventual shift from leasehold to freehold tenures in Ireland, see Wylie, *Irish Land Law*, 29–41; C. F. Bastable, 'The Irish Land Purchase Act of 1903', *The Quarterly Journal of Economics* 18, no. 1 (1903): 1–21; Dunning, 'Irish Land Legislation Since 1845. II', *Political Science Quarterly* 7, no. 3 (1892): 500–521; Varley, Tony, 'Gaining Ground, Losing Ground: The Politics of Land Reform in Twentieth Century Ireland', in *Land Questions in Modern Ireland*, ed. Fergus Campbell and Varley, Tony (Manchester: Manchester University Press, 2013), 25–64.

34 Guinnane and Miller, 'The Limits to Land Reform', 596.

the various land purchase Acts and the associated government financing schemes. If the land reform was meant to weaken the stronghold of Anglo-Irish landlords by chipping away their property rights and assigning them to the tenant cultivators, or what is called the 'redistribution hypothesis', there is a general agreement amongst historians that it achieved the objectives. However, if secure property rights for the cultivators were meant to provide the Irish tenants the incentives to make the necessary investments to improve the productivity of their land holdings (that is the 'efficiency hypothesis'), the available evidence is mixed. For instance, Guttman's study on the Irish Land Act of 1870 shows both efficiency and distribution gains.[35] On the other hand, Solow calls occupancy rights of the 1881 Irish Act as a movement from 'private' to 'communal' property and argues that the act perpetuated 'small uneconomic holdings in the face of economies of scale', which eventually led to inefficient tenants who could not make adequate investments for an increase in productivity'.[36] She suggests that the Irish Act of 1881 was not a sound economic policy but a useful political stroke.[37] The continuing underinvestment by the Irish tenants, even when they had secure property rights, is attributed to the underdeveloped credit markets in Ireland,[38] which were necessary to bring about the beneficial effects of secure and broad property rights.[39]

*****

The brief discussion of the workings of the acts of interest in this study shows that security of tenure for tenant cultivators was institutionalised in the three colonial sites through co-proprietorship or complete proprietorship.[40] Ideological contestations went in favour of those (1) who saw property rights as shifting rather than fixed and thus could be assigned to and shared by different occupiers of land and (2) who believed that improvements were not strictly a function of the size of land holdings and capitalist farming but were dependent on the security of tenure and associated incentives for improvement to actual occupiers/cultivators of the land.

These ideas did not stay confined to the three colonial sites but permeated subsequent land tenure discussions across the Empire. The previous chapters have shown how the Punjab Tenancy Act of 1868, with its provisions of occupancy

[35] Joel M. Guttman, 'The Economics of Tenant Rights in Nineteenth Century Irish Agriculture', *Economic Inquiry; Oxford* 18, no. 3 (July 1, 1980): 408–24.

[36] Barbara Lewis Solow, 'A New Look at the Irish Land Question', *The Economic and Social Review* 12, no. 4 (1981): 312.

[37] Barbara Lewis Solow, *The Land Question and the Irish Economy, 1870–1903* (Cambridge, MA: Harvard University Press, 1971).

[38] Guinnane and Miller, 'The Limits to Land Reform'.

[39] Claire Priest, *Credit Nation: Property Laws and Legal Institutions in Early America* (Princeton, NJ: Princeton University Press, 2021).

[40] My objective here is to demonstrate how the provisions related to security of tenure evolved and were strengthened in subsequent legislation. I rely primarily on secondary sources and outline the broad thrust of the new legislation. Interested reader looking for details can see the provided citations.

rights for tenants, was used as a precedence to achieve a modicum of protection for the Irish tenants through the 1870 Act. More substantial rights (the three Fs of fixity of tenure, fair rent, and freedom of sale) were further established in the Irish Land Act of 1881. It was also shown that the substantial rights granted to Punjab's tenant cultivators were an aberration because the trend in British India after the 1857 mutiny was to take away any proprietary rights afforded to the peasants and restore those of the aristocratic landowning class, best reflected in the province of Oudh where the occupancy tenants were downgraded to tenants-at-will.

Thus, while the occupancy rights in Punjab were being championed in England to address the Irish land question, the rest of British India was falling behind in protecting the tenant cultivators. This led to agricultural discontent and numerous agitations for greater protection of the tenants vis-à-vis exploiting landlords.[41] In rethinking solutions to rural distress, especially in Bengal, where agitations were particularly strong in the 1870s, the British Indian administration sought ways to protect the peasants. In this instance, the Irish precedents came in handy, with Lord Ripon, the newly appointed Governor General of India, writing to Gladstone: 'With regard to Land Tenures we have in many parts of India a state of things to deal with very similar to that which have so long existed in Ireland, except that the landlords here are, I take it, harder and the tenants certainly more patient than they are there. There is therefore all the more need for our interference'.[42] Ripon was an enthusiastic supporter of the Irish Land Act of 1881, with its '3F' provisions, and wanted to see a similar legislation adopted in Bengal. While the eventual Bengal Tenancy Act of 1885 did not go as far as the Irish Act, they shared similarities in their guiding principles of security of tenure through rights of occupancy and fair rents.[43] The Bengal Act built momentum towards greater security of tenure for the peasant cultivators, and eventually, numerous acts were introduced across British India with varying degrees and types of security of tenure (for example, Bihar Tenancy Act of 1885; Orissa Tenancy Act of 1914; Oudh Rent Act of 1921; Agra Tenancy Act of 1926; Madras Estate Land Act of 1908).[44]

[41] Peter G. Robb, *Ancient Rights and Future Comfort: Bihar, the Bengal Tenancy Act of 1885, and British Rule in India* (London: Routledge, 2013).

[42] Letter Lord Ripon to William Gladstone, October 22, 1881. Cited in S. B. Cook, *Imperial Affinities: Nineteenth Century Analogies and Exchanges Between India and Ireland* (New Delhi: Sage Publications, 1993), 100.

[43] For details on the Irish precedents to the Bengal Tenancy Act of 1885, the role of various administrators in British India with Irish sympathies, and the comparative provisions of the two acts, see book length study by Cook, *Imperial Affinities: Nineteenth Century Analogies and Exchanges Between India and Ireland.*

[44] Tajamul Haque and Amar Singh Sirohi, *Agrarian Reforms and Institutional Changes in India* (New Delhi: Concept Publishing Company, 1986); Tirthankar Roy and Anand V. Swamy, *Law and the Economy in Colonial India* (Chicago, London: The University of Chicago Press, 2016); B. H. Baden-Powell, *A Short Account of the Land Revenue and Its Administration in British India; with a Sketch of the Land Tenures* (Oxford, UK: Clarendon Press, 1894); Dietmar Rothermund, 'Government, Landlord and Tenant in India, 1875–1900', *The Indian Economy and Social History Review* 6, no. 4 (1969): 351–67.

The Irish Land Act of 1881 also helped address Scotland's land question. Like Ireland, land ownership was concentrated, and the tenants did the actual land cultivation but without any legal claim to land. During the early nineteenth century, a large portion of land in northern Scotland was cleared from agricultural use (Highland Clearances) to make way for sheep pastures, which were thought to be more economically lucrative. The evicted farmers were forced to settle in small tenant farms or crofts. The crofters lived in miserable conditions that worsened during frequent crop failures. As in Ireland, this led to mass emigration and a land reform movement to get some proprietary rights for the crofters.[45] William Gladstone responded to the agitation through the Crofters Holding Act of 1886, which granted tenants protection in the form of security of tenure, compensation for improvements, and fair rents.[46] The Liberal government took a historicist position that the tenants in the Scottish Highlands had similar customary claims to land as the Ulster tenants in Ireland and thus deserved to convert their customary rights to positive law. This historicist interpretation 'rehabilitated peasant agriculture and customary law' by conferring comprehensive tenant rights to the 'mass of the crofters [in Scotland] and cottiers [in Ireland]'.[47]

The landholding structure in Wales was similar to Ireland, with 60% of the land owned by 571 families in 1873.[48] While the landlord-tenant relationships in Wales were more amicable, nonetheless, a land league was established which 'felt that tenants were entitled, *as of right*, to what they . . . received out of *grace and favour*'.[49] It convinced the minority Gladstone government (his third stint as leader of the Liberal Party) to set up a commission in 1892. The Commission used the Irish Land Act of 1881 and Crofters Holdings (Scotland) Act of 1886 as models to recommend similar rights for the Welsh tenants.[50] However, the Gladstone government fell when the Commission prepared its recommendations, and the new Conservative government shelved the report. Given better conditions of the Welsh tenants, the landlord–tenant problem took a back seat, and the impetus for further

[45] John W. Mason, 'The Duke of Argyll and the Land Question in Late Nineteenth-Century Britain', *Victorian Studies* 21, no. 2 (1978): 149–70.

[46] James Hunter, 'The Politics of Highland Land Reform, 1873–1895', *The Scottish Historical Review* 53, no. 155 (1974): 45–68; Annie Tindley, 'Landed Response to Land Reform in Scotland and Ireland, c. 1860–1903', in *Land Reforms in the British and Irish Isles Since 1800*, ed. Shaun Evans, Tony McCarthy, and Annie Tindley (Edinburgh: Edinburgh University Press, 2022), 237–58; Shaun Evans, Tony McCarthy, and Annie Tindley, 'Introduction: Land Reform, Estates and Society', in *Land Reforms in the British and Irish Isles Since 1800*, ed. Shaun Evans, Tony McCarthy, and Annie Tindley (Edinburgh: Edinburgh University Press, 2022), 1–24.

[47] Clive Dewey, 'Celtic Agrarian Legislation and the Celtic Revival: Historicist Implications of Gladstone's Irish and Scottish Land Acts 1870–1886', *Past & Present*, no. 64 (1974): 34.

[48] Matthew Cragoe, '"A Contemptible Mimic of the Irish": The Land Question in Victorian Wales', in *The Land Question in Britain, 1750–1950*, ed. Matthew Cragoe and Paul Readman (Hampshire: Palgrave Macmillan, 2010), 91–107.

[49] David W. Howell, 'The Land Question in Nineteenth-Century Wales, Ireland and Scotland: A Comparative Study', *Agricultural History Review* 61, no. 1 (June 1, 2013): 90 [italics in original].

[50] Howell, 'The Land Question in Nineteenth-Century Wales, Ireland and Scotland'.

land reform came from some of the changes taking place in England's agrarian system towards the end of the nineteenth century.

*****

> By the second half of the eighteenth century the British were preening themselves on the superiority of their agricultural performance over that of any other major country. They had little hesitation in ascribing this superiority to the beneficial effects of what they considered to be *distinctive, peculiar, and uniquely rational system* of British land tenures. By the beginning of the twentieth century, however, the British were largely convinced of the backwardness and poor performance of their agriculture in comparison with other countries. With some hesitation they ascribed this in large part to the damaging effects of what they considered to be *distinctive, peculiar, and uniquely irrational system* of British land tenures.[51]

The characteristics that made Britain's land tenure system 'distinctive and rational' included large farms owned by improving landlords and cultivated by substantial tenants holding long leases.[52] The tenurial conditions guiding the relationships between landlords and tenants were through mutually structured contracts by the parties. As discussed in Chapter 1 and demonstrated in the contestations around land reform in the three colonial sites, adherents of this land tenure system vehemently opposed attempts to alter these arrangements in England and ensured that legislative efforts to promote owner-cultivator small farms and secure property rights for the tenant farmers were not successful.

Some of the orthodoxy about the superiority of British land tenures began to change during the last few decades of the nineteenth century because of the efforts of political theorists such John Stuart Mill (through the Land Tenure Reform Association he founded in 1868 to promote free trade in land that would lead to peasant proprietorship), the Cobden Club (through the publication of its volume on land tenures around the world in which several chapters foregrounded the economic efficiency of small-scale farming by owner-cultivators),[53] and numerous other farmers' associations,[54] among others.[55] The omnipresence of William

[51] F. M. L. Thompson, 'Changing Perceptions of Land Tenures in Britain, 1750–1914', in *The Political Economy of British Historical Experience, 1688–1914*, ed. Donald Winch and Patrick K. O'Brien (Oxford, UK: Oxford University Press, 2002), 119 [italics mine].

[52] In addition, the large estates 'held together by primogeniture and entail were supposed essential to the maintenance of beneficent political order'. Clive J. Dewey, 'The Rehabilitation of the Peasant Proprietor in Nineteenth-Century Economic Thought', *History of Political Economy* 6, no. 1 (1974): 17.

[53] Cobden Club (London, England) et al., *Systems of Land Tenure in Various Countries* (London: Macmillan, 1870).

[54] J. R. Fisher, 'The Farmers' Alliance: An Agricultural Protest Movement of the 1880's', *The Agricultural History Review* 26, no. 1 (1978): 15–25.

[55] For a more detailed analysis of English land tenures, see A. W. B. Simpson, *A History of Land Law*, Second (Oxford, UK: Oxford University Press, 1986); F. M. L. Thompson, *English Landed Society in*

Gladstone in his four stints as Prime Minister between 1868 and 1894 also boosted the land reformers in England. Gladstone's initial involvement in agrarian reforms stemmed from Ireland's land question, and he wanted to find a local solution by legalising the Ulster tenant-right, which would provide a modicum of security of tenure but not 'shake the stability of property'.[56] His thinking on land tenure evolved, and by the time of the debates on the Irish land question during his second stint as Prime Minister, he was more open to questioning the sanctity of property rights, as reflected in his support for the 3Fs in the Irish land act of 1881.

The change in thinking in England from the 1870s onwards led to land reforms on two fronts: tenants' compensation for improvement and state-assisted peasant proprietorship. The tenant-right movement in England, with its aim of ensuring a 'just claim of a farmer to compensation for any unexhausted improvement made by him and remaining on his holding at the end of the tenancy',[57] was initiated in the 1840s but had not gained much traction for the next three decades. The precedence of legalising the tenant right of compensation in the Irish Act of 1870s and renewed agitation by different farmers' associations led Disraeli's Conservative government to support the Act of 1875, which legalised the tenant right of compensation, but with the clause that it would be voluntary for the landlord to participate in its implementation.[58] The voluntary clause, however, allowed the landlords to circumvent the law. The continuing agitation[59] to put some teeth on the legislation led to the Gladstone-sponsored Agricultural Holdings Act (England) of 1883, which made compensation compulsory and the scale 'determined by the value of the improvements to the incoming tenant'.[60] This Act was a milestone in the history of England's land tenures because it 'marked for the first time the compulsory intervention of the law in the supposedly voluntary bargains made between tenants and landlords, and set in motion a process which culminated in the state

the Nineteenth Century, 1st ed. (London and New York: Routledge, 2007); F. M. L. Thompson, 'Land and Politics in England in the Nineteenth Century', *Transactions of the Royal Historical Society* 15 (December 1965): 23–44. The general weakening of landlord influence in England in the second half of the nineteenth century is also attributed to the three Reform Acts of 1832, 1867, and 1884 which collectively expanded the franchise. For extended analysis, see Sir Llewellyn Woodward, *The Oxford History of England: The Age of Reform 1815–1870*, 2nd 2nd ed., (London: Oxford at the Clarendon Press, 1962); Thompson, *English Landed Society in the Nineteenth Century*; F. M. L. Thompson, 'Epilogue: The Strange Death of the English Land Question', in *The Land Question in Britain, 1750–1950*, ed. Matthew Cragoe and Paul Readman (Hampshire: Palgrave Macmillan, 2010), 257–70.

[56] William Gladstone Speech on the Irish Land Bill of 1870. 'Irish Land Bill. Hansard Third Series CXCIX' (Hansard (3rd Series), 1870), 359.

[57] Julian R. McQuiston, 'Tenant Right: Farmer against Landlord in Victorian England 1847–1883', *Agriculture History* 47, no. 2 (1973): 95. Also see Mason, 'The Duke of Argyll and the Land Question in Late Nineteenth-Century Britain'.

[58] Interestingly, the 1875 Act invoked the presence of customary tenant-right in Lincolnshire to legalise it without facing the criticism that the Act interfered with the freedom of contract. McQuiston, 'Tenant Right: Farmer against Landlord in Victorian England 1847–1883'.

[59] Fisher, 'The Farmers' Alliance'.

[60] McQuiston, 'Tenant Right: Farmer against Landlord in Victorian England 1847–1883', 108.

declaring that the tenant farmer had a species of proprietary interest in his farm as well as the owner'.[61]

The second intervention by the State in England's land tenure system was the creation of owner-operated small farms. The Small Holding Act of 1892, passed under the auspices of Lord Salisbury's Conservative Government,[62] gave County Councils the authority to facilitate through public funds the purchase of small farms (between one and fifty acres) from willing landowners by advancing eighty per cent of the purchase price. The programme did not have many takers because a lack of compulsion on the landowners did not lead to much land on the market for purchase and the difficulty of small farmers in coming up with the 20% down payment. From 1892 to 1907, only 881 acres came up for reallocation. The land acquisition provisions were expanded through another Act in 1907, which better satisfied the objectives of creating peasant proprietors. Between 1907 and 1913, more than fourteen thousand smallholders were settled on 205,103 acres of land.[63] Peasant proprietorship in England began to be seen not only as an answer to a lack of international competitiveness of the traditional English agrarian system of large-scale farms[64] but also 'socially and politically invaluable as reliable and numerous outer defenders of property rights . . . against socialist or communist attack'.[65]

Peasant proprietorship, which until the 1860s had more sceptics than supporters amongst imperial circles at home and in the colonies, had achieved greater acceptance across the political spectrum by the end of the century. In that sense, the British thinking about the socio-political and economic benefits of broader land ownership and security of tenure started converging with land reforms in other parts of the world during the second half of the century. These included the emancipation of serfs in Russia in 1861; the Homestead Act of 1862 and the Southern Homestead Act of 1868 in America, through which an American citizen, first just white and then expanded to African Americans, could claim 160 acres of government land for agriculture; the Dawes Act of 1887 which allowed the Federal government in America to break up land held by Native tribes and reallocate it in smaller parcels.[66]

[61] Thompson, *English Landed Society in the Nineteenth Century*, 196.

[62] Salisbury was not convinced about the economic viability of small farms. He supported the act because he believed that 'things are more important than the economy' and a small farmer is 'the strongest bulwark against revolutionary change'. Cites in Quentin Bone, 'Legislation to Revive Small Farming in England 1887–1914', *Agricultural History* 49, no. 4 (1975): 657–58.

[63] Bone, 'Legislation to Revive Small Farming in England 1887–1914'.

[64] Paul Readman, 'The Edwardian Land Question', in *The Land Question in Britain, 1750–1950*, ed. Matthew Cragoe and Paul Readman (Hampshire: Palgrave Macmillan, 2010), 181–200.

[65] Thompson, 'Changing Perceptions of Land Tenures in Britain, 1750–1914', 134.

[66] For details see Serge A. Zenkovsky, 'The Emancipation of the Serfs in Retrospect', *The Russian Review* 20, no. 4 (1961): 280–93; Jamie L. Bronstein, *Land Reform and Working-Class Experience in Britain and the United States, 1800–1862* (Stanford, CA: Stanford University Press, 1999); Warren Hoffnagle, 'The Southern Homestead Act: Its Origins and Operation', *The Historian*, August 1, 1970; D. S. Otis, *The Dawes Act and the Allotment of Indian Lands* (Norman, OK: University of Oklahoma Press, 2014).

Regarding property, there was greater acceptance of shared rights between landlords and tenants. From a political economy perspective, state intervention in redistributing property rights became an acceptable policy instrument.[67] Even assumptions about the aristocratic classes being indispensable to the stability of the existing political order were challenged, and there was a growing recognition across the political spectrum in England of the political advantage of a content peasantry. The new norms, taken together, represented an institutional change in the British Empire's land tenure system. The change was possible because of small incremental steps on land reform at the peripheries of the British Empire, which reinforced each other and eventually seeped into English land tenures.

In the 1870s, the creation of peasant proprietors through the land acts in Punjab, Ireland, and PEI was seen as *communistic.* By the end of the century, however, the same peasant proprietors became the *bulwarks against communism.*

Intra-Imperial to Inter-Colony Analogies

In his influential book, *Imperial Affinities*, S. B. Cook argued that although 'different in many aspects, Irish and Indian legislation of the 1880s reflected a similar orientation. Each represented a similar confluence of ideology and policy prescriptions based on the accumulated official experience of rural economies and tenurial systems. The scant influence of classical political economy and Anglo-centric models of socio-economic progress on legislation was especially notable ... Through an intellectual and administrative circuit of exchange, one component of the Empire, (Ireland) exerted an extraordinary degree of influence on the development of another, (British India)'.[68] Labelling these as 'intra-imperial analogies',[69] Cook argued that this process entailed 'a recognition that Britain's experience in Ireland was at least remotely relevant to that of other places under British rule', and thus policies introduced in the governance of Ireland could be suitably adapted and applied across its network of colonies.[70]

Numerous historians followed Cook's approach and identified various English principles (land tenure, education, and administration systems) transferred from Ireland to India.[71] This body of work comes to the following broad conclusions: (1)

[67] Avner Offer, 'Farm Tenure and Land Values in England, c. 1750–1950', *The Economic History Review* 44, no. 1 (February 1991): 1–20.

[68] Cook, *Imperial Affinities: Nineteenth Century Analogies and Exchanges Between India and Ireland*, 130, 134.

[69] A widely accepted definition of reasoning by analogy is that structural similarity or isomorphism between analogues being compared increases the 'likelihood that they have some further property in common'. Julian S. Weitzenfeld, 'Valid Reasoning by Analogy', *Philosophy of Science* 51 (1984): 137, 139.

[70] Cook, *Imperial Affinities*, 26–27.

[71] For representative works, see Barry Crosbie, 'Networks of Empire: Linkage and Reciprocity in Nineteenth-Century Irish and Indian History', *History Compass* 7, no. 3 (May 1, 2009): 993–1007; Alan

there was primarily a one-way flow from Ireland to India because 'Ireland acted as the 'colonial point of reference' and a 'laboratory for empire', and thus ideas 'fashioned in Ireland' were applicable in India;[72] and (2) the main objective of these analogies was to justify the transfer or transplant of English principles and policies across the Empire because their applicability in Ireland made them appropriate for adoption in similar colonial contexts. Foregrounding similarities between Ireland and India thus allowed for the diktat that what is good for Ireland is also suitable for India.

Empire and the Peasant Proprietor shows that the institutionalisation of peasant proprietorship across the British Empire was established through inter-colony analogies and precedents. Unlike 'intra-imperial' analogies, which functioned to justify the diffusion of policies based on English principles across the Empire, 'inter-colony' analogies aimed to decouple the colonies from those principles. The latter approach foregrounded shared conditions between the colonies and highlighted how these contrasted with conditions prevalent in England. These differences made English principles unsuited or inappropriate for the colonies.[73] I have argued that developments around property rights, political economy, and political expediency had created conflicting perspectives by the middle of the nineteenth century, which precluded movement on the land question in two colonies (Ireland and PEI) and were in the process of reversing the security of tenure for peasants in Punjab (through the privileging of the landowning class). Part of the stalemate was due to existing norms of viewing colonial land tenures solely through the lens of prevailing practices in England. The challenge for the Imperial Government, whose ideological affinity was more towards the peasants, was to find ways to overcome resistance from the privileged classes in England, which saw any encroachment on rights to property as a threat to their position. The use of 'inter-colony' analogies allowed for a redirection of the debate from one about how far land tenure across the Empire would impact the sanctity of English principles to one where the English principles were considered an anomaly and thus not applicable to the colonies because their situation was akin to each other rather than to the

Lester, 'Imperial Circuits and Networks: Geographies of the British Empire', *History Compass* 4, no. 1 (2006): 124–41; Patrick O'Leary, *Servants of the Empire: The Irish in Punjab 1881–1921* (Manchester, UK: Manchester University Press, 2011).

[72] Jane Ohlmeyer, 'Ireland, India and The British Empire', *Studies in People's History* 2, no. 2 (2015): 169.

[73] J. S. Mill, in his speech on an Irish land bill in 1866 in the British Parliament, had argued that 'Irish circumstances and Irish ideas as to social and agricultural economy are the general ideas and circumstances of the human race; it is English circumstances and English ideas that are peculiar'. John Stuart Mill, 'Speech on Mr. Chichester Fortescue's Land Bill, House of Commons, May 17, 1866', in *Chapters and Speeches on the Irish Land Bill*, by John Stuart Mill (London: Longmans, Green, Reader, and Dyer, 1870), 98. George Campbell also made a similar point in his book where he pointed out 'as the world now stands, it is we [that is, England] who are abnormal, and the Irish system is that which is more general'. George Campbell, *The Irish Land* (London: Trubner and Co., 1869), 16.

metropole. This decoupling of colonial land tenures from England also allowed for multi-directional analogies.

We see evidence of such inter-colony analogies when the Punjab precedent of customary tenures and occupancy rights was cited to legalise the Ulster and related custom-based tenant-right in Ireland in 1870, and subsequently the establishment of security of tenure through the 'three Fs' in 1881; the legalisation of tenant-right in Ireland serving as a model for PEI's Tenants' Compensation Act of 1872; security of tenure was subsequently extended to Scottish Crofters as well as to tenants across numerous provinces in British India. Similarly, compulsory land purchase in Prince Edward Island informed discussions in the push for increasing peasant proprietorship in Ireland in the 1880s and beyond. For example, Charles Stewart Parnell, leader of Ireland's Home League and its Land League in the 1870s[74] called Prince Edward Island the 'New Ireland' which, like its namesake, had struggled under the suffering of landlords and argued that the 'compulsory expropriation of the landlords . . .with full consent of her British Majesty' provided for an 'apt illustration' of a principle that would be suitable for Ireland.[75]

The debates around the various laws examined in this study show that proponents of security of tenure for cultivators increasingly used 'inter-colony' analogies to separate the land tenure issues in each colony from the practices in England. However, defenders of the property rights of landowners were persistent in their attempts to highlight how any security of tenure for the cultivators would impinge on the fundamental English principles about the sanctity of property rights and undermine the contractual arrangements between landlords and tenants. In essence, the debate was between those who believed in the universality of English land tenure principles, which needed to be religiously applied across the Empire (a case for legal transplants from the metropole to the colonies), and others, who saw colonies more like each other and very different from the metropole, thus necessitating solutions that were appropriate for the colonies, even if they diverged from the principles practised at home (a case for decoupling the colonies from the metropole).

*****

Why did the British Empire struggle to reform land tenure in its colonies in the middle of the nineteenth century by finding local solutions that diverged from the practices in England? After all, it had previously accepted significant legal divergences between England and its colonies in the eighteenth century. As argued by Burset, 'Britain's selective denial of English law to its colonies reflected a conscious

[74] 'Charles Stewart Parnell | Irish Nationalist, Politician & Leader | Britannica', June 23, 2024, <https://www.britannica.com/biography/Charles-Stewart-Parnell>.

[75] Charles Stewart Parnell, 'The Irish Land Question', *The North American Review* 130, no. 281 (1880): 400–401.

effort to shape their political and economic development . . . Legal pluralism . . . would keep colonies culturally distinct, politically dependent, and economically subordinate'.[76] Similarly, Ford outlines the legal divergence in policing in the colonies from practices in England to deal with local revolutionary activities. Autocratic policies to keep the peace were initiated in individual colonies and transferred between the colonies.[77]

Even in the context of land tenure, as the following illustrative examples show, the Empire had been open to divergence in land tenure arrangements between the metropole and the colonies and accepted the malleability of the sanctity of property rights and laissez faire principles.[78]

For instance, land in England was considered a 'positional asset' where significant holdings conferred political, social, and economic power and status beyond its 'monetary return'.[79] Its legal institutions restricted creditors' claims on any debts taken by the landowners. However, in 1732, the British Parliament passed the Debt Recovery Act, which allowed creditors to access assets (including land, houses, and enslaved people) to satisfy their claims from debtors in the British colonies in America.[80] It justified a separate law for the colonies because 'the role of the colonies was to benefit the British economy', and thus, the interests of English and Scottish creditors in the colonies had to be prioritised 'over any interest in replicating English law and political society'.[81]

Similarly, the Imperial governments allowed experimentation with different land tenure systems in the colonies. After replicating the English system of privileging landlords with substantial holdings in British India in the eighteenth century, the East India Company used utilitarian principles to experiment with forms of peasant proprietorship in a few provinces in the early part of the nineteenth century.[82] The British also saw economic and political value in widespread land ownership and promoted freehold tenures in its settler colonies around the globe.[83]

[76] Christian R. Burset, *An Empire of Laws: Legal Pluralism in British Colonial Policy* (New Haven, CT: Yale University Press, 2023), 9.

[77] Lisa Ford, *The King's Peace: Law and Order in the British Empire* (Cambridge, MA: Harvard University Press, 2021).

[78] For several other examples whereby the British Parliament allowed legal pluralism in dealing with land issues in the colonies in the eighteenth century, including by showing flexibility on the sanctity of property rights, see P. J. Marshall, 'Parliament and Property Rights in the Late Eighteenth-Century British Empire', in *Early Modern Conceptions of Property*, ed. John Brewer and Susan Staves (London and New York: Routledge, 1995), 530–44.

[79] Offer, 'Farm Tenure and Land Values in England, c. 1750–1950', 2.

[80] Priest, *Credit Nation*.

[81] Priest, *Credit Nation*, 8.

[82] These are discussed in more detail in the following chapters. For an extended discussion, see Baden-Powell, *A Short Account of the Land Revenue and Its Administration in British India; with a Sketch of the Land Tenures*; Roy and Swamy, *Law and the Economy in Colonial India*.

[83] Priest, *Credit Nation*; John C. Weaver, *The Great Land Rush and the Making of the Modern World, 1650–1900* (Montreal & Kingston: McGill-Queen's University Press, 2003); John McLaren,

On questions about the sanctity of property rights, the English landowners were accepting, even if reluctantly, of state intervention if it was justified for the common good (which included economic, political, and ethical grounds), and owners were compensated for confiscating their property. There are numerous examples where private interests in property became subservient to public interests: expropriation of land for building railroads and turnpikes in Britain since the seventeenth century; the abolition of heritable jurisdictions in Scotland in the eighteenth century; the abolition of slave trade and slavery across the Empire by the 1830s.[84] Adequate compensation was essential in all these cases to convince the property holders (whether in land, titles, or people) to relinquish their rights. For instance, Britain's offer of 20 million pounds to abolish slavery 'was the first subsidised emancipation scheme in which tax-payers paid off slave-owners, in cash or in bonds',[85] and 'was crucial to satisfying the broader anti-abolition coalition', with the level of compensation awarded 'attractive to many slave-owners relative to their expected income and social returns from continuing slave-ownership'.[86]

Numerous other developments around land reforms within and beyond the British Empire found some receptive audiences in England. The creation of peasant proprietors of formerly enslaved people after the emancipation in the West Indies and Haiti was seen as a positive outcome to compensate for the historical wrongs of slavery.[87] There was an appreciation for the beneficial political and economic effects of widely held property rights in America.[88] The accumulated evidence of the efficiency of small-scale owner-operated farms in Continental Europe also found favour in certain circles as an alternative agrarian model for England.[89]

The landowning class in England accepted land reforms entailing greater proprietary rights for the cultivators or users of land and the State's role in reallocating these rights if these did not materially impact its own position at home. However, as discussed in Chapter 1, the goals and the related mechanisms of land reform in the colonies started intersecting with land reforms in England by the 1830s. As

A. R. Buck, and Nancy E. Wright, *Despotic Dominion: Property Rights in British Settler Societies* (Vancouver: University of British Columbia Press, 2005).

[84] Julian Hoppit, 'Compulsion, Compensation and Property Rights in Britain, 1688–1833', *Past & Present*, no. 210 (2011): 93–128; Nicholas Draper, *The Price of Emancipation: Slave-Ownership, Compensation and British Society at the End of Slavery* (Cambridge, UK: Cambridge University Press, 2010).

[85] Draper, *The Price of Emancipation*, 270.

[86] Draper, *The Price of Emancipation*, 273.

[87] Carolyn Fick, 'Emancipation in Haiti: From Plantation Labour to Peasant Proprietorship', in *After Slavery: Emancipation and Its Discontents*, ed. Howard Temperley (London: Routledge, 2000), 11–39; Eleanor Marie Brown, 'On the Evolution of Property Ownership Among Former Slaves, Newly Freedmen', SSRN Scholarly Paper, Penn State Law Research Paper (Rochester, NY, June 23, 2016), <https://papers.ssrn.com/abstract = 2799648>.

[88] Priest, *Credit Nation*.

[89] William Thomas Thornton, *A Plea for Peasant Proprietors; with The Outlines of a Plan for Their Establishment in Ireland* (London: John Murray, Albermarle Street, 1848).

argued by Thompson, 'the England land question . . . had historically ridden on the back of the Irish land question. It had been one of the chief fears of English landowners and their allies, and one of the great hopes of English land reformers, that measure adopted to deal with the Irish situation would sooner or later be applied to the British mainland.'[90] England's landowning class made common cause with its brethren in the colonies to put a common front in resisting land reform to protect its political and economic influence. It re-emphasised the universality and sanctity of property rights, whereby the 'property of citizens of the colonies as well as the property of citizens of Great Britain was entitled to the protection which it afforded by applying the criteria of English law to colonial legislation.'[91] While accepting that the English common law needed to be adapted to the contingencies of the different colonies, the Imperial Government disallowed 'what it saw any substantial deviation from the principles of English law. It saw its duty as maintaining the [English rights of property] against what it believed to be irresponsible and self-interested colonial legislatures.'[92] Opposition to diluting landlords' property rights was particularly strong for colonies, such as Ireland and Prince Edward Island, where the Empire had itself assigned property rights to well-connected individuals as rewards for their past and continuing services to the imperial mission. In the previous chapters, we saw evidence of persistent refusal until the 1860s to give proprietary rights to the cultivators in Prince Edward Island by withholding Royal assent for laws passed by the colony's legislature and denying the security of tenure for Irish tenants by opposing almost yearly efforts since the Union by Irish Members of Parliament and their English supporters to bring about needed legislation.

It was only through the decoupling of the land question in the colonies from that in England and the creative use of inter-colony analogies that peasant rights' proponents could overcome resistance in England to colonial land reforms. From a conceptual point of view, the study's findings emphasise the differences between England and the colonies. The purpose of inter-colony analogies was not as much to transplant or transfer laws from one colony to the other[93] but to extricate the land tenure considerations in the colonies from the constraints of English principles. Land laws in the colonies shared an overall goal of security of tenure for the peasants, although the specific provisions of the acts varied considerably.

[90] Thompson, 'Epilogue: The Strange Death of the English Land Question', 261.

[91] Marshall, 'Parliament and Property Rights in the Late Eighteenth-Century British Empire', 539.

[92] Marshall, 'Parliament and Property Rights in the Late Eighteenth-Century British Empire', 539.

[93] The concept of legal transplants continues to evoke considerable debate in the academic literature. For the possibilities and pitfalls of legal transplants, see Toby S. Goldbach, 'Why Legal Transplants?', *Annual Review of Law and Social Science* 15, no. 1 (2019): 583–601; Pierre Legrand, 'The Impossibility of Legal Transplants', *Maastricht Journal of European and Comparative Law* 4, no. 2 (1997): 111–24; Timothy W. Guinnane, 'A Failed Institutional Transplant: Raiffeisen's Credit Cooperatives in Ireland, 1894–1914', *Explorations in Economic History* 31, no. 1 (January 1, 1994): 38–61.

Inter-colony analogies promoted the shared principles behind peasant proprietorship rather than the form it could take.

Governance Ideologies

How do the land reforms examined in this study inform debates on the global logic of the British Empire in the nineteenth century and its underlying ideologies and institutions, in particular, the cohesiveness, consistency, and universality of its overall ideology?[94] There are two sub-themes and related questions: (1) whether the Empire extended the 'civilised' hierarchy that underlined its approach to political representation in the various colonies to considerations about land tenure; and (2) whether the Empire retreated from its liberal principles in institutionalising land tenures around customs and customary rights.[95]

Concerning the first sub-theme, Duncan Bell suggests that 'Victorian thinkers tended to divide the world into different imaginative spheres, each generating radically diverse sociological accounts and competing ethical claims. The most important divide separated the 'civilised' and the 'non-civilised' spheres . . . and this bifocal, though fluid, conception of global order provided the theoretical foundations for justifying Empire'.[96] Karuna Mantena argues that political events in the 1850s and 1860s led to a shift from 'universalist' to a 'culturalist' stance the Empire's governance which 'deep-seated 'cultural' differences between peoples'.[97] An alternative view contests the 'othering' of racialised colonies, and instead sees the British Empire as being 'at least as much about class as it was about race and gender, and at least as much about what we might call 'Saming', or the reproduction of affinities and similarities, as it was about Othering or the production and reproduction of difference'.[98]

The findings from this study point towards a consistent approach across the three colonies by both defenders of landlords' property rights and those who saw the need to provide security of tenure to the cultivators. That is, the *zamindars* or

[94] David Armitage, *The Ideological Origins of the British Empire* (Cambridge, UK: Cambridge University Press, 2000); Duncan Bell, *Reordering the World: Essays on Liberalism and Empire* (Princeton, N.J.: Princeton University Press, 2016); Jennifer Pitts, *A Turn to Empire: The Rise of Imperial Liberalism in Britain and France* (Princeton, N.J.: Princeton University Press, 2005); Uday Singh Mehta, *Liberalism and Empire: A Study in Nineteenth-Century British Liberal Thought* (Chicago, I.L.: University of Chicago Press, 1999); Sartori, *Liberalism in Empire*.

[95] My discussion here is related just to land tenures. For broader discussion around these debates, see Mehta, *Liberalism and Empire*; Sartori, *Liberalism in Empire*; Pitts, *A Turn to Empire*; Bell, *Reordering the World*.

[96] Bell, 'Victorian Visions of Global Order', 9–10.

[97] Mantena, *Alibis of Empire*, 1–2.

[98] Daniel I. O'Neill, *Edmund Burke and the Conservative Logic of Empire* (Oakland, CA: University of California Press, 2016), 6. Also see David Cannadine, *Ornamentalism: How the British Saw Their Empire* (Oxford, UK: Oxford University Press, 2001).

talookdars in Punjab/India, the landlords from the era of conquest and Protestant Ascendancy in Ireland, and the absentee landlords who acquired their landholdings through generous grants for past service to the Empire in Prince Edward Island were all seen to have similar property rights, which needed to be protected by the Empire. Any encroachment was seen as 'communistic' in each colony. On the other side, the yeoman farmer in Punjab, the struggling tenant in Ireland, and the adventurous immigrant farmer of Prince Edward Island were all perceived to be suffering because they could not wholly appropriate the value of their labour and thus needed the security of tenure that recognised their value creation and provided additional incentives for improvement in the land they cultivated. Proponents of both views bolstered their positions by using analogies from different colonies or the metropole. They saw any encroachment to the rights of property and reassignment or redistribution of these rights through similar logics. Foregrounding the 'sameness' of landlords' rights or the tenants' material conditions across the different colonies was an important tool to bolster respective perspectives during the various debates on land tenure.

The argument about abandoning the Empire's liberal pretensions comes from the purported conservative turn towards restoring traditional socio-political hierarchies (including land aristocrats' property rights) in British India and the emphasis on customary tenures in India and Ireland. While it is probably true that a 'crisis of imperialism',[99] emanating from various political movements from East to West during the 1850s and 1860s led to a rethinking of the Empire's aspirations of creating 'little Englands'[100] in its multiple colonies, claims about the abjuration of its objectives are based on a partial understanding of what was happening around the Empire. For example, the literature suggests that in the 1860s, the 'policy in Ireland moved towards greater recognition and protection of the tenant, while in India, the attempt to record and preserve the status of the tenant gave way to a policy more favourable to the rights and interests of superior landholders'.[101] The historiography of the post-Mutiny land tenures in India ignores the happenings in Punjab.[102] The 1868 Act in Punjab protected the occupancy rights of the peasants despite the intense opposition in British India and England amongst the conservatives.

Similarly, much of the Empire literature does not include what was happening in the North American settler colonies, where the efforts in Prince Edward Island

99 Richard Shannon, *The Crisis of Imperialism, 1865–1915* (London: Hart-Davis, MacGibbon, 1974).
100 Mantena, *Alibis of Empire*, 2010, 146.
101 Ronald Hyam, *Britain's Imperial Century, 1815–1914: A Study of Imperial Expansion* (New York: Palgrave Macmillan, 2002), 143.
102 In fact, the Bengal Rent Act of 1859 (discussed at length in Chapter 2), legislated immediately after the 1857 Rebellion, provided a modicum of secure rights for occupancy tenancy in the form of fair rent, which was subsequently expanded to the 'three Fs' in the Punjab Act. For the Bengal Act, see Sartori, *Liberalism in Empire*; S. Ambirajan, *Classical Political Economy and British Policy in India* (Cambridge, UK: Cambridge University Press, 1978).

during that time focused on establishing freehold tenures for the cultivators in line with similar norms in other provinces of the Dominion of Canada. As shown in this study, land tenure legislation in the three colonies during the 1868–1875 period had a common objective: establishing proprietorship for the cultivators through greater tenure security or transferring full property rights from landholders to tenants. One could argue that the institutionalisation of peasant proprietorship based on liberal ideas and championed by William Gladstone's liberal governments during the so-called 'conservative' turn was a defining moment in the Empire's land tenure reform.

Furthermore, this study has shown that a turn to custom in establishing tenants' rights was not an abandonment of the principles of property rights and political economy; instead, it was a valuable tool to bring acceptance of new thinking on property rights (that is, shared and relative rights), and political economy (that is, socio-economic benefits of small landholdings) to overcome the entrenched ideas about absolute rights of landlords and large-scale capital farming as the engine of improvement and economic growth.[103] As argued by Sartori, 'the political vector represented by the liberal discourse of custom is best understood in terms of an expansively radical impulse in later nineteenth-century liberalism, rather than in terms of contractive reaction'.[104]

Nonetheless, the shift from denigrating customs and customary rights to justify the dispossession of land (as foregrounded by several comparative studies)[105] to attempts at their rediscovery to justify the reallocation of property rights (as shown in the current study) provides possibilities for future research that can probe how the Empire dealt with such contradictions in its ideologies and administrative principles and the implications for ongoing agitations amongst Indigenous people in its numerous former colonies. The logic of property rights in land by the end of the Victorian Era had come a full circle: from dispossession of land from original cultivators on the pretext that their traditional practices did not conform to modern English principles to confiscation of land from existing landowners or dilution of their property rights on the pretext that modern English principles could not accommodate cultivators' traditional practices. The Empire could get around these contradictions because, in numerous contexts, the dispossessed people differed

[103] An important recommendation of the Bessborough Commission was to have one law for all tenancy arrangements in Ireland, irrespective of whether the original rights were established through customary tenant-right or through the provisions of the 1870 Act for other arrangements. 'Report of Her Majesty's Commissioners of Inquire into the Working of the Landlord and Tenant (Ireland) Act, 1870'. Moreover, the debates about leasehold tenures in Prince Edward Island during the time did not invoke customs or customary rights, and even in subsequent debates around land tenure legislation in Punjab (Punjab Tenancy Act of 1887) and Ireland (Land Law of 1881) there is minimal resort to customs.

[104] Sartori, *Liberalism in Empire*, 201.

[105] Allan Greer, *Property and Dispossession: Natives, Empires and Land in Early Modern North America* (Cambridge, UK: Cambridge University Press, 2018); Brenna Bhandar, *Colonial Lives of Property: Law, Land, and Racial Regimes of Ownership* (Durham: Duke University Press, 2018); Weaver, *The Great Land Rush and the Making of the Modern World, 1650–1900*.

from the beneficiaries of redistribution.[106] Increasingly, the Indigenous people are trying to reclaim the very land that their ancestors lost through dispossession, thus creating difficulties for post-colonial governments in the former settler colonies of the British Empire, as dealing with these land claims requires confronting the contradictions.

Coda

> Peasants and other people living in rural areas have the right to land individually and or collectively . . . States shall take appropriate measures to provide legal recognition for land tenure rights, including customary land tenure rights not currently protected by law.
>
> —(Article 17 of the Resolution Adopted by the United Nations General Assembly, December 17, 2018)[107]

Secure land rights have long been recognised as a fundamental driver of economic empowerment for many people dependent on agriculture for their livelihoods. Despite efforts by international institutions such as the World Bank[108] and United Nations[109] to prod national governments to secure the rights of peasants/smallholders, encapsulated in Article 17 of the UN Resolution on Peasant Rights adopted in 2018, the goal remains elusive. The difficulty continues to arise because any security of tenure for peasants, as cultivators or users of land, often entails some form of redistribution of proprietary rights. The entrenched and influential owners of the same piece of land fiercely contest attempts to change existing arrangements. How do proponents of peasant rights, with their objective of distributive justice, overcome resistance from existing landowners and their claims around

[106] Tenant right contestations in settler colonies in the nineteenth century were primarily between different settler groups. Reeve Huston, *Land and Freedom: Rural Society, Popular Protest, and Party Politics in Antebellum New York* (New York: Oxford University Press, 2000); Wilson, *New Lease on Life*; Ian Ross Robertson, *The Tenant League of Prince Edward Island, 1864–1867: Leasehold Tenure in the New World* (Toronto; Buffalo; London: University of Toronto Press, 1996). As suggested by Philip Girard, individual property rights debates in the middle of the nineteenth century revolved around different groups of settlers, while the 'First Nations lay outside this dialectic, as their property claims were seen as collective use rights to particular territories or natural resources'. Philip Girard, 'Land Law, Liberalism, and the Agrarian Ideal: British North America, 1750–1920', in *Despotic Dominion: Property Rights in British Settler Societies*, ed. John McLaren, A. R. Buck, and Nancy E. Wright (Vancouver, B.C.: University of British Columia Press, 2005), 122.

[107] 'United Nations Declaration on the Rights of Peasant and Other People Working in Rural Areas', Official Record of the General Assembly, Seventy-Third Session, Supplement No. 53A (A/73/53/Add.1) (United Nations, December 17, 2018).

[108] 'Why Secure Land Rights Matter', World Bank, March 24, 2017, <https://www.worldbank.org/en/news/feature/2017/03/24/why-secure-land-rights-matter>.

[109] 'Secure Land Rights for All | UN-Habitat', 2008, <https://unhabitat.org/secure-land-rights-for-all>.

the sanctity of private property? This question continues to interest policymakers and researchers.[110]

Empire and the Peasant Proprietor attempted to address a similar question in the nineteenth century. Do its findings offer any lessons to the land question that continues to perplex policymakers in the twenty-first century? I will venture to offer two insights, one pessimistic and the other optimistic.

The book shows that landed interest in the colonies, with the support of the powerful landowning class in England, put together a united front to prevent any dilution of its property rights. It resisted land reform, entailing some security of tenure for the cultivators for almost a century, even though broader property rights were becoming acceptable outside the British Empire. A fortuitous alignment of governing bodies with similar ideological bent during the 1868 to 1875 period was what it took to overcome the resistance to land reform in the three colonies. One can conjecture as to the course of history if John Lawrence was not the Governor General of India in 1868 when the Punjab Tenancy Act of 1868 was taking shape. It was his strong will to preserve the occupancy rights of tenants in Punjab (which he had himself established during his earlier stint as the Lieutenant-Governor of Punjab) that stalled the momentum favourable to the landed interest that was taking shape after the 1857 Mutiny in British India. A different Governor-General may have let land tenures in British India take the route of those in Oudh (where proprietary rights of the tenants established just a decade before were rescinded and property rights of the aristocratic class restored in response to the Mutiny) and deprived the Irish land reformers of riding on the Indian precedents.

Similarly, a rare political alignment between the Catholic-supported pro-tenant and Protestant-supported pro-landowner political parties in Prince Edward Island in the 1860s helped the colony make difficult political (joining the Canadian Confederation) and economic decisions (taking an $800,000 loan) to eventually resolve the long-standing land question encompassing tenant-right and freehold tenures. Moreover, the legislature's solution required compulsory land purchase from unwilling landowners, which would have met the same fate of disallowance in England as its earlier attempts with a less liberal government than that of William Gladstone. The central figure that facilitated land reform in the colonies was Gladstone. Although he had not fully grasped the intricacies of the land question in the colonies when he took office in 1868 and was still ambivalent as to

[110] Recent works provide excellent expositions to this enduring question in diverse geographical contexts. Some representative studies include the following: Jo Guldi, *The Long Land War: The Global Struggle for Occupancy Rights* (New Haven and London: Yale University Press, 2021); Catherine Boone, *Property and Political Order in Africa: Land Rights and the Structure of Politics*, Cambridge Studies in Comparative Politics (New York: Cambridge University Press, 2014); Michael Albertus, *Property without Rights: Origins and Consequences of the Property Rights Gap* (Cambridge, UK: Cambridge University Press, 2020); Michael Albertus, *Autocracy and Redistribution* (New York: Cambridge University Press, 2015); Rosa Congost, Jorge Gelman, and Rui Santos, *Property Rights in Land: Issues in Social, Economic and Global History*, 1st ed. (Oxford, UK: Routledge, 2017).

the extent of peasant proprietorship that was feasible on political and conceptual grounds, some of the prominent members of his cabinet and his advisors (which included John Stuart Mill) were firm converts to the peasant proprietorship model. Over time, Gladstone became a fierce proponent of peasant rights, and his presence at the helm of the British government for extended periods in the 1870s and 1880s was critical for the institutionalisation of peasant proprietorship across the Empire and the growing possibility of its acceptance for English land tenures.

The ideological alignments of powerful governing agents across geographies at a given point in time identified in this study are rare. If such alignments are necessary to overcome resistance from entrenched landed interests and establish secure rights for the marginalised, the prospects of land reform are somewhat pessimistic.[111]

On the other hand, this study's findings about the effective use of inter-colony analogies to institutionalise peasant proprietorship across the Empire give cause for optimism on land reform. First, it demonstrates that solutions to intricate problems such as land tenure do not have to originate in the core and then be transplanted or transferred to the periphery. An ongoing difficulty with economic and political reforms worldwide is the Global South's resistance to the Global North's imposed norms (either directly by powerful states or indirectly through organisations such as the International Monetary Fund (IMF), World Bank, and the United Nations (UN), among others). Resistance to some land tenure reforms currently under discussion probably emanates from similar perceptions of being incompatible with local needs. Second, the study shows evidence of periphery-periphery transfer of ideas and reciprocal influences.[112] Taken together, these point towards the optimistic possibilities that impetus and leadership for land reform can originate in the Global South and find solutions through South-South cooperation. I hope that the possibilities to overcome resistance to peasant rights from the past identified in this book prove valuable in tackling similar challenges in the present and the future.

[111] While some institutional theorists have identified role of 'dominant change-agents', with their ability to build power coalitions, to be critical for institutional change (James Mahoney and Kathleen Ann Thelen, *Explaining Institutional Change Ambiguity, Agency, and Power* (Cambridge, UK: Cambridge University Press, 2010), others caution about emphasising 'muscular or heroic actors who somehow have a remarkable capacity to transform institutions', (Evelyn Micelotta, Michael Lounsbury, and Royston Greenwood, 'Pathways of Institutional Change: An Integrative Review and Research Agenda', *Journal of Management* 43, no. 6 (July 1, 2017): 1893.

[112] There is growing evidence of such legal influences in diverse contexts. See Assaf Likhovski, 'Peripheral Vision: Polish-Jewish Lawyers and Early Israeli Law', *Law and History Review* 36, no. 2 (2018): 235–66; T. T. Arvind and Daithí Mac Síthigh, 'Constitutionalism in the Periphery: Revisiting the Roots of Self-Rule Movements in Ireland and India', *Northern Ireland Legal Quarterly* 71, no. 2 (2020): 211–37.

Bibliography

Primary Sources

Manuscripts/Archives

Edward Augustus Prinsep Papers. Mss Eur D488: 1848-1898. British Library, India Office Records.

Edward Augustus Prinsep Petition to Join the Civil Service of the East India Company. IOR/J/1/70/115-24, 1945. British Library, India Office Records.

Fortescue, Chichester. 'Memorandum on the Irish Land Bill to Gladstone', September 13, 1869. Add. MSS 44121. British Library, India Office Records.

Gladstone Papers Vol. XVI. Correspondence with the Duke of Argyll. 1869-1870. Additional MS. 44.IOI. British Library.

Government of India, Department of Revenue, Agriculture and Commerce. 'Land Revenue and Settlements: Working of the Punjab Tenancy Act. Proceedings - Nos. 13 to 16', December 1874. National Archives of India, NAI.

Government of India, Foreign Department, Revenue A. 'Suits under the Punjab Tenancy Act from June to September 1870. K.W. Proceedings, Nos. 16-28', 1871. National Archives of India, NAI.

Government of India, Revenue and Agriculture Department. 'Punjab Revenue Report, 1880-1881, in Amendment of the Punjab Tenancy Act, XXVIII of 1868. Proceedings Nos. 21–22, January 1884', 1884. National Archives of India, NAI.

Government of India Revenue and Agriculture Department. Amendment of the Punjab Tenancy Act, Proceedings- Nos.33 and 34, 1882. National Archives of India, NAI.

Iddesleigh Papers, Letter from John Lawrence to Stafford Northcote, July 7, 1868. Add. MSS. 50226. British Library, India Office Records.

India Council Minute Book, January 1865 to December 1870. C.126. British Library, India Office Records.

India Council Summary Minutes, October 28, 1869. IOR/C/22-23. British Library, India Office Records.

India Political. Collections and Despatches, 1869. L/PS/6/548. British Library, India Office Records.

Ireland: Irish Land Acts, 1881–1929. Their History and Development, H045/13764. The National Archives Kew.

John Lawrence Collection: Viceroy of India 1864-1869. BL IOR/MSS.EUR./F.90/25-73. British Library, India Office Records.

Judicial and Public Department. 'Act XIII of 1900, Punjab Alienation of Land Act 1900'. J&P 2092, 1900. IOR J&P 2092. British Library, India Office Records.

Lieutenant Governor Fonds, 1871–1880. RG1. Prince Edward Island Public Records and Archives.

Letter from Argyll to Mayo, November 1, 1869, n.d. Mss Eur Photo Eur 466, f141. British Library, India Office Records.

Letters and Other Papers from Sir Henry Maine, 1869–1874, 8th Duke of Argyll Papers, n.d. Neg 423–47. British Library, India Office Records.

Letters from Secretary of State, 1849 to 1859, Colonial Office – Prince Edward Island, CO 227. Prince Edward Island Public Records and Archives.

Maine, Henry Sumner. 'The Effects of Observation of India on Modern European Thought. The Rede Lecture Delivered Before the University of Cambridge, May 22, 1875', 1875. MSS Eur F127/238. British Library, India Office Records.

Maine Collection. London School of Economics.
Maine, Sir Henry, Papers. European MSS: MSS.Eur.C.179. British Library. India Office Records.
Papers Regarding Tenant Rights in Oudh, Volume 6. BL IOR/L/PS/6/548 Coll 40/6, 1867. British Library, India Office Records.
Papers and Letters Relating to the Punjab Tenancy Act, 8th Duke of Argyll Papers, 1869. OMF/IOR NEG 4231-4242. British Library, India Office Records.
Prince Edward Island Original Correspondence. CO 226, 1763–1873. Prince Edward Island Public Records and Archives.
Private Letters from the Earl of Mayo to the Duke of Argyll, with Enclosures, 1869-1870, In 8th Duke of Argyll Papers, 1870 1869. IOR/Neg 423-47. British Library, India Office Records.
Richard Temple Collection. European MSS F. 86/84. British Library, India Office Records.
Secretary of State Council of India Proceedings on the Punjab Tenancy Act, October 29, 1869. BL IOR/C/22-23. British Library, India Office Records.
The [Irish] Land Act of 1870, and Proposed Reforms, July 21, 1880. CAB 37/2/37. The National Archives Kew.

Bills and Acts

ACT No. XVIII of 1868, The Punjab Tenancy Act, in A Collection of The Acts Passed by the Governor General of India in Council in the Year 1868: 180-197. Calcutta: Office of the Superintendent of Government Printing, 1868.
Act X. of 1859. *Calcutta Review*, 1864, 278–306.
An Act for settling differences between Landlord and Tenant, and to enable Tenants on certain Townships to purchase the fee simple of their Farms, Pub. L. No. Cap. II, 1864.
An ACT for the purchase of Lands on behalf of the Government of Prince Edward Island, and to regulate the sale and management thereof, and for other purposes therein mentioned, Pub. L. No. CAP. XVIII, 1853.
An Act to alter and amend 'The Tenants' Compensation Act, 1872', Pub. L. No. Cap. XXIV, 1873.
An Act to give effects to the Report of the Commissioners on the Land Question, Pub. L. No. CAP. IV, 1862.
An ACT to secure compensation to Tenants in Prince Edward Island, and thereby to promote the improvement of the Soil, Pub. L. No. CAP. XI, 1855.
Bengal Regulations Vol. 5 1820 to 1825. 'Regulation VII of 1822', 1822. BL IOR V/.
Gladstone, William, Chichester Fortescue, and John Bright. Irish Land: A Bill to Amend the Law relating to the Occupation and Ownership of Land in Ireland, Pub. L. No. 29, 1870.
Land Purchase Act, 1874, Pub. L. No. Cap. III, 1874.
Land Purchase Act, 1875, Pub. L. No. Cap. XXXII, 1875.
Landlord and Tenant Act (Ireland) 1870.
Landlord and Tenant Law Amendment Act (Ireland), 1860. (Deasy Act), 23 and 24 Vic. c. 154, 1860.
Stanley, Lord. Compensation of Tenants (Ireland) Bill, Pub. L. No. Hansard Third Series, Volume 81, 211–235, 1845.
The Punjab Tenancy Act, 1887. A Collection of the Acts Passed by the Governor General of India in Council in the Year 1887. Calcutta: Superintendent of Government Printing, 1888.
The Tenants' Compensation Act, Pub. L. No. Cap. IX (1871), 1871.
The Tenants' Compensation Act, Pub. L. No. Cap. X (1872), 1872.

Official Reports and Proceedings

'A Copy of General Report on the Administration of the Punjab Territories, for the Years 1856-7 and 1857-8', India Office, ordered to be Printed by the House of Commons, April 11, 1859. House of Commons Parliamentary Papers Online.
'Abstract of the Census of the Population and Other Statistical Returns of Prince Edward Island Taken in the Year 1871'. Reilly and Co., Charlottetown, 1871. Prince Edward Island Public Archives and Records Office.

Authority of the Governor-General. 'Abstract of the Proceedings of the Council of Governor-General of India. Assembled for the Purpose of Making Laws and Regulations'. 1869. Calcutta: Office of Superintendent of Government Printing.

Canada Supreme Court. *Judgment of* the *Supreme Court of Canada on the Appeal from the Judgment of the Supreme Court of Prince Edward Island Setting aside the Award of the Commissioners under the Land Purchase Act 1875, in the Case of Charlotte Antonia Sulivan.* Charlottetown, P.E.I.: Henry Lawson, 1877.

'Charles Stewart Parnell | Irish Nationalist, Politician & Leader | Britannica'. June 23, 2024. <https://www.britannica.com/biography/Charles-Stewart-Parnell>.

'Colonial Bills: North America'. The House of Commons, July 26, 1864. House of Commons Parliamentary Papers Online.

'COPY of the ADDRESS to Her Majesty, Adopted by the House of Assembly of Prince Edward Island on the 9th Day of May 1859, Praying for the Appointment of A COMMISSION to Inquire into the Existing Relations of LANDLORD and TENANT in That Colony: And, COPY or EXTRACTS of the Subsequent CORRESPONDENCE of the Secretary of State for the Colonies with the Governor of Prince Edward Island and Landowners and Others of That Colony, Relating to the Same Subject'. 1864. House of Commons Parliamentary Papers.

'Correspondence Relative to the Land Tenure Question in Prince Edward Island'. Presented to both Houses of Parliament by Command of Her Majesty, August 1875. British Parliamentary Papers.

'Debates and Proceedings of the House of Assembly of Prince Edward Island'. 1855–1876. Public Archives and Record Office of Prince Edward Island.

'East India (Progress and Condition); Statement Exhibiting the Moral and Material Progress and Condition of India, During the Year 1867-68'. House of Commons, 1869. House of Commons Parliamentary Papers Online.

British Library, India Office Records. 'East India (Punjab Tenancy): Copies of the Despatch of the Secretary of State for India in Council Dates the 28th Day of October (No. 80) 1869, to the Governor General of India in Council, on the Subject of the India Act No. XXVIII. of 1868, (Punjab Tenancy Act) '. House of Commons, 1870.

'Finance and Revenue Accounts of the Government of India 1862/63'. 1864. House of Commons Parliamentary Papers Online.

'First Report Made to His Majesty By the Commissioners Appointed to Inquire Into the Law of England Respecting Real Property'. House of Commons, May 20, 1829. House of Commons Parliamentary Papers Online.

'Further Correspondence Relative to the Land Tenure Question in Prince Edward Island'. April 1876. House of Commons Parliamentary Papers Online.

'General Report on the Administration of the Punjab for the Years 1849-50 and 1850-51'. London: Printed for the Court of Directors of the East-India Company by J and H. Cox, 1854.

Hancock, W. Neilson. 'Report on the Landlord and Tenant Question in Ireland, from 1860 till 1866; with an Appendix Containing A Report on the Question from 1835 till 1859'. Dublin: Alexander Thom, 1866.

'Irish Land Bill. Hansard Third Series CXCIX'. Hansard (3rd Series), 1870.

Journal of the House of Assembly of Prince Edward Island, 1855-1878.

Lucas, Sir Charles, ed. *Report on the Affairs of British North America from the Earl of Durham, February 11, 1839.* 3 vols. New York: August M. Kelley, 1912.

'Minutes of Conference between the Committee of the Privy Council of Canada, and the Undersigned Delegates from the Colony of Prince Edward Island, on the Subject of the Union of That Province with the Dominion of Canada'. *Royal Gazette.* March 17, 1873.

House of Commons Parliamentary Papers Online. 'Papers on the Subject of Affording the IMPERIAL GUARANTEE to a LOAN for the Service of PRINCE EDWARD ISLAND'. House of Commons, April 16, 1858.

House of Commons Parliamentary Papers Online. 'Papers "Relating to the Mutiny in the Punjab in 1857"'. House of Commons Parliamentary Papers, April 14, 1859.

'Prince Edward Island'. 1864. House of Commons Parliamentary Papers Online.

'Prince Edward Island. Further Correspondence Relative to the Land Tenure Question. Presented to Both Houses of Parliament. February 1881'. London: Her Majesty's Stationary Office, 1881. House of Commons Parliamentary Papers Online.

'Report from Her Majesty's Commissioners of Inquiry into the State of the Law and Practice in Respect of the Occupation to the Land in Ireland (Devon Commission)'. Dublin: Alexander Thom, 1845.

House of Commons Parliamentary Papers Online. 'Report from the Select Committee on Tenure and Improvement of Land (Ireland) Act; Together with the Proceedings of the Committee, Minutes of Evidence'. House of Commons Parliamentary Papers, 1865.

'Report of Her Majesty's Commissioners of Inquire into the Working of the Landlord and Tenant (Ireland) Act, 1870'. Presented to Both Houses of Parliament. Dublin: Alex Thom & Co., 1881.

Robertson, Ian Ross, ed. 'Report of the Commissioners Appointed by the Queen to Inquire into the Differences Prevailing in Prince Edward Island to the Rights of Landowners and Tenants with a View to a Settlement of the Same on Fair and Equitable Principles, July 18, 1861', in *The Prince Edward Land Commission of 1860*, 183–208. Fredericton, NB: Acadiensis Press, 1988.

'Sessional Papers. Second Session of the Third Parliament of the Dominion of Canada, Volume VIII'. 1875. Ottawa : King's Printer.

'Sir H. Elliott's Instructions to Board of Administration as to the Manner of Dealing with Landed Tenures in the Punjab, March 31, 1849'. 1856. House of Lords Papers, Volume XIII, Paper Number 197.

'The Agriculture Statistics of Ireland for the Year 1868'. Dublin: Alexander Thom, 1869. House of Commons Parliamentary Papers Online.

'The Bessborough Commission. Speech Delivered by the Duke of Argyll, During The Debate in the House of Lords on July 1st, 1881'. London: P.S. King, Parliamentary Bookseller, 1881.

'The Irish Land Bill. Speech Delivered by the Rt. Hon. W.E. Gladstone, in the House of Commons, On His Motion Introducing the Land Law (Ireland) Bill, April 7th, 1881'. London: The National Press Agency, Limited, 1881.

'The Parliamentary Reporter: Debates and Proceedings of the Legislative Council and House of Assembly of Prince Edward Island'. Charlottetown: Examiner Office, 1856.

'The Parliamentary Reporter! Or Debates and Proceedings of the House of Assembly of Prince Edward Island for the Year 1870'. Charlottetown: Patriot Book and Job Printing Rooms, 1870.

'The Parliamentary Reporter! Or Debates and Proceedings of the House of Assembly of Prince Edward Island for the Year 1874'. Charlottetown: J.H. Fletcher, 1874.

Wace, Captain E. G. 'Report of the Land Revenue Settlement of the Hazara District of the Punjab 1868-74'. Lahore: Printed at the Central Jail Press, 1875.

Wilson, J. 'Final Report on the Revision of Settlement of the Sirsa District in the Punjab, 1879-83'. Calcutta: Calcutta Central Press Company, 1884.

Primary Published Sources

Baden-Powell, B. H. *The Land-Systems of British India: Being a Manual of the Land-Tenures and of the Systems of Land-Revenue Administration Prevalent in the Several Provinces*. 3 vols. Oxford: Clarendon Press, 1892.

Bentham, Jeremy, Werner Stark, and Robert A. Fenn. *Jeremy Bentham's Economic Writings: Critical Edition Based on His Printed Works and Unprinted Manuscripts*. London: Published for the Royal Economic Society by George Allen & Unwin, 1952.

Bourne, Kenneth, ed. *The Letters of the Third Viscount Palmerston to Laurence and Elizabeth Sulivan, 1804-1863*. London: Offices of the Royal Historical Society, University College London, 1979.

Bright, John. *The Diaries of John Bright, with a Foreword by Philip Bright*. London: Cassell and Company, Limited, 1930.

Butt, Isaac. *Land Tenure in Ireland; A Plea for the Celtic Race*. Third. Dublin: John Falconer, 1866.

Butt, Isaac. *The Irish People and the Irish Land: A Letter to Lord Lifford; with Comments on the Publications of Lord Dufferin and Lord Rosse*. Dublin: John Falconer, 1867.

Caird, James. *The Irish Land Question*. London: Longmans, Green, Reader, and Dyer, 1869.

Cairnes, John Elliott. 'Ireland in Transition: Land Tenure'. *The Economist*, October 14, 1865: 1238–1239.

Cairnes, John Elliott. 'Ireland in Transition: Peasant Proprietorship'. *The Economist*, November 4, 1865: 1333–1334.

Cairnes, John Elliott. 'Ireland in Transition: Tenant-Right'. *The Economist*, October 28, 1865: 1301–03.

Cairnes, John Elliott. 'Ireland in Transition: The Future of Irish Industry'. *The Economist*, October 21, 1865: 1238–1239.

Cairnes, John Elliott. 'Political Economy of Land (Originally Published in Fortnightly Review, January 1870)', in *Essays in Political Economy: Theoretical and Applied*, by John Elliott Cairnes, 187–230. London: Macmillan and Co., 1873.

Campbell, George. *The Irish Land*. London: Trubner and Co., 1869.

Campbell, George. *The Progress of The Land Bill*. London: Trubner and Co., 1870.

Campbell, George. 'The Tenure of Land in India', in *Systems of Land Tenure in Various Countries: A Series of Essays Published under the Sanction of the Cobden Club*, 145–227. London: Macmillan and Co., 1870.

Campbell, Sir George. *Memories of My Indian Career*, edited by Sir Charles E. Bernard. 2 vols. London: Macmillan and Co., 1893.

Cobden Club (London, England). *Systems of Land Tenure in Various Countries*. London: Macmillan, 1870.

Darling, Malcolm Lyall. *The Punjab Peasant in Prosperity and Debt*. Oxford: Oxford University Press, 1928.

Davies, W. G. *Tenant-Right in the Punjab, and the Punjab Tenancy Act*. Allahabad: Pioneer Press, 1882.

De Kiewiet, C. W., and Frank H. Underhill, eds. *Dufferin-Carnarvon Correspondence, 1874-1878*. Toronto: The Champlain Society, 1955.

Douie, J. M. *Punjab Settlement Manual*. Delhi: Daya Publishing House, 1899.

Dufferin, Lord. *Irish Emigration and the Tenure of Land in Ireland*. London: Willis, Sotheran, and Co., 1867.

Dutt, Romesh C., ed. *Sir Philip Francis's Minutes of the Subject of a Permanent Settlement for Bengal, Behar and Orissa*. Calcutta: S.C. Auddy and Co., Booksellers and Publishers, 1901.

Ferguson, William Dwyer. *The Tenure and Improvement of Land in Ireland Considered with Reference to the Relation of Landlord and Tenant and Tenant-Right*. Dublin: E.J. Milliken, 1851.

Finlason, W. F. *The History of Law of Tenures of Land in England and Ireland: With Particular Reference to Inheritable Tenancy; Leasehold Tenure; Tenancy at Will; and Tenant Right*. London: Stevens & Hayes, 1870.

Fitzgibbon, Gerald. *The Land Difficulty of Ireland with and Effort to Solve It*. London: Longmans, Green, Reader, and Dyer, 1869.

Gladstone, William E. '"Our Colonies. An Address Delivered to the Members of the Mechanics' Institute, November 12, 1855"'. London: John W. Parker and Son, West Strand, 1855.

Grenville, William Wyndham. *Substance of the Speech of Lord Grenville on the Motion Made by the Marquis Wellesley, in the House of Lords, on Friday, the 9th of April 1813, for the Production of Certain Papers on Indian Affairs*. London: Printed by C. H. Reynell, 1813.

Hoskyns, C. Wren. 'Land-Laws in England', in *Systems of Land Tenure in Various Countries: A Series of Essays Published Under the Sanction of the Cobden Club*, 92–144. London: Macmillan and Co., 1870.

Kipling, Rudyard. 'The Head of the District', in *Life's Handicap: Being Stories of My Own People*, by Rudyard Kipling, 171–93. Charleston, SC: BiblioBazaar, 2007.

Locke, John. *Two Treatises of Government*. Merchant Books, 1921.

Longfield, M. 'Tenure of Land in Ireland', in *Systems of Land Tenure in Various Countries: A Series of Essays Published Under the Sanction of the Cobden Club*, 1–91. London: Macmillan and Co., 1870.

Maguire, John Francis. *Irish in America*. New York: D&J Sadlier, 1873.

Maine, Henry Sumner. *Ancient Law: Its Connection with the Early History of Society and Its Relation to Modern Ideas*. London: John Murray, 1901.

Maine, Henry Sumner. *Lectures on the Early History of Institutions*. London: John Murray, Albermarle Street, 1905.

Maine, Henry Sumner. *Village-Communities in the East and West: Six Lectures Delivered at Oxford*. London: J. Murray, 1871.

Matthew, H. C. G. *The Gladstone Diaries With Cabinet Minutes and Prime-Ministerial Correspondence: Volume Seven, January 1869-June 1871*. Oxford: Oxford University Press, 1982.

Mill, John Stuart. *England and Ireland*. 2nd ed. London: Longmans, Green, Reader, and Dyer, 1868.

Mill, John Stuart. 'Landed Tenure in Ireland', in *Newspaper Writings December 1847 - July 1873, in Collected Works of John Stuart Mill, Volume XXV*, edited by Ann P. Robson and John B. Robson, 1112–15. Toronto and Buffalo: University of Toronto Press, 1986.

Mill, John Stuart. 'Maine on Village Communities', in *Collected Works of John Stuart Mill: Writings on India*, edited by John B. Robson, Martin Moir, and Zawahir Moir, XXX:213–28. Toronto and Buffalo: University of Toronto Press, 1990.

Mill, John Stuart. 'Speech on Mr. Chichester Fortescue's Land Bill, House of Commons, May 17, 1866', in *Chapters and Speeches on the Irish Land Bill*, by John Stuart Mill, 97–107. London: Longmans, Green, Reader, and Dyer, 1870.

Mill, John Stuart, Jeremy Bentham, John Austin, and Mary Warnock. *Utilitarianism: And, On Liberty: Including Mill's Essay on Bentham, and Selections from the Writings of Jeremy Bentham and John Austin*. 2nd ed. Malden, MA: Blackwell Pub., 2003.

Mill, John Stuart, and Jonathan Riley. *Principles of Political Economy: And Chapters on Socialism*. World's Classics. Oxford; New York: Oxford University Press, 1994.

Mineka, Francis E., and Dwight N. Lindley, eds. 'Letter from J.S. Mill to Henry Maine, January 1, 1869'., in *The Later Letters of John Stuart Mill 1849-1873*, XVII:1536–39. Collected Works of John Stuart Mill. Toronto and Buffalo: University of Toronto Press, 1972.

Mischievous Legislation, Being a Series of Articles on Tenant Right in the Punjab. Reprinted from "Indian Public Opinion," with Appendices. Lahore: Indian Public Opinion Press, 1868.

Opinions of the Press in India on (I) The Tenant Right Controversy in the Punjab. (II) The Action Taken by the Government of India. (III) The Legislative Measure Called "The Punjab Tenancy Act," as Collected from the Newspapers, during the Years 1865 to 1869. Lahore: Indian Public Opinion Press, 1869.

Montgomery, James F. *An Experiment in Communism and Its Results: A Letter to the Right Honorable the Earl of Carnarvon*. Charlottetown: Bremmer Brothers, 1875.

Parnell, Charles Stewart. 'The Irish Land Question'. *The North American Review* 130, no. 281 (1880): 388–406.

Pears, Edwin, ed. *Transactions of the National Association for the Promotion of Social Science, Bristol Meeting 1869*. London: Longmans, Green, Reader, and Dyer, 1870.

Ricardo, David. *The Principles of Political Economy & Taxation*. Everyman's Library. London: New York: J. M. Dent & sons, ltd.; E. P. Dutton & co, 1912.

Richey, Alexander G. *The Irish Land Laws*. London: Macmillan, 1880.

Robson, John M., Michael Laine, and Marion Filipiuk, eds. *Additional Letters of John Stuart Mill*. Toronto: University of Toronto Press, 1991.

Seebohm, F. 'The Historical Claims of Tenant Right'. *The Nineteenth Century: A Monthly Review* 9, no. 47 (January 1881): 19–36.

Seebohm, F. 'The Land Question: Part I. English Tenures in Ireland'. *Fortnightly Review*, December 1869, 626–40.

Seebohm, F. 'The Land Question: Part II. Feudal Tenures in England'. *Fortnightly Review*, January 1870, 89–107.

'Selection from Records of the Government of Punjab, Papers Connected with the Question of Tenant Right in the Punjab'. Lahore: C.H. Voss, 1869.

Smith, Adam, and D. D. Raphael. *The Wealth of Nations*. Everyman's Library 11. New York: Knopf: Distributed by Random House, 1991.

Temple, Richard. *James Thomason*. Oxford: Clarendon Press, 1893.

Temple, Richard. *Lord Lawrence*. London: MacMillan, 1890.

Temple, Richard. *The Story of My Life. In Two Volumes*. London, Paris, Melbourne: Cassell and Company, Limited, 1896.

'The Irish Land Bill. Speech Delivered by the Rt. Hon. W.E. Gladstone, in the House of Commons, On His Motion Introducing the Land Law (Ireland) Bill, April 7th, 1881'. London: The National Press Agency, Limited, 1881.

Thorburn, S. S. *Musalmans and Money-Lenders in the Punjab*. Edinburgh and London: William Blackwood & Sons, 1886.

Thornton, William Thomas. *A Plea for Peasant Proprietors; with The Outlines of a Plan for Their Establishment in Ireland*. London: John Murray, Albermarle Street, 1848.

Tupper, C. L. *Punjab Customary Law: Volume I. A Selection from the Records of the Punjab Government*. Calcutta: Office of the Superintendent of Government Printing, 1881.

Tupper, C. L. *Punjab Customary Law: Volume II. Statements of Customary Laws in Different Districts*. Vol. II. Calcutta: Office of the Superintendent of Government Printing, 1881.

Tupper, C. L. *Punjab Customary Law: Volume III. Questions on Tribal and Local Custom*. Vol. III. Calcutta: Office of the Superintendent of Government Printing, 1881.

Wingfield, Charles. *Observations on Land Tenures and Tenant Right in India*. London: Wm. H. Allen and Co., 1869.

Newspapers

Charlottetown Herald (Prince Edward Island)
Delhi Gazette (India)
The Cork Examiner (Ireland)
The Economist (England)
The Examiner (Prince Edward Island)
Freeman's Journal (Ireland)
The Friend of India (India)
The Globe (England)
The Guam Herald (Ireland)
Indian Public Opinion (India)
The Island Magazine (Prince Edward Island)
Irish Examiner (Ireland)
Irish Times and Daily Advertiser (Ireland)
Lahore Chronicle (India)
The Liverpool Daily (England)
Mayo Examiner (Ireland)
Nation (Ireland)
Patriot (Prince Edward Island)
Paul Mall Gazette (England)
Pioneer (India)
The Punjabee (India)
Royal Gazette (Prince Edward Island)
The Saturday Review (England)
The Spectator (England)
The Tablet (England)
The Times (England)
Times of India (India)

Secondary Sources

Aitchison, Sir Charles. *Rulers of India: Lord Lawrence.* Oxford: The Clarendon Press, 1892.

Albertus, Michael. *Property without Rights: Origins and Consequences of the Property Rights Gap.* Cambridge: Cambridge University Press, 2020.

Albertus, Michael. *Autocracy and Redistribution.* New York: Cambridge University Press, 2015.

Albertus, Michael. *Property without Rights: Origins and Consequences of the Property Rights Gap.* Cambridge, UK: Cambridge University Press, 2020.

Ali, Imran. *The Punjab Under Imperialism, 1885-1947.* Princeton, NJ: Princeton University Press, 2014.

Ali, Imran. 'The Punjab Canal Colonies'. Ph.D. Thesis. The Australian National University, 1979.

Ambirajan, S. *Classical Political Economy and British Policy in India.* Cambridge, UK: Cambridge University Press, 1978.

Armitage, David. *The Ideological Origins of the British Empire.* Cambridge, UK: Cambridge University Press, 2000.

Arnold, Edwin. *The Marquis of Dalhousie's Administration of British India, Volume the First, Containing the Acquisition and Administration of the Punjab.* London: Sauders, Otley, and Co., 1862.

Arvind, T. T., and Daithí Mac Síthigh. 'Constitutionalism in the Periphery: Revisiting the Roots of Self-Rule Movements in Ireland and India', *Northern Ireland Legal Quarterly* 71, no. 2 (2020): 211–37.

Aulakh, Preet S. 'Law, Identity and Imperial Logics of Exclusion: The Case of the Komagata Maru Passengers', *The Journal of Imperial and Commonwealth History* 49, no. 5 (2021): 866–98.

Aydelotte, William O. 'The Country Gentlemen and the Repeal of the Corn Laws', *The English Historical Review* 82, no. 322 (1967): 47–60.

Baglole, Harry. 'Cooper, William (d. 1867)', *Dictionary of Canadian Biography*, Volume IX (1861–1870). University of Toronto/Université Laval, 2003.

Baglole, Harry. 'Patterson, Walter'. *Dictionary of Canadian Biography*, Volume IV (1771–1800). University of Toronto/Université Laval, 2003.

Banerjee, Abhijit, and Lakshmi Iyer. 'History, Institutions, and Economic Performance: The Legacy of Colonial Land Tenure Systems in India', *American Economic Review* 95, no. 4 (2005): 1190–213.

Banerjee, Sukanya. *Becoming Imperial Citizens: Indians in the Late-Victorian Empire.* Durham, NC: Duke University Press, 2010.

Banga, Indu. *Agrarian System of the Sikhs: Late Eighteenth and Early Nineteenth Century.* New Delhi: Manohar, 1978.

Barrier, N. Gerald. 'The Formulation and Enactment of the Punjab Alienation of Land Bill', *The Indian Economic & Social History Review* 2, no. 2 (1965): 145–65.

Barrier, N. Gerald. *The Punjab Alienation of Land Bill of 1900.* Durham, NC: Duke University, 1966.

Barrier, N. Gerald. 'The Punjab Government and Communal Politics, 1870-1908', *The Journal of Asian Studies* 27, no. 3 (1968): 523–39.

Bastable, C. F. 'The Irish Land Purchase Act of 1903', *The Quarterly Journal of Economics* 18, no. 1 (1903): 1–21.

Bayly, C. A. 'Ireland, India and the Empire: 1780-1914', *Transactions of the Royal Historical Society* 10 (2000): 377–97.

Bayly, C. A. 'Maine and Change in Nineteenth-Century India', in *The Victorian Achievement of Sir Henry Maine: A Centennial Reappraisal*, edited by Alan Diamond, 389–97. New York: Cambridge University Press, 1991.

Bayly, C. A. *The Birth of the Modern World 1780-1914.* Malden, MA: Blackwell Publishing, 2004.

Beaglehole, J. C. 'The Colonial Office, 1782-1854', *Australian Historical Studies* 1, no. 3 (1941): 170–89.

Beckert, Jens. "Institutional Isomorphism Revisited: Convergence and Divergence in Institutional Change', *Sociological Theory* 28, no. 2 (2010): 150–66.

Bell, Duncan. 'John Stuart Mill on Colonies', *Political Theory* 38, no. 1 (February 1, 2010): 34–64.
Bell, Duncan. *Reordering the World: Essays on Liberalism and Empire*. Princeton, NJ: Princeton University Press, 2016.
Bell, Duncan. 'Victorian Visions of Global Order: An Introduction', in *Victorian Visions of Global Order: Empire and International Relations in Nineteenth-Century Political Thought*, edited by Duncan Bell, 1–25. Cambridge, NY: Cambridge University Press, 2007.
Besley, Timothy. 'Property Rights and Investment Incentives: Theory and Evidence from Ghana', *Journal of Political Economy* 103, no. 5 (1995): 903–37.
Besley, Timothy J., Konrad B. Burchardi, and Maitreesh Ghatak. 'Incentives and the De Soto Effect', *The Quarterly Journal of Economics* 127, no. 1 (February 1, 2012): 237–82.
Bhandar, Brenna. *Colonial Lives of Property: Law, Land, and Racial Regimes of Ownership*. Durham, NC: Duke University Press, 2018.
Bhatia, Nandi. *Acts of Authority, Acts of Resistance: Theater and Politics in Colonial and Postcolonial India*. Ann Arbor, MI: University of Michigan Press, 2004.
Bhattacharya, Neeladri. *The Great Agrarian Conquest: The Colonial Shaping of a Rural World*. New Delhi: Permanent Black, 2019.
Bittermann, Rusty. 'Lady Landlords and the Final Defence of Landlordism on Prince Edward Island: The Case of Charlotte Sulivan', *Histoire Sociale/Social History* 38, no. 76 (2005): 204–33.
Bittermann, Rusty. *Rural Protest on Prince Edward Island: From British Colonization to the Escheat Movement*. Toronto: University of Toronto Press, 2006.
Bittermann, Rusty, and Margaret McCallum. *Lady Landlords of Prince Edward Island*. Montreal & Kingston: McGill-Queen's University Press, 2008.
Bittermann, Rusty, and Margaret McCallum. 'The Pursuit of Gentility in an Age of Revolution: The Family of Jonathan Worrell', *Acadiensis* 43, no. 2 (2014): 31–56.
Bittermann, Rusty, and Margaret McCallum. 'Upholding the Land Legislation of a "Communistic and Socialist Assembly": The Benefits of Confederation for Prince Edward Island', *The Canadian Historical Review* 81, no. 1–15 (2006): 31–56.
Bittermann, Rusty, and Margaret McCallum. 'When Private Rights Become Public Wrongs: Property and the State in Prince Edward Island in the 1830s', in *Despotic Dominion: Property Rights in British Settler Colonies*, edited by John McLaren, A. R. Buck, and Nancy E. Wright, 144–68. Vancouver, BC: University of British Columbia Press, 2005.
Black, R. D. Collison. 'Cairnes, John Elliot (1823–1875), Economist', *Oxford Dictionary of National Biography*. Oxford, UK: Oxford University Press, 2004. https://www.oxforddnb.com/view/10.1093/ref:odnb/9780198614128.001.0001/odnb-9780198614128-e-4345.
Black, R. D. Collison. 'Economic Policy in Ireland and India in the Time of J. S. Mill', *The Economic History Review* 21, no. 2 (1968): 321–36.
Black, R. D. Collison. *Economic Thought and the Irish Question, 1817-1870*. Cambridge, UK: Cambridge University Press, 2015.
Blakely, Phyllis R. 'Cunard, Sir Samuel', Volume IX (1861–1870), *Dictionary of Canadian Biography*', University of Toronto/Université Laval, 2003.
Bolger, Francis W. P. 'The Beginnings of Independence, 1767-1787', in *Canada's Smallest Province: A History of P.E.I.*, edited by Francis W.P. Bolger, 37–65. Charlottetown, P.E.I.: Prince Edward Island 1973 Centennial Commission, 1973.
Bolger, Francis W. P. 'The Demise of Quit Rents and Escheat, 1824-1842', in *Canada's Smallest Province: A History of P.E.I.*, edited by Francis W. P. Bolger, 95–114. Charlottetown: Prince Edward Island 1973 Centennial Commission, 1973.
Bolger, Francis W. P. 'Long Courted, Won at Last', in *Canada's Smallest Province: A History of P.E.I.*, edited by Francis W. P. Bolger, 207–31. Charlottetown, P.E.I.: Prince Edward Island 1973 Centennial Commission, 1973.
Bolger, Francis W. P. 'Nation Building at Charlottetown, 1864', in *Canada's Smallest Province: A History of P.E.I.*, edited by Francis W. P. Bolger, 135–55. Charlottetown, P.E.I.: Prince Edward Island 1973 Centennial Commission, 1973.
Bolger, Francis W. P. *Prince Edward Island and Confederation, 1863-1873*. Charlottetown, P.E.I.: St. Dunstan's University Press, 1964.

Bolger, Francis W. P. 'Prince Edward Island Rejects Confederation, 1864-1867', in *Canada's Smallest Province: A History of P.E.I.*, edited by Francis W. P. Bolger, 156–84. Charlottetown, P.E.I.: Prince Edward Island 1973 Centennial Commission, 1973.

Bone, Quentin. 'Legislation to Revive Small Farming in England 1887-1914', *Agricultural History* 49, no. 4 (1975): 653–61.

Boone, Catherine. *Property and Political Order in Africa: Land Rights and the Structure of Politics*. Cambridge Studies in Comparative Politics. New York: Cambridge University Press, 2014.

Bourke, P. M. Austin. 'The Agricultural Statistics of the 1841 Census of Ireland. A Critical Review', *The Economic History Review* 18, no. 2 (1965): 376–91.

Boyle, John W. 'Ireland and the First International', *Journal of British Studies* 11, no. 2 (1972): 44–62.

Bronstein, Jamie. 'The Homestead and the Garden Plot: Cultural Pressures on Land Reform in Nineteenth-Century Britain and the USA', *The European Legacy* 6, no. 2 (2001): 159–75.

Bronstein, Jamie L. *Land Reform and Working-Class Experience in Britain and the United States, 1800-1862*. Stanford, CA: Stanford University Press, 1999.

Brann, Henry A. *Gladstone and Irish Grievance. An Essay*. New York: Benj. H. Tyrrel, 1881.

Brown, Eleanor Marie. 'On the Evolution of Property Ownership Among Former Slaves, Newly Freedmen', SSRN Scholarly Paper. Penn State Law Research Paper. Rochester, NY, June 23, 2016. <https://papers.ssrn.com/abstract = 2799648>.

Brown, R. Blake. 'A Taxonomy of Methodological Approaches in Recent Canadian Legal History', *Acadiensis* 34, no. 1 (2004): 145–55.

Buck, A. R. 'Property, Aristocracy and the Reform of the Land Law in Early Nineteenth Century England', *Journal of Legal History* 16, no. 1 (1995): 63–93.

Buck, A. R., John McLaren, and Nancy E. Wright. *Land and Freedom: Law, Property Rights and the British Diaspora*. Aldershot, UK: Ashgate, 2001.

Buckner, Phillip A. ed. *Canada and the British Empire*. Oxford, UK: Oxford University Press, 2010.

Bumsted, J. M. 'Island Resistance: Two Popular Movements for Political Change in the Era of Confederation', *Acadiensis* 27, no. 2 (1998): 135–41.

Bumsted, J. M. *Land, Settlement, and Politics on Eighteenth-Century Prince Edward Island*. Montreal: McGill-Queen's Press - MQUP, 1987.

Bumsted, J. M. 'The Land Question on Prince Edward Island and the Quitrent Controversy of 1802-1806', *Acadiensis* 29, no. 2 (2000): 3–26.

Bumsted, J. M. 'The Origins of the Land Question on Prince Edward Island, 1767-1805', *Acadiensis* 11, no. 1 (1981): 43–56.

Burset, Christian R. *An Empire of Laws: Legal Pluralism in British Colonial Policy*. New Haven, CT: Yale University Press, 2023.

Cairns, John W. *Codification, Transplants and History: Law Reform in Louisiana (1808) and Quebec (1866)*. Clark, New Jersey: Talbot Publishing, an imprint of The Lawbook Exchange, Ltd., 2015.

Cannadine, David. *Ornamentalism: How the British Saw Their Empire*. Oxford, UK: Oxford University Press, 2001.

Caporaso, James A., and David P. Levine. *Theories of Political Economy*. New York: Cambridge University Press, 1992.

Casey, Terence. *The Tenant's Tale: A Chronicle of Life in Rural Ireland during the 19th Century*. Berks, UK: Domlan Scott Ltd, 2013.

Chandra, Bipan. *India's Struggle for Independence, 1857-1947*. New Delhi, India: Penguin Books, 1989.

Chaudhry, Faisal. 'A Rule of Proprietary Right for British India: From Revenue Settlement to Tenant Right in the Age of Classical Legal Thought', *Modern Asian Studies* 50, no. 1 (January 2016): 345–84.

Childers, Edmund Spencer Eardley. *The Life and Correspondence of the Right Hon. Hugh C. E. Childers, 1827-1896*. London: J. Murray, 1901.

Clark, Andrew Hill. *Three Centuries and the Island: A Historical Geography of Settlement and Agriculture in Prince Edward Island, Canada.* Toronto: University of Toronto Press, 1959.

Cole, Daniel H., and Peter Z. Grossman. 'The Meaning of Property Rights: Law versus Economics?', *Land Economics* 78, no. 3 (2002): 317–30.

Condos, Mark. *The Insecurity State: Punjab and the Making of Colonial Power in British India.* Cambridge, UK: Cambridge University Press, 2017.

Cook, S.B. *Imperial Affinities: Nineteenth Century Analogies and Exchanges Between India and Ireland.* New Delhi: Sage Publications, 1993.

Cowell, Herbert. *The History and Constitution of the Courts and Legislative Authorities in India.* Second Edition. Calcutta: Thacker, Spink and Co., 1884.

Cragoe, M., and P. Readman, eds. *The Land Question in Britain, 1750-1950.* New York: Palgrave Macmillan, 2010.

Crawford, W. H. 'Landlord-Tenant Relations in Ulster 1609–1820', *Irish Economic and Social History* 2 (1975): 5–21.

Crosbie, Barry. 'Networks of Empire: Linkage and Reciprocity in Nineteenth-Century Irish and Indian History', *History Compass* 7, no. 3 (May 1, 2009): 993–1007.

Cunningham, John. 'Oliver Cromwell and the 'Cromwellian Settlement' of Ireland', *The Historical Journal* 53, no. 4 (2010): 919–37.

Currie, J. M. *The Economic Theory of Agricultural Land Tenure.* Cambridge; New York: Cambridge University Press, 1981.

Daly, Mary E., and K. Theodore Hoppen, eds. *Gladstone: Ireland and Beyond.* Dublin: Four Courts Press, 2011.

Darling, Malcolm Lyall. *The Punjab Peasant In Prosperity And Debt.* Oxford, UK: Oxford University Press, 1928.

Davenport-Hines, Richard. *Blackwood, Frederick Temple Hamilton-Temple-, First Marquess of Dufferin and Ava (1826–1902), Diplomatist.* London: Oxford University Press, 2008.

Demsetz, Harold. 'Toward a Theory of Property Rights', *The American Economic Review* 57, no. 2 (1967): 347–59.

Dewey, Clive. 'The Influence of Sir Henry Maine on Agrarian Policy in India', in *The Victorian Achievement of Sir Henry Maine: A Centennial Reappraisal*, edited by Alan Diamond, 353–75. New York: Cambridge University Press, 1991.

Dewey, Clive. *The Settlement Literature of the Greater Punjab: A Handbook.* New Delhi: Manohar Publications, 1991.

Dewey, Clive J. 'The Rehabilitation of the Peasant Proprietor in Nineteenth-Century Economic Thought', *History of Political Economy* 6, no. 1 (1974): 17–47.

DiMaggio, Paul J., and Walter W. Powell. 'The Iron Cage Revisited: Institutional Isomorphism and Collective Rationality in Organizational Fields', *American Sociological Review* 48, no. 2 (1983): 147–60.

di Robilant, Anna. 'Property: A Bundle of Sticks or a Tree', *Vanderbilt Law Review* 66, no. 3 (2013): 869–932.

Dirks, Nicholas B. *The Scandal of Empire: India and the Creation of Imperial Britain.* Cambridge, MA: Belknap Press of Harvard University Press, 2006.

Dodwell, H. H., ed. *The Cambridge History of India. Volume VI: The Indian Empire 1858-1918.* Cambridge, UK: Cambridge University Press, 1932.

Dooley, Terence. 'Land and The People', in *the Oxford Handbook of Modern Irish History*, edited by Alvin Jackson, 107–25. Oxford, UK: Oxford University Press, 2014.

Dorsett, Shaunnagh and John McLaren, eds. *Legal Histories of the British Empire: Laws, Engagements and Legacies.* Abingdon, Oxon: Routledge, 2014.

Dowling, Alan. 'The Genesis of Deasy's Act Comments and Notes', *Northern Ireland Legal Quarterly* 40, no. 1 (1989): 53–63.

Dowling, Martin W. *Tenant Right and Agrarian Society in Ulster 1600-1870.* Dublin: Irish Academic Press, 1999.

Draper, Nicholas. *The Price of Emancipation: Slave-Ownership, Compensation and British Society at the End of Slavery.* Cambridge, UK: Cambridge University Press, 2010.

Duncan, Myrl L. 'Reconceiving the Bundle of Sticks: Land as a Community-Based Resource', *Environmental Law* 32, no. 4 (2002): 773–808.

Dunning, Wm. A. 'Irish Land Legislation Since 1845. I', *Political Science Quarterly* 7, no. 1 (1892): 57–79.

Dunning, Wm. A. 'Irish Land Legislation Since 1845. II', *Political Science Quarterly* 7, no. 3 (1892): 500–21.

Eagan, Catherine M. '"White," If "Not Quite": Irish Whiteness in the Nineteenth-Century Irish-American Novel", *Eire-Ireland* 36, no. 1 (2001): 66.81.

Evans, Shaun, Tony McCarthy, and Annie Tindley. 'Introduction: Land Reform, Estates and Society', in *Land Reforms in the British and Irish Isles Since 1800*, edited by Shaun Evans, Tony McCarthy, and Annie Tindley, 1–24. Edinburgh: Edinburgh University Press, 2022.

Eversley, Baron G. Shaw-Lefevre. *Gladstone and Ireland: The Irish Policy of Parliament from 1850-1894.* London: Metheun, 1912.

Fick, Carolyn. 'Emancipation in Haiti: From Plantation Labour to Peasant Proprietorship', in *After Slavery: Emancipation and Its Discontents*, edited by Howard Temperley, 11–39. London: Routledge, 2000.

Fisher, J. R. 'The Farmers' Alliance: An Agricultural Protest Movement of the 1880's', *The Agricultural History Review* 26, no. 1 (1978): 15–25.

Fitzmaurice, Andrew. *Sovereignty, Property and Empire, 1500-2000.* Cambridge, UK: Cambridge University Press, 2014.

Ford, Lisa. *The King's Peace: Law and Order in the British Empire.* Cambridge, MA: Harvard University Press, 2021.

Friedland, Roger, and Robert R. Alford. 'Bringing Society Back In: Symbols, Practices, and Institutional Contradictions', in *The New Institutionalism in Organizational Analysis*, edited by Walter W. Powell and Paul J. DiMaggio, 232–63. Chicago: University of Chicago Press, 1991.

Frost, Mark R. 'Imperial Citizenship or Else: Liberal Ideals and the India Unmaking of Empire, 1890–1919', *The Journal of Imperial and Commonwealth History* 46, no. 5 (September 3, 2018): 845–73.

Gailey, Andrew. *The Lost Imperialist: Lord Dufferin, Memory and Mythmaking in an Age of Celebrity.* London: John Murray Press, 2015.

Gallagher, John, and Ronald Robinson. 'The Imperialism of Free Trade', *The Economic History Review* 6 (1953): 1–15.

Games, Alison. *The Web of Empire: English Cosmopolitans in an Age of Expansion, 1560-1660.* Oxford, UK: Oxford University Press, 2008.

Gandhi, Jennifer, and Adam Przeworski. 'Cooperation, Cooptation, and Rebellion under Dictatorships', *Economics and Politics* 18, no. 1 (2006): 1–26.

Gandhi, Rajmohan. *Punjab: A History from Aurangzeb to Mountbatten.* New Delhi: Aleph Book Company, 2013.

Gerschewski, Johannes. 'The Three Pillars of Stability: Legitimation, Repression, and Co-Optation in Autocratic Regimes', *Democratization* 20, no. 1 (2013): 13–38.

Gibbon, Frederick P. *The Lawrences of the Punjab.* London: J.M. Dent, 1908.

Gibson, James A. 'The Colonial Office View of Canadian Federation, 1856-1868', *The Canadian Historical Review* 35, no. 4 (1954): 279–313.

Girard, Philip. 'Land Law, Liberalism, and the Agrarian Ideal: British North America, 1750-1920', in *Despotic Dominion: Property Rights in British Settler Societies*, edited by John McLaren, A. R. Buck, and Nancy E. Wright, 120–43. Vancouver, BC: University of British Columbia Press, 2005.

Girard, Philip, Jim Phillips, and R. Blake Brown. *A History of Law in Canada.* Toronto; Buffalo; London: Published for The Osgoode Society for Canadian Legal History by University of Toronto Press, 2019.

Goldbach, Toby S. 'Why Legal Transplants?', *Annual Review of Law and Social Science* 15, no. 1 (2019): 583–601.

Gopal, Madan. *The Punjab Tenancy Act, XVI of 1887. With Introduction, Notes, Rules and Debates in Council Second Edition. Revised and Annotated up to End of February 1899.* Lahore: Gulab Singh & Sons, 1899.

Gopal, S. *British Policy in India, 1858-1905*. Cambridge, UK: Cambridge University Press, 1965.

Gordon, Peter. 'Herbert, Henry Howard Molyneux, Fourth Earl of Carnarvon (1831–1890), Politician', *Oxford Dictionary of National Biography*. Oxford, UK: Oxford University Press, 2008.

Gray, J. N. 'John Stuart Mill on the Theory of Property', in *Theories of Property: Aristotle to Present*, edited by Anthony Parel and Thomas Flanagan, 257–82. Waterloo, O.N.: Wilfrid Laurier University Press, 1979.

Greenwood, Royston, Mia Raynard, Farah Kodeih, Evelyn R. Micelotta, and Michael Lounsbury. 'Institutional Complexity and Organizational Responses', *The Academy of Management Annals* 5, no. 1 (2011): 317–71.

Greer, Allan. *Property and Dispossession: Natives, Empires and Land in Early Modern North America*. Cambridge, UK: Cambridge University Press, 2018.

Grewal, J. S. *The Sikhs of the Punjab*. The New Cambridge History of India; II, 3. Cambridge, UK: Cambridge University Press, 1990.

Groenhout, Fiona. 'The History of the Indian Princely States: Bringing the Puppets Back onto Centre Stage', *History Compass* 4, no. 4 (2006): 629–44.

Guha, Ranajit. *A Rule of Property for Bengal: An Essay on the Idea of Permanent Settlement*. Durham, NC: Duke University Press Books, 1996.

Guinnane, Timothy W. 'A Failed Institutional Transplant: Raiffeisen's Credit Cooperatives in Ireland, 1894-1914', *Explorations in Economic History* 31, no. 1 (January 1, 1994): 38–61.

Guinnane, Timothy W., and Ronald I. Miller. 'Bonds without Bondsmen: Tenant-Right in Nineteenth-Century Ireland', *The Journal of Economic History* 56, no. 1 (1996): 113–42.

Guinnane, Timothy W., and Ronald I. Miller. 'The Limits to Land Reform: The Land Acts in Ireland, 1870–1909', *Economic Development and Cultural Change* 45, no. 3 (1997): 591–612.

Guldi, Jo. *The Long Land War: The Global Struggle for Occupancy Rights*. New Haven and London: Yale University Press, 2021.

Gümüsay, Ali Aslan, Michael Smets, and Timothy Morris. '"God at Work": Engaging Central and Incompatible Institutional Logics through Elastic Hybridity', *Academy of Management Journal* 63, no. 1 (2020): 124–54.

Guttman, Joel M. 'The Economics of Tenant Rights in Nineteenth Century Irish Agriculture', *Economic Inquiry* 18, no. 3 (July 1, 1980): 408–24.

Hall, Peter A. 'Aligning Ontology and Methodology in Comparative Research', in *Comparative Historical Analysis in the Social Sciences*, edited by James Mahoney and Dietrich Rueschemeyer, 373–406. New York, NY: Cambridge University Press, 2003.

Hall, Peter A. 'Historical Institutionalism in Rationalist and Sociological Perspective', in *Explaining Institutional Change: Ambiguity, Agency, and Power*, edited by James Mahoney and Kathleen Thelen, 204–24. Cambridge, UK: Cambridge University Press, 2009.

Hambly, G. R. G. 'Richard Temple and the Punjab Tenancy Act of 1868', *The English Historical Review* 79, no. 310 (1964): 47–66.

Haque, Tajamul, and Amar Singh Sirohi. *Agrarian Reforms and Institutional Changes in India*. New Delhi: Concept Publishing Company, 1986.

Hatvany, Matthew G. 'Tenant, Landlord and Historian: A Thematic Review of the "Polarization" Process in the Writing of 19th-Century Prince Edward Island History', *Acadiensis* 27, no. 1 (1997): 109–32.

Hatvany, Matthew G. 'The Proprietary Burden?', *The Island Magazine* 44 (1998): 3–7.

Hatvany, Matthew George. 'Tenant, Landlord, and the New Middle Class: Settlement, Society, and Economy in Early Prince Edward Island, 1798-1848', ProQuest Dissertations Publishing, 1996. <https://search.proquest.com/docview/304265267?pq-origsite = primo>.

Hobsbawm, E. J., and T. O. Ranger, eds. *The Invention of Tradition*. Cambridge; New York: Cambridge University Press, 2012.

Hobson, J. A. *Imperialism: A Study*. London: G. Allen & Unwin ltd, 1902.

Hodgson, Louis-Philippe. 'Kant on Property Rights and the State', *Kantian Review* 15, no. 1 (March 2010): 57–87.

Hoecke, Mark Van. 'Methodology of Comparative Legal Research', *Law and Method*, no. 12 (2015): <https://doi.org/10.5553/REM/.000010>.

Hoffnagle, Warren. 'The Southern Homestead Act: Its Origins and Operation', *The Historian*, August 1, 1970.

Holland, Thomas. *The Elements of Jurisprudence*. New York: Oxford University Press, 1906.

Holmes, Oliver Wendell. 'The Arrangement of Law. Privity', *American Law Review* 7 (1872): 46–65.

Hoppit, Julian. 'Compulsion, Compensation and Property Rights in Britain, 1688-1833', *Past & Present*, no. 210 (2011): 93–128.

Horwitz, Morton J. *The Transformation of American Law, 1780-1860*. Cambridge, MA: Harvard University Press, 1977.

Howe, Anthony. 'The 'Manchester School' and the Landlords: The Failure of Land Reform in Early Victorian Britain', in *The Land Question in Britain, 1750-1950*, edited by Matthew Cragoe and Paul Readman, 74–91. Hampshire: Palgrave Macmillan, 2010.

Howe, Joseph. *Confederation Considered in Relation to the Interests of the Empire*. London: Edward Stanford, 1866.

Howell, David W. 'The Land Question in Nineteenth-Century Wales, Ireland and Scotland: A Comparative Study', *Agricultural History Review* 61, no. 1 (June 1, 2013): 83–110.

Hu, Helen Wei, Lin Cui, and Preet S. Aulakh. 'State Capitalism and Performance Persistence of Business Group-Affiliated Firms: A Comparative Study of China and India', *Journal of International Business Studies* 50, no. 2 (2019): 193–222.

Hunter, James. 'The Politics of Highland Land Reform, 1873-1895', *The Scottish Historical Review* 53, no. 155 (1974): 45–68.

Huston, Reeve. *Land and Freedom: Rural Society, Popular Protest, and Party Politics in Antebellum New York*. New York: Oxford University Press, 2000.

Hyam, Ronald. *Britain's Imperial Century, 1815-1914: A Study of Imperial Expansion*. New York: Palgrave Macmillan, 2002.

Ibbetson, David. 'The Challenges of Comparative Legal History', *Comparative Legal History* 1, no. 1 (May 15, 2013): 1–11.

Ibbetson, David. 'Comparative Legal History: A Methodology', in *Making Legal History: Approaches and Methodologies*, edited by Anthony Musson and Chantal Stebbings, 131–45. Cambridge, England: Cambridge University Press, 2012.

Ince, Onur Ulas. *Colonial Capitalism and the Dilemmas of Liberalism*. Oxford, UK: Oxford University Press, 2018.

Innes, Arthur D., and Charles Gough. *Annexation of Punjab*. Delhi: National Book Shop, 1984.

James, Francis G. 'Irish Colonial Trade in the Eighteenth Century', *The William and Mary Quarterly* 20, no. 4 (1963): 574–84.

Jenkins, Roy. *Gladstone*. London: Macmillan, 1995.

Kamran, Tahir. 'An Orientalist of His Own Ilk: The Uncanny Genius of Letner | Political Economy | Thenews.Com.Pk', May 1, 2016. <https://www.thenews.com.pk/tns/detail/560854-orientalist-ilk>.

Kelly, J. M. *A Short History of Western Legal Theory*. Oxford; New York: Oxford University Press, 1992.

Kelly, Matthew. 'Irish Nationalist Opinion and the British Empire in the 1850s and 1860s', *Past & Present*, no. 204 (2009): 127–54.

Kennedy, Paul. 'Continuity and Discontinuity in British Imperialism 1815-1914', in *British Imperialism in the Nineteenth Century*, edited by C. C. Eldridge, 20–38. London: Macmillan, 1984.

Kenny, Kevin. 'Race, Violence, and Anti-Irish Sentiment in the Nineteenth Century', in *Making the Irish American: History and Heritage of the Irish in the United States*, edited by J. J. Lee and Marion R. Casey, 364–80. New York: New York University Press, 2006.

Khilnani, N. M. *British Power in the Punjab, 1839-1858*. New York: Asia Pub. House, 1972.

Kinzer, Bruce L. *England's Disgrace? J.S. Mill and the Irish Question*. Toronto: University of Toronto Press, 2001.

Knox, Bruce. 'Democracy, Aristocracy and Empire: The Provision of Colonial Honours, 1818–1870', *Australian Historical Studies* 25, no. 99 (1992): 244–64.

Kolbert, C. F., and Timothy O'Brien. *Land Reform in Ireland: A Legal History of the Irish Land Problem and Its Settlement.* Cambridge, UK: University of Cambridge Department of Land Economy, 1975.

Kostal, Rande. W. *A Jurisprudence of Power Victorian Empire and the Rule of Law.* Oxford, UK: Oxford University Press, 2008.

Laidlaw, Zoë. 'Breaking Britannia's Bounds? Law, Settlers, and Space in Britain's Imperial Historiography', *The Historical Journal* 55, no. 3 (September 2012): 807–30.

Lee, Harold. *Brothers in the Raj: The Lives of John and Henry Lawrence.* Oxford, UK: Oxford University Press, 2002.

Lee, Sidney, and Alan O'Day. 'Crawford, William Sharman (1781–1861), Politician and Landlord in Ireland', *Oxford Dictionary of National Biography.* Oxford University Press, 2008. <https://doi.org/10.1093/ref:odnb/6648>.

Legrand, Pierre. 'The Impossibility of Legal Transplants', *Maastricht Journal of European and Comparative Law* 4, no. 2 (1997): 111–24.

Lester, Alan. 'Imperial Circuits and Networks: Geographies of the British Empire', *History Compass* 4, no. 1 (2006): 124–41.

Levine, Philippa. 'Is Comparative History Possible?" *History and Theory* 53, no. October (2014): 331–47.

Levine, Ross. 'Law, Endowments and Property Rights', *Journal of Economic Perspectives* 19, no. 3 (September 2005): 61–88.

Likhovski, Assaf. 'Peripheral Vision: Polish-Jewish Lawyers and Early Israeli Law', *Law and History Review* 36, no. 2 (2018): 235–66.

Liversage, V. *Land Tenure in the Colonies.* Cambridge, UK: Cambridge University Press, 1945.

Long, D. G. 'Bentham on Property', in *Theories of Property: Aristotle to Present*, edited by Anthony Parel and Thomas Flanagan, 221–56. Waterloo, O.N.: Wilfrid Laurier University Press, 1979.

Louis, Wm. Roger, ed. *Imperialism: The Robinson and Gallagher Controversy.* New York: New Viewpoints, 1976.

Lowry, Donal. Review of 'Imperial Affinities: Nineteenth-Century Analogies and Exchanges between India and Ireland. By S.B. Cook. New Delhi, Newbury Park & London: Sage Publications. 1992', *Irish Historical Studies* 30, no. 117 (May 1996): 137–38.

Ludden, David. *The New Cambridge History of India. Volume IV. An Agrarian History of South Asia.* Cambridge, UK: Cambridge University Press, 1999.

Lyall, Andrew. *Land Law in Ireland.* Dublin: Oak Tree Press, 1994.

MacDonald, Edward. 'Who's Afraid of the Fenians? The Fenian Scare on Prince Edward Island, 1865-1867', *Acadiensis* 38, no. 1 (2009): 33–51.

MacKenzie, John M. 'The British Empire: Ramshackle or Rampaging? A Historiographical Reflection', *The Journal of Imperial and Commonwealth History* 43, no. 1 (2015): 99–124.

MacKinnon, Frank. *The Government of Prince Edward Island.* Toronto: University of Toronto Press, 1951.

MacNUTT, W. S. 'Political Advance and Social Reform, 1842-1861', in *Canada's Smallest Province: A History of P.E.I.*, edited by Francis W.P. Bolger, 115–34. Charlottetown: Prince Edward Island 1973 Centennial Commission, 1973.

Macpherson, C. B., ed. *Property, Mainstream and Critical Positions.* Toronto: University of Toronto Press, 1978.

Mahoney, James, and Dietrich Rueschemeyer. *Comparative Historical Analysis in the Social Sciences.* Cambridge, UK: Cambridge University Press, 2003.

Mahoney, James, and Kathleen Ann Thelen, eds. *Explaining Institutional Change: Ambiguity, Agency, and Power.* Cambridge, UK: Cambridge University Press, 2010.

Major, Andrew J. *Return to Empire: Punjab under the Sikhs and British in the Mid-Nineteenth Century.* New Delhi: Sterling Publishers, 1996.

Mann, Michael. 'A Permanent Settlement for the Ceded and Conquered Provinces: Revenue Administration in North India, 1801–1833', *Indian Economic & Social History Review* 32, no. 2 (1995): 245–69.

Mantena, Karuna. *Alibis of Empire: Henry Maine and the Ends of Liberal Imperialism*. Princeton, NJ: Princeton University Press, 2010.

Mantena, Karuna. 'The Crisis of Liberal Imperialism', in *Victorian Visions of Global Order: Empire and International Relations in Nineteenth-Century Political Thought*, edited by Duncan Bell, 113–35. Cambridge, NY: Cambridge University Press, 2007.

Marshall, P.J. 'Parliament and Property Rights in the Late Eighteenth-Century British Empire', in *Early Modern Conceptions of Property*, edited by John Brewer and Susan Staves, 530–44. London and New York: Routledge, 1995.

Martin, Ged. 'Lambton, John George [Nicknamed Radical Jack], First Earl of Durham (1792–1840), Politician', *Oxford Dictionary of National Biography*. Oxford University Press, 2008. <https://doi.org/10.1093/ref:odnb/15947>.

Martin, Ged. 'Was There a British Empire?', *The Historical Journal* 15, no. 3 (September 1972): 562–69.

Mason, John W. 'The Duke of Argyll and the Land Question in Late Nineteenth-Century Britain', *Victorian Studies* 21, no. 2 (1978): 149–70.

Mathur, Yaduvansh Bahadur. *British Administration of Punjab, 1849-75*. Delhi: Surjeet Book Depot, 1973.

Mazumder, Rajit K. *The Indian Army and the Making of Punjab*. Delhi: Permanent Black, 2003.

McCaffrey, Lawrence J. 'Isaac Butt and the Home Rule Movement: A Study in Conservative Nationalism', *The Review of Politics* 22, no. 1 (1960): 72–95.

McCallum, Margaret E. 'The Sacred Rights of Property: Title, Entitlement, and the Land Question in Nineteenth-Century Prince Edward Island', in *Essays in the History of Canadian Law in Honour of R.C.B. Risk*, edited by G. Blaine Baker and Jim Phillips, VIII: 358–97. Toronto: University of Toronto Press, 1999.

McCord, Norman. 'The Fenians and Public Opinion in Great Britain', *University Review* 4, no. 3 (1967): 227–40.

McLaren, John. 'Chasing the Chimera: The Rule of Law in the British Empire and the Comparative Turn in Legal History', *Law in Context* 33, no. 1 (January 2015): 21–36.

McLaren, John, A. R. Buck, and Nancy E. Wright. *Despotic Dominion: Property Rights in British Settler Societies*. Vancouver, BC: University of British Columbia Press, 2005.

McLaren, John, A. R. Buck, and Nancy E. Wright. 'Property Rights in the Colonial Imagination and Experience', in *Despotic Dominion: Property Rights in British Settler Societies*, edited by John McLaren, A. R. Buck, and Nancy E. Wright, 1–21. Vancouver, BC: University of British Columbia Press, 2005.

McQuiston, Julian R. 'Tenant Right: Farmer against Landlord in Victorian England 1847-1883', *Agriculture History* 47, no. 2 (1973): 95–113.

Mehta, Uday Singh. *Liberalism and Empire: A Study in Nineteenth-Century British Liberal Thought*. Chicago: University of Chicago Press, 1999.

Metcalf, Thomas R. *The Aftermath of Revolt: India, 1857-1870*. Princeton, NJ: Princeton University Press, 1964.

Metcalf, Thomas R. *Ideologies of the Raj*. The New Cambridge History of India; III, 4. Cambridge, UK: Cambridge University Press, 1995.

Metcalf, Thomas R. 'The Influence of the Mutiny of 1857 on Land Policy in India', *The Historical Journal* 4, no. 2 (1961): 152–63.

Metcalf, Thomas R. 'Laissez Faire and Tenant Right in Mid-Nineteenth Century India', *The Indian Economic & Social History Review* 1, no. 1 (1963): 74–81.

Metcalf, Thomas R. *Land, Landlords, and the British Raj: Northern India in the Nineteenth Century*. Berkeley and Los Angeles: University of California Press, 1979.

Metcalf, Thomas R. 'The Struggle Over Land Tenure in India, 1860-1868', *The Journal of Asian Studies* 21, no. 3 (1962): 295–307.

Micelotta, Evelyn, Michael Lounsbury, and Royston Greenwood. 'Pathways of Institutional Change: An Integrative Review and Research Agenda', *Journal of Management* 43, no. 6 (July 1, 2017): 1885–1910.

Michalsen, Dag. 'Methodological Perspectives in Comparative Legal History: An Analytical Approach', in *Comparative Legal History*, edited by Oliver Moreteau, Anceto Masfesser, and Kjell A. Modeer, 96–109. Northampton, MA: Edward Elgar Publishing, 2019.

Montgomery, William Ernest. *The History of Land Tenure in Ireland.* Cambridge, UK: At The University Press, 1889.

Mookerjee, Radharomon. *Occupancy Right, Its History and Incidents.* Calcutta: Calcutta University Press, 1919.

Moreteau, Oliver, Anceto Masfesser, and Kjell A. Modeer. *Comparative Legal History.* Northampton, MA: Edward Elgar Publishing, 2019.

Moriarty, Daniel Patrick. '"The Transformation of Rural Ireland: The Irish Land Purchase Policy of the Conservative Party in Britain, 1885-1923', Ph.D., The University of North Carolina at Chapel Hill. Accessed October 15, 2021. <https://www.proquest.com/docview/303577476/abstract/AF2FA97AFDB4B20PQ/1>.

Morley, John. *The Life of William Ewart Gladstone: 1859-1880.* 3 vols. Toronto: George N. Morang & Company, Limited, 1903.

Muir, Sir William. *The Honourable James Thomason, Lieutenant-Governor N.-W. P., India, 1843-1853 A.D.* Edinburgh: T. & T. Clark, 1897.

Mukherjee, Mithi. *India in the Shadows of Empire: A Legal and Political History (1774–1950).* New Delhi: Oxford University Press, 2009.

Murdoch, D. H. 'Land Policy in the Eighteenth-Century British Empire: The Sale of Crown Lands in the Ceded Islands, 1763-1783', *The Historical Journal* 27, no. 3 (1984): 549–74.

Musson, Anthony, and Chantal Stebbings. *Making Legal History: Approaches and Methodologies.* Cambridge, UK: Cambridge University Press, 2012.

Nazir, Pervaiz. 'Origins of Debt, Mortgage and Alienation of Land in Early Modern Punjab', *The Journal of Peasant Studies* 27, no. 3 (April 1, 2000): 55–91.

Nedelsky, Jennifer. *Private Property and the Limits of American Constitutionalism.* Chicago and London: The University of Chicago Press, 1990.

Newsinger, John. 'Fenianism Revisited: Pastime Or Revolutionary Movement?' *Saothar* 17 (1992): 46–52.

Norgate, G. Le G., and John Vint. 'Thornton, William Thomas (1813–1880), Economist and Civil Servant', *Oxford Dictionary of National Biography.* Oxford University Press, 2004. <https://doi.org/10.1093/ref:odnb/27367>.

O'Brien, George. 'William Conner', *Studies: An Irish Quarterly Review* 12, no. 46 (1923): 279–89.

O'Brien, R. B., and Brigitte Anton. 'Duffy, Sir Charles Gavan (1816–1903), Journalist and Politician', *Oxford Dictionary of National Biography.* Oxford University Press, 2008. <https://doi.org/10.1093/ref:odnb/32921>.

O'Brien, R. Barry. *The Parliamentary History of the Irish Land Question. From 1829 to 1869; and The Origin and Results of the Ulster Custom.* London: Sampson Low, Marston, Searle, and Rivington, 1880.

O'Day, Alan. 'Butt, Isaac (1813–1879), Politician and Lawyer', *Oxford Dictionary of National Biography.* Oxford University Press, 2008. <https://doi.org/10.1093/ref:odnb/4222>.

O'Grady, Brendan. *Exiles and Islanders: The Irish Settlers of Prince Edward Island.* Montreal and Kingston: McGill-Queen's Press, 2004.

O'Leary, Patrick. *Servants of the Empire: The Irish in Punjab 1881–1921.* Manchester: Manchester University Press, 2011.

O'Neill, Daniel I. *Edmund Burke and the Conservative Logic of Empire.* Oakland, California: University of California Press, 2016.

Offer, Avner. 'Farm Tenure and Land Values in England, c. 1750-1950', *The Economic History Review* 44, no. 1 (February 1991): 1–20.

Offer, Avner. 'Ricardo's Paradox and the Movement of Rents in England, c. 1870-1910', *The Economic History Review* 33, no. 2 (1980): 236–52.

Ohlmeyer, Jane. 'Ireland, India and The British Empire', *Studies in People's History* 2, no. 2 (2015): 169–88.

Orr, D. Alan. 'From a View to a Discovery: Edmund Spenser, Sir John Davies, and the Defects of Law in the Realm of Ireland', *Canadian Journal of History* XXXVIII (2003): 395–408.

Orr, D. Alan. 'Sir John Davies's Agrarian Law for Ireland', *Journal of the History of Ideas* 75, no. 1 (2014): 91–112.

Osborough, W. N. 'Catholics, Land and the Popery Acts of Anne', in *Endurance and Emergence: Catholics in Ireland in the Eighteenth Century*, edited by T. P. Power and Kevin Whelan, 21–56. Dublin: Irish Academic Press, 1990.

Otis, D. S. *The Dawes Act and the Allotment of Indian Lands*. Norman, OK: University of Oklahoma Press, 2014.

Otto, Jan Michiel. 'Rule of Law Promotion, Land Tenure and Poverty Alleviation: Questioning the Assumptions of Hernando de Soto', *Hague Journal on the Rule of Law* 1, no. 1 (March 2009): 173–94.

Owen, Sidney James. 'The Stability of Our Indian Empire', *The Contemporary Review, 1866-1900* 31, (February 1878): 494–519.

Parnell, Charles Stewart. 'The Irish Land Question', *The North American Review* 130, no. 281 (1880): 388–406.

Percy, Michael B, and Rick Szostak. 'The Political Economy of the Abolition of Seigneurial Tenure in Canada East', *Explorations in Economic History* 29, no. 1 (January 1, 1992): 51–68.

Perrill, Jeffrey Price, and Muḥammad Ikrām Cug̲h̲tā'ī. *Punjab Orientalism: The Anjuman-i-Punjab and Punjab University, 1865-1888*. Lahorē: Pakistan Writers Cooperative Society, 2018.

Phillips, Jim. 'Parliament and Southern India, 1781–3: The Secret Committee of Inquiry and the Prosecution of Sir Thomas Rumbold', *Parliamentary History* 7, no. I (1988): 81–97.

Phillips, Jim. 'A Successor to the Moguls: The Nawab of the Carnatic and the East India Company, 1763-1785', *The International History Review* 7, no. 3 (1985): 364–89.

Pincus, Steven, Tiraana Bains, and A. Zuercher Reichardt. 'Thinking the Empire Whole', *History Australia* 16, no. 4 (October 2, 2019): 610–37.

Pitts, Jennifer. *A Turn to Empire: The Rise of Imperial Liberalism in Britain and France*. Princeton, NJ: Princeton University Press, 2005.

Powell, J. 'Wodehouse, John, first earl of Kimberley (1826–1902), Politician', *Oxford Dictionary of National Biography*. Oxford University Press, 2008. <https://doi.org/10.1093/ref:odnb/36987>.

Priest, Claire. *Credit Nation: Property Laws and Legal Institutions in Early America*. Princeton: Princeton University Press, 2021.

Proudfoot, Lindsay. 'Tenant Right', in *The Oxford Companion to Irish History*. Oxford University Press, 2002. <https://www-oxfordreference-com.ezproxy.library.yorku.ca/view/10.1093/acref/9780199234837.001.0001/acref-9780199234837-e-1846>.

Qiao, Shitong, and Frank Upham. 'Evolution of Relational Property Rights: A Case of Chinese Rural Land Reform', *Iowa Law Review* 100, no. 6 (2015): 2479–2506.

Radaelli, Claudio M. 'Policy Transfer in the European Union: Institutional Isomorphism as a Source of Legitimacy', *Governance: An International Journal of Policy and Administration* 13, no. 1 (2000): 25–43.

Rafferty, O. *The Church, the State and the Fenian Threat 1861–75*. New York: Palgrave, 1999.

Readman, Paul. 'The Edwardian Land Question', in *The Land Question in Britain, 1750-1950*, edited by Matthew Cragoe and Paul Readman, 181–200. Hampshire: Palgrave Macmillan, 2010.

Reay, Trish, and C. R. Hinings. 'Managing the Rivalry of Competing Institutional Logics', *Organization Studies* 30, no. 6 (2009): 629–52.

'Richard Cobden | British Politician & Free Trade Advocate | Britannica', May 30, 2024. <https://www.britannica.com/biography/Richard-Cobden>.

Robb, Peter G. *Peasants, Political Economy, and Law*. New Delhi: Oxford University Press, 2007.

Robertson, Ian Ross. 'Coles, George', *Dictionary of Canadian Biography*, Volume X (1871–1880). University of Toronto/Université Laval, 2003.

Robertson, Ian Ross. 'Introduction', in *The Prince Edward Land Commission of 1860*, edited by Ian Ross Robertson, ix–xxx. Fredericton, NB: Acadiensis Press, 1988.

Robertson, Ian Ross. 'Political Realignment in Pre-Confederation Prince Edward Island, 1863-1870', *Acadiensis* 15, no. 1 (1985): 35–58.

Robertson, Ian Ross. *The Tenant League of Prince Edward Island, 1864-1867: Leasehold Tenure in the New World*. Toronto; Buffalo; London: University of Toronto Press, 1996.

Rothermund, Dietmar. 'Government, Landlord and Tenant in India, 1875–1900', *The Indian Economy and Social History Review* 6, no. 4 (1969): 351–67.

Roy, Tirthankar, and Anand V. Swamy. *Law and the Economy in Colonial India*. Chicago, London: The University of Chicago Press, 2016.

Russett, Bruce M. 'Inequality and Instability: The Relation of Land Tenure to Politics', *World Politics* 16, no. 3 (April 1964): 442–54.

Ryan, Alan. *The Making of Modern Liberalism*. Princeton, NJ: Princeton University Press, 2012.

Ryan, Alan. *Property and Political Theory*. Oxford, UK: B. Blackwell, 1984.

Said, Edward W. *Culture and Imperialism*. London: Vintage, 1994.

Said, Edward W. *Orientalism*. New York: Vintage Books, 1979.

Sartori, Andrew. 'The British Empire and Its Liberal Mission', *The Journal of Modern History* 78, no. 3 (2006): 623–42.

Sartori, Andrew. 'A Liberal Discourse of Custom in Colonial Bengal', *Past & Present*, no. 212 (2011): 163–97.

Sartori, Andrew. *Liberalism in Empire: An Alternative History*. Oakland, CA: University of California Press, 2014.

Schultz, Bart, and Georgios Varouxakis, eds. *Utilitarianism and Empire*. Lanham, MD: Lexington Books, 2005.

'Secure Land Rights for All', United Nations Human Settlements Programme (UN-Habitat), 2008.

Shannon, Richard. *The Crisis of Imperialism, 1865-1915*. London: Hart-Davis, MacGibbon, 1974.

Shannon, Richard T. *Gladstone: Heroic Minister 1865 - 1898*. London: Allen Lane, The Penguin Press, 1999.

Sharpe, Errol. *A People's History of Prince Edward Island*. Toronto: Rail Publishing, 1976.

Simpson, A. W. B. *A History of Land Law*. Oxford, UK: Oxford University Press, 1986.

Smith, Adam, and D. D. Raphael. *The Wealth of Nations*. Everyman's Library 11. New York: Knopf: Distributed by Random House, 1991.

Smith, Richard Saumarez. 'Rule-by-Records and Rule-by-Reports: Complementary Aspects of the British Imperial Rule of Law', *Contributions to Indian Sociology* 19, no. 1 (January 1, 1985): 153–76.

Solow, Barbara Lewis. 'The Irish Land Question After 1870', *The Journal of Economic History* 27, no. 4 (December 1967): 618–20.

Solow, Barbara Lewis. *The Land Question and the Irish Economy, 1870-1903*. Cambridge, MA: Harvard University Press, 1971.

Solow, Barbara Lewis. 'A New Look at the Irish Land Question', *The Economic and Social Review* 12, no. 4 (1981): 301–14.

Steele, David. 'Gray, Sir John (1816–1875), Newspaper Proprietor and Politician', *Oxford Dictionary of National Biography*. Oxford University Press, 2004. <https://doi.org/10.1093/ref:odnb/11343>.

Steele, David. 'Temple, Henry John, Third Viscount Palmerston (1784–1865), Prime Minister', *Oxford Dictionary of National Biography*. Oxford University Press, 2009. <https://doi.org/10.1093/ref:odnb/27112>.

Steele, E. D. 'Gladstone and Ireland', *Irish Historical Studies* 17, no. 65 (1970): 58–88.

Steele, E. D. 'Ireland and the Empire in the 1860s. Imperial Precedents for Gladstone's First Irish Land Act', *The Historical Journal* 11, no. 1 (March 1968): 64–83.

Steele, E. D. *Irish Land and British Politics: Tenant-Right and Nationality 1865-1870*. Cambridge, UK: Cambridge University Press, 1974.

Steele, E. D. 'J. S. Mill and the Irish Question: Reform, and the Integrity of the Empire, 1865–1870', *The Historical Journal* 13, no. 3 (September 1970): 419–50.

Steele, E. D. 'J.S. Mill and the Irish Question: The Principles of Political Economy, 1848–1865', *The Historical Journal* 13, no. 2 (June 1970): 216–36.

Stephen, Leslie. *The English Utilitarians*. New York: London: G. Putnam; Duckworth, 1900.

Stillman, Peter G. 'The Concept of Legitimacy', *Polity* 7, no. 1 (September 1, 1974): 32–56.

Stokes, Eric. *The English Utilitarians and India*. Oxford, UK: Oxford University Press, 1989.

Stokes, Eric. *The Peasant and the Raj: Studies in Agrarian Society and Peasant Rebellion in Colonial India*. Cambridge, UK: Cambridge University Press, 1978.

Suddaby, Roy, Alex Bitektine, and Patrick Haack. 'Legitimacy', *Academy of Management Annals* 11, no. 1 (October 25, 2016): 451–78.

Talbot, Ian. *Punjab and the Raj 1849-1947*. Delhi: Manohar, 1988.

Thompson, F. M. L. 'Changing Perceptions of Land Tenures in Britain, 1750-1914', in *The Political Economy of British Historical Experience, 1688-1914*, edited by Donald Winch and Patrick K. O'Brien, 119–38. Oxford, UK: Oxford University Press, 2002.

Thompson, F. M. L. *English Landed Society in the Nineteenth Century*. 1st ed. London and New York: Routledge, 2007.

Thompson, F. M. L. 'Land and Politics in England in the Nineteenth Century', *Transactions of the Royal Historical Society* 15 (December 1965): 23–44.

Thompson, F. M. L. 'Epilogue: The Strange Death of the English Land Question', in *The Land Question in Britain, 1750-1950*, edited by Matthew Cragoe and Paul Readman, 257–70. Hampshire: Palgrave Macmillan, 2010.

Thorburn, S. S. *Musalmans and Money-Lenders in the Punjab*. Edinburgh and London: William Blackwood & Sons, 1886.

Thornton, Patricia H., and William Ocasio. 'Institutional Logics', in *The SAGE Handbook of Organizational Institutionalism*, edited by Royston Greenwood, Christine Oliver, Roy Suddaby, and Kerstin Sahlin, 99–128. London: SAGE Publications Ltd, 2008.

Tindley, Annie. '"All the Arts of a Radical Agitation": Transnational Perspectives on British and Irish Landowners and Estates, 1800–1921', *Historical Research* 91, no. 254 (2018): 705–22.

Tindley, Annie. *Lord Dufferin, Ireland and the British Empire, c. 1820–1900: Rule by the Best?* London: Routledge, 2021.

Tully, James. *A Discourse on Property: John Locke and His Adversaries*. Cambridge, UK: Cambridge University Press, 1980.

'United Nations Declaration on the Rights of Peasant and Other People Working in Rural Areas', Official Record of the General Assembly, Seventy-Third Session, Supplement No. 53A (A/73/53/Add.1). United Nations, December 17, 2018.

Van den Dungen, P. H. M. *The Punjab Tradition: Influence and Authority in Nineteenth Century India*. London: Allen & Unwin, 1972.

Varley, Tony. 'Gaining Ground, Losing Ground: The Politics of Land Reform in Twentieth-Century Ireland', in *Land Questions in Modern Ireland*, edited by Fergus Campbell and Varley, Tony, 25–64. Manchester: Manchester University Press, 2013.

Vaughan, William Edward. *Landlords and Tenants in Mid-Victorian Ireland*. Oxford, UK: Clarendon Press, 1994.

Wagner, Kim. *Amritsar 1919: An Empire of Fear and the Making of a Massacre*. New Haven, CT: Yale University Press, 2019.

Washbrook, D. A. 'Law, State and Agrarian Society in Colonial India', *Modern Asian Studies* 15, no. 3 (July 1981): 649–721.

Watson, Alan. 'Comparative Law and Legal Change', *The Cambridge Law Journal* 37, no. 2 (November 1978): 313–36.

Weaver, John C. 'Concepts of Economic Improvement and Social Construction of Property Rights: Highlights from the English-Speaking World', in *Despotic Dominion: Property Rights in British Settler Colonies*, edited by John McLaren, A. R. Buck, and Nancy E. Wright, 79–102. Vancouver, BC: University of British Columbia Press, 2005.

Weaver, John C. *The Great Land Rush and the Making of the Modern World, 1650-1900*. Montreal & Kingston: McGill-Queen's University Press, 2003.

Weitzenfeld, Julian S. 'Valid Reasoning by Analogy', *Philosophy of Science* 51 (1984): 137–49.

Williams, Donovan. 'The Council of India and the Relationship Between the Home and the Supreme Governments, 1858-1870', *The English Historical Review* 81, no. 318 (1966): 56–73.

Williams, Robert A. *The American Indian in Western Legal Thought: The Discourses of Conquest.* New York: Oxford University Press, 1990.

Wilson, Catherine Anne. *New Lease on Life: Landlords, Tenants, and Immigrants in Ireland and Canada.* Montreal and Kingston: McGill-Queen's University Press, 1994.

Wilson, Catherine Anne. *Tenants in Time: Family Strategies, Land, and Liberalism in Upper Canada, 1799-1871.* Montreal and Kingston: McGill-Queen's University Press, 2009.

Winstanley, Michael J. *Ireland and the Land Question 1800-1922.* London: Metheun & Co. Ltd., 1984.

Woodward, Sir Llewellyn. *The Oxford History of England: The Age of Reform 1815-1870.* London: Oxford at the Clarendon Press, 1962.

Wylie, J. C. W. *Irish Land Law.* 2nd ed. Abingdon, Oxon: Professional Books, 1986.

Zahid, Masood Akhtar. 'Orientalism's Last Battle in the 19th Century Punjab', *Journal of Pakistan Vision* 10, no. 1 (2009): 27–48.

Zastoupil, Lynn. 'Moral Government: J. S. Mill on Ireland', *The Historical Journal* 26, no. 3 (September 1983): 707–17.

Index

For the benefit of digital users, indexed terms that span two pages (e.g., 52–53) may, on occasion, appear on only one of those pages.

Tables and figures are indicated by an italic *t* or *f*, following the paragraph number.